COLONIAL ITINERARIES OF
CONTEMPORARY MEXICO

Colonial Itineraries of Contemporary Mexico

Literary and Cultural Inquiries

Edited by
OSWALDO ESTRADA AND
ANNA M. NOGAR

THE UNIVERSITY OF
ARIZONA PRESS

TUCSON

The University of Arizona Press
www.uapress.arizona.edu

Printed in the United States of America
19 18 17 16 15 14   6 5 4 3 2 1

Jacket design by Carrie House, HOUSEdesign llc

Publication of this book is made possible in part by the proceeds of a permanent
endowment created with the assistance of a Challenge Grant from the National
Endowment for the Humanities, a federal agency.

Library of Congress Cataloging-in-Publication Data
Colonial itineraries of contemporary Mexico : literary and cultural inquiries / edited
by Oswaldo Estrada and Anna M. Nogar.
        pages cm
   Includes bibliographical references and index.
   ISBN 978-0-8165-3108-0 (cloth : alk. paper)
   1. Mexican literature—21st century—History and criticism.   2. Historical fiction,
Mexican—History and criticism.   3. Colonies in literature.   4. Politics in literature.
5. Motion pictures—Mexico—History—21st century.   6. Colonies in motion pictures.
7. Mexico—In motion pictures.   I. Estrada, Oswaldo, editor of compilation.
II. Nogar, Anna M., editor of compilation.
   PQ7157.C66 2014
   860.9'97209051—dc23
                              2014001577

♾ This paper meets the requirements of ANSI/NISO Z39.48-1992 (Permanence of Paper).

Para Cris, compañera y cómplice de este viaje . . . y los que vendrán.

To Peter, and to Nico, who helped us finish on time.

Contents

Acknowledgments

These colonial itineraries were first broached in March 2010, during the Congreso de Literatura Mexicana Contemporánea at the University of Texas at El Paso. In the company of our friends Ignacio Sánchez Prado, Oswaldo Zavala, Sarah Pollack, José Ramón Ruisánchez, Tamara Williams, and Irma Cantú, we began shaping the focus of our book and thinking of possible contributors who would write on contemporary representations of the Mexican *colonia*. After many e-mail exchanges and discussions, we fleshed out the project at the Latin American Studies Association Conference in Toronto, in October of that same year, amid other close friends and colleagues, such as Mayra Fortes González, Sandra Lorenzano, Brian L. Price, Corinne Pubill, and Berenice Villagómez.

Since then, many people have supported us as we steered this project to completion.

First of all, we want to give special thanks to our authors, whose generosity goes beyond words. Through their thoughtful contributions, this book also belongs to Rolena Adorno, Irma Cantú, Cristina Carrasco, Stuart Day, Guillermo de los Reyes-Heredia, Linda Egan, Josué Gutiérrez-González, Emily Hind, Ilana Dann Luna, the late Seymour Menton, Jeremy Paden, Vinodh Venkatesh, and Tamara Williams. Working with each of you has been a very gratifying experience, indeed.

We are indebted to the many friends who have encouraged us throughout this process, providing advice, useful information, fruitful academic exchanges, and countless words of encouragement. In Chapel Hill, María A. Salgado, Rosa Perelmuter, Lucia Binotti, and Monica Rector have constantly shared their knowledge along with love, warm meals, and many cups of coffee. In New Mexico, the same is true of Enrique Lamadrid, A. Gabriel Meléndez, Miguel Gandert, Karen Patterson, Sarah McKinney, and Chris Holden. To Juan Carlos González-Espitia, Emilio del Valle Escalante, Federico Luisetti, and Samuel Amago: Thank you for our unofficial meetings *en algún lugar de Carrboro, de cuyo nombre no quiero acordarme.* Working on this project has been a rewarding experience in the company of Glynis Cowell, Irene Gómez-Castellano, Bruno Estigarribia, Patrícia Amaral, Laura Halperín, Ariana Vigil, Leila Lehnen, Jeremy Lehnen, Krista Foutz, and Damián Vergara Wilson. Other friends have been there for us too, including Debra Castillo, David William Foster, and Wilfrido Corral, as well as many of the UC-Mexicanistas: Sara Poot-Herrera, Claudia Parodi, Norma Klahn, Michael Schuessler, Pablo Brescia, Beatriz Mariscal, Blanca López de Mariscal, Cheyla Samuelson, Alicia Rueda-Acedo, and Ignacio Ruiz-Pérez.

Agradecimientos are also due to the University of New Mexico, for its generous assistance in the publication process. We cannot give enough thanks to Kristen Buckles, from the University of Arizona Press, for welcoming our manuscript from our very first communications. We also thank our anonymous readers for their positive feedback and constructive criticism. And, of course, many thanks to authors Carmen Boullosa, Luis Felipe Fabre, Mónica Lavín, and Flavio González Mello for giving us permission to reprint their work.

Finally, without the constant love and support of our families and friends in Mexico and New Mexico, California, Texas, North Carolina, Peru, and Spain, this project would have been neither possible nor meaningful. For this, we can never thank you enough.

COLONIAL ITINERARIES OF
CONTEMPORARY MEXICO

Reliving the Mexican Colonia in a New Millennium

Oswaldo Estrada and Anna M. Nogar

Discourse constructs the place of the other,
the meaning of the others, the destiny
of an otherness that it invariably
reads, reorders and assimilates.
—JULIO ORTEGA, *TRANSATLANTIC*
TRANSLATIONS (11)

During the last twenty years—and in response to the quincentennial of Columbus's voyage to America, the bicentennial of Latin American independence, and the first centennial of the Mexican Revolution—Mexico has rearticulated its colonial legacy in numerous poems, short stories, films, plays, chronicles, and novels that confirm the presence of the past as an indelible point of departure or stubborn memory that problematizes unresolved identity matters in the present. The rewriting and reliving of colonial history is part and parcel of the art of "looking back," a living Mexican tradition, as Carlos Monsiváis reminds us in his *Imágenes de la tradición viva* (2006). Today, thousands of Mexican pilgrims continue to visit the shrine of the Virgin of Guadalupe on Tepeyac Hill, driven by the same devotion with which colonial subjects four hundred years ago confirmed their syncretism, difference, and marginality. The image of the *guadalupana* on Juan Diego's *tilma* is neither an obsolete symbol of national independence nor the emblem of countless soldiers and soldaderas of the Mexican Revolution, but rather it continues to be invoked as the perennial mother symbol of virtually *all* Mexicans, even if, as the year 2000 dawned, more than 20 percent of the country did not call itself Catholic (Monsiváis, *Imágenes* 19–40). Consistent with Monsiváis's observations, contemporary expressions of Mexican transculturation bear out Mexico's ongoing return to its coloniality, its uncomfortable Otherness, and its need to challenge and reinterpret the colonial past and its legacy within the paradigms of a new millennium.

Creative works treating Mexico and its past persistently question these continuums, exploring the role of memory and discourse, the difference between literary invention and historical truth, the formation of Otherness in a globalized environment, the destruction of a pre-Columbian world and the birth of mestizo subjects, the creation of new ethnicities and social divisions, and the lasting linkages between Spain and the Americas. In the twenty-first century, a series of "truncated modernities" produced in and outside Mexico invite us to seek out the multiple ways in which contemporary literature continues to articulate a resistant and/or contestatory discourse (Campa 437). When, in 2002, Kimberle S. López studied several Latin American novels that recreate the conquest of Mexico from the fictionalized perspective of the Spanish conquistadors, she noted a clear deconstruction of the rhetoric of empire due to an "anxiety of identification," as well as numerous cases in which "both women and Amerindians remain invisible, silent, and nameless Others . . . despite the corpus's marked emphasis on the representation of marginality" (2, 11–12). Emerging from the political need to combat temporal circularity and historical determinism, contemporary Latin American literature in general— and Mexican literature in particular—has explored new creative horizons that challenge the relationship between history and fiction, and the unfinished aftermath of Spanish conquest and colonization. *Colonial Itineraries of Contemporary Mexico: Literary and Cultural Inquiries* addresses creative innovations of this nature that were produced from the year 2000 onward.

Drawing from present-day realities in which globalization and neoliberalism can be understood as modern manifestations of neocolonialism, and in which capitalism perpetuates coloniality (Moraña et al. 12), the fifteen critics included in this volume carefully analyze how a representative selection of cultural producers manipulate historical evidence and legendary tales, personal and communal stories, discourses of abundance and narratives of scarcity, utopian realities, and traumatic moments of the past and the present. Together, they reveal not only the pervasiveness of Mexico's *colonia* in contemporary discourses but, more importantly, the coloniality that still emerges from a colonial hegemony that imposed social inequality, gender marginalization, ethnic exclusion, economic and cultural dependence, racism, and political instability. (It should be noted that, as opposed to the English definition of the colonia as essentially "an unincorporated settlement [as of Mexican Americans or Mexicans in the U.S.]," this book defines the colonia as the period during which Mexico was under Spanish rule, roughly from the conquest of Tenochtitlán in the early sixteenth century through Mexican Independence in 1821.) Consistent with Mexico's tendency to revert to its (un)official historical past in order to understand its present and future, the representations of the colonia analyzed in this book affirm that the concept of postcoloniality should be read as the continuation of colonialism, while taking into account the forms of resistance generated by colonialism itself (Jáuregui and Moraña 13–14). Analyzed through a transformative interdisciplinary lens, the ultracontemporary works interpreted in these chapters problematize static notions of both personal and national identity within specific cultural palimpsests.

The creative production concerning the Mexican colonia generated from 2000 onward was presaged in the two decades during which Mexican literature successfully recreated the matrix of a dual modern/colonial world, denouncing various strategies utilized over centuries of colonial and neocolonial domination, and challenging postcoloniality as a legitimate Latin American concept (Moraña et al. 11). Through the multiple literary discourses produced during that time, Mexican literature has indeed confronted history and fiction, the language of power, and the many voices that have been consistently ignored since the beginning of American colonization. These earlier works questioned official records and unofficial accounts, as well as private and public memories, which engendered a "double-consciousness," or a colonized sensation of "always looking at one's self through the eyes of the others" (Du Bois 8),[1] rewriting myths and symbols that had historically been abridged by official discourse and setting the stage for post-2000 cultural production. As Fernando Aínsa argued in 2003, the histories or stories that emerged from these literary works reiterated the principles of an unresolved Latin American identity, denounced history's ambivalent silences, and approached the past with a revisionist attitude that sought to destabilize history's hegemonic discourse with the overt use of parody and the grotesque, anachronisms and aesthetic pastiche, interdisciplinary polyphony and transdisciplinary openness (*Reescribir* 26–34).

Not coincident to Aínsa's observations, the evolving real-world political and social conditions in post-2000 Mexico informed the content and tenor of the literary production of this more recent period, as the new millennium marked a significant shift in Mexican politics. The Partido

Revolucionario Institucional (PRI), called "the perfect dictatorship" by Mario Vargas Llosa, lost the presidential election in 2000 after being in power since 1929 and controlling not only every aspect of Mexican politics, but also every "happening" of Mexican society, under the guise of a stable democracy free from the anarchism and brutality of military regimes (63–64). Those seven decades of absolute hegemony and political corruption were deeply internalized by institutions and individuals all over Mexico. Although numerous intellectuals criticized the PRI, many benefited from its power, serving as diplomats, state employees, editors, journalists, and academics in charge of editorial houses, journals and magazines, and important academic institutions. According to Vargas Llosa, the unfortunate complement to México's intense intellectual activity over the course of the twentieth century was "una merma notoria de soberanía y autenticidad en la clase intelectual" (65).[2] Thus in 2000, when the Partido Acción Nacional candidate Vicente Fox Quesada won the presidential election, Mexican society at large anticipated radical changes regarding "the impoverished, backward, and overextended educational system, the desertification of more than a third of the agricultural land, the violence and corruption generated by the United States' inexhaustible preference for illegal intoxicants, the lack of employment opportunities for a population that [had] almost doubled in size in the [previous] thirty years" (Guillermoprieto 302). Though few of these social problems were resolved during the Fox presidency, Mexico's intellectual arena experienced a radical change that profoundly affected its literary and cultural output.

In previous periods of dramatic turns and political turmoil, Latin American literature responded not only by shaping the collective memory of what should not be forgotten, but also by confirming the moral and humanitarian role of the author as the conveyer of unresolved identity problems (Earle 177). Prior to 2000, Mexico's authors bequeathed vivid literary recreations of the Mexican Revolution, the 1968 student movement, the 1985 earthquake, and the 1994 Zapatista anti-NAFTA uprising in Chiapas. In 2001, when the Zapatistas entered Mexico City's Zócalo with the indigenist rhetoric of masked spokesman Subcomandante Marcos—"Somos y seremos uno más en la marcha, la de la dignidad indígena, la del color de la tierra, la que develó y desveló los muchos Méxicos que bajo México se esconden y duelen" (Monsiváis, *Apocalipstick* 395)—the reevaluation of Mexico's perennial state of colonial difference and coloniality, a sociocultural and political construct that invariably constitutes an essential part of modernity (Mignolo 61–63), urgently resurfaced. The same issues emerged in 2006, when Andrés Manuel López Obrador, the presidential candidate from the Partido Revolucionario Democrático, claimed that the elections were a fraud and mobilized large protests throughout the country. The resulting forty-eight-day *plantón* of civil resistance, from July 30 to September 14, 2006, not only blocked Mexico's Paseo de la Reforma and Zócalo, but again exposed the country's antimodernity, its invisible and inaudible side, that side inhabited by millions of marginal and "residual subjects" (Belausteguigoitia 172–73).[3]

Consistent with this pattern of rewriting the past in the face of shifting present conditions, the central objective of many authors and cultural producers in the wake of these post-2000 historical events was to revisit and revise Mexico's inconsistent alignment with modernity, exploring the coexistence of two or more Mexicos defined variously by civilization and barbarism, the urban and the rural, Catholicism and secularism, populism and democracy, or baroque traditions and contestatory discourses (Echeverría 238–42). The forms and genres their works assume both draw from earlier types of literary production and have led to innovations creating entirely new modes of expression. To help provide a critical genealogy that contextualizes the turn these historical rewritings have assumed, it is valuable to engage in a brief discussion of the new historical novel as a discourse that reflects on history and its changes, or as a fictional locus that revises various territories of history, known and unknown, new and old (Perkowska 42).

In 1993, *Colonial Itineraries* contributor Seymour Menton defined Latin America's new historical novel as a narrative whose action takes place in a distant past not directly experienced by its author. Although Menton took into consideration publications such as Alejo Carpentier's *El reino de este mundo* (1949), *El siglo de las luces* (1962), and *Concierto barroco* (1974), the new historical rearticulations that he analyzed—primarily published after Carpentier's work *El arpa y la sombra* (1979)—consistently showed the ambivalent, cyclical, and yet unpredictable nature of history; the conscious distortion of history through exaggerations, omissions, or anachronisms; the use of famous historical characters as protagonists in various processes of metafiction; overt intertextuality; and the fictionalization of Bakhtinian concepts such as the dialogic, the carnivalesque, parody, and heteroglossia (22–24). Following Menton's approach, as well as that of Linda Hutcheon (1988), Noé Jitrik (1995), and Karl Kohut (1997), numerous scholars have studied how Latin America's new historical narratives—particularly texts produced in the eighties and nineties— openly contradict history's official discourse. Their studies of (meta)fictive works demonstrate that such texts illuminate history's neglected discourses; its problematic silences associated with gender, class, and ethnicity; and its inherently changeable nature as an unfinished ideological edifice under ongoing construction.

Other perspectives on late twentieth-century fictional rewritings of Latin American history develop out of the work of these critics as they offer more hemispheric perspectives on such fictions. Building on Raymond Williams's theorizations on Marxism and literature, and Jitrik's reading of the historical novel of the nineteenth century as an identity quest during times of cultural uncertainty and political change, Magdalena Perkowska finds a globalizing trend in the Latin American novel produced between 1985 and 2000. Written in response to Latin America's slow process of redemocratization, regional integration, and economic transnationalization,[4] the historical novels that she analyzes move out of the past to become a new dominant literary form. Perkowska approaches these historical works as sites of negotiation produced in the midst of contemporary social crises and ongoing postmodern debates on history and historical knowledge: "Cada novela traza una imagen o visión no sólo de un acontecimiento pretérito concreto, sino también de la historia y del discurso histórico y su relación con el presente. Un conjunto variado y representativo de estas articulaciones particulares configura una constelación en la que se cifra un concepto de la historia" (37). In his *Cult of Defeat in Mexico's Historical Fiction* (2012), Brian L. Price also argues that historical reconstructions of the nineteenth century acquire deeper meaning in the context of contemporary debates about globalization, neoliberalism, and numerous political challenges of the present.

In Ute Seydel's discussion of new historical fictions written by Mexican women writers such as Elena Garro, Rosa Beltrán, and Carmen Boullosa, Seydel finds several consistent trends: a clear subversion of monolithic historical discourses, hybrid narrative processes that disintegrate essentialisms in regard to culture and identity, the coexistence of cyclical and linear times, the imposition of alternative apocryphal memories and simultaneous narrative voices, ambiguity, and different treatments of gender and marginality. Women writers who work with the historical archive, Seydel notes, reveal a distinct tendency to rearticulate the issues of domestic chores, the portrayal of mothers and wives, general everyday life for women, and the fictionalization of religious practices and women's education, as ways of exploring gender differences in connection to historical experience, language, social class, and power (160–70). Along these lines, Elisabeth Guerrero's recent study of historical novels published in Mexico between

1982 and 1999 encounters not only the humanization of historical figures traditionally elevated to near-hero status—as well as the downplaying or diminishment of European legacies in those works—but also the prominent characterization of women and minorities (6).

The cultural and literary landscape has significantly changed since these literary works and studies were published in the late twentieth century, as present-day cultural producers confront the historical transformations facing Mexico and continue to navigate the hegemonic impositions, historical determinism, and ethnic divisions characterizing the years since 2000. In 2001, Juan José Barrientos noted that, in comparison to more classical fictionalizations of history, new rewritings reflect a shift of narrative perspective, presenting history "behind the scenes" with real and/or imaginary witnesses whose words reconstruct history's inner linings and hidden messages. Simply put: "En todas ellas se trata de presentar la historia *por dentro*; no importa que un personaje histórico nos entregue sus memorias o nos haga confidencias o que sea un personaje imaginario el que nos revele su intimidad" (16, original emphasis). These new recreations of history, according to Barrientos, coincide with various discourses of postmodernity, privilege the subjective experience and discard objective points of view, are irreverent by nature, and come across as the end product of a long process of cultural cleansing (17–20). Consistent with this reading, and drawing from analyses by Germán Gullón, Matías Barchino, and María del Carmen Bobes Naves, among others, Ignacio Corona concurs on the subversive spirit of the "postmodern historical novel" and comments on its intimate undertones, linguistic virtuosity, historical knowledge, and ambiguous, transgressive, and interdisciplinary nature (95–101).

In 2003, Aínsa observed that newer historical discourses eliminate the distancing present in traditional historical novels and facilitate a critical revision of long-standing myths associated with nation building, as well as with social and cultural identity. In an effort to learn what really happened in the past, Aínsa postulates that contemporary authors sacrifice historical accuracy in favor of more introspective and persuasive interpretations of history through which certain facts can be read as intimate occurrences. Via this creative process, Aínsa shows, newer historical novels reread and rewrite history, question historiographic discourses, provide multiple points of view and textual possibilities, and imagine what is almost invisible. Above all, Aínsa recognizes that the most salient characteristic of these texts is that they dig "entre las ruinas de una historia desmantelada por la retórica y la mentira al individuo auténtico perdido detrás de los acontecimientos, [para] descubrir y enlazar al ser humano en su dimensión más vital, aunque parezca inventando, aunque en definitiva lo sea" (*Reescribir* 111–12). In 2011, Aínsa identified this process as a retrospective endeavor confronting different memories, practices of forgetting, historical amnesia, and varying degrees of selective forgetfulness. Thanks to these suggestive encounters between history and fiction, the truth of the past is pluralized, fragmented, and relativized. If our relationship with the past is never neutral, Aínsa suggests, through several new recreations of it, "menos dueños del presente, sentimos cómo el pasado entra en él como cosa viva, obra con fuerza semejante a lo contemporáneo y reactualiza con toda su carga emotiva la ponderosa presencia de la memoria en las contiendas del momento actual" ("Guardianes" 19).

The rewritings of the Mexican colonia discussed in the chapters that follow inevitably question a present reality of marginalities and inequality, of imposed political domination, and of hybrid subjectivities. In their examination of the novels, films, poetry, and chronicles produced in and outside Mexico since 2000, the critics included in *Colonial Itineraries of Contemporary Mexico* produce new interpretations, alternative readings, and different angles of analysis that extend far beyond the theories of the new historical novel of the eighties and nineties, and well beyond the limits of the novel as re-creative genre. Taken together, these incisive readings, as well as the works they examine, open broader conversations about Mexican coloniality as it continues well into the twenty-first century.

Colonial Itineraries's opening section, "Revising Colonial Ruins and Chronicles," presents three chapters that examine the rearticulation of colonial ruins as their interpretations continue to evolve in present-day contexts. The works studied in this first section are heterogeneous in form, from the modern-day chronicle of the public intellectual and the encoded modes of contemporary poetry to a recent historical fiction. Reading Carlos Monsiváis's later reflections on Mexico's conquest and colonization (circa 2006), Linda Egan analyzes how the preeminent twentieth-century cultural commentator rewrites the nation's memory of those paradigms through his contemporary *crónicas*. While Egan reveals Monsiváis's lucid dialogue with the works of Motolinía, Hernán Cortés, Bernal Díaz, Fray Bernardino de Sahagún, and Fray Bartolomé de las Casas, among others, she leads readers to see that Monsiváis rewrites an epoch and a collective mentality rather than a specific text. As she studies Monsiváis's treatment of Mexico's pre-Hispanic and colonial legacy, Egan explores the foundation of modern Mexican life and its principal problems, which include an enduring racism against its indigenous people and a theocratic mindset permeating much of Mexican society. Egan argues that in rewriting early *cronistas'* works for a present-day audience aware of these endemic issues, Monsiváis rewinds the national memory and rebukes the unrepentant conscience of the country's government and privileged classes.

Focusing on the avant-garde poetry of Carmen Boullosa, Jeremy Paden's chapter examines how Boullosa imaginatively treats precolonial and colonial Mexican history in two of her recent poetry compilations, *La bebida* (2002) and *Salto de mantarraya (y otros dos)* (2004). Paying special attention to the poems "Agua," "El son del ángel de la ciudad," and "Los nuevos," Paden observes that Boullosa's reference to the past in these works behaves in startling and disparate manners, sometimes activating a fragmented discourse that voices private, erotic experiences and at other times weaving a story about Mexican history and present-day geopolitics. The fruitful rearticulation of specific elements of Mexico's pre-Columbian history and of Aztec mythology, as well as the constant evocation of the Conquest in Boullosa's poetry, concludes Paden, retells Mexican history and myth as an autobiography of loss and orphanhood that gives voice to a silenced, feminine desire calling into question gender hierarchies and telling the story of the vanquished.

This first section closes with Vinodh Venkatesh's chapter on the confluence of fiction, history, and geography in Héctor de Mauleón's novel *El secreto de la Noche Triste* (2009). Venkatesh studies this rewriting of the colonia not as a new historical novel or even as a historiographic metafiction, but as a literary enterprise that he calls "metafictive historiogeography." He locates the novel within the genealogy of primary texts of La Noche Triste, while distinguishing it from other contemporary rewritings by highlighting its focus on contemporary urban spaces and their relationship to Mexico City's colonial past and its lost treasures, both literal and metaphorical. As Venkatesh unravels a novel that has been called the first New Hispanic thriller, he juxtaposes the fictional text with the writings of Bernal Díaz, Hernán Cortés, and Carlos de Sigüenza y Góngora, in order to reveal a conscious effort on de Mauleón's part to retell the events of the past with an active, self-conscious narrative voice.

Colonial Itineraries's second section, "Queering Gender and Twisting Genres," offers close questioning of how the gendered positionalities and sexualities of the colonia become the foci of critical re-imaginations in contemporary narrative fiction and poetry. The opening chapter, Oswaldo Estrada's reading of Mónica Lavín's *Yo, la peor* (2008), reveals the subtle and yet significant ways in which the colonial epistolary tradition as a metacommentary shapes Sor Juana as a literary character. Her fictional letters, set up by the novelist as having been written during the last six months of her life, are intimately connected not only with the nun's famous *Respuesta a Sor Filotea de la Cruz, Carta atenagórica,* and other renowned real-life epistles, but also with her *Enigmas ofrecidos a la Casa del Placer.* The letters that Lavín crafts for Sor Juana, concludes Estrada, symbolically represent an "alternative testament" that in the twenty-first century compresses her past, describes her present, and projects her into a possible future. The final novelistic act of writing that Lavín implements in this work carries with it the seeds of female transgression, one that speaks against the simulacrum of silence traditionally ascribed to women of the colonia.

Tamara Williams's chapter examines poet Luis Felipe Fabre's innovative redeployment of seventeenth-century historiographical texts dealing with a 1658 Inquisitorial sodomy case that resulted in the execution of fourteen gay men and the punishment of a young boy. In reading *La sodomía de la Nueva España* (2010), Williams finds in the refreshingly irreverent book-length poem that the reordering of fragments from the historical case reconstitutes the silence and invisibility of the homosexual subject in Mexican colonial history. As she teases apart this complex work, composed of chronicles, legal proceedings, letters, diaries, and histories of homosexuality, Williams pays close attention to the section "Retablo de sodomitas novohispanos." In reading this portion of the poem, which is rendered as an *auto sacramental,* she highlights the sacrifice and redemption of the gay transvestite character, Cotita, as that of a thinly veiled Christ-like figure. The poem that we read with Williams poses an antiheteronormative morality that subverts and makes evident what Judith Butler calls "the reiterative power" of seventeenth-century Spanish imperial discourses related to compulsory heterosexuality and phallogocentric knowledge.

Guillermo de los Reyes-Heredia and Josué Gutiérrez-González's chapter explores how Enrique Serna's novel *Ángeles del abismo* (2004) reconstructs a confined, oppressive colonial reality while simultaneously incorporating perspectives missing from the official historiography to create a dialogical critique of the past. De los Reyes-Heredia and Gutiérrez-González elaborate on the way in which the novel, drawing on colonial documents pertaining to the seventeenth-century Inquisitorial process of the *falsa beata* Teresa Romero, reflects upon the rigorous system of *castas* in colonial New Spain, the centralization of power, and the multiple processes of transculturation that have been either ignored or simplified by official history. As they consider the subversive potential of the novel's baroque entanglements of repressed desire, sexual behavior and clandestine idolatry, De los Reyes-Heredia and Gutiérrez-González find that the novel illustrates an oppressive colonial system of power spatially through its representation of an array of increasingly closed spaces.

The book's third movement, "Global and Transatlantic Itineraries," takes to task more wide-ranging approaches to the colonia, its chapters engaging with questions of the multinational production and consumption of Mexico's colonial past and including insightful perspectives on who its consumers are. The section opens with Irma Cantú's chapter on Laura Esquivel's novel *Malinche* (2006), in which the critic exposes the layers of new historical narrative Esquivel uses to attempt to un-write previous patriarchal and nationalistic constructions of Hernán Cortés's interpreter, taking into account Malinche's earliest portrayals in Sahagún's *Florentine Codex*, Cortés's *Cartas de Relación*, and Bernal Díaz's *Historia verdadera*. Cantú identifies Malinche as a political icon that is rewritten for an international readership, but she also finds that Esquivel's effort to construct a different and empowered cultural subject ultimately fails, due to the fact that the novel is written to be a bestseller. Cantú's analysis of the strategies for creating such a novel shows that Esquivel's historical rewriting problematically remythologizes Malinche and perpetuates the misunderstanding of Mexican identity on a global scale.

The chapter that follows, Cristina Carrasco's discussion of Spanish author Inma Chacón's *La princesa india* (2005), explores the way in which the novel draws from several different literary genres to interpret Mexican colonization from a transatlantic perspective. Placing this Spanish novel in the broader context of other Spanish and Mexican novels that re-create the conquest and colonization of Mexico, Carrasco observes in *La princesa india* a reverse discovery of the Americas. Her reading draws parallels between the oppression of the Jews and Muslims in the Iberian Peninsula, both predating and contemporaneous to the conquest of Mexico, and that of the indigenous people in the New World as seen through the eyes of its marginalized female protagonist Ehecatl, an Aztec princess who travels to Spain with her conquistador husband. Carrasco notes that, while on the one hand, Chacón's novel provides an important critical revision of founding myths of early modern Spanish nationalism (namely, blood purity), the portrayal of its indigenous protagonist perpetuates a colonized female archetype rather than demonstrating female agency.

Ilana Dann Luna analyzes the Oscar-nominated Spanish-Mexican-French coproduced film *También la lluvia* (2011) in the third chapter, evaluating the work in light of its metareferential, double "rereading" of the colonial. Set in Bolivia, starring Mexican superstar Gael García Bernal, directed by well-known Spanish actress and director Icíar Bollaín, and written by her partner, Calcutta-born Scotch-Irishman Paul Laverty, Luna avers that the film repositions Spain vis-à-vis its former colonies in a global market, and questions the borders and boundaries of national cinemas, while publicizing and fomenting the unity of indigenous struggles through new media circuits. Taking into consideration a wide range of films that seek to reinscribe marginalized people into the historical record of popular culture, Luna shows that *También la lluvia* draws parallels between colonial practices of enslavement of the indigenous peoples and the present-day, neocolonial, neoliberal economic policies that prioritize the needs of large, capital-amassing global corporations over those of indigenous peoples, relegating the latter once again to the margins of economic subsistence.

Finally, in the section's fourth chapter, Emily Hind analyzes the Mexican colonia as presented in several young readers' texts. Analyzing a rich corpus of children's literature treating the maritime trade route between Acapulco and the Philippines, the Tribunal of the Holy Inquisition, and the biography of Sor Juana Inés de la Cruz, Hind stresses the contradictions inherent in these texts, which waver between treating children as "special" readers and addressing them as mature readers who can handle a stricter, more factual approach. With critical precision, Hind unravels a larger contemporary debate regarding the disputed divisions between childhood and adulthood, pointing out that it is not clear whether children or adults ultimately prove to be more "innocent" when it comes to the difficult legacy of colonial history. In her readings of *El galeón de Manila* (2005), *La Nao de China* (2006), *El Tombuctú* (2000), *De Tenochtitlán a la Nueva España* (2007), and *Sor Juana y don Carlos* (2007), among others, Hind observes that the use and/or suppression of gothic narrative tactics can present the colonia as a period of appalling cruelties that must never be repeated, as well as a warning that present-day realities continue to derive from the colonia, enclosing the past within the present.

The chapters in *Colonial Itineraries*'s final section, "Into the Nineteenth-Century Colonia," draw the collection chronologically from the end of the colonia to the beginning of the nineteenth century, developing points of historical-literary convergence, disjuncture, and continuation into the present day. Anna M. Nogar examines the complex structure of Pablo Soler Frost's 2004 novel *1767*, finding in it both a nineteenth century–style historical novel, as well as a meta-text discussing the impetus for Mexican independence from Spain. Although the novel is ostensibly about the

Jesuit expulsion from New Spain as part of the Bourbon Reforms, Nogar argues that the articulation of the two different literary genres within the work destabilizes the carefully constructed historical novel for the reader, while at the same time proposing alternative possibilities for how the historical event might have related to the fomentation of a Mexican criollo identity. Nogar pinpoints the techniques that Soler Frost employs to construct this historical novel, to create porosity in its reading, and to form a metonymic protagonist representing the late-colonial Mexican everyman on the verge of breaking with his colonial loyalties to Spain.

Stuart Day's chapter considers Flavio González Mello's 2000 play *1822: El año que fuimos imperio* in light of the "ungovernability" of the twenty-first-century Mexican state, seeing in the play's resolution of that crisis of governance a projection of possible futures for contemporary Mexico. In this work's treatment of the eleven years after Mexico's transition from colony to independent state, in which the use of theatrics and religious imagery in politics is parodied, Day uncovers the residual effects of colonial Mexico in the two hundred years since the famous *Grito de Dolores.* Day observers how *1822* enters full force into a complex historical debate as the play conjures the image of the Virgin of Guadalupe on the theatrical stage, through the words of Fray Servando Teresa de Mier (who sought a more egalitarian, pre-Columbian origin for the apparition of the Virgin). It is through these evocations, Day suggests, that the play revisits colonialism and recognizes coloniality: it addresses the overlay of the twentieth and twenty-first centuries and colonial Mexico as they challenge stereotypes and expose political appropriations, revealing the power of the past to cast its myth-making over the present.

The expert on Latin America's new historical novel, Seymour Menton, pens the final chapter reflecting on the historical transition between Mexico's colonial period and its independent era. Drawing on his many years of research, Menton observes that the literary genre he studied and defined in the early nineties has nearly "disappeared," but he notes that several varieties of the historical novel continue to enjoy great popularity among writers and readers today. Menton thus concludes that the rewriting of history through fiction has indeed evolved in the twenty-first century, and he incisively comments on this century's texts' renderings of the nineteenth-century Mexican *colonia*. His reading confirms that, in more than one way, the colonial period extended through the Santa Anna anarchy, the War of the Reform (1857–1860), and the French Intervention (1862–1867), followed by the establishment of the Maximilian-Carlota Empire. Menton closes this section with an analysis of Hernán Lara Zavala's

Península, península (2008), Eduardo Antonio Parra's *Juárez, el rostro de piedra* (2008), Álvaro Uribe's *Expediente del atentado* (2007), and Eraclio Zepeda's *Las grandes lluvias* (2006).

Esteemed Latin American colonial literary scholar Rolena Adorno pens *Colonial Itineraries*'s closing remarks. Her postscriptum, "Specifically Mexican, Universally American: Tales of Colonial Mexico and Their Legacies," points to the necessity of fictional works that re-create the colonial world for their capacity to illuminate certain theoretical problems of significance in the multidisciplinary study of colonial letters. In Adorno's reading, such texts' double value lies in setting forth the importance of the past (and consequently the scholarly importance of colonial-studies research), as well as in inviting new reflections and identifying new conundrums regarding "the prestigious lies of exactitude" bounding historical narrative.

The cronistas of the conquest and colonization of Mexico, as Adorno has argued elsewhere, consistently tried to convince their readers that the experiences they described in writing were indeed real and not invented (*Guancane* 143). In the process of doing so, a chronicler such as Bernal Díaz del Castillo succeeded at re-creating "not only the specific outline of events but also the ethos of the culture of its protagonists" (*Polemics* 188). Several centuries later, poets, novelists, playwrights, and filmmakers in and outside Mexico continue to articulate the colonia in order to produce deeper types of historical truths and lay bare multiple states of coloniality in the midst of a globalized era. This volume provides a sample of ongoing colonial itineraries that, from an interdisciplinary perspective, invite readers to continue "looking back" at Mexico's living tradition.

Notes

1. Drawing from Du Bois, Mignolo considers that "El principio de doble-conciencia es . . . la característica del imaginario del mundo moderno-colonial desde las márgenes de los imperios (desde las Américas, desde el Sureste de Asia, desde África del Norte y del Sur del Sahara). Pero también, como se comprueba hoy por las migraciones masivas a Europa y a Estados Unidos, desde el interior de los países que fueron o que son potencias imperiales: los 'negros' (tanto africanos, como pakistanos como indúes) en Inglaterra; los magrebinos en Francia; los latinos/as en los Estados Unidos. La doble conciencia, en suma, es una consecuencia de la colonialidad del poder y la manifestación de subjetividades forjadas en la diferencia colonial" (64).

2. Enrique Krauze openly denounces this condition in his polemical collection *Textos heréticos* (1992). See, for instance, his chapter on Carlos Fuentes (31–57).

3. We use the term "residual subjects" following Marisa Belausteguigoitia, for whom "la categoría de sujetos del residuo o residuales conlleva una resonancia con la noción de sujeto lacaniana, en su doble carácter: sujetos del discurso, de su creación y rearticulación, y a la vez sujetados al discurso. Estos sujetos se encuentran fijados a su condición de clase 'trabajadora' o 'baja,' pero es esa misma condición la que posibilita su pequeña o mayor 'liberación.' Lo 'residual,' tanto en la sujeción al discurso como en su creación, presenta una posibilidad de lo insondable o lo no representable, lo impronunciable, y que constituye, por lo general, a sujetos raciales, lingüísticos y geográficos descalificados" (161).

4. "[E]n 1983 y 1984, respectivamente, se termina el régimen militar en Argentina y Uruguay; en Brasil, la democracia regresa en 1985; en 1987 empieza el proceso de paz en El Salvador; entre 1988–1990 Chile se sacude de la dictadura de Pinochet; 1989 pone fin al mando absoluto de Stroessner en Paraguay. Otro proceso histórico-político que caracteriza la década es el comienzo de la integración regional a través de la cual los países latinoamericanos buscan respuestas comunes a problemas económicos provocados por la deuda externa y a la creciente competencia económica-tecnológica por parte de (y entre) los países desarrollados que entraron ya en la fase posindustrial y neoliberal de sus economías. Los bloques regionales como la Contadora (Colombia, México, Panamá y Venezuela) y el Grupo de Apoyo (Argentina, Brasil, Perú, Uruguay), que en 1986 se transformaron en el Grupo de Río (o el Grupo de los Ocho), la Comunidad Andina de Naciones o el Mercosur son los principales ejemplos de la creciente transnacionalización de la economía en el contexto de la crisis económica de los años ochenta" (Perkowska 28–29).

Works Cited

Adorno, Rolena. *De Guancane a Macondo: Estudios de literatura hispanoamericana.* Sevilla: Renacimiento, 2008.
———. *The Polemics of Possession in Spanish American Narrative.* New Haven, CT: Yale University Press, 2007.
Aínsa, Fernando. "Los guardianes de la memoria: Novelar contra el olvido." *Cuadernos Americanos* 137.3 (2011): 11–29.
———. *Reescribir el pasado: Historia y ficción en América Latina.* Mérida: Centro de Estudios Latinoamericanos Rómulo Gallegos; Ediciones El Otro, el Mismo, 2003.
Barrientos, Juan José. *Ficción-historia: La nueva novela histórica hispanoamericana.* México, D.F.: Universidad Nacional Autónoma de México (UNAM), 2001.
Belausteguigoitia, Marisa. "El Movimiento de Resistencia Civil Pacífica en la Ciudad de México: Los 48 días del plantón." *Cultura y cambio social en América Latina.* Ed. Mabel Moraña. Madrid: Iberoamericana/Vervuert, 2008. 159–77.
Campa, Román de la. "Postcolonial Sensibility, Latin America, and the Question of Literature." *Coloniality at Large: Latin America and the Postcolonial Debate.* Ed. Mabel Moraña, Enrique Dussel, and Carlos A. Jáuregui. Durham, NC: Duke University Press, 2008. 435–58.
Corona, Ignacio. "El festín de la historia: Abordajes críticos recientes a la novela histórica." *Literatura Mexicana* 12.1 (2001): 87–113.

Du Bois, W. E. B. *The Souls of Black Folk*. 1903. Introduction by John Edgar Wideman. New York: Vintage Books, 1990.

Earle, Peter G. "Memoria e imaginación en hispanoamerica." *Revista Hispánica Moderna* 58.1–2 (2005): 174–84.

Echeverría, Bolívar. *Modernidad y blanquitud*. México, D.F.: Era, 2010.

Guerrero, Elisabeth. *Confronting History and Modernity in Mexican Narrative*. New York: Palgrave Macmillan, 2008.

Guillermoprieto, Alma. *Looking for History: Dispatches from Latin America*. New York: Vintage Books, 2001.

Jáuregui, Carlos A., and Mabel Moraña. Introduction. *Colonialidad y erítica en América Latina: Bases para un debate*. Ed. Carlos A. Jáuregui and Mabel Moraña. Puebla: Universidad de las Américas, 2007. 11–27.

Krauze, Enrique. *Textos heréticos*. México, D.F.: Grijalbo, 1992.

López, Kimberle S. *Latin American Novels of the Conquest: Reinventing the New World*. Columbia: University of Missouri Press, 2002.

Menton, Seymour. *Latin America's New Historical Novel*. Austin: University of Texas Press, 1993.

Mignolo, Walter D. "La colonialidad a lo largo y ancho: El hemisferio occidental en el horizonte colonial de la modernidad." *La colonialidad del saber: Eurocentrismo y ciencias sociales; Perspectivas Latinoamericanas*. Ed. Edgardo Lander. Buenos Aires: Consejo Latinoamericano de Ciencias Sociales (CLASCO), 2003. 55–85.

Monsiváis, Carlos. *Apocalipstick*. México, D.F.: Debate, 2009.

———. *Imágenes de la tradición viva*. México, D.F.: Fondo de Cultúra Económica (FCE)/Landucci/UNAM, 2006.

Moraña, Mabel, Enrique Dussel, and Carlos A. Jáuregui. "Colonialism and Its Replicants." *Coloniality at Large: Latin America and the Postcolonial Debate*. Ed. Mabel Moraña, Enrique Dussel, and Carlos A. Jáuregui. Durham, NC: Duke University Press, 2008. 1–20.

———, eds. *Coloniality at Large: Latin America and the Postcolonial Debate*. Durham, NC: Duke University Press, 2008.

Ortega, Julio. *Transatlantic Translations: Dialogues in Latin American Literature*. Trans. Philip Derbyshire. London: Reaktion, 2006.

Perkowska, Magdalena. *Historias híbridas: La nueva novela histórica latinoamericana (1985–2000) ante las teorías posmodernas de la historia*. Madrid: Iberoamericana/Vervuert, 2008.

Seydel, Ute. *Narrar historia(s): La ficcionalización de temas históricos por las escritoras mexicanas Elena Garro, Rosa Beltrán y Carmen Boullosa*. Madrid: Iberoamericana/Vervuert, 2007.

Vargas Llosa, Mario. *Sables y utopia: Visiones de América Latina*. Ed. Carlos Granés. Lima: Aguilar, 2009.

PART ONE

Revising Colonial Ruins and Chronicles

CHAPTER ONE

Carlos Monsiváis

Rewriting the Nation's Memory, Playing Back the Conscience of a Mexico Remiso

Linda Egan

In 1982, the preeminent Mexican chronicler Carlos Monsiváis's only work of fiction, *Nuevo catecismo para indios remisos*, attracted the attention of few reviewers. Its relentless satire of both colonial and contemporary Mexican religion, government, and culture—basing its humor on the beastly long chronicles of the sixteenth, seventeenth, and eighteenth centuries, and on Church treatises about sin ("esa Interpol de la Colonia"[1])—was apparently too obscure for a popular audience. Still, that slender volume of fables parodying New Spain belongs in the first generation of the cutting-edge genre then given the name "the new historical novel" in Latin America, primarily because of its tendency to "rewrite" the past in critical ways (Menton 42–64; Safati-Arnaud 97). These are the novels that, approximately between the 1970s and 1990s, revisited colonial chronicles, relations, histories, and tracts to give them a "relectura deslegitimadora" (Aínsa 115)—to fill in the blanks and correct, through fiction, what history had failed to set forth or had deliberately distorted (Fuentes 18–22): in short, to read history against the grain (Rabasa 248).[2] In Monsiváis's vast chronicle production, as well as in the darkly humorous *crónica*-stories compiled in the 1982 work to which I have referred above,[3] Monsiváis's emphasis on the theocratic synergy of the colony, which continues to bind Mexico's Catholic Church and state today, exposes the origins of a pervasive society-wide racism permeating class, gender, and economic status.

By definition, the historical *crónica* is an act of rewriting. What we can understand today as chronicle, in-depth feature article, and literary or personal journalism, in its New World inception was a unique discursive practice pioneered by conquerors and missionaries and intended to detail the earthshaking fact of America's existence before it became part of Europe's known reality. Some years ago, I noted that, together with "virtually all Latin American literary giants, Monsiváis fed his moral consciousness and his aesthetic imagination on the Chronicle of the Indies, a genre that sprang into being on the cusp of antiquity and modernity" and whose "textual plenitude" inspired the new historical novels, stories, chronicles, and dramas of the late twentieth century (*Carlos Monsiváis* 87). When Pedro Mártir de Anglería, Bernal Díaz del Castillo, or the Jesuit José de Acosta were penning their massive relations of conquest and colonization in Mexico and Peru, they had to adjust then-received concepts of historiography in order to account adequately for the dumbfounding circumstances that confronted them:[4]

> En el siglo XVI, frailes ávidos de conversiones y soldados de mirada latifundista escriben, con pasmo y escándalo moral, crónicas alucinantes. Hoy los más conocidos son los soldados, Bernal Díaz del Castillo y Álvar Núñez Cabeza de Vaca, pero los más asiduos son los frailes, que viajan enumerativamente a través de paisajes que los aturden y costumbres que, agua bendita en mano, ayudan a destruir. (Monsiváis, "De la Santa Doctrina" 753)

If writers without professional training, such as the conquistador Andrés de Tapia or the Dominican friar Diego Durán, produced magnificent records of their insertion into an alien Amerindian world, they did so with prior trepidation, special assistance, or what we might consider blissful ignorance, because there were so few others qualified for the job. It may go without saying that serious writers in Mexico since the New Spanish territory freed itself of Spanish dominion perforce read their colonial *crónicas*, whether or not evidence of the background knowledge they gained in doing so is explicitly evident in their work. In the texts by Monsiváis published in and after 2000 that I will highlight here, he allows us to see that he has consulted Motolinía, Bernal Díaz, Sahagún, Las Casas, and others. We soon understand that the *cronista* is rewriting an age, an epoch, a collective mentality, rather than a specific text. Monsiváis is rewinding the national memory and playing back the conscience of a country's unrepentant government and privileged classes.

Kimberle López counts a preoccupation with memory among the traits of the new historical novel of the Conquest (5); Walter Mignolo approaches the topic obliquely, reminding us that Indians and Creoles were left out of the story of discovery and later on reduced to generalizations: chroniclers and others wrote of the "Indians" and "Creoles" but almost never singled out any of them to tell their stories as unique human beings (4, 6). Think of how many colonial stories we hear from the point of view of the vanquished, or how often we are made aware of these people's perspective. The writers who marginalize the conquered subject in their works were men of their time, and so we cannot judge them harshly for placing but an *arenga* or two in the mouth of a prominent Indian such as Moctezuma. Today, the Nahua interpreter Malinche is all the rage, but in the sixteenth century, when she played an invaluable role in assuring victory for the greatly smaller Spanish army, she was lucky to get a walk-on part with a line to say. Bernal Díaz clearly adored her, but even he presents her as a spoken-of subject only, the object of a man's creation, never an actor on her own. In five wordy letters addressed to the Spanish monarchs justifying his iron grip on the right to conquer Mexico, Hernán Cortés does not name his interpreter or acknowledge his dependence on her for success; only in the fifth and last letter, an exposition of the despair he encountered as he crashed in circles about the Honduran jungle, does he mention Marina's name a single time (Cortés 242). Even on into the end of the twentieth century, few new-history novelists retell the colonial story from an indigenous point of view (López 2).

On the other hand, suppose you could read all of Carlos Monsiváis, starting with his work in 1959 and finishing in 2010—it might be surprising to note to what frequency and with what conviction he aims his discourse at the plight of Indians, the Indian, this Indian; how often he interviews Indians, listens to and quotes them, goes off into the jungle on foot to have a word with them in the rain, studies their art, music, photography, painting, sculpture, toys, every little thing that makes them the womb and soul of Mexican lived being.[5] Mexico's government, its voters, and its economically capable citizens have never tired of ignoring the Indians of Mexico, even when they could see their suffering.[6] Carlos Monsiváis never tired of writing—and rewriting—to get those sinners to repent. He preached with facts, vivid re-creation of realities made symbols and with the blackest of humor.

That hybrid expressive mode aligns Carlos Monsiváis with the Conquest and colony's intrepid literary founders, whose generic tendency to combine fact and fictionalized discourse characterizes Monsiváis's chronicles as well; truth and emotion team up powerfully to convey lived reality with democratizing impact. Among his chronistic ancestors, "no hay preocupación específicamente literaria en esta urgencia de ampliar los territorios del reino de este mundo y el reino de los cielos, y con todo, el resultado suele ser notable, la belleza expresiva fluye a través de la prédica, del sentido del detalle, del refrendo de lealtades" ("De la Santa Doctrina" 753–54). Neither soldiers turned cronistas of the Conquest nor missionary ethnographers inscribing the life of the Amerindian in voluminous chronicles intended to write either history or literature: "Para ellos cronicar es asir las sensaciones del instante, capturar a Cronos, defenderse de las versiones de los enemigos, celebrar de modo implícito y explícito su propia grandeza, salvar almas y anunciar la salvación colectiva, compartir las experiencias únicas" (754). In the characterizations Monsiváis enumerates in this nuclear text of 1987 titled "De la Santa Doctrina," we glimpse his reading of Bernal Díaz, Cortés, Sahagún, Las Casas, and Fray Toribio de Benavente, "Motolinía, the poor one" (his Indian nickname).

At the heart of the present reading of Monsiváis is a pivotal crónica, one of a triad of texts within a 672-page collection of chronicles called *Imágenes de la tradición viva* (2006). The book is filled with luscious, full-color illustrations, and Carlos Monsiváis's most limpid prose is displayed on thick glossy paper. This giant tome insists with every eloquent paratext that it be savored, taken seriously. The crónica "Los orígenes de la tradición: Los siglos virreinales" reflects on the traditions of New Spain between the Conquest and the Independence; it anchors a three-stage colonial review that begins with the inaugural text of the volume: "La fundación de las tradiciones: La Virgen de Guadalupe" is the first of twenty-nine distinct cultural practices, artifacts, and subjects explored throughout the book. The second chapter, "Las tradiciones fundacionales: El arte indígena," is a cultural analysis mediating the close thematic relationship between the first crónica and the third. Colonial traditions were all the more powerful for being constricted in number. These three chronicles demonstrate their tightly interwoven nature. They also reflect the guiding leitmotif of both *Imágenes* and Carlos Monsiváis's entire oeuvre—which suggests that tradition, as the cronista understands it, is history itself rewritten, reformulated, and thus perpetuated: "Toda tradición funciona con plenitud si se le cree existente desde siempre" (29).[7]

Monsiváis was known as a man of dauntingly diverse and complete knowledge. In his library—his house—in Mexico City, among other topics too numerous to catalog, he read about literary and cultural theory without feeling constrained to pour the jargon into his crónicas in order to prove his knowledge of them. He speaks at length, or in the condensed form of the aphorism, of tradition(s) throughout his work. For the very substantial volume he assembled in *Imágenes de la tradición viva*, Monsiváis attaches a prologue of a single page; the volume's texts will immediately speak for tradition with sufficient eloquence. Somewhat perfunctorily, he places an "objective" definition of tradition on the preliminary page, a brief statement lifted from the English historian Eric Hobsbawm.[8] He excuses himself for presenting a book that is not utterly exhaustive on Mexican traditions, but assures us that all, if living still, are meaningful and, like history, bearers of lessons worth repeating (or not).[9]

If ever there is a Mexican tradition that has remained alive and kicking throughout five eventful centuries, it is the Virgin of Guadalupe, "el principio de la tradición en México" (Monsiváis, *Imágenes* 31)—as Monsiváis sees it, one of perhaps two truly authentic cultural practices that Mexico has created locally since its inception as a Europeanized society (17, 19, 25).[10] Spanning the three centuries of the colonial era and beyond, the Virgin of Guadalupe is "el gran signo de lo nacional" (25, 75, 86). In the beginning, there was the indigenous Virgin,[11] vindicating "la epidermis morena de una nación" (13). Her transcendence and her miraculous powers grow out of the ethnicity of her territory and "el tamaño de la desesperación" (18) of the Amerindian survivors suddenly bereft of gods and sociocultural autonomy. If this local Virgin is the foundation stone of post-Conquest Mexican religion and customs, the racial ambiguity visibly embodied in her Indian-white heritage becomes the sociopolitical base on which colonial life and, later, the Mexican nation are erected (58, 59, 87, 88).

On the latter point, Monsiváis is adamant: the cause-and-effect connection between secular power and religion is undeniable, especially as emblematized by the Virgin venerated by conquered Indians. It is to be read in the chronicles and in the laws, in Church dogma and in public spectacles arranged to mollify the "multitudes harapientas" (*Imágenes* 65, 71)—Indians and many mixed-blood offspring of Spaniards, Indians, and Africans who early on discovered what would be their historically impoverished niche in the Mexican social order. A syncretic reader, Monsiváis can perceive the lines that stretch between Catholicism and its saints' lives—you are rewarded if you suffer beyond endurance—and the Native Americans who survived the battles of conquest. More significantly, he draws links among the Church's expectations, viceregal power, and the indigenous born after the Conquest, yet who still live as the vanquished, still suffer beyond endurance—due to their lack of rights, dignity, well-being, sustenance, rightful belonging in civil society, tolerance by others, education, even basic humanity, in the eyes of the more elite. The religion of the colonial era is not the mystical Neoplatonism of the mind contemplated by the lettered elite; it is the brutally lived suffering of the abject who became the permanently conquered members of Mexican society.[12]

In collections such as *El estado laico y sus malquerientes* (2008) and *Entrada libre* (1987), the cronista comments at length on his society's deeply rooted racism (among other controversial topics). Mexico's unbudging rejection of the Other within began on the day of the European Conquest, achieved institutional status during the three hundred years of colonization, reached epic proportions throughout the nineteenth century, and continues indelibly.[13] As Monsiváis comments acerbically, with respect to the racism that becomes bilateral with immigration from Mexico to the United States: "No es tan exacto alegar que al llegar a Norteamérica los migrantes se ven obligados a interiorizar el racismo, porque si su tez es morena, ya lo traen bien asimilado. En sus lugares de origen, 'los prietitos' sirven, por ejemplo, para que los oligarcas se sientan criollos" ("De los otros aportes" 19). It was thus as a creole society struggled to distinguish itself from the favored Spanish elite in post-Conquest New Spain; it was thus as those triumphant creoles ejected the Spanish from newly independent Mexico, and ever has it been since. Deeply religious, the indigenes who survived Cortés's defeat of Cuauhtémoc proved willing to grasp the efficacy of the Christian goddess who had defeated their deities. During the relatively brief hostilities between Spanish invaders and Amerindian defenders, Mary had claimed a spot on the Great Temple pyramid next to the war god Huitzilopochtli—who so often had steered his charges wrong, while she, dashing into battle with Captain Malinche and his stalwart troops, had tossed dirt into Indian eyes to obviate the advantage of their greater numbers and magically produce victory for the Spanish throughout the land.[14] The broken-hearted Indians needed someone fantastic who had proved herself compassionate and capable. Unwittingly, they took control of Mexico's spiritual future by tucking their goddess mother Tonantzin inside Mary's blue robe. Pretty soon, the creoles in power were using the Virgin of Guadalupe—a paradoxical inversion of European and Native ascendancy—to assert dangerously their sociopolitical autonomy from Spain.

Mexico went forth into independence as a creole and indigenous society, and with Catholicism its one true religion and Guadalupe-Tonantzin its spiritual patroness.[15] With a logic arising from history, Guadalupe became closely associated with poor natives and mestizos—that is, in physical terms, under the adversity that is the norm in Mexico (Monsiváis, qtd. in Furlong 89), and in psychic terms, with unrelieved suffering. As Monsiváis reviews Francis detto Alÿs's photos of the historic center of Mexico

City in 2006, he spies a mongrel dog wandering the square. For him, this sight becomes an evil sign of a society that abandons the least among its members to hunger and depression, the dog a miserable being hunkered down next to where the homeless hang out, a symbol of an unequal citizen in an unequal community (Monsiváis, *Historic Centre* 115).

Only pages away from this somber reflection, the cronista adjusts his attitude and rewrites colonial history from another angle. The Plaza Garibaldi, he tells us, is the "duermevela de los mariachis donde las cenas y las penas se alternan y complementan a la luz de las canciones" (109), and it is also where we can observe "la estupefacción de don Hernán Cortés cuando le preguntó a doña Marina, o Malintzin o Malinche, quiénes eran esos seres extraños e inadmisibles con guitarras, guitarrones y violines y vestuario de ruinas de hacienda, que veían en los conquistadores a clientes a los que les decían de golpe: '¿Qué le vamos a tocar, jefe?'" (109). In its treatment of human beings without access to a sufficient standard of living, or the will to insist on one, Mexico's power culture has not changed since *tlatoani*-slave days. But aspects of its art and culture have evolved—so much so that conquistadors and Mexicas alike would be astonished if they experienced it today.

Nonetheless, Monsiváis makes it clear that in the areas of collective life where it counts, pre-Columbian art traces a continuum from its origins to its adaptation and elaboration in the colonial period to its manifestation from the 1920s "revival" of interest in things pre-Hispanic to the contemporary era ("Arte popular" 21–22, 27). His chronicle on "Arte indígena" (*Imágenes* 53–60) is evidence of the interest he sustained in the roots of indigenous aesthetics flourishing throughout the years of conquest and bureaucratization of New Spain and into the Mexico of his lifelong study (53, 75). He cites two types of astonishment before the spectacle of painting, sculpture, architecture, and ceramics as the Aztecs and other Amerindians created them: the missionaries and land-owning Spaniards "alucinados por el odio a 'lo pagano'" (54) and today's Mexicans who, unable to "entender estas obras desde la perspectiva de sus hacedores," must still feel obligated to at least go see them in a museum and sense a "relación vivísima" with the ancient objects that now form the basis of a tradition (54): the Othering distance of the strange surviving through time.

The indigenous art from before, during, and after the sixteenth century grew out of the practice of human sacrifice and the dance, music, and other elements of spectacle that always attended ritual murder. It is not that Aztec art was based on autochthonous religious rites; Indian art *was* a religious act of cosmogonic intent, "la creatividad extrema . . . que es anhelo de infinito" (Monsiváis, *Imágenes* 53). Not until the twentieth century, for example, did Mexico capture the significance of the great ceremonial centers of Aztec life, "el espacio donde todo culmina y todo se inicia" (53). Mexican scholars and connoisseurs took a new look at the pyramids of Teotihuacán, the Templo Mayor of Tenochtitlán, Chichén Itzá, Palenque, Uxmal, Bonampak, and many more; they began to appreciate "el sentido de grandeza que trasciende la índole guerrera de pueblos al filo inevitable de la violencia y la saña" (53).

Still evident in Mexican crafts is the indigene's love of color and form, veneration of flora and fauna, and "respeto a las potencias sólo asibles en la representación" (53). These characteristics of plastic art in a pre-lettered society inspire a constant theme in Monsiváis's work. He frequently notes that a majority of Mexicans today are—and in light of this crónica, continue to be, since pre-Columbian days—preoccupied with appearances, with the way things seem. As the *Teórico Súbito*, he may slide in among a mass of working-class Mexicans and observe their desperate feeling of the need to conform, to be physically close to an idol they must worship (*Días* 46). While among the masses at concerts, in blue-collar dance dives, at boxing matches or beauty contests, Monsiváis rewrites what he observes, applying and creating theories to account for the collective traits he analyzes. We see him ever on the hunt for transformational patterns of behavior among his compatriots: signs that what has survived since before the Conquest has evolved into a modern way of thinking and behaving. He is almost always disappointed.

The religious, which defines art during the centuries of Amerindian autonomy in Mexican and Central American territories, continues to characterize the indigenous art forms practiced during the colonial period. One form of art that proliferates in the colonial world, for instance, is the convent mural. One may observe throughout Mexico that the convents built by Dominicans, Augustinians, Franciscans, and Jesuits "prescinden de una inspiración netamente europea al demostrarse en ellos claramente la incorporación de imágenes, materiales y técnicas de la tradición prehispánica" (Schuessler 16). Another typical colonial art form, the missionary drama composed to help convert the conquered Indians to Christianity, is also a showpiece of syncretism. Similarly, there existed Nahua theater works that adapted and appropriated Christian discourse (Burkhart 7).

Adoration of form and color—as well as veneration of the invisible made material through the word—permeate the whole of Carlos Monsiváis's writings. His principal focus regarding indigenous art is on its verbal creations, song and poetry, and on the contemporary scholars who devote(d) themselves to preserving and making widely accessible the thought and artistry of Nahua composers. He cites Ángel María Garibay K. at length for his exemplary work on the first friars and chroniclers who dedicated their labor to learning and inventing grammars for some forty indigenous languages, and who also saved many of the pre-Hispanic pictographic books from the zealous fires of less culturally appreciative missionaries (*Imágenes* 56). No doubt Monsiváis was one of Garibay's beneficiaries, grateful to read colonial texts with Garibay's notes and translations. He is beholden, as well, to Miguel León-Portilla for the many books of Náhuatl culture and poetry, as well as the vanquished's moving version of the Conquest (León-Portilla, *Reverso* 53–54). Carlos Monsiváis was famous for his stupendous memory; a significant portion of it was occupied with indigenous poetry that he no doubt was able to absorb from León-Portilla's books. Everywhere in the cronista's writing, lines from *Visión de los vencidos* or from *Las literaturas indígenas de Mesoamérica* show up, either quoted directly or inserted as an intertext. Notably, Monsiváis compares the Aztec practice of sacrifice to the Díaz-Ordaz government's massacre of innocents in the Plaza de Tlaltelolco in 1968, observing that "se renovaba la vieja sangre insomne" (*Días* 303) while citing intertextually the anonymous Aztec who recounts the tragic defeat of his society: "¡Llorad amigos!" (302).[16]

We can trace Monsiváis's reading of and in colonial texts throughout this and the other two chronicles of the trilogy, as well as in many other texts in his overall works. Explicit or implicit, colonial masters Ixtlilxóchitl, Durán, and Bernal Díaz make their presence known among the many whom Monsiváis consults as he "rewrites" the memoirs of his predecessors in order to rearrange the thinking of his contemporaries and—assuredly— his successors. In keeping with his wont and his public's expectations, he will often practice his belief in the virtue of antisolemnity. For instance, while enumerating Mexica and Mayan gods, whose autonomy effectively died with the Conquest, and which thereafter coexisted with Christian gods as part of the national heritage, Monsiváis slips a sly reference to the conquistador Bernal Díaz's *Historia verdadera* into the list. According to our cronista, the indigenous gods represented in buildings, paintings, songs, and plastic arts include Tlaloc, Huehueteotl, Mictlantecuhtli, and Huichilobos. Right there we have to snicker. Bernal Díaz was evidently hard of hearing when Náhuatl words were concerned; a Mexica pronounced the name "Huitzilopochtli" (God of War), and Bernal Díaz heard "Huichilobos," or "God-Wolf," a term that sounds about right if you fight every day in terror of being captured, sacrificed, and eaten (*Historia verdadera* clvi). Monsiváis wrote every other god's name correctly, but he borrowed the conquistador's Huichilobos to entertain the reader and himself.

Many of the books Monsiváis published are exquisite works of art. *Imágenes de la tradición viva* is one of them. Another is *Belleza y poesía en el arte popular mexicano* (1996), from which a part of the crónica on "Arte indígena" of *Imágenes* is based. In the book *Belleza y poesía*, Monsiváis is the first of three authors of texts accompanied by lavish photographic illustrations of the popular arts of Mexico. In Monsiváis's "Arte popular: Lo invisible, lo siempre redescubierto, lo perdurable; Una revisión histórica," this critic of culture focuses on the nature of pre-Columbian indigenous art and its durable links to the viceroyalty and thence to Mexican crafts today (21–22). To speak of popular art in Mexico is to say indigenous culture (27), due to a linkage of the indigenous, picturesque, and locally handmade that has become a Mexican cliché. But, Monsiváis hastens to add, that does *not* mean that the artisan belongs to the national community: "Como ningún otro tema, el del indígena resulta piedra de toque. Allí se refleja y se acrecienta la falsa conciencia de la burguesía que prodiga un mito: el indígena como lastre nacional y raza irredimible" ("Clasismo" 71). What begins with the Conquest persists throughout Mexican history as a tragic dichotomy between pride in the aesthetic artifacts that represent a heroic indigenous past and the "racismo que invisibiliza a los indígenas vivos" (*Imágenes* 59). As a new year dawned in 1994, the "invisible" Indians of Chiapas rose up in arms against historic conditions of poverty and human-rights abuses; Carlos Monsiváis judged that "si algo aclara la rebelión de los indios de Chiapas . . . es el racismo devastador de México. Ser indio . . . es participar de la perpetua desventaja, es la segregación que comienza por el aspecto" ("Espacios" 22). Progress in the arena of human rights has been perceptible but minimal, he notes in a 2005 retrospective on the earthquakes of 1985, which inspired a gratifying altruism among citizens of Mexico City, as well as in the Zapatista rebellion in Chiapas ("*No sin nosotros*").[17] Unlike Guillermo Bonfil Batalla (author of *México profundo*), who would clearly like to turn the clock back to pre-Conquest times of Indian autonomy, Monsiváis's historicist viewpoint remains focused in a forward direction. He deplores sociopolitical and economic oppression of indigenous people as well as of any marginalized sectors of his society, but he looks always for change for the better, and he sees some in Indian communities. For one well-known instance, when women led the movement for political autonomy in the Zapotec town of Juchitán, Oaxaca, Monsiváis was there to capture in *cronos*—in lived, chronological time—the momentous victory of an indigenous group against the political machine and assassins of the monopoly Partido Revolucionario Institucional (Monsiváis, *Entrada* 151–66).

One victory does not a democracy make, of course. Monsiváis takes the humorous approach to social criticism in his last collection of chronicles, *Apocalipstick* (2009). In it, he rewrites the book of Genesis to take yet another swipe at the crippling centralism, which—since Teotihuacán, Tula, and Tenochtitlán; three centuries of viceregal rule; and two centuries of nationalism—has hampered economic development and punished citizens. Mexico has been born again many times in its history, but nothing ever changes, Monsiváis seems to say; thus, the newest (re)creation is brought about by timeworn sameness: the pre-Conquest gods Tláloc, Huitzilopochtli, Coatlicue, and Xipe Tótec (Our Lord the Flayed One) first formed the Center, but they later added the Province so that folks out there would be able to migrate to the capital (*Apocalipstick* 15). Here, as elsewhere, Monsiváis comments snidely on the Mexican predilection for occupying the "good" center and eschewing the "bad" outlying areas. This historical tendency to congregate in vast urban centers causes two unintended problems: overcrowding in a capital whose natural resources are all but depleted, and export of people from the provinces.

Also in *Apocalipstick*, Monsiváis reminds us that the Juchitecs may have won the right to run their own city council, but that did not put them into a higher tax bracket. He imagines the national indigenous community being startled to realize that "carecemos de una aristocracia reconocida internacionalmente" (153). Right away, readers know that the cronista has nothing bad to say about Indians and is instead reminding us that their historic oppression has, indeed, decreed that they should never ascend to the higher classes; he is about to take some mighty swings at the privileged. Case in point: it is enough, apparently, to have your photo published in the celebrity magazine ¡*Hola!* to claim blue blood. The Indians decide, therefore, that if they publish their own glamour mag and call it *Quiubo* or *Quiúbole* (later corrected by aristocratic impulses to *Qué Hubo*), they will slide into the upper-crust club (154). It takes them months to identify a suitable sighting of Mexican aristocrats for their first issue— "*¿Dónde descansaba la sangre azul mexicana*, for God's sake?" (155)—until they settle on Durango (155). Per his custom, Monsiváis has thrown his voice inside an imaginary Indian who notes a dearth of blue-blooded Mexicans. The cronista thus asks us to conclude that Mexico has no aristocracy at all, but is in fact only a nation of wannabes, of which some have more money than most.

Notwithstanding the occasionally jocular presentation of his views on racism and economic inequality, Monsiváis does recognize that dissident actions of the present day include those of indigenous people who "entreveran lo moderno y lo ancestral" (132), by which he indicates that the archaic mentality is gradually being educated into a forward-thrusting, modern attitude. It has taken some indigenous people nearly five hundred years to achieve the will to help themselves into liberty and well-being. Three hundred years of colonial servitude and two hundred years of oppression under the nationalist banner conspired to permanently infantalize the indigene, to keep him fatalistically dependent.

In "Los orígenes de la tradición: los siglos virreinales" (*Imágenes* 65–90), our cronista rests his analysis of the past on "testimonios históricos" (65), which phrase must include the first-person accounts of writers we consider to be chroniclers: Bernal Díaz, Las Casas, Clavijero. He also cites "la historia de la Nueva España" and "información copiosa" (66), as well as specific authors such as Motolinía and the eighteenth-century German travel writer Alexander von Humboldt.

Religion calls to mind morality, but as Monsiváis sees it, the institutionalized version operating through the monolithic Catholic Church does not practice the individualized, ethical morality that marks a modern and democratic mind. It instead imposes a dogmatic will—by force, through the Inquisition—on believers who become victims. In the longest of the colonial trilogy's chapters, this authoritarian religion is once again the first and foremost motif. Colonial Mexican society is presided over by the Virgin of Guadalupe; in these three centuries "no cabe Siglo de las Luces" (84). The Inquisition operates to ensure that no one thinks independently of Church dogma or court dictate; it is the same whether one is a vassal of the viceroy or a parishioner of the Church, for both dominions belong to God (65) and function in tandem. After the first two crónicas in the trilogy of *Imágenes*, the emphasis on religion in this one consolidates Catholicism as one of three ineradicable traditions of Mexico (65, 71–73, 75, 76), which includes in its syncretic heart both the concept and the practice of sacrificial suffering (76). To the latter, Indians and women have almost exclusive rights.

State power in colonial Mexico, as it always was in the same territory prior to conquest, is tightly interwoven with religion. Viceregal society remains as "sacred" from top to bottom as that which the Spanish soldiers conquered; now, it is Catholic rather than "pagan." To be accurate, it is becoming the idiosyncratic mix of "elementos indígenas precolombinos, catolicismo hispano popular del siglo XVI y las enseñanzas oficiales de la

Iglesia" that characterize the majority religious creed throughout Latin America today (Rowe and Schelling 87). This process of transculturation, or occidentalization—terms Monsiváis applies here to the viceroyalty's territorial and spiritual expansion (*Imágenes* 67, 69)—began during the Conquest itself, so that Church and theocratic state were both soon able to solidify their claims to authority. In the religious community that sprang up atop the ruins of Tenochtitlán, the state represented values of the Church as well as the secular precepts governing collective behavior of *gachupines* (Spaniards), creoles, mestizos, Indians, and—promptly—black slaves. An eye-catching tradition that quickly takes deep root in New Spain and to which postcolonial Mexicans cling is the religious fiesta, a spectacle at once theatrical and devotional; this is the only form of civic life to which the Indian has a right in viceregal Spain (71). Churches and street processions are schools for the vanquished: There, they acquire an aesthetic sensibility and "sin desearlo" (71), an ethical orientation dictated by Church will. This is "transculturation" by force for subjects who change their cultural habits "sin necesidad del nomadismo" (75).

At once shrinking from a religious structure they did not seek and seeking it because their own had been stripped from them, Aztec and other indigenous survivors of their holocaust suffered insult added to injury, for "la tradición más radical [de la colonia] es la burocracia, el caos que se forma después de la conquista" (69). Together with Catholicism, heavily bureaucratic governance still shapes Mexican society today, a reality visitors to the Zócalo can take in while viewing the Basílica de Guadalupe and the National Palace, with only the excavated ruins of the demolished Templo Mayor between them—"el poder de la religión y . . . la religión del poder" (Monsiváis, *Historic Centre* 106). If today the historic center of the capital is partly inhabited by homeless people and dogs, the Plaza Mayor of Mexico's eighteenth-century viceregal city boasted some brightly clad members of the elite, but mostly it overflowed with "el desaseo, los puestos y mercados en donde vibran el hambre y los léperos, las calles asimétricas y tortuosas, las acequias que manan aguas pútridas" (87). And a population growth that presses beyond the city limits extends a custom that was already traditional in the Anáhuac Valley before the Spaniards arrived. The phenomenon results in the partial development of the provinces but ultimately establishes a new tradition. When depressed social and economic conditions in the countryside make life untenable for indigenes, they migrate to the capital or to the United States.[18]

Pressured between an unyielding Church and the pitiless court, the Indian, as well as the mestizo and creole, established another enduring tradition during the colonial era: what is known as *relajo*, kicking back, fooling around, blowing off steam, having a good time—or, as Monsiváis puts it: "relajamiento de las costumbres" (*Imágenes* 79); that is, a momentary escape from the suffocating constriction of Custom, of Tradition, of "What Will People Say?" Monsiváis explains that people did not suddenly run wild in the streets. Instead, they simply relaxed—perhaps expressing themselves, for example, by venting their creative impulses in stone, wood, or canvas: "El amor por la decoración es un rechazo evidente del ascetismo de la Contrarreforma que no se acepta porque no se entiende, que no se acata porque limita atrozmente" (79). Thus we learn that in the seventeenth century, one source of the brilliant popular art of both sacred and secular theme is religion itself: the oppressiveness of Counter-Reformation Catholicism and the common citizen's need for a spiritual escape valve. Because this art is principally indigenous, "en el laberinto óptico del barroco novohispano se concilian los principios opuestos de lo devocional y lo pagano" (80).

The three chronicles about Mexico's colonial origins in *Imágenes de la tradición viva* that I highlight here focus on its indigenous genes, cultural aesthetic, sacred imaginary, and the minority powers' unrelenting campaign to suppress the vitalism and free will of the indigenous majority. In this sense, Carlos Monsiváis's trilogy of "*crónicas de Indias*" responds to Kimberle López's observation that few new historical novelists reconstruct the indigenous perspective (2). Among the few who do, Monsiváis here stands out for re-creating a distant social reality with the vanquished in mind at every moment as he explores the dimensions of traditions such as the Virgin of Guadalupe (an indigenous religious conception); the popular art of Mexico (principally indigenous in origin and character); and the society of viceregal New Spain, with its own traditions: religion, religion, and religion. The majority population—the indigenous—is directly and unhappily impacted by all that is invented, erected, practiced, and enforced in the New Spanish "monarchy." The racism under—and overlying—this situation was dismantled neither with independence nor with the Revolution of 1910—nor with Cárdenas's liberal government (1934–1940), nor with any government since. A special report in *Proceso* on the indigenous communities of Mexico provides evidence of the kind of almost "innate" poverty that Monsiváis has long accused his government of cultivating for political gain. The report, published in five multi-article installments in March 2007, relies on documentation and interviews with inhabitants of Mexican states with the highest indices of poverty, unemployment, birth rates, illiteracy, alcoholism, and violence (Caballero;

Martínez; Zamora Briseño; Mandujano; Dávila Valero): in short, "las consecuencias materiales negativas" del racismo (Acosta Córdova 30). The states where *Proceso* reporters fanned out to investigate deep pockets of "La miseria, la terrible miseria" in Mexico are Guerrero, Veracruz, Oaxaca, Chiapas, and Durango. It is this Mexico that sports smart phones and gorgeously illustrated books, hosts luxurious intellectual conferences, frequents swank boutiques, and uses new transportation systems, all of which cannot cover up an anti-democratic truth at its core, which Carlos Monsiváis reviews and rewrites as he returns to pre-Independence Mexico. There, he examines the origins of practices that became traditions, that became ingrained habits. On the topics of theocracy and racism, the two most deadly sins of the religion of reform he believes in, the chronicler's steadfastly optimistic gaze becomes "catastrofista" (qtd. in Furlong 92).

Most of the *cronistas de Indias* sought to represent what they had seen with their own eyes and heard with their own ears as accurately as their sensibilities and the values of their moment in history would permit. The article of faith that most distorted their writings held that God had always chosen Spain to conquer the Americas, that in His Catholic Wisdom, Spanish soldiers and men of the Church were providentially designated to accomplish the work of saving souls for Him. Despite the laudable efforts of a crusader like Bartolomé de las Casas, the people who found themselves quickly herded into the lowest ranks of New Spain society discovered that the churchmen and their spokesmen in the field would do nothing to help them leave that abyss. Over time, they learned in the flesh that Catholic zeal had cursed them forever, that there was no recovering from this loss.

With his analyses of colonial religion, art, and governance as foundational traditions of modern Mexico, Carlos Monsiváis rewrites Catholic providentialism. As he characterizes it in 2006, it is no longer an inevitable consequence of the Catholic kings' political and religious will, expressly authorized by God, to oust non-Catholics from their territory and unite all the fiefdoms under one flag, or to send Columbus across the ocean to get rich and proselytize. Governor Diego Velázquez of Cuba was after gold and slaves when he named Hernán Cortés captain of the 1519 expedition to conquer Mexico. Recall the decisions we made then and have made since, says Monsiváis to the compatriots who read him. Ponder what we should have done, what we did instead, what we have left undone. Between every line of *Imágenes de la tradición viva* and the majority of all else he wrote between 1959 and his death in June 2010, his voice resounds in a wilderness untended for five hundred years: it is never too late to repent. Judgment Day always awaits.

Notes

1. Although the overall tone of the chronicles gathered in the volume I work with for this study is more or less neutral, Monsiváis's humor will not be restrained entirely, especially when dealing with the solemnity of Church officialese. His Interpol quip is from one chronicle I focus on, "Siglos virreinales," in *Imágenes de la tradición viva* (83).

2. The text of Rabasa's that I cite was published at the end of the first generation of colonial rewriting. In it, Rabasa elaborates a revisionist look at a canonical lettered text—Carlos Sigüenza y Góngora's seventeenth-century account of the "Alboroto y motín de los indios de México" in 1692, and of an indigenous codex that was, however, inspired and influenced by the lettered conquering class—the Códex Mendoza, an account of the conquest from the perspective of the vanquished. His goal is to demonstrate how both texts, while purporting to be descriptive, are in fact prescriptive, providing information key to destroying the ways of life they illustrate (247–48).

3. Parallels between colonial and neoliberal times are evident to a careful reader of the mini-fables. The sculptor Bernardo may be contemplating a typical question for Catholics of Counter-Reformation New Spain—How many angels can dance on the head of a pin?—but the fact that he takes the question with scientific seriousness transports our reading to the often sublimely ridiculous investigations carried out today by PhDs. When Bernardo is assailed by demographers clamoring to know the results of his study, Monsiváis's nonserious narrator informs them, "Según cálculos, se igualó el número de ángeles y demógrafos" (26)—clearly a jab at contemporary media mobs who hurl themselves on objects of their fleeting fanaticism. Notwithstanding the humor, when the reader gets it, *Indios remisos* presents a serious rewriting of colonial and nineteenth-century history. Not much has been written on this spunky fiction, but see, for example, Dávila, "*Nuevo catecismo*," and Egan, "Emblematic Revelations."

4. These circumstances of course included the facts (for Europeans, shocking) of human sacrifice and cannibalism, both in Mexico and Peru. The bibliography for this complex and fundamental phenomenon is extensive and not germane to this study. See, for a compact reference to the subject on the eve of the conquest, Fernández-Armesto (289–99). There were, as well, the sociopolitical and cultural aspects of indigenous life that fascinated their European chroniclers. León-Portilla, for example, is prominent among students of pre-Columbian song and poetry in Mexico, as well as all other facets of Nahua culture (see *Literaturas indígenas* and *Toltecáyotl*). In a very recent book, Charles Mann has put in lay—not to say simplistic—terms the evolutionary history of Oaxaca's brilliant pre-Columbian geneticists and inventions in Zapotec territory of not one or two but three calendars, the zero and glyphic writing (236–38).

5. Monsiváis writes frequently about Mexico's indigenous arts, at length or as part of a generalized treatment of popular culture. He may focus on the arts themselves or on an artist/artesan, such as Francisco Toledo. A particularly excellent and beautifully

illustrated overview can be found in the tabletop volume authored by Monsiváis, Fernando del Paso, and José Emilio Pacheco, *Belleza y poesía en el arte popular mexicano*. Monsiváis's text is on "Arte popular: Lo invisble, lo siempre redescubierto, lo perdurable: una revisión histórica." As the title indicates, here as elsewhere, when the cronista considers a baseline element of national identity, he frames his analysis of social and political impacts—of change—within a temporal frame. He looks always for what is lasting, what is good, and what should be changed.

6. Monsiváis suggests that historical, pan-national racism has held back the entire country of Mexico in its ability to provide enough jobs, food, housing, education, clothing, and other necessities for virtually every member of its society. One powerful explanation for Mexico's failure as a state—its failure to lead and to provide for its people's needs—is its insistent relegating of Mexican indigenous peoples to oblivion or to government "help" that in fact worsens an execrable situation. A recent, solidly reported series in Mexico's leading news magazine examines diverse indigenous peoples throughout the country and makes it impossible to ignore the "negative material consequences" of racism. Numbers alone can suggest this impact: Chiapas, Guerrero, and Oaxaca are the states with the highest concentrations of indigenous population and the ones sunk most deeply in poverty, which puts Mexico on a level with undeveloped Africa (Acosta Córdova 30).

7. I will cite in my text the three chronicles of the trilogy by page number(s) in *Imágenes*.

8. Here, Monsivais gives the reader a rare in-text citation of the source he is citing. Chronicles by definition eschew academic apparata. The most Monsiváis generally provides, if anything at all, is a last name—but here, we get all but the page number. He is citing Hobsbawm's *The Invention of Tradition* (1983).

9. The traditions Monsiváis chronicles in *Imágenes* are: the Virgin of Guadalupe; indigenous art; colonial culture; the nineteenth century; religious (Catholic) memory/history; secularization; the dictatorship of Porfirio Díaz; historic memory and popular tradition; José Guadalupe Posada's lively skeletons; landscape, prophesy, and the state of mind: movies; travel; the Mexican Revolution; the Mexican School of Painting; the Historic Center; the province and conservatism; myths; Golden Age of movies; Ramón López Velarde; Mother's Day and other sublime traditions; the Two Origins (Hispanic and Ethnic); Juan Rulfo; the plastic arts; popular music; Frida Kahlo; housing; food; television; comics; and soccer.

10. The other cultural artifact Monsiváis cites as original to the Americas is the baroque ("Fundación" 19), what could be qualified by saying "el barroco de Indias," or the version of the European baroque of the seventeenth century that continued into the eighteenth century. In this baroque expression, the New World demonstrated a much more enthusiastic and long-lived love of ornamentation, in keeping with the pre-Hispanic Indian admiration of flowers, curvy lines, intricately carved details in stone and featherwork that anticipated every frou-frou impulse of the Victorian era. To visit a baroque church in Mexico is to swoon before the sea of angels and flowers and crosses glittering in waves across all its walls and every inch of its ceiling. Its smallest space is inhabited with imagination-made art. All the little angels have Indian faces.

11. The Guadalupan cult is to a Virgin in whom the Aztec's mother goddess Tonantzin is fused with the Catholic virgin mother Mary. As tradition since the seventeenth century holds that the "brown" Virgin appeared to a humble Indian

campesino, the Indian nature of Mexico's patron saint is ever present in the popular mind. Drawing from a copious bibliography on the Virgin of Guadalupe, Jacques Lafaye provides a solid understanding of the cult within the mythical and historical context; the first chapter of Rowe and Schelling provides an efficient summary view. For a history of the Virgin in English, see David Brading's nicely illustrated, coherent, complete account of the two Marys in Mexico, one Spanish and one local, who competed with each other before the *Virgen de Guadalupe*, the indigenous goddess, won the country's heart.

12. In another passage, Monsiváis writes that the power elite, since the Conquest and up to now, has cultivated "el carácter sacro del régimen"; the popular class has obeyed "las tradiciones de la abyección" (*El 68* 215).

13. On the longevity of racism in Mexico, see, for example, Bonfil Batalla's "Quinientos años después." A hundred and fifty years ago, chronicler Guillermo Prieto recognized racism as a pervasive problem in the Mexican nation that was attempting to take form after its wars of independence: "Para Prieto, reafirmar la grandeza del pasado prehispánico, es rehusarse a la mutilación histórica iniciada en la Colonia y proseguida por los conservadores, que hace del criollismo el todo de la nacionalidad" (Monsiváis, *Herencias* 147). Similarly, the sharply critical thinker Ignacio Ramírez called for education and restitution of human rights to the conquered indigene: "Sin ver también en la cultura indígena a la iniciadora de la nacionalidad, no se defiende suficientemente a sus descendientes, calificados por los conservadores y casi todos los liberales de 'peso muerto de México'" (Monsiváis, *Herencias* 205).

14. Among several Marian miracles Bernal Díaz recounts, two involve the Virgin of War (Nebel 45–46), long a tradition in Western Europe. In one account, fifty thousand Mexica warriors excuse their defeat by a handful of Spanish at the Rica Villa de la Vera Cruz (today, Veracruz) because a *gran tecleciguata* rode before the invaders and led them to victory (*Historia verdadera*, xciv). In another Bernal Díaz episode, at the start of the (in)famous series of battles Cortés and his dwindling little army fought to escape from the Aztec capital in mid-Conquest, one of Cortés's captains reports that Indians fighting around their temple claimed to lose the struggle because a Great Lady who looked exactly like the Virgin blinded them with dirt (*Historia verdadera*, cxxv).

15. She was declared patron of Mexico City in 1737 and of all New Spain in 1746. Immediately after declaring Mexico's independence from Spain, creole rebel leaders voted to make Catholicism the official religion of the new country and the Virgin of Guadalupe its patron saint.

16. From the song describing the Nahua people's loss of Tenochtitlán after the seige of the summer of 1521. See *El reverso de la conquista* (53–54).

17. The Ejército Zapatista de Liberación Nacional, or Zapatista Army of National Liberation, aimed its January 1, 1994, armed uprising against the Salinas de Gortari government and historic social attitudes toward Indians in Chiapas and elsewhere in Mexico, dovetailing the attacks with the date that the Tratado de Libre Comercio, or North American Free Trade Agreement took effect among Mexico, the United States, and Canada. The uprising was as much about neoliberal economics and its effects on the poor as it was specifically about the tradition of anti-Indian racism in Mexico.

18. There is a very large bibliography on the U.S.-Mexico border and, in particular, migration across it to access the U.S. job market. In the context of this study, in

which Christianity plays a central role, readers may find Rodney Stark's comparison of the Mexican socioeconomic reality interesting. On immigation, see pages 212–13.

Works Cited

Acosta, José de. *Historia natural y moral de las Indias.* 1590. Ed. Edmundo O'Gorman. México, D.F.: Fondo de Cultura Económica (FCE), 1962.

Acosta Córdova, Carlos. "Ni para comer . . ." *Proceso* 1679 (2009): 28–31.

Aínsa, Fernando. "Invención literaria y 'reconstrucción' histórica en la nueva narrativa latinoamericana." *La invención del pasado: La novela histórica en el marco de la posmodernidad.* Ed. Karl Kohut. Madrid: Iberoamericana/Vervuert, 1997. 111–21.

Bonfil Batalla, Guillermo. *México profundo: Una civilización negada.* México, D.F.: Grijalbo; Consejo Nacional para la Cultura y las Artes (Conaculta), 1990.

——. "Quinientos años después: ¿Llegaremos finalmente a un pacto de civilizaciones?" *México a fines de siglo.* Ed. José Joaquín Blanco and José Woldenberg. 2 vols. México, D.F.: FCE, 1993. 377–98.

Brading, David A. *Mexican Phoenix: Our Lady of Guadalupe: Image and Tradition Across Five Centuries.* Cambridge: Cambridge University Press, 2001.

Burkhart, Louise M. *Holy Wednesday: A Nahua Drama from Early Colonial Mexico.* Philadelphia: University of Pennsylvania Press, 1996.

Caballero, Alejandro. "Miseria, la terrible miseria." *Proceso* 1583 (2007): 15–18.

Cortés, Hernán. *Cartas de relación.* 1522. Introduction by Manuel Alcalá. México, D.F.: Porrúa, 1994.

Dávila, Arturo. "*Nuevo catecismo para indios remisos* o las trampas de la Reverenda fe." *El arte de la ironía: Carlos Monsiváis ante la crítica.* Ed. Mabel Moraña and Ignacio Sánchez Prado. México, D.F.: Universidad Nacional Autónoma de México (UNAM)/Era, 2007. 204–34.

Dávila Valero, Patricia. "Caminos hacia la nada." *Proceso* 1587 (2007): 37–39.

Díaz del Castillo, Bernal. *Historia verdadera de la conquista de la Nueva España.* 1632. Ed. Miguel León-Portilla. Madrid: Historia 16, 1984.

Durán, Diego de. *Historia de las Indias de Nueva-España y islas de Tierra Firme.* México, D.F.: Imprenta de J. M. Andrade y F. Escalante, 1867–1880.

Egan, Linda. *Carlos Monsiváis: Culture and Chronicle in Contemporary Mexico.* Tucson: University of Arizona Press, 2001.

——. "Emblematic Revelations of a Just World to Come in Carlos Monsiváis's *Nuevo catecismo para indios remisos.*" *Revista Canadiense de Estudios Hispánicos* 32.2 (2008): 333–61.

Fernández-Armesto, Felipe. *1492: The Year the World Began.* New York: HarperOne, 2009.

Fuentes, Carlos. *Geografía de la novela.* México, D.F.: FCE, 1993.

Furlong, Julie. "Carlos Monsiváis." *Testimonios de fin de siglo: 25 entrevistas que definen el acontecer nacional, realizadas por Julie Furlong.* México, D.F.: Planeta, 2000. 87–92.

Lafaye, Jacques. *Quetzalcóatl y Guadalupe.* México, D.F.: FCE, 1997.

Las Casas, Bartolomé de. *Brevísima relación de la destrucción de las Indias.* 1552. Ed. Consuelo Varela. Madrid: Castalia, 1999.

——. *Historia de las Indias.* 1875. Ed. Lewis Hanke. México, D.F.: FCE, 1951.

León-Portilla, Miguel. *Las literaturas indígenas de Mesoamérica.* México, D.F.: FCE, 1992.

——. *El reverso de la conquista.* México, D.F.: Joaquín Mortiz, 1964.

——. *Toltecáyotl: Aspectos de la cultura náhuatl.* México, D.F.: FCE, 1980.

——. *Visión de los vencidos.* La Habana: Casa de las Américas, 1969.

López, Kimberle S. *Latin American Novels of the Conquest: Reinventing the New World.* Columbia: University of Missouri Press, 2002.

Mandujano, Isaín. "Los últimos." *Proceso* 1586 (2007): 40–43.

Mann, Charles C. *1491: New Revelations of the Americas Before Columbus.* New York: Knopf, 2005.

Martínez, Regina. " '¿Pos qué le hacemos?' " *Proceso* 1584 (2007): 22–24.

Menton, Seymour. *La nueva novela histórica de la América Latina, 1979–1992.* Trans. Seymour Menton. México, D.F.: FCE, 1993.

Mignolo, Walter D. *The Idea of Latin America.* Oxford: Blackwell, 2005.

Monsiváis, Carlos. *Apocalipstick.* México, D.F.: Random House Mondadori, 2009.

——. "Arte popular: Lo invisible, lo siempre redescubierto, lo perdurable. Una revisión histórica." *Belleza y poesía en el arte popular mexicano.* By Carlos Monsiváis, Fernando del Paso, and José Emilio Pacheco. México, D.F.: Tiempo Imaginario; CVS Publicaciones, 1996. 19–29.

——. "Carlos Monsiváis." *Testimonios de fin de siglo: 25 entrevistas con los personajes que definen el acontecer nacional, realizadas por Julie Furlong.* Interview by Julie Furlong. México, D.F.: Planeta, 2000. 87–92.

——. "Clasismo y novela en México." *Cuadernos Políticos* 1 (1974): 67–79.

——. "De la Santa Doctrina al espíritu público." *Nueva Revista de Filología Hispánica* 35 (1987): 753–71.

——. "De los otros aportes de los migrantes." *La compañía de los libres* 2 (2002): 18–19.

——. *Días de guardar.* México, D.F.: Era, 1970.

——. *Entrada libre: Crónicas de la sociedad que se organiza.* México, D.F.: Era, 1987.

——. *El Estado laico y sus malquerientes (crónica/antología).* México, D.F.: UNAM, 2008.

——. "La fundación de las tradiciones: La Virgen de Guadalupe." *Imágenes* 12–49.

——. *Las herencias ocultas: Del pensamiento liberal del siglo XIX.* México, D.F.: Instituto de Estudios Educativos y Sindicales de América, 2000.

——. "Los espacios marginales." *Debate Feminista* 18 (1998): 20–28.

——. *The Historic Centre of Mexico City.* Texts in Spanish by Carlos Monsiváis. Trans. Susan Meredith and Caroline Haslett. Images by Francis detto Alÿs. Madrid: Turner, 2006. 99–116.

——. *Imágenes de la tradición viva.* México, D.F.: FCE/Landucci/UNAM, 2006.

——. "No sin nosotros": Los días del terremoto (1985–2005). México, D.F.: Era; Santiago de Chile: Lom; Montevideo: Trilce; Tafalla: Txalaparta, 2005.

——. *Nuevo catecismo para indios remisos.* México, D.F.: Siglo XXI, 1982.

——. "Los orígenes de la tradición: Los siglos virreinales." *Imágenes* 64–90.

——. *El 68: La tradición de la resistencia.* México, D.F.: Era, 2008.

——. "Las tradiciones fundacionales: El arte indígena." *Imágenes* 50–63.

Motolinía, Toribio de Benavente. *Historia de los indios de la Nueva España.* 1848. Ed. Georges Baudot. Madrid: Castalia, 1985.

Nebel, Richard. *Santa María Tonantzin, "Virgen de María": Continuidad y transformación religiosa en México.* Trans. Carlos Warnholtz Bustillos with Irma Ochoa de Nebel. México, D.F.: FCE, 1995.

Paz, Octavio. "Mexico and the United States." *The New Yorker,* September 17, 1979: 136–53.

Rabasa, José. "Pre-Columbian Pasts and Indian Presents in Mexican History." *Dispositio/n* 19.46 (1994): 245–70.

Rowe, William, and Vivian Schelling. *Memoria y modernidad: Cultura popular en América Latina.* Trans. Hélène Lévesque Dion. México, D.F.: Grijalbo, 1993.

Safati-Arnaud, Monique. "*Gonzalo Guerrero,* de la crónica a la novela." *Texto Crítico* 42–43 (1990): 97–104.

Sahagún, Bernardino de. *Historia general de las cosas de la Nueva España.* ca. 1575–80. Ed. Alfredo López-Austin and Josefina García Quintana. Madrid: Alianza Editorial, 1988.

Schuessler, Michael K. *Artes de fundación: Teatro evangelizador y pintura mural en la Nueva España.* México, D.F.: UNAM, 2009.

Stark, Rodney. *The Victory of Reason: How Christianity Led to Freedom, Capitalism, and Western Success.* New York: Random House, 2005.

Tapia, Andrés de. *Relación de la conquista de México.* México, D.F.: 1866.

Zamora Briseño, Pedro. "Hambre ancestral." *Proceso* 1585 (2007): 36–41.

CHAPTER TWO

Reading Colonial Ruins in Carmen Boullosa's Poetry

Jeremy Paden

Carmen Boullosa began her literary career in 1979 as a poet and has continued to consistently publish poetry. However, she is better known as a leading Mexican novelist. Indeed, since the publication of her first novel in 1987, she has written everything from science fiction to coming-of-age novels and has set her stories in places as diverse as contemporary Mexico and New York; ancient Egypt; seventeenth-century Spain; and post-apocalyptic, dystopian futures. She is especially known for her three novels from the 1990s—*Llanto: Novelas imposibles* (1992), *Duerme* (1994), and *Cielos de la tierra* (1997)—that directly rewrite colonial Latin American history using intertextuality, palimpsest, parody, heteroglossia, and metafiction.[1] Despite her prolific career as a poet, Boullosa's verse remains virtually unread by U.S. critics.[2] Even Julio Ortega, in a brief essay on her "identidad literaria," defines her first and foremost as a novelist, reserving only a few sentences for her poetry, which he considers to be "no menos inventiva" (143) than the rest of her work. Curiously, at the time of his essay, Boullosa had already published more than ten volumes of poetry. Aside from this comment concerning the creativeness of her poetry, Ortega's only assessment of her verse in this essay is that it contains "su voz más personal . . . hecho entre voces de fábula y pasajes oníricos" (143). His description of her poetry stands in stark contrast to his assessment of her novelistic discourse. This, he believes, forms part of a literary tradition initiated by Octavio Paz and Carlos Fuentes, among others, and effects a revision of the literary tradition at the same time that it takes up the question of "la experiencia mexicana" (139).

Academic interest in Boullosa's fiction has especially concentrated on her three already mentioned postcolonial, historiographical novels. These, as Oswaldo Estrada has pointed out, are concerned with "acts of remembering the past" that "expose and contest Mexico's (and therefore Latin America's) permanent state of *coloniality*" (146). These acts of remembering and of writing a contestatory history are by nature allegorical.[3] Kate Jenckes, in *Reading Borges After Benjamin*, brings out an important aspect of allegory that helps explain why this trope, especially following Walter Benjamin's reformulation of it, is so very useful in political readings of historical novels—and, in this case, of historical poetry. Benjamin's view of allegory, Jenckes asserts, "concerns a sense of life that cannot be fully represented, but rather gestures beyond itself to . . . the 'secrets of history'— that is, a conception of history that can never be appropriated by those [whom he] calls history's victors" (xiii). Allegory resists appropriation by the victors because, among other things, it is a practice that "interrupts representations that seek to fix it into naturalized narratives of linearity and identity" (xiv). Or, again, as Jenckes writes later on, allegory intervenes in "historical representations by opening them up to their constitutive distortion, to what they tend to exclude" (77). Indeed, Boullosa's novels try to interrupt the naturalized narratives of Mexican identity by revealing the secrets of Mexican history. It is my contention that her poetry can be understood to operate in a similar manner.

Though it might be unfair to Ortega to draw generalizations from his characterization of Boullosa's poetry as an expression of her most personal voice and her fiction as a public intervention in Mexican literary history, it is true that Boullosa's poetry has garnered much less critical interest than her poetry, as I have suggested—despite it not being any less interesting. In fact, Ortega's characterization of lyric poetry as personal, private, emotional discourse, and the novel as public, political, and historical, reproduces the traditional characterizations of these two genres. Part of what I would like to call into question in this chapter is this generic distinction. Because of the nature of this volume, I will concentrate only on those references to colonial and precolonial Mexico made since the year 2000.[4] A cursory glance at those Boullosa poems that make references to the colonial and precolonial would have us note that there are two principal ways these references operate. On the one hand, the historical fragment is inserted as one of many references within a highly personal and private lyrical mode. This first mode would seem to reinforce Ortega's characterization of her poetry as the site of her more personal voice. On the other hand, she has also written a long persona poem that rewrites Mexican history, giving voice to the voiceless and commenting on contemporary Mexican politics, much in the same way she does in her novels.

Before moving on to Boullosa's poems, the fraught relationship between history and the lyric should be examined. Octavio Paz, in the preface to *Children of the Mire*, states that "the poem is a device that produces anti-history"; that is, he believes poetry and history are in "contradiction" (v). In the introduction to *Lyric Poetry and Modern Politics*, Clare Cavanagh notes that this opposition or contradiction, to use Paz's word, between history and poetry, is commonplace in modern post-Romantic conceptions of poetry. According to Cavanagh, this distinction is read both in terms of genre (history is narrative, whereas lyric poetry is circular or timeless) and in terms of subject orientation (history is public and treats the sociopolitical realm, while poetry retreats to the private, the individual). Likewise, Wolosky notes that contemporary discussions of lyric poetry tend to stress either history, aesthetic movements, and historical referents, or "formal analysis and theoretical reflection" (651). The latter tends to stress poetry as "a self-referring language artifact" (651) or "a timeless, formal purity" (652).

This divide between lyric poetry and history gets spun in different ways. On the one hand, summarizing the critique of lyric poetry by New Historicism, Cavanagh writes, "With its single speaking voice privileging the private over public experience, individual autonomy over civic responsibility, and aesthetic independence over social engagement, the lyric becomes a metonym or synecdoche for the bourgeois subject in all its illusory, self-sufficient glory" (11). The novel, on the other hand, especially the postmodern, historiographic novel, because of its heteroglossia, parody, and questioning of history as a discipline, among other things, has been understood by definition to be a political genre concerned with history and subverting dominant discourse. On the other hand, Susan Stanford Friedman shows how feminist critics and avant-garde poets have tended to exploit poetry's circular, timeless, non-narrative discourse as a means of transgressing against patriarchy and the symbolic order. Indeed, there is a long tradition of avant-garde women's poetry in Latin America that, as Mario Campaña has recently argued, understands poetry as a site of critical discourse that carries out a "crítica del lenguaje, de la ética y de la estética, de la política y de la erótica, de la cultura y de la ontología, de la vida cotidiana y de la vida espiritual trascendente" (92, 93). Mariana Libertad Suárez Velázquez reads *La salvaja* within this tradition. For her, the hermetic, highly lyrical language of the collection is an aesthetic attempt to "responder y desarticular el falogocentrismo que le dio origen" (128). In fact, Suárez Velázquez proposes that Boullosa's circular, non-narrative, emotive discourse, which Suárez Velázquez believes to be centered in hysteria, is "la intención de apropiarse de la prosa fundacional latinoamericana y reescribirla" (114). That is, this critic understands Boullosa's poetry, its fragmentation and hermetic language—its use of emotion-charged, lyrical language—as an interrogation of history and politics, especially the politics of gender and the history of patriarchy.

One last point regarding lyrical poetry and narrative discourse should be made. Though feminist critics and avant-garde poets have often understood poetic discourse to be transgressive, this does not mean that narrative poetry or narrative techniques cannot be deployed as subversive. Friedman, in fact, notes that the long poem has been used by women as a means of resisting patriarchy for a relatively long time. She goes on to say that narrative and lyric modes do not "exist in a fixed binary where lyric is (always) the revolutionary force that transgresses (inherent) narrative tyranny. Rather, they coexist in a collaborative interchange of different and interdependent discourses" (23). She claims that in contemporary women's poetry, narrative functions as a way to claim historical and mythic discourse—that is, poetry in its epic mode. Historically, the epic, whether dealing with myth or history, has excluded the voice of women. Yet she argues that women have been "engaged in a revisionist reconstruction of narrative by setting in play a collaborative dialogue between narrative and lyric" (22). Boullosa's poems should be understood within this context. They all fall under the rubric of the long poem, though length is relative. More importantly, perhaps, they all bring together narrative and lyric, history and poetry.

In two of Boullosa's more recent collections, *La bebida* (2002) and *Salto de mantarraya (y otros dos)* (2004), she has incorporated explicit references to precolonial and colonial Mexican history. These appear in three long poems: in "Agua" and "El son del angel de la ciudad," the second poem and the last poem, respectively, from *La bebida*—as well as in "Los nuevos," the two-part poem that concludes *El salto de mantarraya (y otros dos)*. In both "Los nuevos" and "Agua," the references to precolonial and colonial Mexico are fleeting. In these poems, the historical reference is not part of an overt political discourse that tries to reread and rewrite Mexican history. Instead, they are images that work within the fragmented discourse of lyrical poetry and try to give voice to private, erotic experience. This is not to say that these poems cannot be read in the same manner in which Suárez Velázquez has read *La salvaja*; indeed, they should be seen as attempts to contest patriarchy. However, because of the primacy given to the private, lyrical experience, understanding how history and politics relate in the poem is more difficult than simply noting the incorporation of a historical referent. In contrast to the poems just mentioned, "El son del angel de la ciudad" is a long persona poem that speaks in the voice of the Angel of Mexico City and juxtaposes historical scenes and images with contemporary ones to show how modern Mexico is something like a palimpsest, where glimpses of its glorious pre-Columbian past and the plundering of its splendor show through. This poem is no less fragmented or lyrical than the others. Instead, it uses the fragmented, lyrical discourse of poetry in order to weave a story about Mexican history and present-day geopolitics. In this sense, it is similar to Boullosa's fictional discourse, in which fragmented narratives juxtapose colonial and modern-day Mexico.

As noted, the pre-Columbian reference in "Agua" is fleeting. The poem, like much of Boullosa's verse, is a love poem that revels in dream-logic and evades rational discourse. It begins, "Los dos lejanos, los separados, van hacia el agua a que su sed los guía" (27). The water, or love, is what the two lovers most ardently desire; at the same time, it is a lie that will lead them astray. Love, in this poem, as Martha Canfield argues, is a utopia that humans are unable to reach. Though the poem largely unfolds in the third person, there is an abrupt switch to the first person in the poem's fourth fragment. It reads,

Si Huitzilopochtli la bebiera, con su casco de colibrí sobre la cabeza y en su pie
    de xhuihcoatl, serpiente de fuego,
        en lugar de guiarnos de Aztlán a Tenochtitlán, se clavaría en el primer charco para
            boquear también, agitando sus brazos, lerdas alas.
Esa agua es engaño, es el desorden, es el fin del instinto . . . (31)

These lines affirm that Huitzilopochtli, the patron god of the Aztecs and Tenochtitlán, would have failed to guide the people to Texcoco and failed to found Tenochtitlán had he drunk from this water. This historical referent ostensibly serves to reinforce the point that love is "agua rota, mochada . . . hipócrita" (27); that it leads to loss. But when read within the context of Suárez Velázquez's reading of *La salvaja* and Friedman's proposal that women's long poems need to be understood as a way to rearticulate the epic, especially in light of their exclusion, this reference to a possible failed founding of Tenochtitlán takes on a new meaning. Huitzilopochtli, in order to carry out his epic adventure and mythic task, did not drink the water of love. By extension, this excludes the woman's voice, as love poetry, or lyric, is her permitted genre. As Suárez Velázquez writes, "La lírica no ha sido presentada nunca como un discurso fundacional" (113). Yet Boullosa in this erotic love poem, where both the man and the woman are presented as desiring subjects, finds a way to incorporate the feminine into a foundational discourse that presumably had excluded it. In fact, the fragment—which immediately follows the Huitzilopochtli reference—mentions "la mujer que aquí escribe" (32), marking the author of the poem as woman.

Similar to "Agua," the poem "Los nuevos"—from *Salto de mantarraya y otros dos*—contains only brief mentions of both the precolonial and colonial in Mexico. "Los nuevos" is a poem in two parts, the first of which is a seventy-three page confessional, autobiographic monologue. For Friedman, the long autobiographical poem can also be a means of history making. She writes, "Some autobiographical long poems demonstrate a sense of the self-in-history supplemented by a reflexive awareness of the self-as-history" (28). And this poem, though it takes place within the mind of the speaker while walking the streets of New York, ranges far and wide. It references herself as a child going to school, her grandparents and their life, the story of Amistad and Cinque, the sack of Antwerp in 1576 by the Spanish, and a host of other historical events, all brought together by the stream of consciousness of the speaker, who confesses to have fallen in love again—and in falling, to have been born anew. Among the many things referenced by the speaker, she describes a kiss between the lovers:

Este beso equivale a lo que Pizarro quería encontrar,
Es todo oro, otorga la juventud perpetua,
Vence la enfermedad, provoca la risa,
Y desespera y abrasa, y abraza
Y da sustento y raíz.
Vence la cautela, es lento y es apetito desaforado,
Saquea, incendia, construye y calma.
Golpea, arrasa, pela, desholla, lima el hueso,
Transfigura, trasvasa, restaura, sacia,
Viste, adorna, desnuda, da sentido. Habla.
Es el silencio y sus lenguajes.
¡Es beso! Pesado, sólido,
La piedra que el azteca puso en la boca del cadáver
Para que no se le fuera a escapar el alma
Antes de emprender el viaje con el cuerpo. (93–94)

I have cited the entire section because it employs metaphors that allude to both Spanish and Aztec history/practices. The kiss is both the elusive treasure sought by Pizarro (an unattainable utopia, a transfiguring madness, a life-giving force that also pillages, burns, and beats up the lovers) and the Aztec stone placed in the mouth during funerary rites to help protect the soul on its journey in the afterlife. As with the previous poem, here, the references to colonial Latin America and pre-Columbian Mexico work within the logic of the poem to illustrate and expand upon the point being made. The colonial and/or pre-Columbian fragment is subordinated to the argument of a poem that inserts images from the Mexican cultural imaginary into the private symbolic language of love.

Quite differently than "Agua," this poem presents love in a positive light, as it does the loss of self in love. Though there is violence, even a violence that refers to colonial practices—"Saquea, incendia, construye y calma. / Golpea, arrasa, pela, desholla, lima el hueso"—it also provides sustenance and sense, among other positive attributes. Indeed, there is no judgment passed on Pizarro. The kiss is simply what he was looking for, pure gold; it is the jade that helps the soul make the transit to the other life. This is not to say that in this later poem, Boullosa is less radical. In fact, if a characteristic of *La salvaja* and "Agua" is a wandering about without maps, in "Los nuevos," a new path has been forged—"No somos lo que sigue las huellas. / No lo natural, y esto tienes que entenderlo, / Mira cómo te tiendes ahora bajo mí como una doncella" (115). The new path the poem's characters have embarked upon is one that questions traditional gender roles. What we see in the use of these two fragments—the Huitzilopochtli and the Pizarro/Aztec stone—is Boullosa's freedom to do what she will with those images the nation-state has used to mark her as Mexican.

"El son del ángel de la ciudad," the last poem of the collection *La bebida*, is also a fragmented first-person monologue. Only, in this case, the speaker is a feminine angel—specifically, the Angel of the City of Mexico.[5] Despite being a first-person monologue that opens with a confession, the poem does not move smoothly through the act of soul bearing. It jumps among an autobiographical narrative, a lament over lost splendor, and the narration of scenes taken from modern urban life. It is divided into two larger sections, each subdivided further into shorter lyrical passages without any obvious unifying logic beyond loss and mourning. The first section allegorically narrates the story of the Angel's fall through the use of emblems and vignettes that call upon mythology, Christian symbols, national monuments, and autobiography. The second section provides a picture of life in modern-day Mexico City. To use Friedman's typology, the poem "construct[s] a fusion" (25) between history and myth in order to give voice to Mexico's cultural, political, and economic orphanhood.

"El son" begins confessing that the Angel cannot hear her own song. "No oigo lo que tengo que decirles," is the poem's first line (57). She states, "Estoy sorda" (57). Rather than being able to hear herself speak, she is able only to hear "el llanto de la triste langosta canadiense" (57) screaming as she is being killed by those who swallow any and everything: a flayed dog, opened coconuts, split papayas, whole bulls, even the lows emitted by the bulls: "Ahora mismo tragan el mugido / se lo están manducando" (58). Near the middle of the opening fragment, the Angel comments again on her deafness, "No escucho las palabras que quiero confiarles" (58). In this instance, that deafness extends to the Angel's audience as well. She goes on to say, "No podrán escucharlas, y por esto no aparecen. / Quiero decirlas para ustedes, aunque sea imposible" (58). It is not that the Angel is deaf; in fact, the second section begins with the Angel proclaiming "Oigo el zumbar de la ciudad" (67) and proceeds to enumerate things heard throughout the city. The stories told are small, insignificant moments—a dog dreaming in the early morning, the hustle and bustle of a metro station, a lost shoe being dragged by a car, children saluting the flag at the beginning of school, children playing ball in a park, the coupling of lovers in a park. The list, which appears to be a random collection of things seen, is organized like a timeline that begins near daybreak and moves forward during the day. It also, as we will see, tends to focus on orphanhood and loss.

As the Angel states in the last vignette of the poem, the poem is only a brief sketch of her song. The concluding lines of the poem read,

Cae un poco de tinga de la orilla del taco
y en el piso suena a risa su salsa
junto al puesto de jugos.
Los colibríes, en el parque, bailan al son del exprimidor, al del
    chasquido de la
salsa que cayó y sigue cayendo de la tortilla.
Ellos fueron guerreros cuando aquí estaban los lagos, los ríos y
    aquellos templos.
Yo fui un ángel, tuve alas y una diosa cuidando mi sueño
mientras siseaban los seres de su falda.
Los colibríes perdieron su escudo y su imperio.
Yo gané un son, que aquí, solo un poco, solo de asomo, reseño. (73)

This closing segment is a good example of how the poem works. The rather banal and mundane scene of stewed pork falling and splattering on the sidewalk beside a juice stand and of *colibríes* (hummingbirds) darting about in the park contain echoes of Mexico's loss. In fact, the birds are allegories of this loss. The stanza presents them as emblems, first the images of the hummingbirds, then the explanation of what they mean: they were once warriors. This reading of the colibríes follows Aztec mythology believing that brave warriors of Huitzilopochtli, the hummingbird god of war, would return as hummingbirds. Along with the gloss of the image, the Angel reminds us that this city once contained Aztec temples. This is not the first and only mention made of these temples, now ruins, in the poem. In fact, the Angel has hovered over and about these ruins and used them to tell her story. Now at the close of the poem, she states that her song is bound to the loss of empire—"Los colibríes perdieron su escudo y su imperio. / Yo gané un son." Modern Mexico, as seen in this segment and entire poem, is shot through with physical reminders of this loss. The poem evidences what Boullosa writes about Mexico in her essay "El que gira la cabeza," "el ayer, en esta ciudad, forma parte presente del presente. Si el paso de los años cierra cicatrices, en México las abre. Si el paso de los años entierra lo ocurrido, en México el paso de los años saca a luz lo que otros años enterraron" (9). Mexico is a city built on the ruins of another and these ruins, as Boullosa makes known in this poem, the essay, and her novels, keep pushing their way to the surface.

For Walter Benjamin history and allegory come together in the ruin: "In allegory the observer is confronted with the *facies hippocratica* of history as a petrified, primordial landscape. Everything about history that, from the very beginning, has been untimely, sorrowful, unsuccessful, is expressed in a face—or rather in a death's head" (166). And a little later,

> The word "history" stands written on the countenance of nature in the characters of transience. The allegorical physiognomy of the nature-history, which is put on stage in the *Trauerspiel*, is present in reality in the form of the ruin. In the ruin history has physically merged into the setting. And in this guise history does not assume the form of the process of an eternal life so much as that of irresistible decay. . . . Allegories are, in the realm of thoughts, what ruins are in the realm of things. (177, 178)

Central to this relationship is transience and decay. The ruin, testament to the grandeur of a past era, becomes part of the landscape. This transformation of the ruin into natural history, however, does not make the ruin any more readable. Furthermore, the ruin still suffers decay, still continues to lose meaning. Despite this loss, though, a trace of the ruin is left, and it becomes part of the present as it is integrated into the landscape. The ruin is the afterlife of the past, an afterlife that points to death.

The reference to the ruined temples of Tenochtitlán with which the poem ends is not the first time that these ruins have been mentioned. Section one of the poem contains three references to colonial Mexico and/or pre-encounter Tenochtitlán. Two of these references concentrate on the city as infrastructure, monument, architecture, and ruin. The first of these is in the opening lyrical fragment. After the Angel confesses that she cannot hear what she is telling us because she is deafened by the screams of the lobster's slaughter, she states that we, her audience, will not be able to hear her words either. Our inability to hear is because we gave her "dos días para morir en un puerto de lagos que era el centro, el ombligo del mundo" (58). The reference is to Texcoco, the lake at the center of the Aztec world. Curiously, the founding of Tenochtitlán is glossed over. The following line simply reads, "y en uno tercero, cuando me resucitaron en una ciudad fincada sobre el agua" (58). Her status as city does not last long; again, she is killed. She speaks of this second death as both "pago de regreso a los hombres" and "regalo." Immediately after telling the story once, she tells it again and underlines even more forcefully the Christological reference. Yet, as the lowercase "c" implies ("Viernes y sábado muerta estuve, como el cristo"), the reference to Christ is not one to him as deity, but to a story. In this particular case, given that resurrection leads to an even worse death, the reference to Christ is devoid of redemptive power:

> Viernes y sábado muerta estuve, como el cristo, y el domingo caminé
> entre las
> personas, sólo para regresar a una muerte más terrible, sin ascensión ni
> tumba,
> y ya no se veían entonces el Popo y el Itza, ni la cordillera del Ajusco,
> ni el Cerro
> de la Estrella cuidando los bordes luminosos del valle. (58)

This section moves from a lacustrine port, center of the Aztec world, to a city built over water, to a valley so choked—presumably with pollution, though the poem does not say—that the iconic volcanoes and mountains can no longer be seen. This death without ascension and without glorification that leaves the Angel trapped below, in a world now separated from the volcanoes Popocatepetl, Iztaccihuatl, and Ajusco, is worse than any previous death. She is neither in heaven nor properly buried, but now she haunts a world with few, if any, connections to her origins. It should be noted that among the mountains and volcanos mentioned, she includes the Cerro de la Estrella, the site of the Aztec New Fire ceremony, where priests would sacrifice a human being to keep the sun alive.

In his *Trauerspeil* study, Benjamin notes that allegory turns the old gods into ideas and concepts, principally emblems of virtue. This transformation of the gods into palatable images for Christian consumption is the very origin of allegory. A similar transformation—old gods turned into national allegories—occurs in the second mention of Aztec ruins. In the second fragment of the first section of "El son," the Angel loses her wings and is turned into a gilded angel placed on top of a column made from the ruins of Tenochtitlán. The passage reads:

> desparramaron las piedras talladas que hacían los altos templos
> y vaciaron en ríos y lagos la sangre de las venas de los míos,
> dejando una larga columna
> arriba de la cual me plantaron, inmóvil, dorada, toda ojos. (60)

The image of a golden angel fixed atop a column is reminiscent of the Ángel de la Independencia, the gilded angel erected during the Porfiriato to celebrate the centennial of Mexican Independence. Boullosa's description of how this monument was fashioned, though, moves beyond the celebration of Mexican Independence itself to include the conquest of Tenochtitlán. The same men that place her on the column also turn the temples into rubble and empty the blood of her people into the rivers and lakes of the valley. The ruin of these temples essentially comprises the column on which she is placed. The connection established between the modern monument and the pillaging of Tenochtitlán is one that indicts Spanish colonizer and Mexican oligarch alike. Though she has stated she has no tomb, in essence, the statute acts as such. Like a tomb or a sarcophagus, it keeps her immobile. The one difference is that she is all eyes—witness to everything.

As noted, the first section of the work contains an autobiographical narrative. In this thread, the Angel remembers formative scenes with her grandmother and, as a way of explaining who she is, tells the story of her parents' origins. Her mother, she notes, comes from Mexico's Gulf Coast, while her father is Spanish, born in Galicia. Yet these domestic scenes quickly unfold into the larger story of Tenochtitlán and Mexico. The grandmother scene is part of the second section of the first part of the poem, the section where she refers to herself as a gilded angel on a column made of Aztec stones. This is also the segment in which she first mentions her fall. Wondering if she deserved her fall, the Angel asks if it is her fault: "¿Gané yo mi muerte?" (59). As part of this line of questioning, she asks if "mi rostro se llenó de cabezas de víboras" (59). This question leads her to recount a strange story in which, "De la falda de mi nana brincaron [las culebras] a la cara, / y fueron las dos garras de ella quienes acariciaron mi torso" (59). This reference to serpents on a skirt worn by a grandmother is quite possibly a reference to the Aztec goddess Coatlicue, Huitzilopochtli's mother, whose name means "snake-skirt."

Immediately after this account, she loses her wings and falls "más ásperamente que Ícaro" (59). The reference to Icarus, on the one hand, is simply a reference to a fall and to hubris. However, it is hard not to hear echoes also of Sor Juana's failed dream flight, in which the soul falls twice, once like Icarus and a second time like Phaeton. Also, it is hard not to establish a connection with the family drama at the heart of the original story, in which Daedalus has fashioned wings to help his son and himself escape their entrapment on Crete. In this case, though, the drama is between grandmother and granddaughter. The story repeats, in encrypted language, the foundational scene of Tenochtitlán. Only, in this iteration of it, the grandmother, trying to care for her Medusa-headed granddaughter, grabs her in her talons and brings about her fall—a fall that ends with her being forced into the shape of a golden angel.

The next fragment continues the autobiography, only the family narrative becomes even more explicit. Now, the Angel tells the story of her parents. Up to now, the Angel has been repeating the story of Tenochtitlán with variations that never quite fully tell the story of the Mexica migration from Aztlán to Texcoco—there is a city founded on a lake in the valley of Mexico, there is a Medusa trapped by eagle talons. This next vignette, though, tells the story of *mestizaje*, but sets it sometime after the founding of the Mexican state. However, given that it is the story of the Angel's parents, it, too, is a story of origin.

Her mother, the Angel says, was born on the shores "del dorado mar del Golfo"; spent her days eating thick turtle and crocodile soup, stewed chicken, and fish tamales; and when not eating, working, or resting from the heat, would drink cocoa or coffee. Her father, born in Galicia, brought with him "la memoria de otros continentes" and came looking for gold and chocolate. This last reference—to both the gold and the chocolate—is an obvious allusion to Cortés. The basic structure of the story coincides with the historical record of the encounter. However, the Angel's mother— born on the coast, imbiber of nonnative coffee—is not Malintzín, just as the father is not Cortés. Not only is the Marquez from Extremadura rather than Galicia—the temporal setting seems to be the twentieth century. The Angel concludes the vignette announcing that she, the Angel, was born in opposition to her father—"en su contra" (61). In fact, her narration highlights her father's incomprehension of Mexico and, by proxy, of his daughter. Having come from Europe, "Ignoró la riqueza de los moles y los pipianes, las tortillas y los panes complicados de mi pueblo. / Nunca miró de quién era la efigie dibujada en los billetes de diez o veinte pesos. No supo la historia del cura Hidalgo, de Morelos, de Villa" (61). The Angel clearly employs the first-person possessive to align herself with Mexico, "mi pueblo," not her father's land. Furthermore, the whole segment begins with the phrase, "Todo había sido pertenencia cuando llegó el despojo" (61). Thus, this story of genealogy and origin, a domestic tale of parents from drastically different backgrounds and father/daughter conflicts, is both framed by dispossession and loss, and haunted by the story of Cortés and La Malinche.

Idelber Avelar, in the introduction to *The Untimely Present*, notes that "allegory flourishes in a world abandoned by the Gods, one which pre- serves, however, a trace of memory of such abandonment and therefore has not been eaten away by oblivion quite yet" (7). As we have seen, con- temporary Mexico is a world without gods, a world inhabited by a fallen Angel, a world where the city is a Christ raised only to die again and haunt the earth. The second section of the Angel's poem lists those sounds she heard on a typical day in Mexico City. Though mainly an enumeration of sounds perceived as the day progresses, the images are related to each other. They characterize modern day Mexico as a place of orphanhood and loss: a car kills a pedestrian, "un zapato huérfano" (68) is dragged through the streets by tires, a baby sleeps in a cardboard shoebox. Along with the modern, contemporary images and sounds described, others are given. In fact, "todo se escucha" (68), past and present: the sounds (and accompanying images) of reeds and forests that used to inhabit the land, the waves that used to lap at the shores of the lake, the abandoned leper colony. The private family drama told in the first section of the poem— the girl's struggle with her father—finds an echo in these images of orphanhood.

The penultimate and antepenultimate sections of the poem focus not on the mass of humanity going about its day but on schoolchildren saluting the flag and the clandestine coupling of two of these children in a park. It should be remembered that the flag's representation of the eagle and the snake on the nopal contains a visual allusion to another of the family dramas from the poem's first section—about the girl's struggle with her grandmother. As the schoolchildren salute the flag, the Angel records their secrets: the fleas on the head of one, a girl whose skirt is stained "de caramelo o menstruo" (70), a boy who silently cries because his father has beat him, a girl who'd had neither breakfast nor dinner, and another, a fourteen-year-old girl named Luisa, who "trae un soldado en cada / hijo en la panza. / Es la del parque" (70). While other children play ball in the park, Luisa and an unnamed boy make out on a bench. He convinces her to let him have sex with her. She ends up pregnant and in a state where "nadie la querrá casar" (71). The city and the city's children live in a world marked by abandon; even intimate acts of coming together lead to eventual abandonment and orphanhood. Though the city has an angel watching over it, this angel only stands as a witness that speaks without being heard.

Even though section two of the poem simply tends to list images of contemporary life in rapid succession without much commentary, the fragment in which the schoolchildren salute the flag contains an explanatory aside that establishes another link between sections one and two. When noting the hungry girl, the Angel states that the lobster's cries at the beginning of the poem were not for the lobster, but for this hungry girl. The lobster, it should be remembered, is described as a "langosta canadiense." When describing the Angel's fall in the first section, one of the reasons given for it is the increasing smallness of the globe: "se ha vuelto pequeño el globo. / No podemos rastrear sitio alguno en el mapa diminuto" (62). Two sections later, she reiterates the sentiment, saying, "Soy la presa por expulsión, la condenada al afuera. Mi jaula es del tamaño del mundo" (64). The reference to the killing and eating of the Canadian lobster and the connection made between the tears of the lobster and the girl's hunger, coupled with the smallness of the globe, point to globalization as one of the reasons for the Angel's fall and the abandonment that characterizes modern-day Mexico. At the same time, though, this is not a poem that simply points outward toward the plunder of Mexico by Europe and the United States as the reason for the state of the world. Though there are clear references to globalization, to the exploitation of the land, resources, and people by the greedy and the powerful, there are just as many references inculpating the Angel for this loss and diminishment: "Perdí sola mis alas" (64) is the opening line of the segment that first mentions the shrinking of the world. And when she first describes her fall in the segment where her grandmother grabs her in her talons, she wonders, "¿Qué hubo en mí para cambiarme de aquel ángel que fui en un pájaro negro y mudo?" (59). This insistence on the Angel's own culpability (after all, what the war-rior/hummingbirds lost was an empire built on bellicose expansionism) pulls back from a facile reading that would lay the blame solely outside Mexico.

One of the characteristics of the Baroque allegory that Benjamin laments is the way in which its "intention does not faithfully rest in the contemplation of bones, but faithlessly leaps forward to the idea of resur-rection" (233). No such faithless leap happens in "El son del ángel de la ciudad." There are no grand narratives of salvation. Before concluding the discussion of this poem, I would like to return to the closing stanza that I cited at the beginning. In the last line of the poem, the Angel affirms, "Yo gané un son." The winning of this song is directly tied to the loss of empire suffered by the hummingbirds. The final line of the poem con-nects directly to the title of the poem, "El son del ángel de la ciudad." But, "son" is also used in one other place in this section. It describes the sound of the electric juicer to which the hummingbirds in the park are dancing. Given that the hummingbirds were once mighty Aztec warriors, given that the Angel's song arises out of the loss and ruin of their empire, it would seem that the birds would be dancing to the music of the poem, the music of the song of the Angel, rather than to the electric buzz of the juicer. But no one, truth be told, hears the Angel's song, not even herself. The inability of the hummingbirds to hear the Angel's song is foreshadowed in the opening fragment of the poem. "El son" begins confessing that the Angel cannot hear her own song: "No oigo lo que tengo que decirles" is the poem's first line (57). Near the middle of the opening fragment, the Angel comments again on her deafness, "No escucho las palabras que quiero confiarles." In this instance, that deafness extends to the Angel's audience as well. She goes on to say, "No podrán escucharlas, y por esto no apare-cen. / Quiero decirlas para ustedes, aunque sea imposible" (58). The poem offers no hope for the audience that the world might change, be different, that the Angel might regain her wings and Mexico return to the ancient splendor of Tenochtitlán.

It is not the Angel's task to trace out a return path on the map. Instead, she sits in contemplation of ruin and decay. In doing so, she brings to light the transience of life, the fact that all natural, cultural, historical life moves toward death. Jenckes concludes her discussion of allegory, history, and ideology by arguing:

Allegory signifies the possibility of representing history without the ide-
alization of a redemptive wholeness characteristic of ideology. It would
intervene in such historical representations by opening them up to their
constitutive distortion, to what they tend to exclude. . . . Rather than destabilizing representations of identity only to suture them back into
ideal "futures of social totality," allegory would trace paths of a history
not reducible to such ideals, opening the ideological concept of history
to its unrecognized exclusions. (77)

The Angel, rather than presenting herself solely as victim, ponders the
extent to which she might have brought about the fall. Rather than simply
lamenting the losses suffered at the hands of foreigners, she narrates the
lives of the marginalized and excluded, focusing on both how they have
been exploited and how they take advantage of themselves. Furthermore,
she does this in a broken and failed song. Immediately following the strong
statement "Yo gané un son," which seems to refer directly to the poem, the
Angel qualifies her statement: the poem is not her song, only a summary
of it. The poem itself is a ruin, a song that, because of the passage of history, because of the white noise of contemporary life, is only a sketch.

The Angel employs a host of typical allegorical tropes (of ruins, monuments, religious and mythological emblems, family) to sketch out her song
of loss. In this grand though fragmented narrative, history and politics
are not considered separate and apart from the mundane, the domestic,
the private realms of life. Instead, the two are held together in such a way
that loss is felt all the more acutely. The hunger of the children is related
to the gluttony of the powerful. The indictment of the poem is directed
not only at foreigners who have exploited Mexico, but also at Mexican
nationals.

Boullosa employs colonial and precolonial ruins in both historical persona poems that retell Mexican history and myth as an autobiography of
loss and orphanhood, and in more so-called private lyrical poems. In
Boullosa's verse, the ruins of history and the national, foundational myths
are brought in contact with lyrical, confessional, erotic, autobiographical
poetry in order to give voice to silenced, feminine desire, to call into question gender hierarchies, and to tell the story of the vanquished. Furthermore, her historical poetry calls into question the notion that lyrical poetry
is a private discourse, whereas the novel is public. Indeed, we see in her
poetry how the ruin brings together both the personal and the public,
and how it shows the way in which lyric poem can be a space for political
commentary.

Notes

1. The critical literature on Boullosa's fiction is considerable and includes essays by Jean Franco, Verónica Salles-Reese, Yolanda Martínez-San Miguel, Julio Ortega, Anna Reid, and Oswaldo Estrada, among many others.

2. The Modern Languages Association database registers only two essays on Boullosa's poetry, both published in a German anthology of essays dedicated to her work. Her website mentions two more essays, one of these a book review rather than a critical reading.

3. Ute Seydel—in an oft-cited essay on *Duerme*—does, in fact, call the protagonist an allegory for a multiethnic, multiracial, and multicultural Mexico, and Rosana Blanco-Cano notes the way in which Boullosa's fictions contest patriarchal allegories of the nation.

4. I should note, though, that references to this period in Boullosa's poetry—before 2000—are rather uncommon.

5. Canfield and Suárez Velázquez have both noted Boullosa's common manner of marking the gender of her books, poems, and poetic speakers with the feminine article: *La salvaja*, *La delirios*, *La infiel*, and so on.

Works Cited

Avelar, Idelber. *The Untimely Present: Postdictatorial Fiction and the Task of Mourning*. Durham, NC: Duke University Press, 1999.

Benjamin, Walter. *The Origin of German Tragic Drama*. Trans. John Osborn. London: Verso, 1998.

Blanco-Cano, Rosana. "Revisiones a las narraciones históricas mexicanas en *Duerme* (1994) e 'Isabel' (2000) de Carmen Boullosa." *Espéculo* 40 (2008): n. pag. pendientedemigracion.ucm.es/info/especulo/numero40/boullosa.html. Accessed April 30, 2010.

Boullosa, Carmen. "El que gira la cabeza y el fuego: Historia y novela." *Revista de Literatura Hispanoamericana* 30 (1995): 5–16.

———. *La bebida*. México, D.F.: Fondo de Cultura Económica (FCE), 2002.

———. *Salto de Mantarraya y otros dos*. México, D.F.: FCE, 2004.

Campaña, Mario. *De la flor al tallo: El discurso crítico de las poetas hispanoamericanas*. Maryland: Q'Antaty Enterprises, 2010.

Canfield, Martha. "Carmen Boullosa: Las mujeres de hoy entre el amor y la furia." *Fórnix: Revista de Creación y Crítica* 8–9 (2008): 250–52.

Cavanagh, Clare. *Lyric Poetry and Modern Politics: Russia, Poland and the West*. New Haven, CT: Yale University Press, 2010.

Estrada, Oswaldo. "(Re)constructions of Memory and Identity Formation in Carmen Boullosa's Postcolonial Writings." *South Atlantic Review* 74.4 (2009): 131–48.

Friedman, Susan Stanford. "Craving Stories: Narrative and Lyric in Contemporary Theory and Women's Long Poems." *Feminist Measures: Soundings in Poetry and Theory*. Ed. Lynn Keller and Cristanne Miller. Ann Arbor: University of Michigan Press, 1994. 15–42.

Jenckes, Kate. *Reading Borges After Benjamin: Allegory, Afterlife, and the Writing of History.* Albany: State University of New York Press, 2007.

Ortega, Julio. "La identidad literaria de Carmen Boullosa." *Texto Crítico* 5 (1999): 139–44.

Paz, Octavio. *Children of the Mire: Modern Poetry from Romanticism to the Avant-Garde.* Trans. Rachel Phillips. Cambridge, MA: Harvard University Press, 1974.

Suárez Velázquez, Mariana Libertad. "La verdadera perversión: La histeria como recurso contrahistórico en *La salvaja*, de Carmen Boullosa." *Escritos: Revista del Centro de Ciencias del Lenguaje* 26 (2002): 111–29.

Wolosky, Shira. "The Lyric, History, and the Avant-Garde: Theorizing Paul Celan." *Poetics Today* 2.3 (2001): 651–68.

CHAPTER THREE

Fiction, History, and Geography

Colonial Returns to Mexico City in Héctor de Mauleón's El secreto de la Noche Triste

Vinodh Venkatesh

The young narrator in Héctor de Mauleón's *El secreto de la Noche Triste* (2009), Juan de Ircio, "vecino y natural" (7) of the city of Mexico, wastes no time in engaging the twenty-first-century reader in a historical labyrinth of secrets, murders, and urban legends with the sole purpose of telling a story that other *cronistas*, he notes, have chosen to ignore (9). What seems at first a simple recounting of the lives and events of the year 1600, marked by a torrential rain and flooding, becomes a life-and-death struggle between the criollos and a stealthy assassin who prowls the streets of the young megacity, deftly slicing the throats of a group of men who share a common link to the city's razing and subsequent founding. It comes as no surprise, then, that Mauleón's tale, as witnessed by the surrounding chapters of this edited volume, has been lumped together with other contemporary rewritings of the Mexican colony. What sets the novel apart, however, and what I seek to elucidate in this chapter, is that this rewriting of the colony is not specifically geared toward or dialogued with traditional notions of the (new) historical novel—that is to say, the tangential lines that we, as critics, draw between contemporary workings of the past and their antecedents. Instead, it builds a separate site of contact that traces an altogether distinct line of inquiry from traditional approaches to Linda Hutcheon's notion of historiographic metafiction employed in other (new) historical fictions. What distinguishes *El secreto* from other rewritings of the colony—and what its true secret is, I argue—is its acute focus on urban space and the role of the flaneur, or urban observer, in textualizing its crevices and alleyways, putting forth a spatialization of discourse that I term "metafictive historiogeography."

Rich in detail and archival investigation, the novel has been billed as the first New Hispanic thriller. The author presents the story of Juan, a native of Mexico City who writes his memoirs in 1637 at the age of forty-nine. The timeline of his narrative follows what has traditionally been considered a period of stabilization in Latin American colonial history defined by the establishment and functioning of colonial centers and structures. Current scholarship on the period, however, has unearthed a rich and fruitful epoch, as "the old tendency to view the era as inert or lethargic has fallen away, displaced by awareness that defining aspects of present-day Latin America took shape during the approximately 150-year period of stabilization" (Merrim 14). The narrator largely focuses his memory on the events circa 1600, when a slew of murders set him and his family in the sights of a killer who slit the throats of the grandsons of the original conquistadors who sacked and then left Tenochtitlán during Hernán Cortés's Noche Triste. In keeping with the techniques and narrative strategies of historiographic metafiction, Mauleón frequently incorporates historical documents and popular myths to unveil the secret of the Aztec gold that the Spaniards are rumored to have hidden in 1520 as they left Tenochtitlán. This detail is evidenced when the narrator's aunt, Beatriz, discovers a parchment painting in a copy of Francisco Cervantes de Salazar's *México en 1554: Tres diálogos latinos*, which is a replica of an actual work in the church of Santa Cruz de Tlatelolco, illustrating the torture inflicted upon the natives by the gold-hungry Spaniards. Juan's memories of the time period attempt to unveil the secret behind the murders and the parchment found in *México en 1554.*

Hypotheses as to the final resting place of the treasure abound, and the novel does not necessarily provide a more original or peculiar interpretation than Disney's popular *Pirates of the Caribbean* series of Hollywood blockbusters. The focus on the mythic gold confirms what Beatriz Pastor terms the "base de un proyecto colonial concreto que se apoyaba en la percepción y caracterización de América como botín" (75), placing the contemporary text within a historical archive that emphasizes the role of and search for treasure in conceiving the New World. The use of La Noche Triste in Mauleón's novel as a backdrop to enter a critical cross-examination, that is, a theme or topic that goes beyond the events lived on the night, is, furthermore, nothing new, as it has been previously attempted by Ignacio Ramírez's nineteenth-century play, *La Noche Triste.* This earlier piece uses the context of the flight of the Spaniards and the

offensive mounted by the indigenous locals to permit a critical undermining of the Catholic belief system vis-à-vis indigenous religions (Ruiz Bañuls 211). In the twenty-first century, Arturo Pérez Reverte's *Ojos azules*
(2009), for its part, "pone el énfasis . . . en la imposibilidad de simbolizar
la conquista ya que ésta desborda las capacidades del lenguaje" (Gómez
López-Quiñones 113). Keeping these examples in mind, we can place
Mauleón's work in a literary genealogy that attempts a discursive challenge within a carefully framed historic episode.

   This strategy is masterfully implemented in *El secreto de la Noche
Triste*, as Mauleón, known more for his journalistic pieces and urban accounts of eighteenth- through twentieth-century Mexico City, uses the
purported "secret" of La Noche Triste as a ruse to undertake the critically
challenging task of interrogating the trajectories and lines of contact that
emanate from the dialectic between space/history—not time/history, on
which traditional historical narratives have tended to focus. The author,
furthermore, stops at the many unlit and dangerous intersections of the
dirt roads of seventeenth-century Mexico City to ponder the ability of language to conceive and encapsulate the urban and the urban experience,
decentering the text from a traditional (new) historical reading. My point
of entry into Mauleón's text follows a path first posited by Edward Soja
when he commented that "life-stories have a geography too; they have mi-
lieux, immediate locales, provocative emplacements which affect thought
and action. The historical imagination is never completely spaceless"
(*Postmodern Geographies* 14).

   This postmodern geographer's assertions reaffirm Michel Foucault's
observation that "space [is] treated as the dead, the fixed, the undialecti-
cal, the immobile. Time, on the contrary, [is] richness, fecundity, life, dialectic" (70). It comes as no surprise, then, that any look at the historicity
or processes of historiography in contemporary Mexican fiction is focused
on the issue of time and chronology. I, too, am guilty of this methodology,
as only a few paragraphs above, I connected the rewriting of La Noche
Triste to Ramírez's nineteenth-century play. This route of critical thinking, used by scholars such as Linda Hutcheon, Seymour Menton, María
Cristina Pons, and Ramón Luis Acevedo—to name a few—contextualizes
historical and new historical fictions and underlines Foucault's preoccupation with the role of space. That being said, though, can we produc-
tively look at these rewritings of the colonial period without taking time
into account?

   It is convenient to stop at this juncture to analyze the historical imagination of Mauleón as he puts the pen in the hand of Juan the cronista, a

figure who is consciously placed within a tradition of writings of the colony and the Spanish withdrawal from the city. The earliest extant narratives of the eventful night of June 30, 1520, are unsurprisingly contradictory. Describing the night and its aftermath in his *Historia verdadera de la conquista de la Nueva España* (first published in 1632), Bernal Díaz notes how "no quedamos sino cuatrocientos y cuarenta [soldados] con veinte caballos y doce ballesteros y siete escopeteros, y no teníamos pólvora, y todos heridos y cojos y mancos" (93). Cortés's version in his second *Carta de relación*, however, reframes the Spaniards' withdrawal in simple terms: the natives had no real motive for rebelling against the Spanish yoke— they were in a position he would later reaffirm in the third *Carta*. Cortés's version, as Pastor outlines, contradicts Bernal Díaz's chronicle of the same night:

> Cortés, por el contrario, creando su versión a posteriori y sobre la decisión previa de silenciar el incidente de la matanza, organiza su ficción en torno a la alegría del reencuentro con sus hombres, convirtiendo la desagradable escena de acusaciones y justificaciones narrada por Bernal en una idílica ilustración de la armonía, solidaridad y camaradería reinantes entre él y su ejército. (110)

This third version of the events was expanded by Carlos de Sigüenza y Góngora in *Alboroto y motín de México del 8 de junio de 1692*, an important piece in the nascent corpus of creole literature. The relationship between the creole citizen and early narratives of La Noche Triste is commented upon by Kathleen Ross when she notes that the "derrotado de aquella noche de 1520 se ha convertido en el honrado símbolo de la fuerza y el poder" (185) in *Alboroto*, reflecting on the way in which the appropriation of previous chronicles "no sólo se trata de una conquista militar del indio por el español, sino de una conquista textual del español por el criollo" (188).

This connection between Cortés and Sigüenza y Góngora exemplifies the many rewritings of the colony that have emanated from the New World from its first Eurocentric narratives. It is on this core of previous narratives that Mauleón flexes his pen to situate *El secreto de la Noche Triste* within a literary family tree that is built on both content and style. The content aspect needs no explanation, as the retelling of an event so well known in Hispanic cultures does not require extensive detective work on the part of the critic. The issue of style, however, poses a more encompassing hermeneutic challenge.

The structure of the novel certainly lends itself to analysis, as the older narrator who has lived the events to be narrated sits down to write his memoirs with the objective of setting the story straight, as did Bernal Díaz before him. There is a stark focus on remembering and memory, evocative of Bernal Díaz's canonical work that portrays a soldier chronicling his involvement in the events of the Conquest (Flores 143). A further connection can be made between *El secreto de la Noche Triste* and Bernal Díaz's *Historia verdadera* when we take into consideration the intratextual narrators implicit in the two texts. Both write into their narratives a direct influence of the *novelas de caballería* such as *Amadís de Gaula* (first printed in 1508) and have a sense of impending terror and suspense that goads the text along from page to page (Flores 146). The sensations of terror and suspense that the *Historia verdadera* evokes in the reader leads Enrique Flores to call the text a thriller (147). Connecting Bernal Díaz to *El secreto*, Mauleón seizes upon this characteristic of the earlier chronicle as he unabashedly writes a thriller situated in the colonial era, thereby directly referencing the nature of the *Historia verdadera* in relation to La Noche Triste and its subsequent textual genealogy.

The most overt connection between the contemporary rewrite and the first narratives to come from the colony, however, can be evidenced by the repeated citation of passages and descriptions from Bernal Díaz's original text. It is here that *El secreto de la Noche Triste* implicates a direct relation between the events narrated and the historical documentations of the colony, evoking Hutcheon's thesis on historiographic metafiction and the possibilities of questioning the past and what we know of it. Writing on the poetics of postmodernism, Hutcheon argues that the genre knowingly mixes registers and facts, History and histories (106–14), confusing the "generic lines between history and fiction" (Estrada, "Textos y pretextos" 97), with the end result of showing just how "history and fiction have always been notoriously porous genres" (Hutcheon 106). What we observe, then, in the search for the truth behind the *secreto* is a conscious effort to retell the events of the past with an active, self-conscious narrative voice that intermingles previous narratives of the era to, on the one hand, lend historical veracity to the text, and on the other, to inculcate a self-reflexivity of the power of language and the text behind discourses of the past. By including direct citations from the *Historia verdadera*, Mauleón channels a critical line of inquiry into why and to what effect colonial narratives of New Spain were written.

Here we stumble upon a small problem of chronology, as the *Historia verdadera* was only first published in 1632 in Spain, though the manuscript was finished in 1568, thereby shining a suspicion of anachronism on Mauleón's interpretation, as the events narrated purportedly take place immediately after 1600. What is to note regarding this detail, however, is that Bernal Díaz's text, like so many of its time, first circulated as unedited manuscripts among the creole intelligentsia in the urban enclaves of the New World prior to gaining official status when printed. It comes as no surprise, then, that sections from the *Historia verdadera* are cited by both Juan, Mauleón's narrator, and Arias de Villalobos, a local poet who is inserted into *El secreto de la Noche Triste* as an authoritative source of the past, since he "conocía las gestas del pasado como si en ellas hubiese participado" (41). This detail is important because Bernal Díaz underlines in his original text the reading of his manuscript by others as a form of lending credibility to his version of events.

A further linkage between Mauleón's and Bernal Díaz's texts can be made when we consider the many novelistic characteristics of the *Historia verdadera*, which have been catalogued by Oswaldo Estrada in *La imaginación novelesca* as the presence of round and flat characters (45), character development (50), the inclusion of substories (47), and the presence of an autobiographical "I" (55) who lends testimony to the interested and often mentioned reader. The "I," furthermore, enables what Yanira Angulo-Cano calls Bernal Díaz's desire to "*write* himself and his fellow soldiers into the history of the conquest" (289, my emphasis). She goes on to perform a structural analysis of the *Historia verdadera* and elicits an understanding of the way in which autobiography functions in relation to Bernal Díaz's textual self, noting that "when autobiographers review their lives, they are quite serious about adding meaning to their existences" (292). Mauleón's Juan shares this tendency in his attempts to lend meaning to events of 1600 that real writers of the period have left untouched. Angulo-Cano further expands her analysis to say that the autobiographer tends to gravitate toward the project of self-justification, highlighting chapters 207–214 in the *Historia verdadera* as showing examples of the enaction of this goal. The placement of these chapters toward the end of the *Historia verdadera* contrasts with Mauleón's insistence on lending meaning to Juan's life from the first pages of the novel. This difference, which at first may seem to dislocate *El secreto de la Noche Triste* from the textual genealogy headed by Bernal Díaz, is quite secondary when we consider the similarities that abound in reference to the textual "I" that both writers create.

The "I" in the *Historia verdadera* is carefully collocated in line with a paternal lineage that establishes the subject in relation to a sanguine temporality that justifies its existence. In this context, Karl Weintraub notes the subject gains subjectivity through "una fusión excepcional de lo que le fue dado al principio [y] lo que selecciona de ese mundo" (25), summarized by Angulo-Cano through the rhetorical equivalency of "I am A, son of B, who in turn was the son of C" (295). This strategy sets the "I" to consider itself "a mere extension of . . . society" (Angulo-Cano 295), which is evident throughout the introductory chapter of the *Historia verdadera*. A similar conception of the "I" occurs in *El secreto de la Noche Triste*, as Mauleón shows a lucid reworking of the patrilineal framework expressed through Juan's detective work to find the perpetrator of a series of mysterious murders of creoles in the city. The dead men, Juan Fernández de Maldonado, Gonzalo Guzmán, Juan Solís, Juanes de Fuenterrabia, and Francisco Dazco (El Entonado) all share a common bond, as their grandfathers are rumored to have belonged to a clique that knows the true resting place of the gold. Following popular lore, Mauleón writes about how the secret was divulged under the duress of torture by the Spaniards, which Solís's grandfather, known as "Tras-de-la-puerta," hears and keeps within the group. Each member of the original band, beginning with Solís, is then tortured and killed by the processes of the Inquisition in Mexico, leading to the first whisperings of a curse of the gold. The use of nicknames in *El secreto de la Noche Triste* harkens to a similar stylistic strategy in the *Historia verdadera* (Estrada, *Imaginación* 24). By connecting the contemporary murders in *El secreto de la Noche Triste* to a maligned common ancestor, Mauleón upholds the narrative strategy of viewing the subjectified "I" through the equally desubjectifying genealogical mechanism that triggers a supernatural reading of the events, as they are not simply murders but are connected, instead, to an ancient betrayal.

The descendants of the original group headed by Solís, going back to Weintraub's schematic of order and belonging, meet equally damning fates years later, highlighted by the spree of serial killings by a skilled swordsman who slices their throats. It comes as no surprise that the narrator's grandfather, Martín de Ircio, also plays a role in the narrative, as he met Cortés in 1519 in what is present-day Cuba and becomes a crucial figure in the local machinations of the Inquisition. Mauleón follows the family system of naming and identity used in the *Historia verdadera* but actively excludes the name of the narrator's father. This character appears regularly in the narrative, but goes nameless and is often absent in crucial situations, always away on business. This break from the model established in colonial literature gives us a first signal of the way in which Mauleón chooses to refocus the colony under a different optic, as the principal "I" is excised from the genealogical mechanism.

Returning to the structural and stylistic similarities between Mauleón's text and Bernal Díaz's autobiographical account, we can further note that both narrators fashion the detailed representation of a heroic act (Weintraub 26), instead of simply jotting down the intimate details of their memories. Their testimonies are less a recollection of their lives lived and more a carefully constructed compendium of events and characters that underline their personal importance to the reader. Juan inserts himself into the notion of a genealogical *crónica* by asserting his own importance in regard to the legend of the hidden gold and the series of murders purportedly associated with it, though it is unclear as to his exact role in finding the treasure. What this inclusion does achieve, however, is the strengthening of a sense of doom and impending death, both also characteristics of large sections of the *Historia verdadera* (Angulo-Cano 296–97). The effervescence of suspense propels the narrative forward, as Juan unmasks and solves a series of mysteries to get to the bottom of the creole murders. The active narrator, furthermore, both in diegetic and metaliterary terms, necessitates a resourceful and interested reading akin to Bernal's strategies of telling the tale in the *Historia verdadera* (Estrada, *Imaginación* 56).

Keeping in mind these direct allusions to the *Historia verdadera* and to the author's own acknowledgement of using the *Diario de sucesos notables* (1665–1703) by Antonio de Robles (Aguilar), the linkages between *El secreto de la Noche Triste* and colonial texts cannot be more explicit. By carefully placing Juan de Ircio within a tradition of narrators and narratives, the author successfully concretizes a contemporary return to the streets and to the events of the years immediately following the establishment of a thriving and stable colonial structure. Synchronicity, diachronicity, and anachronicity are also concepts with which the author plays in crafting the thriller to unmask the secret of La Noche Triste. We can pause here to return to the original question of what really is the secret of Mauleón's text. Is it the recurring questioning of how and who first reported the events of La Noche Triste that lies at the core of his literary project? This line of inquiry seems almost banal, as the inclusion of direct quotes and descriptions from the *Historia verdadera* suggest a critical knowledge of the character of historiographic metafiction. The relation to Bernal Díaz and Cortés are, furthermore, trumped by that narrative's incessant need to bring to light an almost foregone conclusion in the mind of the reader as to why the killings of the grandsons of the conquerors are taking place. The narrator repeatedly creates a sense of suspense around the murders, as though there is another possibility besides the search for the Aztec gold as a motivation for the killings.

Could the secret be in relation to the actual hiding place of the lost gold? The replica that Beatriz finds in the tome by Cervantes de Salazar holds the inscription "CGIRANCIACSAMRLJAMCEOS," suggesting in its code the location of the loot. The suspense created by the written code in connection to the painted image creates a semantic guessing game for the reader, not far removed from Dan Brown's narrative strategy in *Angels and Demons* (2000) and *The Da Vinci Code* (2003). In fact, the first reading of *El secreto de la Noche Triste* prompts a pop-culture comparison to the mystery-solving adventures of Brown's protagonist, Robert Langdon, albeit now in the dark and less glamorous streets of New Spain. For those readers versed in the research and fictive representations of the Aztec gold, the ending to the Mexican novel comes as no surprise, analogous to the reader's disappointment upon discovering the connections among Da Vinci, Jesus, and Mary Magdalene in Brown's novels. The secret of the location of the gold, therefore, is not a real secret, leading us back to the original question of what Mauleón is truly trying to elucidate.

The key to Mauleón's purpose, I argue, lies in the mystery of the parchment that Beatriz finds. She is asked by Juan's nameless father to come to New Spain to educate his son after the inopportune death of his wife. The father cunningly includes in his request the text by Cervantes, *México en 1554*, which chronicles the many wonders of the city for the perusal of Cervantes's European readers as part of his project of establishing a new university in the colony. The original manuscript is composed of a series of Latin grammar exercises penned by Luis Vives, with the addition of seven dialogues written by Cervantes, three of which make reference to the New Spanish city. These three dialogues, some of the first chronicles of the new colonial space, were separated and republished by Joaquín García Icazbalceta in a separate volume in the nineteenth century. The version that Beatriz has access to is likely the original compilation of seven dialogues, though she pays particular attention to the dialogues on Mexico City.

The dialogues recount the urban experience of three men who ride through the ordered and uncontaminated streets of the new capital on horseback. The two locals, Zuazo and Zamora, parade through the streets and buildings of Mexico as though it were a modern interpretation of the classical city, highlighting for the newly arrived Spaniard, Alfaro, its many wonders. They tour the university, the central area known as *la traza*, a main road leaving the city, and the panoramic view afforded from Chapultepec, in order to show Alfaro that New Spain is second to none in its embodiment of the Renaissance ideals of law and order. These dialogues, according to Ivonne del Valle, make up:

a paradigmatic text of a colonial order embedded in writing, bent on imposing its design upon a given reality. Their author attempts to frame the city within a superior structure of Renaissance knowledge, culture, and urbanism, thereby overwriting Tenochtitlán to become Mexico City. For this purpose, the "guided tour" of the Hispanic city has as its preamble a visit to the recently inaugurated university. (201)

The representation of the cityspace in the dialogues has been contextualized by Stephanie Merrim within a chronology of development that traces city-texts from the structured and hygienic streets and markets of the City of Order (9) to the Spectacular City of the New World Baroque that is inaugurated by Bernardo de Balbuena's "lengthy, elitist, convoluted poem" (8) *Grandeza Mexicana* (1604). Merrim argues that Cervantes's text follows an established model that collocates New World urban centers in direct comparison to their European kin. Following Bernal Díaz's and Cortés's repeated likenings of what they see to referents from across the Atlantic, Cervantes's descriptions of the streets, buildings, and markets of Mexico City are ordered along European imperatives of civilization. In their dialogues, Alfaro and the two natives "dissolve Mexico City into a panoply of resemblances to the classical world, Europe, and Spain. The filigree of comparisons inserts New Spain into a diachronic and synchronic constellation, a transhistoric global network" (Merrim 72).

The dialogues become, in essence, an example in a colonial Mexican setting of Michel Foucault's notion of heterotopias, further developed by Soja in his study of the metropolis. Soja articulates a triadic understanding of spatiality beginning with firstspace, defined as "a set of materialized 'spatial practices' that work together to produce and reproduce the concrete forms and specific patternings of urbanism as a way of life" (*Postmetropolis* 10), followed by secondspace, which occupies a dialectic position where cityspace becomes "more of a mental or ideational field, conceptualized in imagery, reflexive thought, and symbolic representation, a *conceived* space of the imagination" (11). This second notion is the realm of an "urban epistemology, a formal framework and method for obtaining knowledge about cityspace and explaining its specific geography" (11). The combination of both spaces, the hypothesized thirdspace, occupies a third axis where the urban space is "a simultaneously real-and-imagined, actual-and-virtual locus of structured individual and collective experience and agency" (11).

By hiding the parchment that is supposed to signal the secret of La Noche Triste and the subsequent murders of the creole descendants of the conquerors, Mauleón coyly emphasizes the importance of the many textual representations or "propagandistic and/or touristic city texts" (Merrim 9) of the City of Order as being the real metafictional referents to the narrative exercise of *El secreto*. What we unearth in this reading is an acute narrative focus on the role and prominence of space over time, as the author focuses his metatextual exercise on representations of geography. It is not the obvious, often cited antecedent penned by Bernal Díaz, but the relatively unstudied colonial works of Cervantes, Juan de la Cueva, and Eugenio de Salazar y Alarcón that merit our attention in the historical, and necessarily spatial, reading of Mauleón's novel. The City of Order presented in Cervantes, like the notion of an authoritative History, comes under the microscope as Juan interrogates its verisimilitude in relation to the events of the creole murders. Just as he managed the nuances, stylistics, and registers of historiographic metafiction, Mauleón showcases a precise handling of the critical work done on the dialogues, as criticism has surprisingly left them unanalyzed, preferring instead to merely annotate them.

What follows in this narrative probing is a stark demythification of Cervantes's city of the university and la traza, the city center inhabited by creole and Spanish conquistadors, as Beatriz arrives in the capital of New Spain on March 26, 1597. She carries with her an "ejemplar roto y descosido" (15) of the dialogues, suggesting that the pages to follow will swiftly unbind the book in the interest of excavating a spatial knowledge of the city that is independent of, yet dialogued with, the colonial text. This possibility is quickly realized, as "la ciudad que el doctor Cervantes cantaba en sus diálogos, con su Plaza Mayor sin paralelo en el mundo, con sus calles amplias y bien trazadas, con sus elevados palacios de tezontle rojizo y sus frescos paseos de aroma perfumado, era en realidad un albañal inmundo" (15–16). By referring to the space as a sewer, De Mauleón calls into question not only Cervantes's misleading representation of the capital but also the colonial exclusion of pre-Hispanic cultures and knowledge that were central to the founding and functioning of the city upon a lake, thereby stressing the coloniality of discourse in its attempt to construct a foundational space. Ivonne del Valle traces this omission when she argues that the problems of hydrography and hydraulics were essential in imagining a nonindigenous city (216), as the initial omission of hydrography and hydraulics cements the colonial regiment's gesture of resemanticizing colonized geographies. By calling the space a sewer, Mauleón dislocates the City of Order in Cervantes and replaces it with an acutely different space that is aware of the effects of colonial rule. The city in *El secreto* is not the new, brilliant space conceived by the Spaniards on the site of the destroyed territory of Tenochtitlán, but is instead a thirdspace where plural and polyvalenced lines of being, seeing, writing, and imagining are intersected. By challenging the dialogues within a self-conscious discourse of coloniality and historical (re)appropriation, Mauleón follows Soja's intention of "not [erasing] the historical hermeneutic but [opening it] up and [recomposing] the territory of the historical imagination through a critical spatialization" (*Postmodern Geographies* 12). The geophilosopher goes on to affirm that this "cannot be accomplished simply by appending spatial highlights to inherited critical perspectives and sitting back to watch them glow with logical conviction. The stranglehold of a still addictive historicism must first be loosened" (12). This latter step is brought to fruition in *El secreto,* in concordance with the many other historical reimaginings of space that Mauleón undertakes in other narrative works such as *La perfecta espiral* (1999), *El tiempo repentino* (2005), and *El derrumbe de los ídolos* (2010), as he lubricates a disjunction from historicism through the conceptual framework of historiographical metafiction as a genre and site of hermeneutic epistemology. By juxtaposing the filthy sewer with the descriptions of the City of Order, within the textual exercise of historiographic fiction, the author emulates the critical spatialization that Soja calls for.

The conversation with Cervantes's dialogues continues, as Beatriz's carriage on her initial ride into the city is pummeled by a mass of "indios, negros y mulatos" (16). This racial detail is important, as Cervantes is careful to trace a notion of Mexico that is limited to la traza. In her reading on the role of what space embodies in the dialogues, Del Valle notes:

> Cervantes administers spatial and human resources by dividing the space available—discriminating the space of the city proper—and by hierarchically assigning it to different populations. In his narration, Creoles are the city's rightful inhabitants, while the Spaniards are treated as visitors and Indians relegated to a marginal place outside the city's limits. . . . The wayfarers hardly encounter anyone along their route. What they do note are the buildings (and the echo of their inhabitants' names) from which the colonial state imposes its law. (204)

The native presence is visibly absent in the dialogues, though the Spaniard Alfaro is quick to note that European colonialism transformed the indigenous peoples from misery/slavery to happiness/liberty. The dialogues, furthermore, reflect the colonial authority's city-planning ordinances of establishing a developed center, which Indians on the periphery could contemplate and understand that newly arrived Europeans were settling permanently and not temporarily (García Gallo 244). The unity of this vision that Alfaro affirms in the dialogues, however, is idealistic and naïve at best, as the real space, like all cities in their chaotic and always-changing morphosyntax, did not adhere to city planning. Instead, "the same servitude and commerce that divided society, ironically enough, increasingly rendered the city a contact zone" (Merrim 21). The inclusion, therefore, of "indios, negros y mulatos" (16) in Mauleón's narrative of the city in the final years of the sixteenth century is illustrative of the nonsegregated topography of race-space that is conveniently excised from the historiogeography of Mexico City in the Cervantes dialogues.

A further demythification of Cervantes's City of Order is carried out as Juan articulates a sensorial description of its spaces. In opposition to Alfaro, who emphasizes the feats of engineering and architecture that create a modern and grandiose urban space, Juan provides a much darker and pungent description: "Las plantas del lago apestaban en las secas. Los canales, menguados, se llenaban de basura y animales muertos en los meses cálidos. En las calles donde había mataderos, zahúrdas y pescaderías, el aire esparcía su putrefacción amarga. No había quién se supiera a salvo del tabardillo, las calenturas podridas, las fiebres malignas y las disenterías" (16). This sharp contrast in descriptions highlights the demythifying tone of the novel, as by means of a reimagined geography, complete with topologic sensorial markings and formations, Mauleón attempts a recalibration of Cervantes's original writing of the space.

Beatriz's arrival in New Spain portends a series of events that lead Juan to believe that something sinister is taking place with the murders of the creoles. The Ircio household is informed of the daily workings and events of the city through the written chronicles of the blind ex-soldier Dueñas, who comes to their door and sips some warm wine while writing down all that he observes during the day. He is an old, war-broken soul who has lived through "seis virreyes, tres fiebres virulentas y cuatro pestilencias universales" (13). The subjective genealogy that Mauleón traces in this character evokes a startled break from the notion of urban Order and, instead, puts forward an alternative geography, where life is defined by the political, but more importantly, by disease and chaos. Aside from providing information that is later vital in the detective work to find the killer of the creoles, Dueñas serves as a reminder of the importance of the chronicler in the literary life of the city. Mauleón signals the prominence of this role when, upon Dueñas's death, the poet Arias comments that "no habrá ya quién recoja la memoria de los días que se pierden para siempre" (92). The centrality of the flaneur is further expanded by Juan when he notes that "entre la gentía . . . la ciudad [le] resultó más amplia. La [sintió] lejana, confusa, indescifrable. [Supo], oscuramente, que ya no [le] iba a ser posible entenderla. Desde la muerte del ciego, un mundo entero se [le] escapaba" (95). The irony here, of course, is that the urban chronicler is blind, forcing the reader to question the mimetic process of writing the city and its events. Are all chroniclers, both colonial and modern—such as Mauleón—blind? What do their words really represent, and how can we "see" through their narratives?

After Dueñas's visit one evening, Juan and Beatriz realize that the painting in the Cervantes text is a replica of a painting in the church of Santa Cruz de Tlatelolco. They journey quickly to its freshly painted walls one morning in a carriage, where Beatriz decides to entertain herself by spotting the seven Cs that Juan de la Cueva notes abound in the city: "calles, calzadas, caballos, carrozas, canoas, capas negras y criaturas" (36), further emphasizing the literary connection between Mauleón and the colonial urban chroniclers. In the church, they realize that the print is of a painting that depicts the torture of the Indians as the Spaniards searched for gold. It is in the church and afterward, during Juan's repeated visits to study the painting, that we see a further demythification of the textual dialogues. In addition to propagating an ordered blueprint of the city, "each dialogue on Mexico contains a . . . profession of allegiance to the evangelizing, draconian, teleological Spanish mission that set out to perfect the Indians, absolving them of the putative stain of paganism" (Merrim 69). The young protagonist desacralizes the authority and space of the church by beginning a relationship with a young Indian girl who works there. He returns time and again to enjoy her flesh, while excusing himself from his aunt with the alibi of studying the painting. Mauleón decenters the authority of the institution over colonial culture by housing within its walls the act of *mestizaje*, the breaking of Cervantes's ordered racial topography. This process culminates with Dueñas later reporting that the church's priest was apprehended for having multiple affairs with women, and with Juan declaring that he "había oído muchas veces de los sacerdotes solicitantes. La carne les quemaba. Las calles de la Nueva España estaban llenas de sus historias" (72).

Mauleón does not stop at dialoguing with and demythifying Cervantes's Ordered city, but goes further by including a metaliterary Bernardo de Balbuena in a scene with the fictional and lesser-known Arias. The two participate in a meeting of poets held at the press of Juan de Alcázar, where a court of old-timers visited the press from afternoon to afternoon (136) to keep up to date on the literary life of the colony. It is here that Juan, on an errand to collect a treaty on art for his mentor, the renowned New World painter Andrés de Concha, encounters the two poets discussing the use of spectacles. Balbuena, "ganador de concursos literarios en la juventud" (137), had spent the last few years of his life in a church in New Galicia, "separado por completo de los vicios y placeres de la vida intelectual" (137). He comes to Mexico City on what he describes as a "sagrada encomienda" (137) to write a long poem to a certain widow of San Miguel de Culiacán, to whom he had promised to reveal how the city is the "joya mayor de la Nueva España" (137). Given *El secreto de la Noche Triste*'s articulate historiography, it comes as no surprise that the poet is hatching "aquella tarde de 1601" (137), the first verses of what will become his most read work, *Grandeza Mexicana*.

The poet reveals how he has written some verses to describe the grandeur of the streets in the flowery diction of the Baroque. His verses, however, are quickly deposed of their authority when we learn that he has been writing and walking without spectacles and that he, therefore, cannot really see the events and buildings on the streets. Balbuena argues that his vanity does not allow him to use the spectacles, as they tend to "convertir a su usuario en objeto de burla, al ser llevados generalmente por hombres de edad avanzada, suelen indicar la proximidad a la muerte. Fácilmente se comprenderá que no pueden escribir buenos versos personas cuya descomposición se encuentra ya muy avanzada" (138). The secret to Balbuena's verse, it seems, emanates from his lack of clarity and vision when writing about the grandeur of the city, as it is not very grand at all, given Mauleón's introduction to its streets with the arrival of Beatriz. The narrative reference to Balbuena, however, is not fortuitous, as his version of the city dialogues effusively with the earlier model of the City of Order. His Spectacular City (Merrim 92) stands at the crossroads between the natural and manmade. This resemanticized space is a conglomeration of opposing lines of flight that signal an urban epistemology that attempts to reconcile competing essences in urban planning and experience. If Cervantes was concerned with establishing a mimetic space of the European in the New World, Balbuena focuses his verse as a "paean to mercantile capitalism, textualized objects [that] at once execute and emblematize the disruption of the Renaissance Ordered City" (92). The Spectacular City is not about regimented order, but is instead a locus of uncontrollable and unruly intricacies, signaling a discursive break with the colonizing necessity for calm and stability.

The contradictions arise when we consider how Balbuena envisions a Mexico City that is a "pivotal place on the globe," that "rejects its Aztec past, [and] surpasses the classical world" (132). The irony of this assertion, however, is swiftly put to rest by a clear-sighted Beatriz, who opines that "la Roma del Nuevo Mundo haría llorar a Vitruvio" (16). The poet's inability to truly see Mexico City is further developed in his discussions with Arias about the use of spectacles, particularly when the latter asserts, "en la ciudad de México el uso de anteojos es privilegio exclusive de los nobles y los sabios" (139). Balbuena's response is unsurprisingly illogical, as he affirms that "esos endiablados instrumentos hacen que las cosas pequeñas se vuelvan grandes, que los enanos aparezcan como gigantes y que las lagañas sean miradas como perlas. Falsean la realidad de tal modo, que hacen ver mayores a escritores que son, en realidad, menores" (139). The humor in *El secreto*'s pages cannot be ignored in these lines, as it is the myopic Balbuena who is truly guilty of blowing the grandeur of all things observed out of proportion. The narrator reflects upon this, albeit in a sarcastic tone, when he wonders if the poet wrote *Grandeza Mexicana* with glasses on, as its verses "dibuja[n] una ciudad más honda, más pura, más bella" (143). This beautified city, however, is relative. When compared to Cervantes's praise of its ordered walkways and centers of learning, yes, Balbuena does provide a more holistic understanding of its workings and peoples. Yet at the same time, the poet is guilty of glossing the stench, sickness, and detritus of the streets of the city, something that Juan, writing his memoirs in 1637 with a pair of glasses "contra [sus] ojos" (143), is not guilty of committing. He gives us an account of the city and its spaces with all its details and imperfections as, unlike Balbuena, he chooses to enjoy perfect vision.

Mauleón does not stop at simply claiming that Balbuena's Baroque city is an outlandish and exaggerated version of real veins and arteries of its body. He goes on to demythify the poem as being nothing more than a clerical love note to an unattainable widow, as Balbuena's commitment to the Church did not allow him to openly court the fairer sex. The fictional Arias, like the historical poet who, according to Merrim, "put[s] pressure on Balbuena's sublime, elite city" (10), deciphers the real meaning behind the imperfect stanzas of a sonnet in one of Balbuena's earlier pieces, *Siglo de Oro*. He notes that the first letter of each verse spells the name "DONA YSABEL DE TOBAR" (141), the name of the young widow who entrusts Balbuena with capturing the aura of Mexico City in *Grandeza Mexicana*. The novel suggests that Balbuena's eccentric take on the urban is nothing more than a ruse for some other hidden amorous message, and thereby it discounts his contribution from clearly representing and understanding the true spaces of Mexico.

The figure of Arias within this dialogue further merits attention, as he provides a narrative ploy to gain authority over the events that transpire. He first appears during the celebration of Beatriz's birthday, with an intertextual fragment of the *Canto titulado Mercurio* (1623) in his pocket. The novel intersperses a literary history of Mexico beyond simply quoting sections of the *Historia verdadera*, and thereby incubates a literary historiography within its pages through such intertextual citations. The *Canto*, like the sections of Bernal Díaz's text, appears prior to publication and furthers the notion of *El secreto* being an archaeology of the first textualizations of Mexico City, as the version of the *Canto* we evidence in the novel is a purported pre-published version. Mauleón not only effectively illustrates the literary products of the time but also provides a candid narration of the literary process of writing, sharing, and editing manuscripts in the colonial period. The lines that Arias reads to Beatriz allude to the *Canto*'s and his own importance to the diegesis, as he recounts how Cortés and his men retreated from Tenochtitlán on La Noche Triste. He provides a Spartan description of the event, noting that "aquí perdió Cortés, en grande ultraje, / con la reputación, todo el tesoro, / los tiros, prisioneros y fardaje, / y la ciudad, que es causa de más lloro . . ." (42). In his description, the focus is on being "aquí," privileging the site of the events of that fateful night. In the eyes of the young Arias, "pálido, alto, joven aún, con el aspecto de un monje que acabara de escapar del seminario" (42), the most important element of the narrative is the city and not the treasure, which further hints at what the real secret of Mauleón's *El secreto* really is.

The inclusion of Arias in the text, albeit prior to the publication of the *Canto*—his major work dealing with the city—is not accidental either, as his verses directly interact with and rearticulate Balbuena's work. The *Canto* is divided into two sections: the first, a dramatic and grandiose epic poem that celebrates the conquest of colonial Mexico; the second, a touristic and ekphrastic walkthrough of Mexico City during the viceroy's celebrated 1603 entry. The relationship between this second section and Mauleón's text is ontologically poignant, as its verses are seemingly composed immediately after Arias's fictional involvement with Juan and Beatriz to uncover the mystery of the serial killings. The relationship between Arias and Balbuena, furthermore, is developed beyond the pages of the novel as the second section of *Canto* rehashes many topics from *Grandeza*, appropriating the latter's Baroque style, diction, and disposition to favor artifice and the sublime over the natural and real.

More importantly, *Canto* disarticulates Balbuena's *Grandeza* through its rearticulation, evidencing a belligerent criollismo (Blanco 203) when it "maneuvers 'Grandeza' into an ironic counterpoint to its ideological platform as it implies that all of the wealth standing at the heart of Balbuena's poem eludes creoles in 1623" (Merrim 143), underlying the newly formed division in the colony between creole wishes and imperial desires. Arias's masterpiece, therefore, emblemizes the power struggle between competing groups that sets in motion the murder of the grandsons of the first conquistadors, and serves as a key historio-literary referent to Mauleón's excavation of the city. Keeping this tension of the text in mind, it comes as no surprise, then, that Arias's *Canto* disarticulates its literary antecedents, that is, the accounts of the city before *Grandeza*, as it deranges the sanitized and regimented spaces of the Ordered city through a disjunctive, heterogeneous, and inconclusive portrayal and characterization of Mexico City.

The poet's role in the novel, furthermore, demonstrates just how far Cervantes's version of the Ordered City is from the truth of the space, as the novel ends with Juan and Arias walking through the plaza in front of the city's cathedral. Juan, who by now has decoded the inscription beneath the replica found in *México en 1554*, asks Arias where the mythical Cincalco is—that is, where the Aztec gold is said to be hidden. The poet points to the hill of Chapultepec in the distance, informing the narrator that beneath it lies the Aztec underworld. The spatiality of this scene at the end of *El secreto de la Noche Triste* is fundamental to the polyvalenced interrogation of the city text in *México en 1554*, as it stands diametrically opposite to the final scene of Cervantes's text. In the latter, Chapultepec is where Alfaro and the two locals stand in disbelief at the city below them. It is where Zamora instructs the foreigner to "[tender] ahora la vista y [abarcar] por entero la ciudad de México" (74), a space that is aesthetically pleasing in its natural bounty and beauty. Mauleón, however, urges us away from the hill on the horizon, as even the best spectacles cannot make up for the obscureness that spatial distance naturally creates. He, instead, locates his characters and narrative within the city, as they walk through its streets and smell its scents, see its murders and poverty, and feel the wretched threat of danger at every turn. More importantly, Arias's revelation at the end of the novel accounts for, and emphasizes the importance of, an indigenous past that was buried beneath layers of Western discourse and urbanization, as represented by Cervantes's dialogues. Mauleón pushes aside the Eurocentric conception of the (New) space to remind the reader that below the streets, avenues, and buildings of Mexico City's firstspace lies an imaginative and indigenous secondspace that can never be erased.

These examples of a narrative juggling of texts, writers, poets, and portrayals of the cityspace are what I argue to be the true secret of Mauleón's *El secreto de la Noche Triste*. The writer critically articulates the tenets of historiographic metafiction, and he does not shy away from including his piece within a genealogy and genre of contemporary texts that serve as a site of contact for varied trajectories of inquiry into the connections between fiction and history. Like others of its kind, the novel beckons the reader to question the first—and all subsequent—accounts of the colonial period in Mexico, and it lays bare a structural framework that elucidates a potent reading of how La Noche Triste was represented and conceived of by different authors who managed to mingle their own intents and conditions into the text. What is new, however, in the recourse to historiography and metafiction is the attention placed on a series of texts that focus on the growing and nascent space that was built upon, and elided: the ancient Aztec center. This strategy or approach, termed metafictive historiogeography, I argue, poses a distinctive and fruitful site of research that reconsiders the forgetting or sublimation of space that Foucault and Soja elucidate in their work. These depictions of space and spatiality enrich the already fertile field of historiographic inquiries into fiction, but they further combine an acute awareness of space and geography, calling to mind Soja's need to "recompose the territory of the historical imagination through a critical spatialization" (*Postmodern Geographies* 12). Mauleón's fiction is historiographic and metafictive, yet it manages to assemble a narrative geography of Mexico City that transcends traditional historical imaginations.

The importance of space is captured in a seemingly innocuous conversation between Juan and Arias one day as they go from church to church to uncover more details of the killings. The poet bows to his knees and kisses the ground of a street corner near the church of Santo Domingo, explaining that the renowned poet Gutierre de Cetina was murdered on that very spot. He goes on to recount the events of one fateful night of 1554 when de Cetina was murdered by two hitmen who mistakenly thought the Sevillian poet was having an affair with a newly married bride who lived doorsteps from the corner. Further investigations proved that de Cetina was indeed innocent and that his murder had been an unfortunate mistake, robbing poetry of one of its "grandes maestros" (110). The implications of the terrain of the street corner to the history of the city's literary life is not lost on Arias, as he renders it a memorial to a writer who never fully blossomed. Juan, however, is ignorant and naïve of the importance of the secondspace that emanates from the street, and instead thinks of "aquella esquina cubierta de lodo, en la que sólo habían quedado impresos los pies de los transeúntes, las ruedas de los coches, las pezuñas de los caballos" (110). The novel, however, seems to argue otherwise, as Mauleón forces the reader to reconsider the images, histories, peoples, and events that once and forever have left a mark on the intrepid and boisterous streets of Tenochtitlán.

Works Cited

Aguilar, Yanet. "De Mauleón en busca del tesoro perdido." *El Universal*, October 21, 2009. http://www.eluniversal.com.mx/cultura/60960.html. Accessed November 9, 2011.

Angulo-Cano, Yanira. "The Modern Autobiographical 'I' in Bernal Díaz del Castillo." *Modern Language Notes* 125.2 (2010): 287–304.

Balbuena, Bernardo. *Grandeza Mexicana y compendio apologético en alabanza de la poesía.* 1604. México, D.F.: Porrúa, 1971.

Blanco, José Joaquín. *La literatura en la Nueva España.* México, D.F.: Cal y Arena, 1989.

Cervantes de Salazar, Francisco. *México en 1554. Tres diálogos latinos que Francisco Cervántes Salazar escribió é imprimió en México en dicho año.* México, D.F.: F. Díaz de León y S. White, 1875.

Del Valle, Ivonne. "On Shaky Ground: Hydraulics, State Formation, and Colonialism in Sixteenth-Century Mexico." *Hispanic Review* 77.2 (2009): 197–220.

Díaz del Castillo, Bernal. *Historia verdadera de la conquista de la Nueva España.* Tomo II. 1632. Ed. Joaquín Ramírez Cabañas. México, D.F.: Pedro Robredo, 1939.

Estrada, Oswaldo. *La imaginación novelesca: Bernal Díaz entre géneros y épocas.* Madrid: Iberoamericana/Vervuert, 2009.

———. "Textos y pretextos entre la *Historia verdadera* y *Nen, la inútil* de Ignacio Solares." *Revista de Literatura Mexicana Contemporánea* 29 (2006): 95–103.

Flores, Enrique. "El silencio de la conquista: Poéticas de Bernal Díaz." *Revista de Crítica Literaria Latinoamericana* 57 (2003): 143–50.

Foucault, Michel. "Questions on Geography." *Power/Knowledge: Selected Interviews and Other Writings 1972–1977.* Ed. C. Gordon. New York: Pantheon, 1980. 63–77.

García Gallo, Alfonso, ed. *Cedulario indiano, Libro cuarto.* Facsimile of 1596 edition. Madrid: Ediciones Cultura Hispánica, 1946.

Gómez López-Quiñones, Antonio. "La conquista y el problema de la modernidad hispánica: Dos discursos sobre el pasado (post)colonial en la democracia española." *Anales de la Literatura Española Contemporánea* 36 (2011): 101–31.

Hutcheon, Linda. *A Poetics of Postmodernism: History, Theory, Fiction.* New York: Routledge, 1988.

Mauleón, Héctor de. *El secreto de la Noche Triste.* México, D.F.: Planeta, 2009.

Merrim, Stephanie. *The Spectacular City, Mexico, and Colonial Hispanic Literary Culture.* Austin: University of Texas Press, 2010.

Pastor, Beatriz. *Discursos narrativos de la conquista: Mitificación y emergencia.* Hanover, NH: Ediciones del Norte, 1988.

Ross, Kathleen. *"Alboroto y motín de México*: Una noche triste criolla." *Hispanic Review* 56.2 (1988): 181–90.

Ruiz Bañuls, Mónica. "Cortés y otros héroes de la conquista en el teatro mexicano del siglo XIX." *América sin nombre* 5–6 (2004): 208–15.

Soja, Edward W. *Postmetropolis: Critical Studies of Cities and Regions.* Malden, MA: Blackwell, 2000.

——. *Postmodern Geographies: The Reassertion of Space in Critical Social Theory.* London: Verso, 1989.

Villalobos, Arias de. "Canto intitulado Mercurio." *Documentos inéditos o muy raros para la historia de México.* Ed. Genaro García and Carlos Pereyra. México, D.F.: Vda. de C. Bouret, 1905–1911.

Weintraub, Karl J. "Autobiografía y conciencia histórica." *Suplementos Anthropos* 29 (1991): 18–33.

PART TWO

Queering Gender and Twisting Genres

Four Letters and a Funeral

Sor Juana's Writing in Yo, la peor

Oswaldo Estrada

No mi voluntad, mi poca salud y mi justo temor
han suspendido tantos días mi respuesta . . .
—SOR JUANA INÉS DE LA CRUZ (*RESPUESTA* 38)

Certainly, one of the most fascinating documents that Sor Juana (1648–1695) produced during her lifetime was her well-articulated *Respuesta a Sor Filotea de la Cruz* (1691). Unlike her philosophical sonnets and playful villancicos, her enigmatic *Sueño* of 975 Baroque lines, or her intricate allegorical compositions, the letter that she addresses to the bishop of Puebla, Manuel Fernández de Santa Cruz, still attracts contemporary audiences with the familiar tone of what appears to be an honest autobiography or the secret confession of a religious woman who defends her intellectualism. Even though several critics have studied this letter as a rhetorical construction that mimics the structure of the forensic discourse (Perelmuter 25–41), as a literary process of self-textualization (Luciani 80–126), or as an ingenious display of the strategies employed by the disempowered (Ludmer 86–93), the vast majority of contemporary novels that recreate Sor Juana's life take her *Respuesta* as a true historical source, or as a point of fictional departure. This is evident, for instance, in Mónica Zagal's *La venganza de Sor Juana* (2007),[1] José Luis Gómez's *El beso de la virreina* (2008), and Kyra Galván's *Los indecibles pecados de Sor Juana* (2010). In line with this trend, Mónica Lavín also returns to Sor Juana's famous letter defending the right of women to read, think, and be intellectual when crafting her novel *Yo, la peor* (2009). In Lavín's novel, however, the fictional Sor Juana composes four additional letters during the last six months of her life—the ultimate evidence of her commitment to read and write—as she is forced to stay silent and away from her studies.

The novelistic presence of these letters reminds us that Sor Juana composed several such epistles throughout her life, as evidenced by her *Carta atenagórica* or *Crisis de un sermón* (1690), the aforementioned *Respuesta a Sor Filotea de la Cruz*, and her *Carta al Padre Núñez* (discovered in 1981). The fictional letters inserted in Lavín's work also allude to the fact that Sor Juana exchanged a good number of them with prominent figures in Europe and Spanish America, such as the poet Juan del Valle y Caviedes, the Portuguese nuns of the *Casa del Placer*, and the mysterious author of the *Carta de Serafina de Cristo*.[2] The fact that many letters and poems of praise were written about Sor Juana's impressive work on both sides of the Atlantic during her lifetime and for many years after her death is no mystery, either.[3] To this extent, the set of four letters in the novel that Sor Juana addresses to the former vicereine María Luisa Manrique de Lara, Countess of Paredes, residing in Spain, symbolically represents an *alternative testament* that compresses her past, describes her present, and projects her into a possible future (Lavrin, "*Femenino*" 169). Consistent with colonial female writings and recorded testimonies that expressed a woman's reaffirmation of her faith, the recounting of her life, the disposition of her belongings, and an overall (if frequently mediated) view of female life (Lavrin, "*Femenino*" 169), Lavín's Sor Juana uses her last letters to reflect on her lifelong accomplishments as a writer, and also on her diminished position after being confronted by repressive ecclesiastical authorities. Metaphorically speaking, then, this final novelistic act of writing carries with it the seeds of female transgression, one that combats women's traditional simulacrum of silence (Porzecanski 53).

The association of these fictional transatlantic letters with Sor Juana in a contemporary context can be somewhat thorny if we consider that the epistolary form itself has been historically related to domesticity, femininity, and various private modes of experience (Gilroy and Verhoeven 2). At least since the sixteenth century, when the familiar letter acquires the status of a literary form, European male commentators note, disparagingly, that the epistolary genre "seem[s] particularly suited to the female voice" (Goldsmith vii). Apparently aligned with this particular view of the epistolary genre, Lavín's letters privilege the alleged domestic nature of the letter, sacrificing the scholastic arguments or the forensic rhetoric that the nun employed to craft original masterpieces. Consequently, although the letters in *Yo, la peor* denote Sor Juana's intellectuality, they come across as confessional, having nothing to do with the conscious and premeditated effort underpinning the art of letter writing that the historical Sor Juana practiced in order to explain her philosophical and/or theological reasoning (Perelmuter 32). And yet, seen from a feminist point of view, each letter is undeniably crafted against silence and misrepresentation. As readers, we may not like the end product, especially if we compare the literary caliber of these imagined letters to Sor Juana's actual writing. In their own right, however, these letters fictionalize a painful writing exercise that runs through a woman's body and challenges an assigned domesticity. Lavín's ultimate goal is to create through the letters an empowered identity that can combat enduring cycles of emptiness and historical absence (Lorenzano 371).

Since *Yo, la peor* primarily fictionalizes the lives of Sor Juana's mother and grandmother, older sister, and aunt—as well as the mentor who teaches her how to read and write and the vicereine who becomes her lifelong protector, friend, and literary accomplice—it is easy for most critics to highlight the novel's feminine perspective, consistent with trends in the late Hispanic *feminine* boom (Guillén 97; Madrid Moctezuma 95). While the re-creation of Sor Juana's life in the context of a strong female community clearly articulates the novel's overt feminism, Lavín reaches a higher level of female empowerment and transgression as she allows Sor Juana to identify herself as a woman writer in the four letters that she addresses to the Countess of Paredes. If letters offer an optimal space for uncensored expression in the absence of a face-to face interlocutor (Schaefer 70), Sor Juana's first fictional letter to the vicereine, dated November 17, 1694, immediately validates the author's true intention to break the silence that has been imposed on the nun by New Spanish authorities. "Querida y admirada María Luisa," begins Lavín's Sor Juana, "Te escribo con la certeza de que no tenemos tiempo. Es preciso que procedas de prisa para que los lobos se den cuenta de que su plan ha fallado. Han seguido acorralándome y yo he dado muestras de que me han convencido, pero tú bien sabes la verdad" (13).

The defensive tone of this epistolary introduction prepares readers of *Yo, la peor* for the unfolding of various unresolved mysteries surrounding Sor Juana's final years. For several decades, an entire community of *sorjuanistas* has debated whether during the last years of her life the nun renounced her studies, lived as a typical nun, wrote mystical compositions, or had a final moment of true conversion (Paz 602–8; Lavrin, "Unlike" 86–87; Xirau 54). Although we now assume that Sor Juana continued to read and write virtually until her death on April 17, 1695, a conclusion drawn in part thanks to the inventory of her cell at the time of her death that reveals the presence of several unfinished poems and approximately 180 volumes of selected works (Trabulse, *Memoria* 26), Lavín gives the fictional nun the opportunity to refute her hypothetical pious conversion. In order to accomplish this, the character Sor Juana recalls how her life has changed, "desde la publicación de la *Carta atenagórica*, tres años atrás" (14). The allusion to this historical document invites readers to recall and revisit the production and reception of a set of letters that dramatically affect Sor Juana's life.

In 1690, the bishop of Puebla published the nun's *Carta atenagórica*, a private letter in which Sor Juana contests the 1650 sermon of the famous Portuguese Jesuit preacher, Antonio de Vieira. This letter, as is well known, was prefaced by the bishop's *Carta de Sor Filotea*, in which, under the pseudonym Sor Filotea, Fernández de Santa Cruz commands Sor Juana to act like a true nun, devoting all of her energy to the study of divine and exclusively religious matters, in order to become more holy, "dulcemente herida de amor de su Dios" (*Respuesta* 228). The letter described by Fernández de Santa Cruz as "worthy of Athena," in which Sor Juana behaves like a theologian capable of discussing, with admirable reasoning, Jesus Christ's highest favor to humanity, represents a real threat to the men of the Church, even more so than her already problematic love poems (Arenal and Powell 12). If the bishop published this letter to publicly reprimand and silence Sor Juana, the nun countered with the elaborate *Respuesta*, arguing with affected modesty, "No quiero ruido con el Santo Oficio, que soy ignorante y tiemblo de decir alguna proposición malsonante o torcer la genuina inteligencia de algún lugar. Yo no estudio para escribir, ni menos para enseñar (que fuera en mí desmedida soberbia), sino sólo por ver si con estudiar ignoro menos" (*Respuesta* 46).

Sor Juana's *Respuesta a Sor Filotea de la Cruz* was published posthumously in 1700, but in 1691, the year she wrote the letter, she claimed "el escribir nunca ha sido dictamen propio, sino fuerza ajena" (46); she published her villancicos to Saint Catherine of Alexandria in Puebla; and the second volume of her works was printed in Seville in 1692, including the *Crisis de un sermón*, as the nun's critique of Vieira was now called. Between 1692—when she sold her library—and 1694, when she renewed her religious vows and signed a statement of self-condemnation with her own blood, a mysterious aura of silence surrounds the nun and her public writing.[4] Taking into account the *Petición que en forma causídica presenta al Tribunal Divino la Madre Juana Inés de la Cruz, por impetrar perdón de sus culpas*, her first biographer, Diego Calleja in Spain, depicts the nun as a woman of saintly attributes, "tan deseable para esperar la muerte quien no la teme como fin de la vida, sino como principio de la eternidad . . . despidiéndose de su esposo a más ver y presto" (26).

In response to this portrayal of an exemplary *vida* for Sor Juana, most likely as a contemporary reinterpretation of her own desire that "Dios me haga santa" (*Obras Completas* [hereafter OC] 4: 522), as expressed on February 24, 1669, when the nun takes her religious vows in the convent of San Jerónimo; and definitely in reaction to her secret trial, "el pleito que se sigue en el Tribunal de vuestra justicia contra mis graves, enormes y siniguales pecados" (*OC* 4: 520), Lavín's Sor Juana writes in her first letter:

> Ahora me piden que sea otra de la que soy, que me corte la lengua, que me nuble la vista, que me ampute los dedos, el corazón, que no piense, que no sienta más que lo que es menester y propio de una religiosa, de una esposa de Cristo. ¿Quién ha decidido que no pensar es propio de la mujer del Altísimo?
>
> La ira me vence, me abate el ánimo disfrazarme de otra cosa; te reitero que he aceptado a mi antiguo confesor para sosegarlos y por lo mismo he pretendido silencio. (17–18)

This fictional discourse is moving and simultaneously subversive, as it implicitly confronts the bishop of Puebla who reprimands Sor Juana, "Lástima es que un tan gran entendimiento, de tal manera se abata a las rateras noticias de la tierra, que no desee penetrar lo que pasa en el cielo" (*Respuesta* 228). At the same time, the words that Lavín fictionally attributes to Sor Juana undeniably reflect the combative spirit with which the historical nun had dismissed her confessor Núñez de Miranda between 1681 and 1682, arguing, "¿Había de ser santa a pura fuerza? Ojalá y la santidad fuera cosa que se pudiera mandar, que con eso la tuviera yo segura . . . pero santos, sólo la gracia, y auxilios de Dios saben hacerlos" (*Poesía* . . . 1416).[5]

In keeping with the historical Sor Juana's self-protective rhetoric, the nun writes her first letter in *Yo, la peor* to thank her friend María Luisa for arranging the publication of *Los enigmas de la Casa del Placer,* a set of twenty redondillas on the nature of love originally composed for a group of Portuguese nuns. The significance of this textual reference to these enigmas is twofold. On the one hand, it confirms Sor Juana's determination not only to continue writing, but also to do so with a set of "preguntas destinadas a hacer pensar" (Cruz, *Enigmas* 13), at a time when her superiors order "que no piense" (17). On the other hand, the mention of the enigmas in the novel immediately evokes Sor Juana's fame and multiple transatlantic connections with the Iberian Peninsula, particularly with a community of women devoted to (her) poetry (Cruz, *Poesía* 529). When the fictional Sor Juana reflects on *"Los enigmas* que he escrito y enviado a las monjas portuguesas" (16), readers are invited to recall the elaborate handmade manuscript produced in Lisbon in 1695, the same year in which the nun died. With this deftly positioned intertext, Lavín pushes to the forefront the fact that, at least toward the end of her life, Sor Juana was closely involved with a "female literary academy formed by a group of aristocratic Portuguese nuns from various convents in Lisbon" (Kirk, *Convent* 143).

What is disguised in the letter as a heartfelt reflection on the poems that "comfort" Sor Juana in the midst of her "tribulations," to the extent that they symbolize (as she explains to María Luisa) "una manera de agradecerte mi salvación, la única posible" (16), actually unwraps a metaphorical box of enigmas regarding Sor Juana's final years. Originally presented "en su disfraz" (*Enigmas* 73), in order to entertain the Portuguese nuns—"Divertiros sólo un rato / es quanto aspirar podrá" (*Enigmas* 73)—Sor Juana's book of riddles guards hidden messages that speak of hope, jealousy, absence, amorous passion, and various types of (courtly) love (Cruz, "Contemporáneos" 215–44). These compositions are indeed enigmatic, as their title suggests, particularly because they must have been crafted around the time when Sor Juana signed her *Protesta* with her own blood on March 5, 1694, supposedly "al tiempo de abandonar los estudios humanos para proseguir, desembarazada de este afecto, en el camino de la perfección" (*OC* 4: 518).

True to the historical nun's lifelong passion for the exploration of knowledge, Lavín's Sor Juana, by alluding to her own *enigmas*, defines herself as an intellectual who is always on the move, someone who can speak truth to power—as uncomfortable as that may be—even from a marginal position (Said 8–12). Echoing the defensive tone of the *Respuesta a Sor Filotea de la Cruz*—in which the nun argues, "Desde que me rayó la primera luz de la razón, fue tan vehemente y poderosa la inclinación a las letras, que ni ajenas reprensiones—que he tenido muchas—ni propias reflejas—que he hecho no pocas, han bastado a que deje de seguir este natural impulso que Dios puso en mí" (*Respuesta* 46)—in *Yo, la peor*, a courageous Sor Juana also defines her intellectuality, but with a modern twist:

> Soy un animal acorralado, un animal acusado de su naturaleza: tener colmillos y usarlos, tener garras y encontrar su sitio en el mundo. Si la bestia se alimenta de otros animales, lo mío es alimentarme del pensamiento de los demás, de sus maneras de mirar el mundo, lo mío es

apresar el entendimiento en palabras. Encontrar las metáforas del in-
telecto que me hagan estirar el cuello a las alturas donde la gracia divina lo permita. (15)

Furthermore, echoing the arguments that the nun eloquently articulated in her *Carta al Padre Núñez*, in which she protests against women's
limited access to knowledge—"¿Qué revelación divina, que determinación
de la Iglesia, qué dictamen de la razón hizo para nosotras tan severa ley?"
(*Poesía* . . . 1415)—in her first letter to the former vicereine the character
Sor Juana also complains, "¿Quién ha decidido que no pensar es propio de
la mujer del Altísimo?" (17). In both instances—historical and fictional—
Sor Juana's is the voice of a true intellectual endowed with the special
faculty of representing and embodying a firm attitude or message to, and
for, a public (Said 11). Although Sor Juana is described in other passages of
Lavín's novel as a *rara avis*, for being simultaneously intelligent, eloquent,
beautiful, and elegant, this first letter expands and restores the nun's intellectual legacy, contained within those texts in which she assembles a complex semantic puzzle that situates the feminine within the privileged
realm of official discourse (Martínez-San Miguel 53). Ultimately, what
matters the most in *Yo, la peor* is that a woman is writing another woman's
life to contest women's historical silence and misrepresentation, to recu-
perate the lost voices of a female individual or group, and to situate their
life stories within a safe place that is different from the one that has been
consistently assigned to an entire female population over centuries of male
domination (Lorenzano 351).

The letters that Sor Juana writes to the Countess María Luisa in *Yo, la
peor* are all crafted with the sensibility of one who seeks comfort and refuge in a friend and literary interlocutor. Sor Juana calls María Luisa
"amiga" (16), "leal amiga" (79), "imprescindible amiga" (213), and finally,
"entrañable amiga y poeta" (365). While, on the one hand, this intimate
language reflects the personal manner in which letters in general seek to
overcome the loss or absence of a special individual (Schaefer 69), on the
other hand, their deceptively feminine and domestic tone disentangles a
complex network of literary friendships and various polemics surrounding
the life and works of Sor Juana Inés de la Cruz. Like the historical lettered
nun who established close friendships first with the vicereine Leonor
Carreto and then with María Luisa Manrique de Lara, the fictional protagonist of *Yo, la peor* also attracts the attention of both women through
the poems she composes to each of them. In the novel, Sor Juana writes
"notables sonetos" (226) to the first vicereine, the Marquise of Mancera,

who protects her in the viceregal palace and continues to protect her after she enters the convent where she professes. The nun also writes a good number of poems to the Countess of Paredes and, in the first letter she writes to her, Sor Juana accurately remembers: "Cuántos versos te escribí en los tiempos en que estuviste en Palacio, tan cerca de mi celda en San Jerónimo, tan arropada por los volcanes como yo" (13).

These words—and the fact that Sor Juana displays throughout the novel a series of "fineza(s) política(s)" (257) aimed particularly at pleasing the vicereine, María Luisa (who feels ambiguously attracted to the nun's intelligence)—confirm the courtly strategies that the nun employed in order to secure a small but privileged place of her own within the political matrix of New Spain (Paz 249). In view of Sor Juana's subtle empowerment in real life, Sara Poot Herrera affirms:

> Una de las finezas de Sor Juana Inés de la Cruz hacia las mujeres de las que estuvo cerca fue dedicarles varios romances de su poesía; la poeta también recibió finas respuestas, entre otras, romances escritos especialmente para ella. Estos "romances de amiga" son los hilos visibles e invisibles de una urdimbre textual de relaciones y afectos que se va tejiendo desde la segunda mitad de la década de los años setenta del siglo diecisiete—época inicial de las ediciones sueltas de los villancicos de Sor Juana—hasta 1695, año de "impresión" de los *Enigmas* que dedica a las monjas portuguesas de La Casa del Placer, y 1700, que es cuando se publica su *Fama y Obras póstumas*. (277–78)[6]

Consistent with these historical and literary relationships, the novel's Sor Juana appears to craft her second, third, and fourth letter to the vicereine as a true humanist of the Early Modern era who privileges the written word over oral conversation, at the same time appearing to have used the letter as a necessary but imperfect substitute for an in-person meeting (Van Houdt and Papy 4). Not only does she use these letters to define herself as a scholar by means of self-presentation—"aquí en el papel, en las lides de los retos y acertijos de palabras me encuentro a mis anchas, respiro" (79)—she also unveils an intricate "coded language" that implies a notion of "reciprocality" (Altman 120–21), an *I-you* relationship that revives Sor Juana and the vicereine María Luisa in the twenty-first century, as well as a number of crucial protagonists and events that, for better or worse, directly affected the famous nun.[7]

As Sor Juana thanks the former vicereine for the great "tejido que has logrado entre las monjas portuguesas y mi persona" (82)—particularly a fruitful exchange of poems with Sor Feliciana de Milâo and Sor María de Céu—the nun also takes the opportunity to personally thank María Luisa for writing one of the poems that will serve as a preface to her *Enigmas*. Echoing the "spontaneous," "non-literary," and "daily" language found in numerous letters written by nuns of the colonial era (Lavrin, "Celda" 140), the fictional Sor Juana writes in a most simple manner: "Debo decirte, por cierto, que el poema que acompaña el libro y que me has hecho llegar para mis enmiendas es de una factura sorprendente y que tu modestia es infinita cuando sólo incluyes uno, en lugar de tener el mismo espacio que a mí me ha sido concedido" (81). More than just another expression of gratitude, the brief and subtle allusion to the poem written by the Countess of Paredes exposes their close relationship and literary complicity. Acting as contemporary literary detectives of Sor Juana's life and works (Kirk, "Genealogical" 357), we turn our attention to the *Enigmas*, where the vicereine writes: "Amiga, este libro tuyo / es tan hijo de tu ingenio, / que correspondió, leído, / a la esperanza el efecto" (83). María Luisa's poem may or may not be, as she herself argues, "destemplado, / ronco, indigno, torpe" (85). What matters more, however, is that the vicereine's voice in the book, the one that gathers Sor Juana's enigmas, transforms Lavín's novel into a "pensive text" insofar as it seems to keep "in reserve," as Roland Barthes would certainly argue, an implicit yet higher level of meaning, thanks to the almost invisible presence of unspoken and unwritten language (216–17).

The inferential process through which we recognize the vicereine who speaks to Sor Juana with the *tú* used between two close friends (Cruz, *Enigmas* 32), brings with it the realization that the same woman was responsible for the publication of the nun's first volume, *Inundación castálida* (1689). That book made Sor Juana famous, and also allowed her to speak out against those who blamed her for being an intellectual (Sabat de Rivers, *En busca* 121). In her letters to María Luisa, Sor Juana remembers their literary *tertulias*, the reading and discussion of controversial texts, and the stagings of her own plays; she thanks the vicereine for sending the bishop of Puebla her *Segundo volumen* (1692), a book produced by both women with the help of several churchmen—Jesuits, Carmelites, Trinitarians, and even *calificadores* of the Santo Oficio—who openly defended Sor Juana's intellectualism (Glantz 158–61); and she consistently refers to Fernandez de Santa Cruz, the archbishop Aguiar y Seixas, and her confessor Núñez de Miranda as "los lobos" (13, 79, 213, 365). These comments, and specifically the reference to the men of the Church as wolves who chase after her, are not gratuitous. On the contrary, the allusion is charged with "pensiveness," and the printed text suddenly appears supplemented by "an *et cetera* of plenitudes" (Barthes 217); it becomes more expressive as it alludes to various sources of implicit knowledge that endow the literary text with a greater sense of interiority.

In the midst of many explicit references to some of Sor Juana's works in the novel—the *Neptuno Alegórico* (17, 249, 257), the *loa* to the *Sacred Sacrament* (44, 59), the play *Los empeños de una casa* (271), "Un papelillo llamado *El sueño*" (287–90), and the *Inundación castálida* (318), among others, and several allusions to her villancicos (14, 314, 319) or to the poems "[Éste que ves] *engaño colorido*" (214), "*Hombres necios*" (215) and so on—the carefully inserted reference to the "wolves" reveals a hidden document that silently appears in the text as a form of secret or forbidden knowledge that immediately sparks curiosity: the *Carta de Serafina de Cristo* that I mentioned at the beginning of this chapter.[8] Unlike the *Respuesta a Sor Filotea de la Cruz*, which is heavily used throughout the novel in order to reconstruct Sor Juana's biography—from her childhood in Panoayan and her attendance to the Amigas school at the age of three until she enters the convent in order to live alone, without any obligations that would disturb her freedom to read and write—the *Carta de Serafina de Cristo* is never mentioned. And yet, each time Sor Juana speaks of the wolves pursuing her in the four letters to the vicereine, we are invited to revisit Serafina's letter, a cryptic text that refers to one of the opponents of "Madre Cruz" (43) as a wolf in disguise:

No la cara, la cabeza
sacó de lobo a Camila;
y aunque los dientes afila,
queda *in albis* su fiereza.

Lobo se ha mostrado, y es
que imagina ser cordera
su adalid, como si fuera
aquella Camila YNÉS. (39)

Dated 1691, the *Carta de Serafina de Cristo* was first published in 1996 by Elías Trabulse and stands as a clear example of several pieces of writing that circulated in manuscript form during Sor Juana's lifetime, in order to discredit or to defend the theological arguments that the nun exposes in her problematic *Carta atenagórica* (Rodríguez Garrido 21; Buxó 374). Although originally attributed to Sor Juana by Trabulse (*El enigma* 9), in

1998 Antonio Alatorre and Marta Lilia Tenorio discarded that possibility in their study *Serafina y Sor Juana*, and suggested that the real author could very well have been Juan Ignacio de Castorena y Ursúa (140). In support of Trabulse's hypothesis, however, in 1999, Sara Poot Herrera concluded, "Si Sor Juana no es Serafina, nadie más lo podría ser, a no ser que en San Jerónimo—donde se fechó la carta, donde se escuchó a Palavicino, donde se aprobó su sermón, donde se escribió la *Atenagórica*, la *Respuesta*—se inventara el nombre para dejar un testimonio de que Sor Juana—como Núñez de Miranda—tampoco estaba sola" (*Guardaditos* 177). In agreement with this latter reading, Lavín implicitly supports the hypothesis that Serafina is none other than Sor Juana. She does this from the moment that she presents a young Juana Inés in possession of a doll named Serafina, which she leaves with her sister Josefa when she moves to Mexico City (41), and Lavín continues to develop this unspoken connection between Serafina and Sor Juana in the letters in which the nun, empowered by the forthcoming publication of her *Enigmas*, is depicted as the "loba sagaz" who treats her enemies—namely Fernández de Santa Cruz, Aguiar y Seixas, and Núñez de Miranda—as "ovejas engañadas" (213).

In the end, the implicit intertext—of *los lobos*—that connects Sor Juana's fictional letters to the historical *Carta de Serafina* (still of dubious authorship in the twenty-first century) alludes not only to the ferocity of one of her enemies, but also to the uncomfortable tension surrounding the nun in the wake of the publication of her *Carta atenagórica*. By and large, this letter that appears only implicitly between the lines that Sor Juana crafts for the vicereine, and produces the same effect as Serafina's actual letter, according to Alatorre and Tenorio:

> Nos deja oír el rumor de los comentarios que en el mundillo de la cultura—teólogos, predicadores, catedráticos, frailes, "tertulios," y tal vez hasta una parte del "público en general"—se hacían sobre la *Crisis* del Sermón del Mandato. Esa monja tan aplaudida por el ingenio de sus villancicos, por la erudición de su *Neptuno Alegórico*, por la inventiva de sus loas y autos, por la gracia del "festejo" de *Los empeños de una casa* (la comedia, los sainetes y todo lo demás), entraba ahora, de manera sorprendente, en un terreno menos pisado aún por pies femeninos: el debate teológico, y no contra cualquiera, sino contra el célebre P. Vieira. (91)

Taking as its literary models the "discursive battle" (Moraña 84–85) found in the *Carta al Padre Núñez* (also known as the *Carta de Monterrey*), in which Sor Juana questions her confessor's authority to interpret God's will for her (Myers 99), and the famous *Respuesta*, a document clearly articulated as "una lograda *defensa*, un discurso que encuadra perfectamente en la línea de la oratoria forense" (Perelmuter 29), Lavín's Sor Juana empowers herself with a discourse of her own, one that allows her to fight with the word as her only weapon against the men that try to clip her intellectual wings. Here, in her second letter to María Luisa, the nun imagines what she would say to the bishop Manuel Fernández de Santa Cruz, if he were to visit her in San Jerónimo after he used his own letter to publicly reprimand her:

> Manuel . . . yo no acusé de hereje a nadie, ni de vanidad, sólo di argumentos para inclinarme hacia una u otra teoría. Sí, algo había de complacencia, ¿quién es inmune a ello? Yo mejor que nadie lo puedo entender. Pero las formas importan, las lealtades íntimas también y tú fuiste cobarde. Te llamaste Filotea, aunque debo agradecerte que me permitiste responder y aclarar mi posición en el mundo. Si me han de excomulgar o quemar en la hoguera tú serás responsable, pero quedará esa carta a Filotea, para que la sinceridad de mi corazón sirva y dé luz a quienes sean reprendidos y silenciados injustamente. (82)

In reaction to the portrait of a nun who finally submits to authority and officially assumes "the cross of the nun"—a portrayal of Sor Juana that Asunción Lavrin promotes well into the twenty-first century (*Brides* 348)— in Lavín's third letter Sor Juana resuscitates the arguments she presented both in her *Carta al Padre Núñez* and the *Respuesta a Sor Filotea de la Cruz*, working within and reshaping the conventions and ideological possibilities of the epistle and the confessional *vida*, as she did in real life in order to strengthen her arguments (Myers 99). An eloquent Sor Juana now protests:

> ¿O sea que hay temas que no son para nosotras las mujeres ni aun cuando religiosas y en clausura hemos renunciado al mundo y el bullicio? ¿O sea que nosotras en virtud de un cuerpo que se distingue del de varón, no debemos acariciar palabras, dudar, pensar, indagar? Si nos es dado experimentar en la cocina y ver *que un huevo se fríe y une en la manteca y aceite y, por contrario, se despedaza en el almíbar*, ¿por qué no es posible indagar los terrenos de lo sagrado, donde ellos por permiso de su anatomía sí lo pueden hacer? Quiera Dios y la inteligencia de las mujeres que su encierro sea por voluntad y la extensión de su mirada

también derive de sus propias decisiones. ¿A quién ofende leer? ¿A quién el asombro y el debate de las ideas? (214, original emphasis)

Quoting directly from her own *Respuesta*, in which the kitchen is depicted as an empirical laboratory (Ochoa 230), and invoking the same words with which she defended her right to study in the letter to her confessor—"¿Qué revelación divina, qué determinación de la Iglesia, qué dictamen de la razón hizo para nosotras tan severa ley?" (*Poesía* . . . 1415)—Lavín's Sor Juana further argues: "Yo no pienso esconderme en calzas de hombre, bajo barbas y bigotes para que el mundo de las palabras sea mío" (215).

These words remind us of the historical Sor Juana's authoritative use of her personal talent to defend herself (Franco 78), as when she bluntly told her confessor, "Yo tengo este genio, si es malo, yo [no] me hice racional, nací con él y con él he de morir" (*Poesía* . . . 1415). The fictional Sor Juana likewise validates contemporary women's writing as a political act of "desborde, ruptura e intersticio," in as much as it crosses the limits imposed on women within male-dominated societies, rewrites or does away with conventional hegemonic discourses, and even finds new points of departure that reconfigure marginal, liminal, and/or peripheral zones of female subordination (Porzecanski 55). By the time we read the fourth letter, it is clear not only that each one is inserted in *Yo, la peor* as part of an intentional "feminine epistolary narrative" (Baquero Escudero 20),[9] but that each part of the composite whole is crafted using a poetics of eloquent silence. If Sor Juana withdraws from the public eye during the last two years of her life and, in fact, gives the impression that she has taken the ascetic path that Núñez de Miranda had previously prescribed for her (Arenal and Powell 14), in the novel she behaves like an artist whose silence produces something dialectical: "an enriching emptiness," as Susan Sontag would call it, a resonating or eloquent silence that remains a form of speech and an element in a dialogue (11).[10]

First of all—and this is what most readers will undoubtedly notice when they first approach *Yo, la peor*—in her last letter to the vicereine, Sor Juana confirms the true nature of her public silence:

Ha sido necesario actuar. Accedí a celebrar mis bodas de plata por todo lo alto, me tiré al piso de nuevo con los brazos abiertos pero sin la emoción antigua, y grité mis pecados: me acusé de vanidosa, de haber descuidado mis deberes de esposa, de haber desobedecido, de haber tenido vida mundana, de violentar la clausura con los intercambios en el locutorio y las epístolas, juré no dedicar mi entendimiento a lo terreno, ni tener

transacciones con el mundo muros afuera, juré no escribir una sola carta
ni una palabra más que no fuera en los versos religiosos, juré ser quien
no era y fingí dolor, el dolor era real, claro, y los convenció, aunque las
razones del mismo son otras. (367)

More important, however, and less explicit, is the fact that she immediately reinforces this illusion of silence with a rhetoric that indicates her determination to pursue her lifelong passion more cunningly and skillfully
than she did before (Sontag 12). She calls her male authorities "pobres ilusos"; reiterates her desire to "sobrevivir por la palabra y con la palabra. Pen-
sando a través de los signos del idioma"; and thanks her "bien amada amiga
y benefactora" for helping her to tell the world, although in the most subtle
of ways, that she continues to be true to herself (367). Simply put:

> Los tres lobos y el resto del mundo deben saber la verdad. . . . Deben
> saber que si firmé Yo, la peor de todas con mi sangre fue por rubricar
> dramáticamente aquella representación. Sé que los enigmas de la Casa
> del Placer ha sido terminado el mes pasado, por tu empeño y entrega,
> como bien me indicas, y que muy pronto estará impreso. . . . Esos enig-
> mas, escritos para que la inteligencia de las monjas portuguesas los
> complete y descifre, serán prueba de que el despojo de mis libros y la
> intención de matar a la que yo soy, no ha sido posible. (368)

Through the fictionalization of an aesthetic of silence, *Yo, la peor* invites us to reconsider the notion of emptiness and reduction around the
work of an artist with the aid of new prescriptions for looking, reading,
hearing, and interpreting, "which either promote a more immediate, sen-
suous experience of art or confront the artwork in a more conscious, conceptual way" (Sontag 13). Lavín's Sor Juana does this by turning the
reader's attention, one last time, to the book of enigmas, which in turn re-
directs that attention back onto the nun herself. As she finishes her fourth
letter to María Luisa, hoping "que el libro llegue pronto a término para
que arribe a estas tierras y sea elocuente la gozosa complicidad de las mujeres para las que la palabra es extensión de nuestra persona, de nuestro
aprecio del mundo, de nuestra alianza con lo divino desde lo terreno"
(368), we are once again invited to examine this curious book of riddles, in
search of a possible resolution to the mystery of Sor Juana's final silence.
    While it is undeniably true that Sor Juana's *Enigmas ofrecidos a la Casa
del Placer* places her in a transatlantic context of countless women who
took up the pen to challenge male dominance and dismantle gender inequality (Vollendorf 101), the intertext becomes even more suggestive if we

think, along with Georgina Sabat de Rivers, that the nun "les sugería a las monjas que las respuestas a sus enigmas, pasatiempo y diversión, podían encontrarse en su propia obra ya publicada, la cual, por supuesto, las monjas conocían muy bien" (*En busca* 222). In the presentation to her book of *Enigmas*, Sor Juana writes:

> Reverente a vuestras plantas,
> solicita, en su disfraz,
> no daros qué discurrir,
> sino sólo qué explicar.
> . . .
>
> Todo quanto incluye en sí
> por descrifrado lo da,
> porque no es yerro en la fe
> proponer, sino dudar.
> . . .
>
> Y si por naturaleza
> quanto oculta penetráis,
> tolo lo que es conocer
> ya no será adivinar. (73–76)

Not only does Sor Juana imply that the book has no secrets for the Portuguese nuns of the Casa del Placer, but also, and more importantly, she suggests that nothing needs to be deciphered; whatever these enigmas hide is already known and/or has been previously explored (Cruz, *Enigmas* 47). If the answer to these enigmas can be found in Sor Juana's own works, as Sabat de Rivers proposes, the twenty redondillas that she presents to her transatlantic interlocutors are not only a condensed and representative sample of her whole poetic project, but also an actual invitation to reread and revise everything that she has published. A task that should only require "instantes de atención" (for the Portuguese nuns already know her works) would turn into "siglos de vanidad" (73–74).

If, according to Sóror Francisca Xavier (one of the nuns who writes a "romance de arte mayor" for the *Enigmas*), Sor Juana successfully reduces "al breve mapa de este corto libro / el vasto imperio de tu metro acorde" (*Enigmas* 88); if the book is, as Sóror Mariana de Santo Antonio considers in another laudatory composition, so representative of Sor Juana's work, "que están quantos lo leen / viendo en sus hojas palpitar tu vena" (*Enigmas* 80); if each enigma reflects, as Doña Simoa de Castillo writes in her congratulatory endechas, how "el rayo de tu ingenio / quiso cegar lo mismo que alumbró" (*Enigmas* 91); then we must interpret that what Sor Juana wishes for the book in particular is also what she wants for her entire oeuvre (and literary persona) in general:

> Hazerse inmortal procura,
> que favor tan celestial
> se mide en la estimación
> a precios de eternidad. (74)

Lavín hints at this possibility as she portrays Sor Juana not defeated by her ecclesiastical authorities, but quite triumphant: "de que su astucia había rebasado el silencio al que la creían condenada y que *Los enigmas de la Casa del Placer* ya estaba listo para publicarse" (369).

The novel ends with a brief chapter in which the narrator outlines Sor Juana's death on April 17, 1695, "en que murió por una epidemia en el convento" (369), but the metaphorical funeral that we attend is quite different from that of a woman who leaves this world with the saintly radiance that her first biographer imagined for her, "despidiéndose de su esposo a más ver y presto" (26). The very last image of the intellectual who feigned satisfying the demands of "los lobos" with a series of rituals through which she was reformulated into an "ejemplo de la renuncia y el sacrificio" (369) is accompanied by her smile, as the nun remembers "el gozo primero de descifrar lo que los trazos en papel develaban a sus ojos" (370). This fictional portrayal certainly agrees with the life of the historical nun who ends her writing career with a set of enigmas that seek explanation, further research, literary analysis, and reading between times and lines—all in order to decipher the intellectual passion, the hunger for knowledge, and the female agency of the historical protagonist who signs her last fictional letter:

> Tuya por siempre,
> Juana Inés de la Cruz (368)

Notes

1. The novel was written by Héctor Zagal, but he published it under the pseudonym Mónica Zagal to demonstrate that men can also write feminist novels. For further information, see his interview on YouTube.

2. I will come back to this letter in the second part of this analysis.

3. See Alatorre's *Sor Juana a través de los siglos (1668–1910)*.

4. For a closer look at Sor Juana's "final conversion" and current debates regarding her last years, see Alejandro Soriano Vallès, *La hora más bella de Sor Juana* (2008), and Geoff Guevara-Geer, "The Final Silence of Sor Juana" (2007).

5. In "Exploraciones del conocimiento místico," I analyze these and other passages that raise Sor Juana's (in)direct involvement with various rhetorical constructions of mysticism (77–79).

6. In order to further study Sor Juana's close (literary) connections with important noblewomen of her time, see Georgina Sabat de Rivers's "Mujeres nobles del entorno de Sor Juana."

7. I speak of these letters' "coded language" following Janet Gurkin Altman's postulates: "The creator of fictional letter narrative must produce an impression of authenticity without hopelessly losing his outside reader. To do so he not only establishes a code that is particular to the *I-you* messages but also ultimately makes this code accessible to others, . . . Epistolary discourse is thus a coded—although not necessarily an obscure—language, whose code is determined by the specific relationship of the *I-you*" (120).

8. In his book *Forbidden Knowledge*, Roger Shattuck provides several categories for the study of inaccessible or unattainable knowledge, one that can be fragile, ambiguous, or even dangerous and destructive, as it causes uncertainty and implies a potential limit on human curiosity (165–66).

9. I use the term "feminine epistolary narrative" following Ana L. Baquero Escudero's explanation: "Por narrativa epistolar femenina entiendo, en definitiva, esos relatos construidos sobre el artificio epistolar y protagonizados por personajes femeninos" (20).

10. According to Sontag, "'Silence' never ceases to imply its opposite and to depend on its presence: just as there can't be 'up' without 'down' or 'left' without 'right,' so one must acknowledge a surrounding environment of sound or language in order to recognize silence" (11).

Works Cited

Alatorre, Antonio. *Sor Juana a través de los siglos (1668–1910)*. 2 vols. México, D.F.: El Colegio de México/El Colegio Nacional/Universidad Nacional Autónoma de México (UNAM), 2007.

Alatorre, Antonio, and Martha Lilia Tenorio. *Serafina y Sor Juana (con tres apéndices)*. México, D.F.: El Colegio de México, 1998.

Altman, Janet Gurkin. *Epistolarity: Approaches to a Form*. Columbus: Ohio State University Press, 1982.

Arenal, Electa, and Amanda Powell. Introduction. *The Answer / La Respuesta. Including Sor Filotea's Letter and New Selected Poems*. Ed. and trans. Electa Arenal and Amanda Powell. New York: The Feminist Press at the City University of New York, 2009. 1–37.

Baquero Escudero, Ana L. *La voz femenina en la narrativa epistolar*. Cádiz: Universidad de Cádiz, 2003.

Barthes, Roland. *S/Z*. Trans. Richard Miller. New York: Hill and Wang, 1974.

Bergmann, Emilie L., and Stacey Schlau, eds. *Approaches to Teaching the Works of Sor Juana Inés de la Cruz*. New York: Modern Languages Association, 2007.

Buxó, José Pascual. "Las lágrimas de Sor Juana: Nuevos textos de una polémica inconclusa." *Revista de Estudios Hispánicos* 44 (2010): 363–97.

Calleja, Diego. *Vida de Sor Juana*. Ed. Ermilo Abreu Gómez. Toluca: Instituto Mexiquense de Cultura, 1996.

Cruz, Sor Juana Inés de la. *The Answer/La Respuesta: Including Sor Filotea's Letter and New Selected Poems*. Ed. and trans. Electa Arenal and Amanda Powell. New York: The Feminist Press at the City University of New York, 2009.

———. *Enigmas ofrecidos a la Casa del Placer*. Ed. Antonio Alatorre. México, D.F.: El Colegio de México, 1995.

———. *Obras completas*. Vols. 1–3. Ed. Alfonso Méndez Plancarte. México, D.F.: Fondo de Cultura Económica (FCE), 1995.

———. *Obras completas*. Vol. 4. Ed. Alberto G. Salceda. México, D.F.: Fondo de Cultura Económica (FCE), 1995.

———. *Poesía, teatro, pensamiento*. Ed. Georgina Sabat de Rivers and Elias Rivers. Madrid: Espasa Calpe, 2004.

Estrada, Oswaldo. "Exploraciones del conocimiento místico en tres romances de Sor Juana Inés de la Cruz." *Calíope: Journal of the Society for Renaissance and Baroque Hispanic Poetry* 14.2 (2008): 69–86.

Franco, Jean. *Las conspiradoras: La representación de la mujer en México*. Trans. Mercedes Córdoba. México, D.F.: El Colegio de México/FCE, 2004.

Gilroy, Amanda, and W. M. Verhoeven. *Epistolary Histories: Letters, Fiction, Culture*. Charlottesville: University Press of Virginia, 2000.

Glantz, Margo. *Sor Juana: La comparación y la hipérbole*. México, D.F.: Consejo Nacional para la Cultura y las Artes (Conaculta), 2000.

Goldsmith, Elizabeth C., ed. *Writing the Female Voice: Essays on Epistolary Literature*. Boston: Northeastern University Press, 1989.

Guevara-Geer, Geoff. "The Final Silence of Sor Juana: The Abysmal Remove of Her Closing Night." *Approaches to Teaching the Works of Sor Juana Inés de la* Cruz. Ed. Emilie L. Bergmann and Stacey Schlau. New York: Modern Languages Association, 2007. 201–8.

Guillén, Claudia. "Sor Juana en el centro de las miradas." *Revista de la Universidad de México* 64 (2009): 97–98.

Kirk, Stephanie. *Convent Life in Colonial Mexico: A Tale of Two Communities*. Gainsville: University of Florida Press, 2007.

———. "Genealogical Searches: Sor Juana Studies Today." *Revista de Estudios Hispánicos* 44 (2010): 357–62.

Lavín, Mónica. *Yo, la peor*. México, D.F.: Grijalbo, 2009.

Lavrin, Asunción. *Brides of Christ: Conventual Life in Colonial Mexico*. Stanford, CA: Stanford University Press, 2008.

———. "La celda y el siglo: Epístolas conventuales." *Mujer y cultura en la colonia hispanoamericana*. Ed. Mabel Moraña. Pittsburgh, PA: Instituto Internacional de Literatura Iberoamericana, 1996. 139–59.

———. "*Lo femenino*: Women in Colonial Historical Sources." *Coded Encounters: Writing, Gender, and Ethnicity in Colonial Latin America*. Ed. Francisco Javier

Cevallos-Candau, Jeffrey A. Cole, Nina M. Scott, and Nicomedes Suárez-Araúz. Amherst: University of Massachusetts Press, 1994. 153–76.

———. "Unlike Sor Juana?: The Model Nun in the Religious Literature of Colonial Mexico." *The University of Dayton Review* 16.2 (1983): 75–92.

Lorenzano, Sandra. "*Hay que inventarnos*: Mujer y narrativa en el siglo XX." *Miradas feministas sobre las mexicanas del siglo XX*. Ed. Marta Lamas. México, D.F.: FCE; Conaculta, 2007. 349–85.

Luciani, Frederick. *Literary Self-Fashioning in Sor Juana Inés de la Cruz*. Lewisburg, PA: Bucknell University Press, 2004.

Ludmer, Josefina. "Tricks of the Weak." Trans. Stephanie Merrim. *Feminist Perspectives on Sor Juana Inés de la Cruz*. Ed. Stephanie Merrim. Detroit: Wayne State University Press, 1999. 86–93.

Madrid Moctezuma, Paola. "Sor Juana Inés de la Cruz y el barroco novohispano a través de los modelos narrativos de la ficción histórica y del *boom* hispánico femenino." *América sin nombre* 15 (2010): 93–106.

Martínez-San Miguel, Yolanda. *Saberes americanos: Subalternidad y epistemología en los escritos de Sor Juana*. Pittsburgh, PA: Instituto Internacional de Literatura Iberoamericana, 1999.

Moraña, Mabel. *Viaje al silencio: Exploraciones del discurso barroco*. México, D.F.: UNAM, 1998.

Myers, Kathleen Ann. *Neither Saints nor Sinners: Writing the Lives of Women in Spanish America*. New York: Oxford University Press, 2003.

Ochoa, John. "Sor Juana, Food, and the Life of the Mind." *Approaches to Teaching the Works of Sor Juana Inés de la* Cruz. Ed. Emilie L. Bergmann and Stacey Schlau. New York: Modern Languages Association, 2007. 229–37.

Paz, Octavio. *Sor Juana Inés de la Cruz o las trampas de la fe*. México, D.F.: FCE, 1998.

Perelmuter, Rosa. *Los límites de la femineidad en Sor Juana Inés de la Cruz*. Madrid: Iberoamericana/Vervuert, 2004.

Poot Herrera, Sara. *Los guardaditos de Sor Juana*. México, D.F.: UNAM, 1999.

Porzecanski, Teresa. "El silencio, la palabra y la construcción de lo femenino." *El salto de Minerva. Intelectuales, género y Estado en América Latina*. Ed. Mabel Moraña and María Rosa Olivera-Williams. Madrid: Iberoamericana/Vervuert, 2005. 47–57.

Rodríguez Garrido, José Antonio. *La Carta Atenagórica de Sor Juana. Textos inéditos de una polémica*. México, D.F.: UNAM, 2004.

Sabat de Rivers, Georgina. "Contemporáneos de Sor Juana: Las monjas portuguesas y los *Enigmas* (con soluciones)." *Sor Juana Inés de la Cruz y sus contemporáneos*. Ed. Margo Glantz. México D.F.: Condumex, 1998. 215–44.

———. *En busca de Sor Juana*. México, D.F.: UNAM, 1998.

———. "Mujeres nobles del entorno de Sor Juana." *"Y diversa de mí misma / entre vuestras plumas ando": Homenaje internacional a Sor Juana Inés de la Cruz*. Ed. Sara Poot Herrera. México, D.F.: El Colegio de México, 1993. 1–19.

Said, Edward W. *Representations of the Intellectual*. New York: Vintage, 1996.

Schaefer, Claudia. *Textured Lives: Women, Art, and Representation in Modern Mexico*. Tucson: University of Arizona Press, 1992.

Shattuck, Roger. *Forbidden Knowledge: From Prometheus to Pornography*. New York: St. Martin's, 1996.

Sontag, Susan. "The Aesthetics of Silence." *Styles of Radical Will*. New York: Vintage, 2001. 3–34.

Soriano Vallès, Alejandro. *La hora más bella de Sor Juana*. México, D.F.: Conaculta, 2008.

Trabulse, Elías. *El enigma de Serafina de Cristo: Acerca de un manuscrito inédito de Sor Juana Inés de la Cruz*. 1691. Toluca: Instituto Mexiquense de Cultura, 1995.

———. *La memoria transfigurada: Tres imágenes históricas de Sor Juana*. México, D.F.: Universidad del Claustro de Sor Juana, 1996.

Van Houdt, Toon, and Jan Papy. Introduction. *Self-Presentation and Social Identification: The Rhetoric and Pragmatics of Letter Writing in Early Modern Times*. Ed. Toon Van Houdt, Jan Papy, Gilbert Tournoy, and Constant Matheeussen. Leuven, Belgium: Leuven University Press, 2002. 1–13.

Vollendorf, Lisa. "Across the Atlantic: Sor Juana, *La respuesta*, and the Hispanic Women's Canon." *Approaches to Teaching the Works of Sor Juana Inés de la* Cruz. Ed. Emilie L. Bergmann and Stacey Schlau. New York: Modern Languages Association, 2007. 95–102.

Xirau, Ramón. *Genio y figura de Sor Juana Inés de la Cruz*. México, D.F.: El Colegio Nacional/UNAM, 1997.

Zagal, Héctor. "La venganza de sor Juana." YouTube, November 3, 2009. http://www.youtube.com/watch?v=VUT7o2UzhCE. Accessed January 6, 2013.

CHAPTER FIVE

Queering the Auto Sacramental

Anti-Heteronormative Parody and the Specter of Silence in Luis Felipe Fabre's La sodomía en la Nueva España

Tamara R. Williams

We imagine the lives under the mortar,
but how do we recognize the end
of a bottomless silence?
— MICHEL-ROLPH TROUILLOT

"A hole," writes Mexican poet Luis Felipe Fabre (1974), "is a space that occupies a place in matter. In truth, it is to get to the heart of the matter." A hole, he continues, is a gap, a hollow, an absence; to read holes is to understand that the gaps and hollows that wound a text are also writing: "They are the braille of the disappeared" (*Agujeros* 11–12).

In this chapter, I examine the literary return of an absence—a hole—in seventeenth-century colonial historical texts dealing with the prosecution and death by burning of fourteen men and a boy—all alleged sodomites—in *La sodomía de la Nueva España* (2010) by Luis Felipe Fabre. A distinctive feature of *La sodomía* is Fabre's reconfiguration and deployment of fragments of texts—from chronicles, legal proceedings, letters, diaries, and histories of homosexuality in colonial Mexico—into a poignant, refreshingly irreverent book-length poem that contains three interrelated parts. The poem's main part and the focus of this chapter is the "Retablo de sodomitas novohispanos," which is rendered explicitly as an *auto sacramental,* a one-act morality play written in verse and generally associated with the Feast of Corpus Christi, a Holy Day of Obligation in the Roman

Catholic liturgical calendar that celebrates the Eucharist, that is, the sacrifice and redemption of the body and blood of Christ. The "Retablo," in turn, is followed by two appendices: "Villancicos del Santo Niño de las Quemaduras" and the "Monumento fúnebre a Gerónimo Calbo," which together remind readers of, and engage them with, the Spanish celebratory music and rituals related to Christmas and the Triduum, respectively. Viewed as a whole, therefore, the three-part *La sodomía* evokes the key events in the Catholic liturgical calendar—the death, the burial, and the resurrection of Christ. The difference, of course, is that Fabre's poetic employment of the archival materials related to the group execution of alleged sodomites features the sacrifice and redemption of the gay transvestite, Cotita, as a thinly veiled Jesus character. It can be read, therefore, as a gay version of "the greatest story ever told."[1]

With the text thus understood, I explore *La sodomía* as an allegorical parody. Grounded in Judith Butler's understanding of parody as a troubling return, as a strategy of subversive repetition that exposes "the foundational categories of sex, gender and desire as a specific formation of power" (*Gender* xix), I argue that Fabre's poetic reworking of the archival material related to the group execution engages his readers in a complex transgressive exploration of an anti-heteronormative morality that subverts and makes evident what Butler refers to as "the reiterative power" of seventeenth-century Spanish imperial discourses—of its systems and practices—to produce and regulate compulsory heterosexuality and naturalize a phallogocentric knowledge of gender (185). This same redeployment, moreover, operates metaleptically. That is, by saying without saying, the poet lays bare the degree to which Spanish imperial discourses silenced, concealed, and misrepresented the homosexual and/or transvestite subject as a "sex" that is not one; "a sex that cannot be thought, a linguistic absence, an opacity" (Butler, *Gender* 14). Ultimately, the poet resignifies them as systemically injurious (indeed, deadly), thereby opening a discursive space (Fabre might say "widening the hole") wherein the abject bodies of the fourteen burned and disappeared sodomites and of the scourged boy are able to return and make their claim.

Following a brief introduction to the documented facts related to the group execution of the fourteen gay men and the punishment of the young boy, this chapter will examine three layers of interrelated and mutually supporting subversive repetitions operating in Fabre's text. The starting point will be the redeployment of a literary genre, the auto sacramental, as a key structural platform for the activation of the poem's parodic interplay. I continue with a description of the way in which the poem redeploys colonial history, both in terms of the poem's narrative or story and in terms of the poem's discursive quality, mainly its extensive use of quotations of historical text. I conclude by looking beyond the density of the parody to what remains, which is an absence, that is, a violent voiding of homosexual identity that was the explicit goal of the parodied discourse. Out of and through this absence, finally, I dwell briefly on how Fabre's text evolves a poetics of silence, a kind of threshold reading/writing in which a third eye traces the fissures—the wounds—in the homosexual *corpus*, understood here in Butler's sense as the "materiality" of the homosexual body as constituted by the law, that is, the heterosexual imperative that regulates and signifies the intelligibility of gender and sex (Butler, *Bodies* 2–3).

"Abramos un agujero: abramos una ausencia en memoria de los sodomitas ajusticiados"

On November 6, 1658, at eleven o'clock in the morning, fourteen men and a young boy were removed from His Majesty's Prison of the High Court of the Viceroyalty of New Spain in Mexico City. They were led along the Calle del Reloj and paraded in front of the home of the Marquise of Villamayor. They were then taken to the wall of San Lázaro, six blocks east of the Zócalo, but not before being subject to physical examination by two surgeons of "great and indisputable repute, who found the bodies quite used and corrupted" (Garza Carvajal 167). Once at San Lázaro, they first administered garrote to Juan de la Vega, a mulatto who called himself "Cotita de la Encarnación" (167). Then they roasted him alive. He was followed by Juan de Correa, a mestizo recognized as more than seventy years of age and known as "la Estanpa" [*sic*], the name of "a very graceful lady who had lived in the city" (Garza Carvajal 101). Because of the young boy's age, he was sentenced to two hundred lashings and six years of hard labor instead of to death. Magistrates and neighborhood commissioners attended the men's executions, and the entire city and surrounding villages emptied out as crowds thronged to San Lázaro to see the "spectacle of justice" for those found guilty of *pecado nefando*—the abominable crime against nature of the sin of sodomy. It took until eight o'clock to finish with the fourteen men and punish the boy because each punished subject had to hear his sentence and make declarations. The fire after their punishments, though, burned through that night.

Documented in the *Archivo General de Indias* and in Gregorio Martín de Guijo's *Diario: 1648–1664*, among other sources, this public execution by burning for the "crime and sin of sodomy" was not unusual. Henry Kamen notes that in Spain, since the Middle Ages, sodomy—referred to in standard definitions of the time as "the unspeakable" or "abominable" crime—"was treated as the ultimate crime against morality" and that "the punishment was burning alive for all those over twenty-five years of age" (268). In New Spain from the Conquest onward, public executions persisted. In the seventeenth century, however, persecution and repression of alleged sodomites, especially of mulattos or mestizos deemed unmanly and "effeminate," intensified. As historian Federico Garza Carvajal has noted, the same year that Cotita de la Encarnación, la Estanpa, and twelve other men were burned at the stake, the High Court of the Viceroyalty of New Spain "accused and ordered the apprehension of another one hundred and three men in an unprecedented, brutally repressive program and active pursuit of sodomites in the early modern Metropole of México" (167). Indeed, the historian continues, claiming that he had uncovered a network of homosexual activity that had persisted in the city for several generations, the newly appointed viceroy of New Spain, the duke of Alburquerque, wrote to King Charles II that "never in the history of mankind had he heard of such complicity" (Garza Carvajal 166); the viceroy would proceed to send three additional letters describing in obsessive detail the incidents pertaining to the equally unprecedented 1657–1658 sodomy cases. Concluding his investigation and prosecution of the cases, Juan Manuel de Sotomayor, magistrate of His Majesty's High Court, intensified the scurrilous attacks, asserting that sodomy had become "an endemic cancer" that had "extensively contaminated the provinces of New Spain" (Garza Carvajal 206).

Finally, as Garza Carvajal makes evident, the prosecution of sodomites, theological and moral treatises to justify such prosecutions, and extensive juridical and historical documentation of such cases, were anything but marginal: "Descriptions of *sodomie* and sodomites," affirms the historian, "were firmly anchored within the realm of early modern Spanish Imperial politics" (3). Spain's principal ideological concern beginning in the sixteenth century, the historian continues, citing Pagden, was to be the self-appointed guardian of universal Christendom, and to act in accordance with Christian ethicopolitical principles enacted by theologians and jurists (25). To carry out this task required the construction of the idyllic man, or Vir, a man of courage and Christian virtue; "a symbol of honor, strength, the seducer and owner of his wife"; a "loyal vassal possessed by virile bravado that predisposed him to enlist and fight in wars for his prince" (76). Deployed in New Spain, and reconstituted in the dramatic increase of juridical and theological discourses related to empire building and the Inquisition, the identity and subject position of the Spanish Vir would be fortified by actively constituting, repressing, and burning the sodomite as an Other, racialized as mulatto or mestizo, physically and intellectually inferior, perverted, vile, lazy, lascivious, and, most notably, effeminate (28).

Absent from the theological and moral treatises from the Spanish colonial period is any trace of the repression and violence, of the sexual practices, gender relations, and desires of those whose bodies burned that November. "Silence," asserts anthropologist Serge Gruzinski, persists in its concealment of the existence and experiences of those whose gender affinity called into question the prevailing heteronormative gender norms in Imperial New Spain. "While many," he argues, "have raised their voices to denounce—with all good reason—the plight of the indigenous, of black slaves, of Jews, and more recently of women, few have questioned or question the fate of those men who desired and loved those of their own sex. These were the only ones that paid with their lives what was a manifestation of their being" (225).

"Hagamos un altar donde todas las imágenes estén de cabeza"

Fabre's choice to break this silence through a poetic version of the auto sacramental, a dramatic genre associated with imperial Spain, is not surprising. A poet, gay activist, and performance artist, this young Mexican writer is gaining increasing notoriety for his extraordinary capacity for the assimilation and poetic and parodic transformation of a wide range of literary and nonliterary genres from an array of traditions and periods both canonical and noncanonical. These include, but are not limited to, history, archaeology, journalism, mass media, cinema, theater, performance, and the visual arts generated in the lettered city and in popular culture, subcultures, and countercultures. Indeed, Fabre's poetic reworkings rely extensively on the careful selection and juxtaposition of quotations or paraphrased fragments from pre-existing texts. His poems, therefore, are largely parodic, more often than not irreverent; their tonal register is ironic, frequently unsettling. These aspects combined with his carefully researched knowledge of the source texts as objects of literary play, his formal rigor, his technical virtuosity and lyrical poignancy, have quickly established his oeuvre among the most distinctive, relevant, thoughtfully entertaining, and disquieting poetry being written in Mexico today.

La sodomía is no exception. As the title makes clear, in the first and main part of the three-part poem, "Retablo de sodomitas novohispanos (auto sacramental)" alternatively called "La nueva sodoma: El poema de los agujeros," the poet explicitly evokes the "horizon of expectations" for the auto sacramental, thus inviting the reader to take into account the nature and purpose of the auto qua auto. A brief review of the genre's defining characteristics—of its purpose and history—makes evident that Fabre's explicit redeployment of the auto sacramental is not gratuitous but strategic. Indeed, while on the one hand, it might strike the reader as a logical choice to revive the auto as a model for representing historical events related to the trial and execution of sodomites in mid-seventeenth-century Spain, it is also the case that the repetition of the genre nudges the reader to consider the auto's complicity with, and privileged status in, imperial Spain's field of cultural production. Indeed, the auto played a significant role in representing, sustaining, and perpetuating the repressive discourses and prosecutorial practices of Spain's Inquisition, and ultimately, of her broader imperialist and colonialist politics, which sought to erect Spain as a "Universal World Monarchy and Champion of Christendom" (Garza Carvajal 4) through the marginalization and elimination of those whose race, class, religion, gender, and/or sexuality were perceived as Other to the perfect Spanish man, or Vir—in fact, the masculine embodiment of all that the empire aspired to stand for.

A type of allegorical drama traditionally performed for the Feast of Corpus Christi, a solemn Latin rite that celebrates the Eucharist, the auto sacramental was performed as a reminder of the sacrifice and redemption of the "Most Holy Body and Blood of Christ." While it originated in medieval Spain, it reached its peak in the late seventeenth century in the works of Calderón de la Barca, one of the genre's indisputable masters. Rendered in one act and in verse, it was typically staged as part of liturgical celebrations and performed in the streets on floats carrying decorative scenery, and it was presented under the auspices of civic and Church authorities. Its primary purpose was didactic, as it sought to exalt the true Catholic faith—and the Church as the guardian of that faith—and to combat her enemies, mainly those from other faith traditions (Islam, Judaism, and later Protestantism), as well as from a range of sins and heresies (Parker 62), including, of course, sodomy.

The autos were Church and state sanctioned; these subsidized street spectacles encouraged proliferation and innovation of the genre. "The Church's own ambivalence towards performances in places of worship," notes critic Malveena McKendrick, "may well have encouraged the growth of pageant drama in the streets and marketplaces. The Corpus drama from its earliest days, therefore, played a much more prominent and spectacular role in public life than the church-bound Christmas and Easter plays" (239). To the extent that the writing, production, and performance of the auto was propelled by civic and Church authorities, the genre held a privileged position in the field of Spanish cultural production in imperial Spain. This privilege, no doubt, undergirded the extraordinary success of the genre's most notable Golden Age authors, including Lope de Vega, who wrote four hundred autos, and the aforementioned Calderón de la Barca, who authored approximately seventy.

The staggering number of autos produced in the lifetime of each of these outstanding Spanish playwrights underscores the prominence and popularity of the genre as both a didactic platform and a performative showcase for the dissemination and reiteration of core values and beliefs, as well as for the exclusionary and repressive discourses and practices of Church and civic authorities. Inevitably, censorship and civic and Church control over messaging accompanied the proliferation of auto production, as did the proliferation of ancillary texts by playwrights such as Lope and Calderón regarding the definition, form, appropriate content, and guidelines for performance of an auto.

Two notable scholars of the auto tradition, A. A. Parker and Bruce Wardropper, agree that among the divergent and contradictory definitions of the auto sacramental, especially those having to do with the nature and degree of the auto's unique focus on Eucharistic doctrine and Catholic dogma, the most reliable guide is Calderón de la Barca, whose clarification regarding the distinction between the auto's required *asunto* and the *argumento* provided a flexible framework, or formula, for controlling the message and form of the seventeenth-century auto. For Calderón, all autos are "similar in their *asunto*, dissimilar in their *argumentos*. The *asunto* of every *acto* is therefore the Eucharist, but the *argumento* can vary from one to another: it can be any 'historia divina'—historical, legendary, or fictitious—provided that it throws light on some aspect of the *asunto*" (60). The Eucharist, Parker continues, was the one Catholic dogma that could offer the widest scope to the theological dramatist. The central themes of sacrifice and redemption constituted the theme, or asunto, of the auto, but its treatment, or argumento, could vary extensively from one to another according to the nature of the allegories employed to achieve the genre's didactic purpose (Parker 36). Parker goes on to say: "The *auto* can therefore treat Christianity apologetically and historically. [It] can deal with the acceptance and rejection of Faith, with the Church as the guardian of that

Faith, with her foundation, with her struggles against her enemies, with the different world religions, and with heresies" (62).

As this quotation and the brief history of the genre make evident, the auto—its function, form, and content—was complicit with Spain's imperial discourses in repressing, distorting, and voiding or negating, ultimately, homosexual identities. This darker side of the genre's literary history is not lost on Fabre and should not be overlooked, as it becomes the backdrop or platform for the transgressive redeployment—the perversion—of the traditional auto, which is *La sodomía*. Placed within and against the auto's history, *La sodomía* gains density and relevance, as it not only brings into existence the silenced view of the genre's history with power—it also exposes the limits of Spanish imperial discourse and its literary appendages disguised as the "true (and total) interpretation of events" (Mignolo 33).

"Sale el Fuego
y ardiente besa a Juan de la Vega en los labios: aplausos"

Like the traditional auto, Fabre's *La sodomía* is structured as a one-act allegorical drama rendered in verse that is didactic in form and function while still retaining the popular carnivalesque "regocijo" of the public spectacle. In keeping with Calderón de la Barca's aforementioned guidelines, *La sodomía*'s central theme, or asunto, is sacrifice and redemption broadly understood. Its difference resides in what can best be described as the queering of the argumento, which traces, in poignant allegorical form, the history of the life, trial, and death at the stake of the gay transvestite Juan de la Vega (alias Cotita de la Encarnación) as a propitiatory victim whose sacrifice and redemption ultimately celebrate the sacramental nature of human sexuality, including—indeed, privileging—queer sex (Goss 158).

A remarkable feature of *La sodomía* is the degree to which Fabre relies explicitly on fragments of historical texts—histories, diaries, letters, confessions, edicts, testimonies—related to the group execution to give flesh to the play's argumento. In a gesture that is as much an acknowledgment of sources and invitation to further reading as it is a reminder to his readers that the narrated events in the poem are historically documented and true, Fabre also makes clear, in the notes at the end of the book, that his ultimate objective in writing *La sodomía* was to bring to light the verbal material—the historical corpus—related to the "la encarnizada persecución de homosexuales registrados en España durante 1657–1658" (81). So, through a process of careful selection, rearrangement, repetition, and variation of historical fragments, Fabre breathes life into the gnawed and moth-eaten annals of forgotten history, giving shape to a story that, through a combination of poetry, allegory, and dramatic structure, rewrites the death of Cotita de la Encarnación as, on the one hand, a denunciation of the sexual ideology that created the condition of possibility for the continued persecution and violence aimed at sexual minorities. On the other hand, it remembers the life and death of Cotita as a calling for the rights of love and lust for all.

The dramatic tension in Fabre's auto hinges on Juan de la Vega's unapologetic defiance of heteronormative gender roles. Relying extensively on trial proceedings, *La sodomía* dramatizes the accusation of Vega of the crime of sodomy, understood here in the strictest legal sense as the act of anal intercourse, "the crime against nature" known also as *"pecado nefando,"* the sin that cannot be named or spoken. As the drama unfolds, however, it becomes unclear whether the crime of sodomy was ever actually committed. Indeed, Juana de Herrera, documented as the lead witness for the prosecution and a character in the play, reports having seen two men, both naked, one mounted on top of the other: "Estaban / el uno encima del otro quitados los calzones ambos" (16). When pressed, however, de Herrera reveals that the person she presumed to be the second man was cloaked and not visible to the eye:

Dice
Juana de Herrera: Juan de la Vega
Tapaba al de abajo con la capa que traía puesta. (16–17)

Beyond underscoring the arbitrariness of the regulatory rules that govern sex, gender, and desire in colonial New Spain, what the cloaking—the concealment or disguise—of the alleged crime reveals is that it is Juan de la Vega's unintelligibility as neither man nor woman; his overt cultivation of minority sexual practices; and, most significantly, his leadership in, and claim over, an alternative economy based on a communal homosocial solidarity, which, more than the crime of sodomy in and of itself, disorganize, and hence, deeply threaten, Inquisitorial authorities.

It is through the character, voice, and text of a seventeenth-century presbyter and secretary of the cathedral of Mexico City, Martín de Guijo, that we learn of Juan de la Vega's coincidental and ironic preference for a woman's name, Cotita de la Encarnación. His self-naming represents a key site for the queering of Fabre's auto sacramental. Cotita rhymes with "jotita"—in Mexico, a feminized diminutive version of "joto," a colloquial term for a homosexual male.[2] Combined with the tag "de la Encarnación"—"the Embodiment/Embodied One"—Cotita's renaming rewrites and decenters the standard theological teachings related to the Eucharist and Incarnation in numerous ways. The iconoclastic reclaiming involved in the renaming embodies and sanctifies the transvestite body of Cotita while celebrating the homosexual erotic, as both *encarnar* and *encarnación* are words that circulate in the gay community to refer to the actions, effects, and pleasures of homoerotic desire. By extension, and as in the Jesus story, Cotita also incarnates the pain of his persecuted community, bears his community's suffering, and ultimately dies for its "sins."

Among these "sins" is Cotita's being a transvestite mulatto—dressing like a woman. He ties his hair in a ribbon, wears a white doublet like the one used by women, and through openings in his sleeves dons colorful bracelets and charms. He is, finally, singled out by Inquisitorial authorities for gathering around his hearth other men and boys and for providing them with friendship, sustenance, protection, and visibility in homoerotic solidarity. Citing from the record of the historical proceedings, the Indian character, second witness to the prosecution, Tomás de Santiago, makes his own statement:

Dice
Tomás de Santiago:
De ordinario a Juan de la Vega le visitaban
unos mozuelos a quienes llamaba mi alma, mi vida,
mi corazón, y Juan de la Vega se ofendía si no le llamaban
Cotita.

Dice:
Juan de la Vega se sentaba
en el suelo en un estado como mujer
y hacía tortillas y lavaba y guisaba y los mozuelos
se sentaban con él y dormían en un aposento. (24)

Among those who frequented Cotita's circle are the thirteen men and the young boy, who, as a group, recall Christ's disciples. In *La sodomía*, however, the disciples are revisited as a circle of men drawn together by a homosocial bond. Men gather to sing and dance with each other; some of them dressed like women, calling to each other using women's names. Borrowing from historical documents, Fabre's text reads: "Dice el Alcalde: Los acusados / confesaron que se convidaban en sus casas / y se regalaban chocolate y decían requiebros y bailaban" (27). Historically, the existence of this community suggested the presence of a broader homosocial subculture, a subculture that, as Gruzinski has described, enjoyed its own geography, information and communication network, language and codes. More importantly, and from the standpoint of Inquisitorial authorities, these homosexual communities forged an alternative economy that dispensed with institutional networks and ties, mainly the traditional nuclear family and the Church, and deeply threatened the status quo of colonial sexual and economic ideology.

La sodomía explores these communities, their alternative economy, and the threat they presented to the Inquisitorial authorities. They are made evident by Santa Doctrina's accusation, in scene 12, that the gatherings of Juan de la Vega and his friends were motivated by profit, by the circulation and exchange of money possibly—but not necessarily—for gay sex. She further claims that these took place during religious celebrations. The power and threat of this alternative economy is represented in Santa Doctrina's envisioning of a third side of a coin stamped with the image of Juan de la Vega:

> Dice la Santa Doctrina: Si las monedas tuvieran
> además de anverso y reverso,
> inverso,
>
> en esa cara veríamos acuñada la cara
> de Juan de la Vega: la descarada
> reina de los invertidos. (26)

Fabre's subsequent and mischievous repetition and variation of the noun "moneda," and the verbs "troquelar" and "acuñar," engage the reader in a series of semantic twistings that blend the sexual and the economic. Through artful verbal play, the lines between Santa Doctrina's anxious obsession with Juan de la Vega's capacity for producing and exchanging value, and Carne and Naturaleza's relentless sexual innuendo, are blurred, for both "troquelar" and "acuñar"—while related to the mint and coining—also recall the phallic-shaped minting die and its related actions of penetration and perforation:

> Monedas, dice la Naturaleza
> Monedas, dice la Carne
> Monedas, dice la Santa Doctrina.
>
> Dice
> la Santa Doctrina
> Juan de la Vega y sus bujarrones troquelaban.

Dice: En las festividades de Nuestra Señora
y en las festividades de los santos
y en ocasión de celebrarlos:
¡troquelaban! (26)

In sum, and as these lines from scene 12 make evident, Fabre's *La sodomía* casts Cotita de la Encarnación as a victim of Inquisitorial authorities, whose steadfast refusal to conform to the strict gender binaries imposed by Spanish imperial ideology costs him his life. Cotita's crime, therefore, was not the act of sodomy per se, but rather his disavowal of the masculine signifying economy (Butler, *Gender* 17)—in particular, the Spanish imperial ideal of the Vir, and by extension the role of the Vir in the traditional nuclear family, which in turn was a structure that emerged from, and was complicit with, the narrow, profit-oriented interests of the burgeoning colonial economy.

Cotita's only crime, then, was that even as a young boy, he had projected himself into the "disparaged female sphere" (Butler, *Gender* 24). To paraphrase Judith Butler, Cotita represented "a specter of discontinuity and incoherence" in relation to the existing sexual ideology that sought to establish, maintain, and enforce "causal and expressive lines of connection between 'feminine' and 'masculine,' where these are understood as expressive attributes of 'male' and 'female'" (Butler, *Gender* 24). In this cultural matrix, through which gender identity became intelligible, men like Cotita, "whose gender did not 'follow' from either sex or gender" could not exist. Indeed, when men like Cotita made themselves known as extant, they provoked a "convergence and disorganization of the rules that govern sex, gender and desire" (Butler, *Gender* 24) to which Spanish imperial law invariably responded with punishment and, in Cotita's case, annihilation.

It is, therefore, no coincidence that Fabre structures *La sodomía* as an allegorical trial—a dramatic structure, it should be noted, not unusual in a traditional auto, as it is lends itself well to its didactic function. In Fabre, however, the trial is a mockery of the law and a parodic indictment of its annihilative power. The farcical trial combines historical characters (historian Gregorio Martín de Guijo, the Alcalde Montemayor, and informant Juana de Herrera, among others) and allegorical characters (such as La Santa Doctrina, El Escribano, La Carne, La Naturaleza, La Justicia, and La Fortuna) engaged in a sustained series of accusations and counteraccusations rendered largely as repetitions and variations of fragments culled from the trial records and proceedings. The result is the forging of a provocative and irreverent multivocalic discourse that progressively undermines the reiterative power of the same juridical discourse that it cites through a relentless deployment of double entendres and innuendos.

Dramatic intensity, humor, pathos, and chaos bordering on absurdity mount as Santa Doctrina's initial report of Juan de la Vega's crime gains traction. The drama culminates when the allegorical characters Justicia (Santa Doctrina's puppet) and the capricious Fortuna spin the wheel to cast the fate of Cotita and the thirteen men and young boy being punished along with Cotita. Amidst the mounting chaos and accusations, Cotita maintains his innocence until the very end, when he utters his only two lines in the entire play: "Llámame Cotita. . . . Nada, yo no he hecho nada de lo que se me acusa" (23). In scenes 17 and 18, finally—and drawing on the entry for November 6, 1658, in Martín de Guijo's *Diario*—Cotita is administered garrote, and his body, along with the bodies of thirteen other men, are tossed in the pyre.

At this point, Fabre's auto takes another subversive turn, as Cotita's punishment by fire is rewritten as an erotic encounter with the allegorical character Fuego, who "ardiente besa a Juan de la Vega en los labios" (36). In what might be described as Fabre's ultimate queering of the traditional auto's Eucharistic message, Fabre redeploys the Christian images of flame, fire, and light—all sacred symbols, within the Catholic tradition, for the living truth of Christ and eternal presence of God—as a the return of gay lust and passion. The allegorical gives way to the supernatural when a dark and chaotic orgy ensues, symbolizing the spectral return—dare I say, the resurrection—of the repressed homoerotic flame and its menacing claim to the rights of love and lust personified in these haunting images of phantoms and witches that emerge from burning embers:

> *Nada guardes para luego*
> *pues ya, entre requiebros tantos,*
> *morimos pariendo espantos:*
> *se desatan de nosotras,*
> *que en la pira ardemos, otras:*
> *brujas de humo y leves mantos.* (37)

In a manner consistent with the didactic function and tonal range of the auto, in scene 23 there is another abrupt shift in mood to that of carnivalesque "regocijo." In a gesture of false modesty, Escribano pleads with the audience that they overlook the play's "yerros, sus ripios, sus versos farragosos" (43), calls for the play to end and life to begin anew, and Escribano summons all to make music and sing hymns of celebration. And so *La sodomía* concludes with a final parodic gesture, the replacement of hymns of praise and exaltation with the witty, burlesque, and highly transgressive light verse of "La Tirana" sung by victims and executioners alike. Like the haunting scene of Cotita's orgiastic encounter with Fuego, "La Tirana" portends, albeit in a relatively more comic and profane register, the oneiric return of the repressed eros to haunt the albarrada de San Lázaro, the place of the group execution:

En San Lázaro han sembrado
de Gomorra las simientes:
caminante, no te sientes
que seguro brota un nabo. (44)

To end with "La Tirana" further complicates *La sodomía's* richly layered parody by activating an association with the mythohistorical figure from the Andean region, La Virgen del Carmen de la Tirana, known also as La Virgen de la Tirana, La Reina de Tamarugal—or by her indigenous name, Ñusta Huillac. La Tirana is described by one source as an indigenous woman, daughter of a high priest descended from the sovereign Inca princes of Tahuantinsuyo, whose father had been killed by the Spanish conquistador of Chile, Diego de Almagro. Consequently, she became notoriously fierce—the Chilean poet, Enrique Lihn, uses the word "virile" ("Un lenguaje violento")—as a member of the anticolonial indigenous resistance known to have special powers and feared by many. Eventually, however, she falls in love with a man whom her own community had taken prisoner, a Portuguese miner named Vasco de Almeida. Her resolute love for Almeida leads her to free him from prison. She marries him and converts to Christianity—both activities that ignite the ire of her former comrades, who ultimately kill her. After her death, she is beatified as La Virgen del Carmen de la Tirana, but she is most often referred to by the shorter, much more ironic, and highly unlikely name of La Virgen de la Tirana.

There are, therefore, relevant parallels between "La Reina de Tamarugal" and *La sodomía's* "La Tirana." Like Cotita, La Virgen de la Tirana is a "specter of discontinuity and incoherence" (Butler, *Gender* 24) whose blurring of gender, religious, and racial lines cost her her own life. Large popular street festivals, reminiscent of the auto's street performances, are held annually in July and affirm La Tirana's in-between-ness as they emerge from the synthesis of Catholic and indigenous beliefs and feature, as their central ritual, the colorful and elaborately costumed "Danza de la Tirana." The dance, too, reenacts the confrontation between, and ultimately the rebalancing of, good and evil, which in turn signals the beginning of a new era. La Virgen de la Tirana is revered for her steadfast and resolute love and passion, as well as for her martyrdom—and she is, of course, venerated among some as the patron saint of prisoners.

While it is possible that Fabre's source for *La sodomía*'s "La Tirana" was the Andean region's beloved Virgen de la Tirana and the carnivalesque street festivals that celebrate her annually, it is more likely that it is Chilean poet Diego Maquieira's poetic parody of La Reina, "La Tirana" (1983), that inspired Fabre's burlesque and irreverent closing. According to Chilean poet Enrique Lihn, Maquieira's "Tirana" is a renegade, a sexual tyrant alienated by the Inquisition who, at the peak of her life, had two vocations: sainthood and prostitution. In the spirit of Don Francisco de Quevedo at his most vicious, Lihn continues, Maquieira's poetry is ferocious, irreverent, and brilliantly executed (Lihn, "Un lenguaje violento"). Thus, Fabre's "La Tirana" would appear to be a parodic homage to a kindred poetic spirit. It is then, moreover, a parody twice removed—that is, a parody of Maquieira's parody—a parody that displaces and subverts any remaining traces of the sacred in both the auto sacramental and La Virgen de la Tirana, replacing them with a profane burlesque spectacle. Indeed, like the character Fuego, Fabre's redeployment of "La Tirana" represents an ironic, humorous, and witty return of the implacable specter of absence and negation whose geography extends beyond Mexico to include Chile and the entire former territories of Imperial Spain.

Following this reading of the auto's ending, some caution is in order because, tempting as it might be to interpret *La sodomía*'s subversive reenactment of scenes reminiscent of the scourged Christ's death and redemption as a liberationist feminist affirmation of transcendent Christian beliefs and values, to do so would be misguided. In *La sodomía*'s exploration of the correspondences between the figures of Jesus and the transvestite Cotita, Fabre's central concern is, at the very most, to revisit and expose—via Cotita's tragic story—the ambiguity, obscurity, negation, and inevitable silence surrounding alternative sexualities in the Jesus story. Thus exposed, the more accurate reading of *La sodomía* is as a performative affirmation—a requiem and celebration—not of any one truth, but rather of the absence (repression, negation, distortion, silence) of the homosexual subject in the theological and juridical discourses of seventeenth-century imperial Spain—which, it must be noted, persists to this day. Put another way, whatever density and relevance *La sodomía* gains when read as a text that brings into existence the silenced view of the auto's history with power, it gains even more in irreverence and provocation, dimension and implication, when it nudges the reader toward a rereading of the persistent silence regarding Jesus's ambiguous sexuality, the same Jesus in whose name Cotita de la Encarnación and countless others were burned at the stake.

"De cómo decir lo que no se puede decir"

That silencing and voiding of, and violence toward, homosexual identities is the central focus of Fabre's poem is made explicit in the text's *loa* or prelude, which is numbered 0 or zero. Naming the loa "0" is a graphic and symbolic representation of the abyss between the memory of, and the desire for, the homosexual erotic that *La sodomía* ultimately celebrates. The "0," therefore, is an absence, that is, the "sex" that is not one—but it also re-signifies the anal orifice, the site of the *pecado nefando* (the sin that shall not be named or spoken) as nothing less than a ground zero. Even while "0" represents an absence, however, it is also a hole that must be opened—penetrated—in order for the story of the life and death of Cotita, and by extension the violent repression of homosexuals in colonial Mexico, to be told. To underscore this point, it is the character Carne who issues the call to open/penetrate this absence/hole in memory of the condemned sodomites, in poignant and eschatological irreverence that is signature Fabre:

> Dice
> la Carne: En memoria
> de los catorce ajusticiados abramos
> el culo del mundo: la boca del infierno.
> Abramos un agujero, dice la Carne,
> y el Otro, cantando,
> remata:
>
> *Para que no se nos escape un pedo,*
> *meta primero el Anticristo un dedo.* (4)

Scene 0, most importantly, introduces Silencio, a spectral character that enters the stage covered head to toe in blank pages and donning the wound of a violent kiss: "a pin driven through his cheek, through his

tongue, and out the other side; another pin sealing his lips forming a cross"
(Greenblatt 241) and bridling his speech:

> Sale
> el Silencio
> vestido de papeles en blanco:
> trae puesto un beso atroz: el candado
> que hiriente atraviesa y mantiene juntos sus labios:
>
> sale el Silencio y se queda callado
> durante el resto de la página: (11)

The use of an open-ended colon as a conclusion to Silencio's speechless
prelude suggests that the story about to be told is his, and it leads the reader
to therefore anticipate his presence throughout the text. The character Silencio, however, never reappears. Rather, it is his spectral absence and the
memory of his wounded and bridled lips that persists throughout the play
as an absence from where, and against which, the drama unfolds.

Indeed, a retroactive reading of the dense parodic carapace that is *La
sodomía* through the lens of the violently muzzled Silencio, yields a reading that exposes the wound—the poignancy and sadness—underlying the
text's pain-filled laughter. It is the absence of words—silence—and therefore,
the pervasive condition of nothingness, the state of being forgotten or of
ontological oblivion, that is the core of the affliction and longing so palpable
in Fabre's verse.

The character Silencio—who, it is worth recalling, is "vestido de
papeles en blanco" (11)—personifies this affliction through his spectral
absence. More extraordinary, however, is how Fabre gives expression to
Silencio and his affliction. In much the same way a painter might foreground negative space (Smith 1–2), the poet mobilizes silence in, around,
in between, and within the words on the page. The effect is to activate silence and oblivion as a disquieting, perhaps even menacing discursive
power that refracts—alters and distorts—the density of the words on the
page: words that in *La sodomía* represent the law. *Merriam-Webster's Dictionary and Thesaurus* reminds us that the verb *refract* derives "from the
Latin *refractus*, past participle of *refringere*, to break open, break up, from
re + *refrangere*, to break." Read another way, then, Fabre activates silence to
break open the words on the page, exposing their holes and gaps. It is no
wonder, then, that in scene 22, the poetic voice renames *La sodomía* "el
poema de los agujeros" (41).

To produce this effect, Fabre relies on a variety of strategies. Aside from foregrounding silence in the remarkable character Silencio, it is underscored in the narrative or plot as silence and its consequences—neglect, exclusion, invisibility, distortion, violence, and annihilation—play out in the tragic story of the senseless deaths of Cotita and his friends. Moreover, nothingness, absence, and silence also are reiterated throughout the text thematically as a looming power to be reckoned with and in the recurrence of the word "Nada" imaged as a hole, or "agujero," as can be appreciated in scene 22:

Dice el Escribano:

A la manera de los agujeros son los sodomitas.
A la manera de los agujeros:
estigmas de la Nada en la materia.

Dice el Escribano:

Mas nada puede un escribano contra la Nada:
contra la Nada todo el latín
es en vano. (42)

Most striking, however, is the way in which Fabre mobilizes silence in the texture of the poetic discourse itself, generating a kind of threshold writing that traces the rims and explores the holes—the nothingness or absence—in the historical record related to the experience of the persecution of homosexuals in Mexico beyond their identification by the law as perpetrators of the crime *contra natura*.

Silence is mobilized even through the privileging of blank space in the very printing and layout of each of the twenty-five scenes or poems of *La sodomía*. The visual effect of the blank space is to magnify and therefore contain/constrain the words on the page. Abrupt and unorthodox line breaks, as well as intentional manipulation of punctuation marks, further disrupt the words on the page, drawing the reader's eye and internal ear toward silence. Fabre's use of what might be described as a "colon to nowhere," as in the aforementioned loa 0, to indicate discontinuity and rupture, is especially effective.

A more substantial source of silence in the text is mobilized in Fabre's explicit and extensive borrowing and redeployment of fragments of texts both from within and outside of the poem. By their very nature, fragments of any kind, but textual fragments in particular, signify "a piece broken off, detached, isolated, incomplete" (*Merriam-Webster's Dictionary and The-saurus*). The fragments, therefore, also signify separation and disconnection from their source texts, as well as the space or emptiness between fragment and source. As José Ramón Ruisánchez Serra has argued, beyond another illustration of what Antoine Compagnon calls *récriture* or what Marjorie Perloff identifies as the twenty-first-century hegemonic tendency toward *citationality*, of a "dialectic of removal and graft, disjunction and conjunction, its interpenetration of origin and destruction," Fabre exploits the fragment to breathe silence/nothingness into the space between the source and its always parodic intertextual redeployment (Ruisánchez Serra 1–3).

It is in this space and from this silence that the struggle for Cotita's claim to legitimacy and intelligibility ensues. Redeployed fragments do battle with the very same discourses and texts that would cast Cotita into oblivion: the theological and juridical discourses, all ultimately related to "dogmatic heteronormative constructions of Christ" (Goss 160), which were—and continue to be—complicit in the silencing and sanctioned violence directed toward all those who cross the binary lines imposed by compulsory heterosexuality.

The first scenes of *La sodomía* offer an example of this discursive struggle. Following the loa 0, the auto proceeds with Santa Doctrina entering the stage and demanding, "Silence!" Escribano, her minion, follows dutifully, parroting much of what she says. Given the character Silencio's aforementioned appearance in the introductory loa, Santa Doctrina's command takes on multiple meanings. Her command for silence imposes quiet, while simultaneously calling forth the spectral absence of the violently bridled Silencio, who in turn embodies the silence/absence of all those who have died for committing the sin that cannot be named, the sin of sodomy. La Carne then enters the stage, and defying Santa Doctrina's command, he announces the title of the auto—"Retablo de los sodomitas novohispanos"—and calls for the show to begin.

Henceforth, and in a manner consistent with the didactic function of the traditional auto, the antagonism or polarity between the repressive Santa Doctrina (along with her minion, Escribano, and puppet, Justicia), on the one hand, and the defiant Carne (along with her side-kick Naturaleza), on the other, frames the core issue of the play, which is the relegation of homosexual identity to a state of silence—oblivion—before the law. With exquisite subtlety, the unfolding dialogue among the polarized characters reinforces this core theme metadramatically by making it evident that the language that Carne and Naturaleza speak is not their own. Indeed, when Carne and Naturaleza speak, they repeat the same language that they oppose.

This repetition is often verbatim. However, it can also include a variation: a gloss or chide, an interruption or contestation, or it may appear in the form of a paraphrase or embellishment.

Scene 3, for example, begins by citing a fragment from Cotita's trial proceedings, this time from the chief witness of the prosecution, Juana de Herrera, whose original accusation initiates his prosecution and trial: "¡Estaban dos hombres cometiendo el pecado nefando!" (14). Escribano follows by restating her testimony, adding some factual details pertaining to herself and the location of the witnessed event:

> El Escribano
> lee otro papel en voz alta:
> Juana de Herrera, mestiza, lavandera, declara
>
> que en la albarrada de San Lázaro, a las afueras
> de la Ciudad de México,
> estaban
>
> dos hombres cometiendo el pecado nefando. (14)

Carne proceeds by restating Herrera's testimony as modified by Escribano. Carne's subtle changes, however, reveal her allegiance to Cotita as they underscore the "naturalness"—that is, sameness, with heterosexual sex—of the encounter as he and another man unite as "of one flesh" under the shade of willow trees in a clandestine meeting fraught with passion and danger. Any pleasantries suggested by the scene, however, are unsettled by the extended image of the penetration of a flesh dagger, which signifies, on the one hand, the desire for—and pleasure in—the interpenetration of flesh daggers, or penises. On the other, however, it portends the wounding and death of these same men by the castrating dagger or punishing law:

> Dice la Carne: En la albarrada de San Lázaro,
> a las afueras de la Ciudad de México,
> bajo los sauces,
> estaban
> dos hombres a la manera de una carne
> herida por un cuchillo a su vez
> hecho de carne. (14)

Repetitive sequences such as these, which characterize most of the dialogue in the "Retablo," reveal Fabre's masterful manipulation of what Butler terms the "radical proliferation of gender" as a strategy that displaces the very gender norms that enable repetition itself (*Gender* 189). The parodic death nail, though, consists of the nearly one hundred repetitions of the third-person singular form of the verb "decir" or "dice," which appear throughout *La sodomía*. The proliferation of "dice" shapes a continuous stream of "he says, she says" that ultimately rewrites the cited juridical proceedings, and by extension, its legal and theological rationale and justifications, as gossip or hearsay. Subverted and displaced, the iron grip of the authoritative discourse gives way to free play—a place—for Cotita and his friends to stake a territorial claim. The first appendixed poem to *La sodomía*, the "Villancicos del Santo Niño de las Quemaduras," reads, "Cuiloni, chimouhqui, cucuxqui," citing Bernardo de Sahagún's litany of indigenous terms used to refer to homosexuals and homosexuality. "Hagan plaza, hagan plaza" (62), the poem ends, as if to say: We have been here always. Make room! Make room!

"Dice
la Carne: Hagamos un requiem
que sea al mismo tiempo lo contrario: la canción
del deseo: la dolorosa canción del deseo en la voz de un
castrati"

To conclude, in *La sodomía*, repetition in its myriad forms—of genre, story, and text—engages the reader in a process that Robert Goss refers to as "an unmooring" (Butler would use "decentering") or the foundations of compulsory heteronormativity. Put another way, it is the space between Escribano's repressive and coercive discourses, and its repetition and variation by Carne and Naturaleza, which exposes the gaps—widens the "0"—in the homosexuals' *corpus* "through and against," as Butler would argue, "the same discourse that sought their repudiation" (*Bodies* 224). It is in this space, finally, where the melancholy of the graphically muzzled Silencio and the writhings of the burning bodies of Cotita and his friends become audible as "the mournful song of desire in the voice of a castrati" (39) that is both light verse and dirge.

Notes

1. See Robert Goss (158). I note, with gratitude, that this provocative study on Terrence McNally's *Corpus Christi* through the lens of Marcella Althaus-Reid's *Indecent Theology* was invaluable in the elaboration of this chapter.

2. See Serge Gruzinski: "Pensamos, por ejemplo, en los apodos que designan a muchos de estos hombres, 'El Mitre Pulquero, Camarones. . . .' También cabría recordar el uso de términos mariquita, cotita, puto, guapo, etc., o la intervención anónima que informó al mulato Benito de Cuebas de su inminente aprehensión" (278).

Works Cited

Althaus-Reid, Marcella. *Indecent Theology: Theological Perversions in Sex, Gender and Politics.* London: Routledge, 2000.

Arellano, Ignacio, and Enrique J. Duarte. *El auto sacramental.* Madrid: Ediciones del Laberinto, 2003.

Badenes, José Ignacio, "This is My Body Which Will Be Given up for You: Federico García Lorca's *Amor de Don Perlimplín* and the *Auto Sacramental* Tradition." *Hispania* 92.4 (2009): 688–95.

Baudot, Georges, and María Agueda Méndez, eds. Prologue and Introducción. *Amores híbridos: La palabra condenada en el México de los virreyes.* México, D.F.: Siglo XXI, 1997. 9–21.

Bethencourt, Francisco. "The Auto de Fé: Ritual and Imagery." *Journal of the Warburg and Courtauld Institutes* 55 (1992): 155–68.

Butler, Judith. *Bodies that Matter.* New York: Routledge, 1993.

——. *Gender Trouble.* New York: Routledge, 1999.

Fabre, Luis Felipe. *Leyendo agujeros.* México, D.F.: Fondo Cultural Tierra Adentro, 2005.

——. *La sodomía en la Nueva España.* Valencia: PRE-TEXTOS, 2010.

Garza Carvajal, Federico. *Vir: Perceptions of Manliness in Andalucía and Mexico, 1561–1699.* Geneva: ACADEMISCH PROEFSCHRIFT, 2000.

Goss, Robert E. "Marcelus Althaus-Reid's 'Obscenity no. 1: Bi/Christ': Expanding Christ's Wardrobe of Dresses." *Feminist Theology* 11.2 (2003): 157–66.

Greenblatt, Stephen. *The Swerve: How the World Became Modern.* New York: Norton, 2011.

Gruzinski, Serge. "Las cenizas del deseo: Homosexuales novohispanos a mediados del siglo XVII." *De la santidad a la perversión.* Ed. Sergio Ortega. México D.F.: Grijalbo, 1985. 255–79.

Guijo, Gregorio Martín de. *Diario: 1648–1664.* Ed. Manuel Romero de Terreros. México, D.F.: Porrúa, 1952.

Kamen, Henry. *The Spanish Inquisition.* New Haven: Yale University Press, 1997.

Lihn, Enrique. "Diego Maquieira: Escribir es rayarse." *Letras.s5.com.* http://www.letras.s5.com/maquieira100403.htm. Accessed November 19, 2012.

——. "Un lenguaje violento y 'chilensis': *La Tirana* de Diego Maquieira." *Letras.s5.com.* http://www.letras.s5.com/maquieira100403.htm. Accessed November 19, 2012.

Maquieira, Diego. *La Tirana, Los Sea Harrier.* Santiago: Tajamar, 2003.

McKendrick, Melveena. *Theatre in Spain: 1490–1700.* Cambridge: Cambridge University Press, 1989.

McNally, Terrence. *Corpus Christi.* New York: Grove Press, 1999.

Merriam-Webster's Dictionary and Thesaurus. http://www.merriam-webster.com. Accessed November 19, 2012.

Mignolo, Walter. *The Idea of Latin America*. Oxford: Wiley-Blackwell, 2005.

Parker, Alexander A. *The Allegorical Drama of Calderón: An Introduction to the Autos Sacramentales*. Oxford, UK: Dolphin, 1943.

Ruisánchez Serra, José Ramón. "Fabre: El fragmento que no acaba." Simposio Internacional *Imágenes y Realismos* en América Latina, Universiteit Leiden, September 29, 2011. Unpublished Conference Proceedings.

Schuessler, Michael K., and Miguel Capistrán. *México se escribe con "J."* México, D.F.: Temas de Hoy, 2010.

Smith, Alex. "Porque se lo dice." Pacific Lutheran University, October 4, 2011. Unpublished paper.

Taylor, Diana, and Sarah J. Townsend, eds. *Stages of Conflict: A Critical Anthology of Latin American Theater and Performance*. Ann Arbor: University of Michigan Press, 2008.

Wardropper, Bruce. *Introducción al teatro religioso del Siglo de Oro*. Salamanca: Anaya, 1967.

CHAPTER SIX

Colonial Confinement, Confession, and Resistance in Ángeles del abismo by Enrique Serna

Guillermo de los Reyes-Heredia and
Josué Gutiérrez-González
Translated by Bradley L. Drew

Confinement, resistance, confession, and transgression are recurrent themes that make up a significant portion of the corpus of Spanish American colonial texts studied and read by contemporary scholars. We find these topics in numerous diaries, Inquisitorial *procesos*, and court proceedings of all sorts, in particular those written by women. Canonical authors of the colonial period such as Sor Juana Inés de la Cruz, as well as other individuals persecuted by the Inquisition, such as Catalina de San Juan (better known as the *china poblana*) and *beatas* like Teresa Romero or Marina de San Miguel have been associated with closed and gendered spaces, such as the cloister, the convent, and even individual rooms. Mediated through these private spaces, resistance and transgression are successfully expressed from marginal spaces and by marginalized individuals. As is well known, Josefina Ludmer calls these articulations of resistance "*tretas del débil*," strategies used from a powerless position in order to survive within a regime that is hierarchical, Inquisitorial, and oppressive. Taking this critical paradigm as a point of departure, we argue that in his novel *Ángeles del abismo* (2004), Enrique Serna reconstructs a colonial Mexican society framed as a tyrannical reality that, at least metaphorically, speaks to contemporary Mexico. We examine how the interplay between confinement, and the mechanisms the protagonists use to transgress, subvert, or accept such confinement, highlight how the postcolonial mind imagines these spaces and reinvents them for the contemporary reader. The best model for describing the novel's genre, and for explaining the transmission of its message, is "historiographic metafiction," a self-reflexive and yet historical genre theorized by Linda Hutcheon.

Serna's novel produces a symbolic image of the colonial past to reflect upon the rigorous system of *castas* in colonial Mexico, the centralization of power, the subversive potential of historiographic metafiction, and the multiple processes of transculturation that have been either ignored or simplified by official history (Juan-Navarro and Young 21). In *Ángeles del abismo*, as Oswaldo Estrada argues, critics will certainly find the use of carnivalesque and polyphonic language, anachronisms, irony, metafiction, and parody, but they may in fact miss the subtle ways in which Serna creates a truly revolutionary text that stirs and subverts our conception of the Mexican *colonia* (27–28).

Situated in seventeenth-century Mexico, the novel fictionalizes the lives of Crisanta Cruz, a false *beata*, and Tlacotzin, an acculturated Indian. Crisanta is a criolla, the daughter of a working-class, alcoholic Spaniard, and Tlacotzin is a Mexican Indian who has grown up in the Christian faith, but slowly begins to question it, until he finally converts back to his indigenous beliefs. Crisanta and Tlacotzin develop a strong will to survive and a sophisticated way of subverting the establishment and mocking their oppressors. These characters lie at the heart of a hilarious plot that reveals the public virtues and private vices of colonial Mexican society. Among the main themes are the drama of mysticism and spirituality, baroque entanglements of repressed desire and sexual behavior, clandestine idolatry, and the constant struggle for power not only between religious and secular authorities, but also between the Dominican and Jesuit orders. This rich and picaresque novel proposes a critical, novel, and revolutionary approach to Mexico's colonial past presented from multiple marginal perspectives.

As a historiographic metafiction, *Ángeles del abismo* has a plot revolving around the Inquisitorial process pursued against Teresa Romero in seventeenth-century New Spain. Romero was known as the "*falsa Teresa de Jesús*," and was prosecuted for being a false beata, a trickster, and an opportunist. While Serna acknowledges his use of the historical archive pertaining to Romero's case in his "créditos de salida" (535), the innovation in his novel resides in the re-creation of an oppressive colonial system of power through a complex array of closed spaces, such as the prison, the palace, the bedroom, and the monastery. Imitating his colonial predecessors, Serna revives personalized forms of narration, such as epistolary discourse and confession, in order to posit his own versions of resistance and to offer his characters an escape route from the oppression of the colonial regime.

In addition to examining how oppression is represented by successively more diminishing enclosures, and how a potential escape from that condition is imagined by Serna, we also analyze the contradictory role of colonial confessional discourse. In the novel, confession becomes an unstable discursive practice that functions as an instrument for maintaining control of the mind, as well as a mechanism of resistance that lays bare the contradictions and fissures of the colonial system. Ultimately, Serna's text allows us to view the processes of control exercised by a disciplinary state through a narrative of confinement. We use this term, following the observations of Ioan Davies, Victor Brombert and Jorge Marturano, to refer to those stories in which a particular subject is confined, whether voluntarily or by force, to a physical or imaginary space. In the case of Crisanta, she is confined to her bedroom (both at home and at the Marqués de Selva Nevada's palace); in the case of Tlacotzin, not only is he physically unable to see Crisanta—the restrictions on his movement are imposed by the Catholic Church.

Confinement in the Narrative

In *Ángeles del abismo*, Serna manipulates a stark vision of the social and cultural contradictions that are produced within a conflictive and multifaceted New Spain. Thus, the novel presents itself as a multilayered discourse featuring irony, parody, and satire. A good example of the way in which these elements are manipulated in the novel is shown when Sandoval de Zapata, the Spanish poet, playwright, and director of a play in which Crisanta performs, tries to adapt one of his *autos* to attract the Indians' attention:

> Para seducir a los indios y facilitarles la comprensión del auto, Sandoval Zapata había caracterizado como nahuales a los ángeles del abismo— una pareja de cómicos jóvenes, él con máscara de jaguar, ella con antifaz de lechuza—, que danzaban en cuatro patas y recitaban ululantes endechas alrededor del Hombre, para tentarlo con riquezas, placeres y honores. Al verlos aparecer entre una nube de copal, los indios aplaudieron de pie. (148)

With seductive descriptions such as this one, Serna exposes the social and cultural contradictions produced in a world characterized by diversity. A significant example of this appears at the beginning of the novel, when Crisanta, the co-protagonist, frustrated by the fact that her father does not provide her with a better lifestyle, complains before the mirror: "¡Que me aspen si la indiada nos quita el pan! En este reino ya no se respetan las jerarquías. ¿Dónde se ha visto que los naturales tengan más derecho que los españoles?" (16).

At the same time, the novel criticizes the mechanisms that political and religious powers utilize to regulate sexual conduct and to take control of their colonial subjects' minds. Several examples of this all-encompassing control are illustrated throughout the novel; a good example of this is present in Inquisitor Fray Juan de Cárcamo's soliloquy, as he describes the pleasure he experiences from taking an enema:

> Sólo puedo alegar en mi descargo, que a pesar de haber gozado en forma tan sucia, no por ello soy marica, ni utilizo el clíster como sustituto del miembro viril. En lo que se refiere al acto carnal, mi voto de castidad sigue incólume, pues jamás he tenido la tentación de holgar con hombre ni con mujer. Apruebo con entusiasmo la ordenanza episcopal de quemar a los sométicos en el atrio de San Juan, y en modo alguno me siento acreedor a esa pena, porque no pervierto a nadie con mi pecado. (267)

Thus, in *Ángeles del abismo*, Serna provides the reader with spaces in which transgression is tolerated only because it poses no threat to the established order, such as the bedrooms where Crisanta has several *arrobos*, either at her father's house or at her protectors' palace.

This vision of the viceroyalty as an oppressive reality is constructed not only through the characters' actions, as we can see in Cárcamo's characterization, but also by the way in which the physical spaces of power are depicted. This becomes more evident when we take a closer look at the novel's spatial and structural configuration. The novel's plot and its individual chapters are presented as a geographical journey that conveys an increasing restriction of space. The novel is laid out in three sections. In the first one, "Cruce de caminos," Crisanta and her lover Tlacotzin travel from the Tacuba neighborhood, and the Amecameca region and its surrounding areas, to other cities, such as Puebla. In the second part, "Tres años después," the geographical perimeter is drastically reduced, and the novel's action takes place primarily in the center of Mexico City (the house of the Marqués de Selva Nevada, the Plaza de Santo Domingo, and the Plaza Mayor), including Tlacotzin's occasional journeys within the city's center and the neighborhood of La Candelaria. The third section, "El proceso," is not only shorter than its predecessors but takes place almost exclusively within the Inquisitorial prison, and, in the end, Crisanta and Tlacotzin escape from their confinement through very tight (and smelly) tunnels. This process of progressive reduction of the geographical space where the action takes place can be read as the result of a system of relationships established between colonial authorities and the spaces at which power is centralized.

Due to this spatial configuration, each character almost naturally moves toward the political and cultural center of New Spain. While this centralization of power reflects the political situation of the colonia, it might also be interpreted as a critique of Mexico's current centralization. The image that best illustrates the perverse relationship established between space and power can be found in the finale of "Cruce de caminos" when, impressed by the dialogue of a Eucharistic play, Crisanta interprets her coming to the city and the life that awaits her there, with Tlacotzin, as arriving at the entrance to hell:

> Sin hacerle mal a nadie, tendrían que vivir en los oscuros antros del pecado, como enfermos de lepra o mal gálico, y de tanto apretarles el cuello, la culpa impuesta desde afuera llegaría a formar parte de su carácter. Ahora comprendía mejor el astuto rencor del personaje que había interpretado en el auto. El abismo no era un destino elegido: hacia allá los empujaba la tiranía de los justos, como a los ángeles réprobos expulsados del paraíso. (194)

As Crisanta enters the city, she becomes aware of the clandestine situation in which she must physically live under a colonial system of power and repression. Therefore, the novel as a whole begins to construct itself as a narrative of confinement, as the characters, especially those who find themselves close to authority, are controlled by a disciplinary state that isolates, contains, and immobilizes them. As the book moves forward, the narration reproduces a colonial reality that controls the body and sexuality, pleasure and gender roles. The New Spanish society that Serna reconstructs is based on several relationships of power, and colonial authority exercises its influence beyond the political sphere so as to impose itself into the private space and even onto the consciousness of the main characters.

As we mentioned above, the emphasis placed on the dynamics of imprisonment associates this novel with the discursive modality that Jorge Marturano named "narratives of confinement." For his part, Hernán Díaz notes that these types of narratives, which he calls "island narratives," are centered around the subjective experience of confinement, and they generate an impulse to overcome it by the use of language:

> Island narratives are, to a large extent, the account of desperate attempts at inventing an interlocutor. The maroon's first impulse is, then, to resort to the magical arithmetic of monologue, thanks to which one becomes at least two—speaker and listener. An alternative solution in the same direction is the invention of another, an artificial echo, someone who, quite literally, speaks back. (97–98)

Díaz's idea suggests the presence of a dialogic structure within narratives of confinement that manifests textually through highly personalized discursive forms (diaries, blogs, letters, wills, and other records) that transmit a subject's attempt to narrate his own state of immobility.

The literary representation of confinement is not limited to the characters' increasing physical restraint within various spaces. That mechanism symbolizes or alludes to the construction of the colonized mind. Serna fictionalizes this process and its attendant ramifications every time colonial authorities demand confession, presenting that process as yet another form of confinement.

Spaces of Control and Discipline

The novelistic construction of an oppressive reality marked by outside control and other inequalities that characterized colonial Mexico is best summarized in this passage:

> El Tribunal del Santo Oficio, presidido con celo apostólico por el ilustre y docto don Juan de Ortega Montáñez, ha emprendido una persecución concienzuda y tenaz de los monstruos que cometieron esta diabólica fechoría. . . . Debemos, pues, ayudar a los defensores de la Iglesia, delatando a los sujetos que por la impureza de su sangre o su modo deshonesto de vida caigan bajo la sospecha de haber incurrido en herética pravedad. México y la Nueva España hierven de hebreos que imitan en lo exterior las acciones católicas y disimulan su mentira con una continuada perfidia. (327)

In the novel, Fray Juan de Cárcamo, as a representative of the Santo Oficio, is after the "heretics" who have "violated" the Church of the Virgen de los Remedios. This persecution of supposed offenders against the Church is what first keeps Tlacotzin—the person who commits the "sacrílego despojo a la Virgen de los Remedios" (326)—away from Crisanta, in a journey of displacement away from the center of the city that nonetheless brings him to the doors of the Inquisition. This is how Serna represents some of the spaces in which colonial power is materialized, using the narrative space as a symbolic scenario to represent his ideological perspective (Pimentel 87–88).

In *Ángeles del abismo*, not only does the chapter layout coincide with the geographic journey of the characters, as mentioned earlier, but their individual actions are organized in terms of power and spaces. As we have seen, the novel proposes a displacement of the protagonists from diverse peripheral spaces toward the political and cultural center of New Spain. Crisanta needs to move to a better neighborhood in order to have more people witness her arrobos: "Necesitamos mudarnos a un barrio más elegante, para que venga a verte gente de calidad," Nicolasa comments (230). She moves to the Palace of the Marqueses de Selva Nevada to be close to the marquis, don Manuel, in order to cure him with her supposedly special curative powers. After an initial visit, don Manuel testifies: "Ella me salvó, ella hizo el milagro" (283). His words and Cristanta's move coincide with her growing power. Suddenly, she has a new life full of privileges because of her allegedly special communication with God and, as expected, several members of Mexico City's aristocracy go to the Selva Nevada Palace to witness her amazing abilities, bringing her jewelry and all sorts of gifts.

But just when she feels more powerful within a structure of power, the Santo Oficio attempts to constrain her:

> Como medida precautoria, en las semanas posteriores al nombramiento de Cárcamo [Crisanta] evitó mostrarse en público y tener arrobos en casas ajenas, pues su relumbrón social era, sin duda, lo que más podría molestar a los adustos inquisidores. . . . Pero en vez de quitarle notoriedad, el encierro le granjeó nuevas legiones de admiradores, pues cuanto menos se dejaba ver, más crecía su leyenda. (363–64)

And, as the protagonists are transferred to the very center of the city, they actually become prisoners of institutions that considerably limit their actions and that eventually impose relentless punishment for any deviations from the social order in the form of idolatry, or heretical or immoral behavior.

If Crisanta wants to enjoy some of her existing power, she needs to keep "cierta expectación a su alrededor para seguir recibiendo buenos regalos" (364). The only problem is that she cannot deal with "las penitencias, los ayunos, los tullimientos y, sobre todo, la tensión de representar a diario el mismo papel sin poder quitarse la máscara" (364). With these words, which immediately evoke a contemporary Mexican identity—calling to mind the way in which Octavio Paz portrays Mexicans hiding behind an eternal mask in his *Laberinto de la soledad*—Serna presents the colonial system as a highly restrictive society, formed by concentric circles that seduce and attract subjects in search of possible alternatives to their subaltern condition. This happens, for instance, when Tlacotzin is arrested by the Santo Oficio and remains trapped in a labyrinth of labels and ethnicities:

> Según la ley, Cárcamo hubiera debido poner a Tlacotzin a disposición de los jueces seglares, pues el Santo Oficio, por una antigua cédula real, tenía prohibido conocer causas de indios. . . . Pero la sola idea de entregar a su presa, para que otros se ufanaran de haber resuelto el caso, le revolvió las víceras. . . . Recurrió, pues, al sencillo expediente de presentar al reo como mestizo y aunque Tlacotzin, desde su primera deposición, declaró en náhuatl ser indio puro por parte de madre y padre, no lo pudo comprobar con su fe de bautizo, que había extraviado cuando huyó de Amecameca. (479)

Gradually, it is revealed that the areas of control remain in the city, specifically in those spaces that harbor political-religious power: palaces, prisons, and the houses of the aristocrats. Within this narrative of confinement, the main characters associate freedom with spaces away from Mexico City and its zone of influence. Understandably, then, Havana—the city where Crisanta's mother goes after she leaves her and her father—is portrayed throughout the text as a symbol of freedom.

The bedroom in the Palace of Selva Nevada, the Inquisitorial prison, and the places where Tlacotzin hides are not the only spaces of confinement introduced in the novel. The convent and the *manicomio* also transmit the idea of a ruthless colonial order that nonetheless allows certain transgressions and scandal. The Dominican monastery, for instance, is represented as an institution that despite its rigorous nature permits some forms of transgression. In this space, the friars' nocturnal incursions are silenced with bribes, as can be seen in the following exchange when Leonor, the daughter of the Marqueses de Selva Nevada, is snuck into the cloister:

Cuando llegaron al portal de Santo Domingo. . . . Pedro la [Leonor] ayudó a bajarse del caballo. . . . Recárguese en mi hombre como si estuviera borracha. . . . Pedro tocó el aldabón y cuando Melchor, el portero, se asomó por el torno, le dijo entre jadeos, como si trajera un cuerpo a rastras:

—Fray Gervasio volvió a las andadas. Viene borracho como una cuba.

—Si quiere pasar, que bendiga las llaves de san Pedro [replied Melchor].

—Aquí tienes hermano. Es todo lo que hallé en su talega. Pedro hizo la señal de la cruz y colocó en el torno dos escudos de oro. Hubo un tenso compás de espera mientras Melchor probaba las monedas con los dientes. Pasado el trámite, el portón se abrió como por ensalmo. (385–86)

The curious dialogue above shows Serna's critique of a colonial system that, even within the walls of a monastery, has room for transgression and corruption. Only a major transgression—in this case, Leonor's stealthy entrance into the convent of Santo Domingo—unleashes disciplinary measures, but the punishment is limited to expelling the offender, the poet Luis de Sandoval Zapata, from the monastery.

Serna here shows how those in control manipulate the system to their advantage: "Por la gravedad de lo sucedido, el arzobispo Sagade Bugueiro llamó a las partes en conflicto para buscar un arreglo conciliatorio, que dejara bien parada a la Iglesia sin agrandar el escándalo" (455). The archbishop manages to repair the prestige of the Church (and receives financial compensation), stating, "Ni la Iglesia ganaba nada con ventilar en público asuntos tan escabrosos como la entrada de una mujer a un convento de clausura, ni los nobles apellidos del marqués merecían andar en boca de los maldicientes" (458). When doña Pura finds out that her daughter Leonor has lost her virginity and is involved in the scandal, she decides to cancel all social events and confines herself to her oratory with Crisanta, "la hija virtuosa que nunca le faltaría" (458). Thus, doña Pura creates her own confinement, "encerrada en un mutismo sepulcral, pasaba tardes enteras en el oratorio con su protegida" (458). After several days, she decides that in order to save her family's reputation without giving up her own social life, she must confine Leonor to the Casa de Mujeres Dementes del Divino Salvador (the Divine Savior Home for Insane Women). Consequently, Leonor goes from one cloister to another to pay for her moral transgressions.

The Casa de Mujeres Dementes serves as a synecdoche for New Spain's hierarchical system. As in the case of the Inquisition jail, a rigorous distribution of spaces according to the social status of the inmates

exists here: "Un patio en forma de anfiteatro, parecido a un circo romano, con jaulas de madera para las locas furiosas, que se estrellan como fieras en las tablas. . . . Otro patio con un jardín en el centro, el destinado a las reclusas distinguidas" (459). Likewise, the prison order reveals a strict distribution of time and conduct: "desayuno a las seis de la mañana, a las nueve distribución de medicinas con pena de latigazos a quien escupa el brebaje; a mediodía, salida al asoleadero, enseguida el almuerzo y a las cinco de la tarde el rosario en la capilla" (459). Finally, the violent means of discipline also vary, although they do not spare the privileged women: "Todos los días las monjas le aplican vomitivos, laxantes, cauterios y estornutarios para provocar la expulsión de los vapores superfluos que según el médico le han nublado las potencias intelectivas" (459).

Given this layout of discipline and order, it is clear that Serna portrays the manicomio, the convent, and the Inquisitorial prison as spaces where colonial power acts to systematically regulate women's transgressive and rebellious conduct. At the Casa de Mujeres Dementes, Leonor suffers a new confinement, one that does not afford her the luxury and comfort she had in her other confinement (her house, as we will discuss later), although, ironically, this place gives her a new opportunity to fall in love again: "y al caer la tarde, recién bañada, se sienta en el alféizar a esperar el regreso de su galán" (460). The private mental ward—which Gastón Bachelard, in his phenomenological approach to the poetic imagination, interprets as the great metaphor for escape (1–3)—is no alternative to the other authoritarian spaces that Serna creates. The convent and the home are represented as parallel contexts in which power—this time patriarchal (whether one marries God or a man)—is exercised relentlessly. In both scenarios, a woman remains imprisoned by religious authorities (in the Casa de Mujeres Dementes) and/or by her family (in the home of the Marqueses de Selva Nevada) until the moment she marries and follows her husband's wishes.

When Crisanta is cornered by Cárcamo, who argues that he considers it his responsibility to "preseguir la santidad fingida" to be "un deber perseguir la santidad fingida, lo mismo que las visiones imaginadas inspiradas por el demonio" (408), Father Pedraza offers her entrance into the order as her only possible escape. The Jesuit's words are very telling: "Mientras vivas en el siglo serás vulnerable a cualquier ataque" (419). Crisanta has no other option and, naturally, accepts his offer. She goes along with doña Pura, who cannot be more excited to see her joining the Convento de las Carmelitas with an ostentatious dowry. And yet Crisanta feels imprisoned:

Si Dios la hubiera puesto en libertad de escoger, tal vez habría elegido la suerte de Leonor. Enloquecer por un amor prohibido era un bello gesto de rebeldía, el golpe teatral que toda actriz anhelaba para salir de escena con una gran ovación. Ella en cambio, no había tenido la suerte de elegir su destino: otras voluntades más fuertes, ocultas en la sombra, habían escrito la tragedia secreta que le tocaba representar. (462)

For Crisanta, the cloistered life of the Carmelite nuns seems like an endless punishment of forced labor: "Se vio envejecer haciendo vainillas y labor blanca, en oscuras crujías con paredes mohosas, donde los ecos lejanos del mundo exterior . . . atizarían todas las noches el hervidero de sus antojos" (464). Crisanta sees the convent as: "reclusiones injustas en celdas de castigo con goteras sobre el camastro, jetas hostiles espiándola por el ventanuco, enfermedades, vómitos, gritos de auxilio que nadie escucha" (464–65).

Marriage has historically fit within the regulatory institutions of the colonial order as well: women were conceived of as the husband's property, and as subjects that were considered likely to give in to sinful temptations— thus, it was believed that only through marriage (human or divine) could the feminine soul be protected from the world. In the colonial world, as Asunción Lavrin states, marriage of any sort becomes a form of guardianship, a confinement that protects a woman from the dangers of the world— above all from herself—and protects the honor of the men related to her; it may even be thought of as a sort of cell in which women have to live, a space of protection supervised by the husband (1–5). Thanks to ecclesiastical safeguarding, a nun is kept safe from the many dangers that threaten her virtue, much as a wife is protected by her husband. Therefore, doña Pura welcomes Crisanta's desire to enter the convent so that Crisanta may avoid repeating Leonor's mistakes. The models of *virgen/no madre* for single women and *madre/no virgen* for the married ones (Franco 95) are clearly represented in Serna's novel by Crisanta, Leonor, and doña Pura. As long as Crisanta—as a devout woman with spiritual gifts—remains in the secular world, she represents a threat to the ecclesiastical order of the community. And, in a way, her entrance into the convent symbolizes confinement: "Sólo tenía dos puertas para escapar del mundo: la de la gloria o la de la infamia. El convento, su tabla de salvación, en realidad era una antecámara del infierno, más benigna, eso sí, que las cárceles secretas del Santo Oficio. . . . Ella no tenía madera de monja, ni paciencia para sepultarse en vida" (420). In the novel, monastic life is portrayed as a seclusion that affects not only the body but also the very soul of the future novice.

Thus, the spatial form of the convent becomes a concrete representation of the colonial system and its societal control.

The most reliable example of the impact of power in the domestic environment is evident in the case of Crisanta and her father, Onésimo: "La primera víctima de las prenurias familiares fue Crisanta, pues Onésimo la condenó a comer sobras o raciones ínfimas de la comida que ella misma guisaba" (91). Onésimo's house represents the place where various types of violence take place, including Crisanta's rape by her own father. When the family moves to Tacuba, on the other side of the city, their second house becomes a place of exploitation and confinement for Crisanta. When her father finds out that she has performed in a play and that she has faked a mystic ecstasy, he almost kills her, although he soon finds a way to exploit her supposedly saintly attributes. Due to her potential as "una mina de oro que no hemos sabido explotar" (92), Crisanta is kept within the private space by her father and his lover, Lorenza, so as to avoid any contact with the faithful, who rush to see her arrobos. Because of the resulting controlled performance, their home is transformed into a prison, a space where discipline is exercised—and, like a prison might, it contains the live body and the conscience of a woman.

These same prison-like characteristics apply to other representations of the colonial home and family, including that of the nobility. With its luxury and privileges, the residence of the Marqués de Selva Nevada also represents a prison for Leonor's intimate desires and sexuality. Her transgressive passion for Fray Juan de Cárcamo places her in a position that allows her to become aware of her confinement. Despite her prohibitions and her fears, Leonor devises a plan to steal into the Dominican convent; as she plans, she reflects, "Dichosas putas: a cambio de la deshonra y el repudio social, ¡cuánta libertad para hacer su regalada gana! Era una cruel paradoja que la doncella más rica del reino, propietaria de ingenios, minas y haciendas, no fuera dueña de su propio cuerpo, el único bien terrenal que de verdad le importaba" (378). This excerpt shows how, with respect to domestic imprisonment, Leonor voices the restrictions that the colonial system imposes upon women within privileged groups—at the same time pointing out the spaces of transgressive freedom enjoyed by certain groups because of their peripheral or openly marginal position (Franco 52; Dopico-Black 68). It is only logical, then, that both Crisanta and Leonor develop—despite their social differences—a fascination for don Luis de Sandoval Zapata, the poet, playwright, and theatrical businessman who embodies a complex model of mobility and, more importantly, political and intellectual resistance.

Confession

The narrative of confinement becomes more visible in *Ángeles del abismo* as it rearticulates the Inquisitorial process pursued against Teresa Romero in the seventeenth century. The document, written in legal form for official use during a trial, can be read from a contemporary point of view as an expression of a subaltern identity that confronts, by means of words, one of the institutions of the colonial system (Alberro 528). This is revealing, since Serna attempts to recapture, with every license available to the novelist, various strategies of self-representation of subaltern voices. In order to do this, Serna incorporates the confessional register as a privileged discursive model within the narration in a way that metaphorically creates an escape route for the imprisoned conscience in the rigid colonial order.

For Michel Foucault, confession constitutes one of the technologies of the ego; in other words, one of those mechanisms generated by culture "that permit individuals to carry out, by themselves or with the help of others, a certain number of operations on their body and their soul, thoughts, conduct, or whatever form of being, thus obtaining a transformation of themselves with the aim of reaching a particular state of happiness, purity, wisdom, or immortality" (49). Although in Western context, confession is a practice originating in the classical world, for Foucault it does not acquire its current dimensions until the Middle Ages, with the rise of the Christian model of confession. It is a model to which Serna's novel constantly alludes through various characters who feel forced to exhibit their beliefs before a representative of power, to verbalize their desires, and to recognize misconduct—all within the network of spaces where power is exercised.

Ángeles del abismo makes use of confession—religious and legal—as a privileged textual referent that can transmit a subjective vision of confinement. To do this, the model of confession is reformulated to allow the perspective of a personal voice. In her commentary about Teresa Romero's original Inquisitorial documents, Solange Alberro shows that a third-person narrative perspective is employed to express the experiences of the colonial subject through the fictionalized filter of official discourse (526). In his adaptation of the original Inquisitorial *proceso*, Serna radically transforms the confession of Teresa Romero, and the mediation of the third person dims until a model of personal and intimate confession is produced. As Foucault would certainly argue, confession is one of the premodern mechanisms par excellence for the exhibition and control of conscience (89). Serna takes advantage of this a priori and reproduces the confessional modality from the colonial period in order to show not only negative impressions about the colonial system, but also the ways in which characters resist their physical and symbolic confinement.

The presence of confessional segments in *Ángeles del abismo* involves various characters and covers different aspects of the colonial order. Control of the body is one of the motifs that frequently coincides with this personalized discourse. Fray Juan de Cárcamo offers an interesting example of the complex relationship between the exercise of colonial power and confession as a discursive practice. Cárcamo not only represents the villain who opposes Crisanta's and Tlacotzin's love; he also embodies various levels of colonial authority. Cárcamo is a member of the metropolis sent out to more distant communities, where he is a representative of the high ecclesiastical hierarchy in his role as an Inquisitor of the Holy Office. But even in these more remote locations, at the top of the social pyramid, Cárcamo cannot extract himself from the atmosphere of control imposed upon him. Therefore, when Tlacotzin assists him with the application of one of his regular enemas, he confesses, "Gracias, hijo, para ser tu primera vez lo hiciste muy bien. . . . Pero quiero pedirte un favor: esto debe quedar entre tú y yo. Ni una palabra a nadie, ¿entendido?" (113). Even as a Grand Inquisitor (a title he eventually earns), Fray Juan must be persistently vigilant of his conscience. Of the multiple forms of confession that appear in the novel, Cárcamo's most openly contradict the confessional model and, by extension, the system of institutions that implement it. Although he has a confessor, Fray Gabriel de Villalpando, Cárcamo tells only God his most precious secrets.

For Leigh Gilmore, "confession produces unintended effects, including the exposure of the confessor, who is typically hidden within the logic and practices of confession" (186). We see this in Serna's novel when Cárcamo uses various methods to avoid confession and its consequences: "En cuanto al pecado de la gula, cada viernes primero lo confesaba sin rodeo a fray Gabriel de Villalpando, mi subalterno y compañero de bacanales, quien me imponía una penitencia benigna a cambio de que yo le diera el mismo trato cuando se confesaba conmigo" (265). This confessional avoidance is even more significant when read within the parameters of the Catholic Church, which may consider such actions invalid, false, and even sacrilegious. If, according to Peter Brooks, within the Western imaginary, public acceptance of guilt provides a form of restoration of the social connection broken by improper conduct, the act of confessing (before a religious or civil authority) implicitly carries some sort of punishment, including exclusion, either momentary or permanent, from the subject's community

(1–5). As Grand Inquisitor, Cárcamo knows this quite well and opts for a safe confession, without the public display and physical torment that he himself requires of his penitents.

Nevertheless, Fray Juan de Cárcamo, like Crisanta and Tlacotzin, is inevitably a prisoner of the restrictive logic that controls the body and its desires in colonial Mexico. His simulated confession revolves around the proscription of worldly pleasures, those suspicious forms of desire that are ultimately unacceptable for all colonial subjects:

> Acúsome, Señor, de haber contraído un raro apetito concupiscente, que hasta donde llegan mis lecturas, no aparece consignado en ninguna guía de pecadores y, sin embargo, inficiona el alma tanto como el fornicio o el pecado de Onán. Soy afecto a las lavativas y gozo hasta la ignominia cuando me aplican el clíster en salva sea la parte. (264)

His words disentangle an ample and detailed series of personal confessions that recreate what Brooks identifies as the tendency of the confessional discourse to reproduce itself endlessly once it has begun (6). Employing an ironic point of view to describe the autoeroticism of the priests, the author evidences the fear colonial subjects held in regard to the body:

> Nunca antes había derramado mi simiente, ni practiqué jamás la masturbación—sólo había tenido poluciones nocturnas en sueños, que la Iglesia perdona por su carácter involuntario—y al verme en tal embarazo comprendí cegado por una revelación luminosa, con la que san Pablo encontró en el camino a Damasco, de que el solo y único fin de todas mis comilonas, había sido provocar esa efusión sacrílega. Por fortuna el semen se derramó en mi sotana, y como estábamos a oscuras, creo que fray Andrés no se percató de lo sucedido. (266)

This first private confession encourages Cárcamo to recall a long history of transgressions that include the discovery of sexual pleasure, his constant fear of having his transgressions made public, his silent battles to dominate the body, his tactics for avoiding his own conscience, and the constant failures of a body that has supposedly become a demonical space or, worse yet, the playground of prohibited passions that keep virtue under constant siege.

Metaphorically speaking, Cárcamo's revealing words display the fissures of imperial morality, whose foundations seem more and more improper and contradictory: "Se me podrá acusar de cualquier cosa, menos

de revolcar mi sagrada investidura en la ciénega del fornicio, y si mañana ardiera en el Tártaro, me quedaría el consuelo de no haber corrompido a ningún Cristiano" (267). In a desperate attempt to restore the order that he sees under constant threat, the Inquisitor blames his own transgressions on the relaxation of institutional discipline outside the Mexican metropolis: "Cuando los superiores, en reconocimiento a mis méritos, me enviaron al Nuevo Mundo, con el honroso cargo de prior del convento de Amecameca, quedé librado a mi propio arbitrio, sin el freno de ninguna autoridad superior" (265). Through Cárcamo, then, the novel shows a New Spanish authority that is simultaneously terrorized and seduced by its own "body."

Along these lines, Leonor also exemplifies the relationship between the confessional mode and the ever-vigilant state of the colonial world. Like Cárcamo, Leonor lives enduring a continual conflict between her illicit passion and her fear of this passion being discovered—by anybody. The young woman finds herself permanently subject to the scrutiny of others, and her sexual transgressions fall under the divine gaze: "Deslizaba la otra mano por debajo de su basquiña, en busca de la húmeda entrepierna, cuando se sintió observada por el Cristo de la cabecera, y alzó las manos como un rufián sorprendido en flagrancia" (215). The idea of a watchful deity is not the exclusive domain of a Catholic religion that controls the lives of criollos, *peninsulares*, and mestizos; a similar idea is also represented within the indigenous community, as we see in Tlacotzin's experience of native religion. After renouncing Christianity, he reconciles with his ancestral gods, but this does not free him from the oppressive atmosphere that touches all sectors of the colonial world: "Terminada la ceremonia iniciática, Tlacotzin recibió la orden de someterse al ritual purificatorio con duración de cuarenta días, similar al de los viejos guerreros que se ofrecían como voluntarios para morir en la piedra de los sacrificios" (312).

Tlacotzin is also constantly preoccupied with offending his Aztec gods: "Perdóname, señora [Coatlicue], por haberle rezado a tu enemiga con esta boca perjura, que solo debe abrirse para adorarte" (324). The Aztec gods are portrayed in the novel as vigilant and punishing entities that silently speak to Tlacotzin from the dungeons of his own soul—for example: "Mira nomás en lo que has venido a parar, semilla podrida, caballero de tepuzque. ¿Es así como honras la palabra empanada? No mereces ser hijo del bravo Axotécatl, ni pertenecer al círculo de las cuatro cañas" (467). When Crisanta wants proof of his Christian faith, "con tal de apaciguarla, Tlacotzin accedió, si bien rezó en voz muy queda, con la pueril esperanza de pasar inadvertido a los oídos de Coatlicue" (324). Episodes such as this

appeasal by Tlacotzin are repeated throughout the text, particularly during the proceso, and although Tlacotzin passes through several moments of doubt regarding his native religion, in the end he is reconciled with his old gods, to whom he attributes the salvation of his family. Tlacotzin prays to Coatlicue, and asks her to save him and Citlali (a Nahuatl name that he gives to the "Mujer Blanca," Crisanta): "No la rechaces por ser Cristiana, ella es carne de mi carne y antes de ir a tus brazos, Xiuhtecutli la limpiará de impurezas con un bautizo de fuego" (512).

Interestingly, both Crisanta and Tlacotzin feel that they must be true to their religious beliefs. Toward the end of the novel, Crisanta wants to baptize their child in the church, while Tlacotzin also remains true to his roots: "En su fuero interno sabía que estaban libres gracias a la intervención de Coatlicue, pero guardó silencio, para no reavivar una discordia que debía quedar sepultada. Ya saldrían sus deudas de gratitud en Cuba, cuando tuviera un momento a solas para encender copal" (529).

With this last image of a family that can only have a happy ending away from the center of power—in Cuba—*Ángeles del abismo* ultimately confirms the inequalities of the colonial landscape. Such inequalities, as we have seen, take place at all levels of the social pyramid and develop because those who have control privilege certain members of society, while disenfranchising others, a practice Aníbal Quijano has defined as the coloniality of power (113). This state of coloniality, fictionalized in a contemporary novel published in 2004, reminds us that this colonized condition is not exclusive to the colonial period, as Walter Mignolo has discussed extensively (58–59). Our contemporary relationships have been influenced by this matrix of power to such an extent that we sometimes lose sight of this fact, just as many of Serna's characters actively contribute to their own states of coloniality. As this novel unfolds, and problematic issues related to religion and syncretism, social class, race and ethnicity, *mestizaje*, transculturation and hybridity, assigned gender roles and sexual control, we wonder to what extent they still have an impact on the life and behavior of "postcolonial" Mexico.

Works Cited

Alberro, Solange. *Inquisición y sociedad en México, 1571–1700*. México, D.F.: Fondo de Cultura Económica (FCE), 1988.
Bachelard, Gastón. *La poética del espacio*. Trans. Ernestina de Champourcin. México, D.F.: FCE, 2000.

Brombert, Victor. *La prison romantique: Essai sur l'imaginaire.* Paris: Librairie José Corti, 1975.

Brooks, Peter. *Troubling Confessions: Speaking Guilt in Law and Literature.* Chicago: University of Chicago Press, 2000.

Davies, Ioan. *Writers in Prison.* Oxford, UK: Basil Blackwell, 1990.

Díaz, Hernán. "Figures of Confinement: Literature and Claustrophilia." Diss. New York University, 2007.

Dopico-Black, Georgina. *Perfect Wives, Other Women: Adultery and Inquisition in Early Modern Spain.* Durham, NC: Duke University Press, 2001.

Estrada, Oswaldo. "Revolución de pícaros y beatas coloniales en *Ángeles del abismo* de Enrique Serna." *Revista de Literatura Mexicana Contemporánea* 46 (2010): 27–35.

Foucault, Michel. *Historia de la sexualidad 1: La voluntad de saber.* Trans. Ulises Guiñazú. México, D.F.: Siglo XXI, 1990.

Franco, Jean. *Plotting Women: Gender and Representation in Mexico.* New York: Columbia University Press, 1989.

Gilmore, Leigh. "How We Confess Now: Reading the Abu Ghraib Archive." *Modern Confessional Writing: New Critical Essays.* Ed. Jo Gil. London: Routledge, 2006. 180–91.

Holler, Jacqueline. "The Spiritual and Physical Ecstasies of a Sixteenth-Century Beata: Marina de San Miguel Confesses Before the Mexican Inquisition." *Colonial Lives: Documents on Latin American History, 1550–1850.* Ed. Richard Boyer and Geoffrey Spurling. Oxford: Oxford University Press, 2000. 77–100.

Hutcheon, Linda. *A Poetics of Postmodernism: History, Theory, Fiction.* New York: Routledge, 1988.

Juan-Navarro, Santiago, and Theodore Robert Young. *A Twice-Told Tale: Reinventing the Encounter in Iberian-Iberian American Literature and Film.* Newark: University of Delaware Press, 2001.

Lavrin, Asunción, ed. *Sexuality and Marriage in Colonial Latin America.* Lincoln: University of Nebraska Press, 1989.

Ludmer, Josefina. "Tretas del débil." *La sartén por el mango: Encuentro de escritoras latinoamericanas.* Ed. Patricia Elena González and Eliana Ortega. Río Piedras, Puerto Rico: Huracán, 1984. 47–54.

Martin, Luther H., et al. *Technologies of the Self: A Seminar with Michel Foucault.* London: Tavistock, 1988.

Marturano, Jorge Gustavo. "Vampiros en la Habana: Discursos intelectuales, políticas de la cultura y narrativas de encierro en la república (1934–1958)." Diss. Durham, NC: Duke University Press, 2006.

Mignolo, Walter. "La colonialidad a lo largo y a lo ancho: El hemisferio occidental en el horizonte colonial de la modernidad." *La colonialidad del saber: Eurocentrismo y ciencias sociales; Perspectivas latinoamericanas.* Ed. Edgardo Lander. Buenos Aires: Consejo Latinoamericano de las Ciencias Sociales (CLASCO), 2003. 55–85.

Pimentel, Luz Aurora. *El espacio en la ficción.* México, D.F.: Universidad Nacional Autónoma de México (UNAM); Siglo XXI, 2001.

Quijano, Aníbal. "Colonialidad del poder, cultura y conocimiento en América Latina." *Anuario Mariateguiano* 9 (1997): 113–21.

Serna, Enrique. *Ángeles del abismo.* México, D.F.: Joaquín Mortiz, 2004.

PART THREE

Global and Transatlantic Itineraries

CHAPTER SEVEN

Malinche as Cinderellatl

Sweeping Female Agency in Search of a Global Readership

Irma Cantú

Malinche, from Chingada to Chingona

On November 8, 1519, the first encounter between Spanish conquistador Hernán Cortés and Aztec Emperor Moctezuma occurred, at the confluence of what were the two principal avenues of Tenochtitlán, streets that today are República de El Salvador Street and Pino Suárez Avenue. In the midst of this meeting between the two paradigmatic figures of the Mexican Conquest, a goddess-like woman materializes: doña Marina, "the Tongue," so named by Cortés because she was his translator. This, at least, is the vision of the encounter presented by Fray Bernardino de Sahagún's informants in the *Florentine Codex*. In that work, of the three individuals represented, she is the tallest and located at the center of the image his work projects, between Cortés and Moctezuma.

In contemporary criticism and literature, however, Malintzin is positioned in two major ways: first, as a historical figure in the making, and second, as a potential myth of origin, a protomyth. The limited amount of first-hand information about Malintzin's role is predominantly provided by three sources: the *Florentine Codex* by Sahagún and his informants, the *Cartas de Relación* by Cortés, and the *Historia verdadera de la Conquista de la Nueva España* by Bernal Díaz del Castillo. Comparing all these historical texts to each other, it appears that the indigenous informants had a knowledgeable but distant vision of Malintzin. In contrast, Cortés had the closest relationship but the most silent one: he mentions her by name as doña Marina once in his fifth *Carta*, and in previous *Cartas*, he refers to her as "my tongue," but beyond that, he offers little detail about her. Bernal Díaz's recounting stands out; he provides the most detailed version of her life. Nevertheless, the *Historia verdadera* is seen now as a hyperhybrid text in which history, ethnography, and literature are intertwined; it is more than a historical recount. In fact, it is precisely its lack of historical information that allows for the constant reimagining of Malintzin. She has became a cultural icon of post-Conquest America, and the notion of her has nurtured literature, philosophy, and history, with her personage appearring everywhere from legends to novels to identity theories.

In part because so little historical documentation informs Malintzin's background, her figure became malleable. Thus, every time a major historical change occurs in Mexico, the country's history needs to be retold to conform with a new national agenda, and Malintzin's story is reshaped as a result. In the past two centuries, four major historical events shaped the idea of her as a *vendepatrias*. First, in 1861, the liberal ideologue Ignacio Ramírez categorized Malintzin as a traitor and referred to her as Cortés's *barragana*, a derogatory term equivalent to concubine. According to Monsiváis, this categorization of Malintzin provides a new reading of post-Independence Mexico "porque la inculpación de doña Marina es parte del proceso de desespañolización general, que requiere el proceso contra los aliados indígenas de los conquistadores, trátese de los tlaxcaltecas o Malinche, y porque al centrarse el proceso en una mujer, a la causa política se suman prejuicios de la época" (189). Second, after the Mexican Revolution of 1910, as part of the cultural nationalist project, Malintzin/Malinche would become a noun, *malinchismo*, designating any preference for a foreign idea or product as a type of treason. In 1950, Octavio Paz converted the national soul into a national conscience in his seminal book *El laberinto de la soledad*. In the famous chapter "Los hijos de la Chingada," Malinche became the incarnation of motherhood through rape; therefore her "hijos"—understood as all Mexicans—carry with them the historical consequence of that rape in the form of guiltiness and solitude.

A more recent national effort must be made to reconcile Mexicans and Mexican identity with its colonial past. A case in point is author and critic Margo Glantz's approach, which contradicts Paz's perspective, as shown here by scholar Claudia Leitner:

> Margo Glantz llega a asociarla con el sobrenombre de Malinche, Tenepal—que permite la asociación con "labios fuertes" y "facilidad de palabra"—y le da un fundamento firme arraigándola en el cuerpo

mismo de Malinche. . . . Este cuerpo evidentemente no comparte la
"fatalidad anatómica" de la Malinche/Chingada del *Laberinto,* no está
abierto al gran agresor; este cuerpo posee labios fuertes y una lengua
muy aguda—y podríamos concluir: fálica—para penetrar. *Tales metáfo-*
ras van en contra de las bases epistémicas del Laberinto y su texto precursor, incluso en contra de una tradición más larga de simbolismo sexual
en el mundo occidental. (233, my emphasis)

The evolution shown here from Chingada to Chingona, or from dominated to dominating, was mainly possible due to the contributions from
Chicana writers previous to Glantz that have revitalized Malinche in
reaction to the androcentric Chicano movement of the late 1960s and
1970s. The Plan Espiritual de Aztlán, produced in 1969 as a result of the
first ever Mexican American Congress, was extremely male oriented;
therefore, in 1971, Chicana writers and activists demanded additions
and corrections to the original Plan Espiritual through a manifesto titled
"Chicanas Speak Out" (Vidal). Their demands were never included.
Consequently, Malinche became a paradigmatic figure of the growing
Chicana movement:

> In the ensuing years, Chicana writers often invoked the figure of La
> Malinche as a vital, resonant site through which to respond to andro-
> centric ethno-nationalism and to claim a gendered oppositional iden-
> tity and history. This has involved negotiating complex self-definitions
> with respect to the two forces that defined the cultural and political
> space around them: ethno-nationalism, whose masculine and patriar-
> chal values oppressed them, and Anglo-American feminism, whose white
> and middle class biases erased the class and race dimensions of their
> struggle. (Pratt 861–62)

In that political atmosphere, Malinche as a figure who represents ongoing negotiations of meaning and has contradicted ideologies of resistance
emerges as an emancipatory icon for a women's movement struggling with
gender and national identity in the United States. In the 1980s and 1990s,
the Chicana activists' appropriation of Malinche as a resistive figure nurtured the Mexican national feminist agenda. This new perspective on Malinche is thoroughly developed in *La Malinche, sus padres y sus hijos*
(2001), coordinated by Glantz. This collection offers a nonmisogynistic
approach to Malinche beyond previous nationalistic readings and well-
established patriarchal versions.

With this reconstructive precedent in mind, the analysis of a contemporary novel written by a female Mexican author in which Malinche was the main character is intriguing, and might focus in particular on the ways in which new academic approaches would have been incorporated into a contemporary literary representation. *Malinche* by Laura Esquivel revisits the topic of Malinche as a politically inscribed figure and rewrites it for contemporary readers, looking to influence the broadest spectrum of international readership through a major publishing house. Nevertheless, despite Esquivel's inclusions of strong female characters with certain feminist practices in previous works, her attempt to construct a cultural subject out of the mainstream mythologization ultimately fails in this 2006 novel. Regardless of her objective to invent a less blameworthy Malinche, her novel reveals its major ambition: to become a best seller. After the international success of Esquivel's first novel, *Like Water for Chocolate* (1989), the author acknowledges the required series of strategies to warrant a global readership. The aim of my work is to examine how the strategies for creating a best-selling novel were implemented in *Malinche*, and also to illustrate how, instead of imagining a more historical, less patriarchal-manipulated Malinche, they do not successfully demythologize the figure.

Malinche, Globalizing Narrative Strategies

On April 6, 2006—one week prior to *Malinche's* arrival at bookstores—the author gave an interview to Mónica Mateos-Vega of the Mexican newspaper *La Jornada* titled "*Malinche*, de Laura Esquivel se enfila para ser un éxito editorial." In it, Esquivel clarifies her intent to locate Malinche out of the process of blaming: "¿Por qué el afán de culpar a una sola mujer de un proceso que fue tan complejo?" she wonders. The author does not hold responsible previous patriarchal tendencies in categorizing Malinche, instead assigning blame to the complete obliteration of pre-Columbian cultures, as well as addressing the immense loss of this cosmovision:

> más que la reivindicación de un personaje es la revaloración de todo lo que somos los mexicanos [porque], como nación, tenemos un nudo atorado que tiene que ver con la integración de esa visión del mundo que acepta un orden cósmico. Una parte de la profunda espiritualidad de los pueblos indígenas se basa en ello, en presencias y deidades, donde el agua, el fuego y el aire hablan, nos dicen cosas. Esa creencia absoluta

de formar parte del todo, de estar en la intemporalidad, se contrapone a la visión de la temporalidad que llegó con los españoles. Es la idea del imperio, donde éste no forma parte de nada ni de nadie, sino que todo le pertenece. La tierra deja de ser la madre para convertirse en algo apropiable, expropiable, al igual que el espacio aéreo, las telecomunicaciones, el agua, el petróleo. Todo es parte del imperio, eso lo estamos viviendo. (qtd. in Mateos-Vega)

Esquivel attempts to reframe Malinche in a manner that takes into account her original pre-Columbian culture as the character learns to adapt to a new one. Esquivel's assessment of the colonial Mexican's two contrasting cultural influences or worlds is revealed to be manipulative, as she constructs *Malinche* as a series of rites of passages for her main character, from baptism to womanhood to marriage to death. In the novel, Cronos is the name assigned to the pre-Columbian world, and its relevance and bearing on her life is limited to her first baptism, to fantasies and dreams during her life, and to her death when she recovers her original and "clean" name of Malinalli. Through her second baptism as Marina, she enters "el mundo de Cortés" to perform her predestined historical role. When she is about to be Christianized by the Spaniards, she reflects on her original name:

Curiosamente, fue con [la flor de] malinalli, la fibra de que estaba hecha la manta que Juan Diego portaba el día en que en el año 1531 se le apareció la Virgen de Guadalupe sostenida por la luna, el día doce del doceavo mes y a los doce años de la llegada de Cortés a México. . . . Malinalli estaba tan orgullosa de todos estos conceptos contenidos en el significado de su nombre. (41)

In the vision of Malinche as a Mexican Eve, Esquivel proposes to reverse a common association between Malinche and the Virgin of Guadalupe. This is a move designed to symbolically remove the guilt associated with Malinche since the nineteenth century, but it does not dislodge her from the mythologization that indirectly promotes a dehumanization of female figures, as they are relegated to myths and legends. According to Roger Bartra, this mythologization promotes disdain for all indigenous cultures in favor of nationalistic notions:

Ya en el siglo XIX el aspecto romántico de la relación entre la Malinche y Cortés es visto como el prototipo de la traición, el deshonor y la ilegitimidad: por obra y por gracia de los diversos nacionalismos, Malintzin se convierte en la Chingada Madre, y llega a ser desplazada por otra madre, virginal y casta, la virgen de Guadalupe. Los mestizos fueron convertidos en símbolos de esa sustancia esencial que es, supuestamente, la identidad nacional . . . Este mito nacionalista—racista y excluyente—ha ocultado la gran diversidad étnica de México. (199)

Contrary to her stated purpose—to achieve the "revalorización de todo lo que somos"—Esquivel plays with the same patriarchal and nationalistic elements already well-established in the official version of Mexican history. It seems that questioning history and challenging the reader are not the proper narrative strategies to successfully appeal to a global market. The novel's structure and selected topics of focus make it into a modern fairy tale. According to the author, the Mexican *cronistas'* accounts serve as a dramatic structure and provide the historical facts that frame her novel. One can infer that this dramatic structure derives from Bernal Díaz's *Historia verdadera,* since his text provides the only extant historical information about Malinche's childhood and adolescence.

Recently, Sonia Rose de Fuggle has questioned the labeling of short stories to include those that are found in historical accounts: "[Los episodios] . . . pueden ser vistos por su estructura y su técnica narrativa como cuentos independientes. En la *Historia verdadera* . . . de Bernal Díaz del Castillo nos encontramos con muchos episodios de este tipo" (939). According to this critique, Malinche's story as told by Bernal Díaz in the *Historia verdadera* might be seen as a traditional folktale. The connection between use of archetypical characters in the *novelas de caballería* (a popular literary genre during Bernal Díaz's lifetime), to those found in folk and fairy tales was recognized in early philology and psychology studies as part of a nationalist historical project that commenced with literary Romanticism. In the section of his book dedicated to Malinche as a novelistic character, Oswaldo Estrada underlines Bernal Díaz's skillful management of Malinche as a heroine from a *novela de caballería*: from Bernal Díaz addressing her as "*doña*," to her disdain and celestinesque control over the *alcahueta*, to the biblical-scale pardon she bestows on her mother and brother. Estrada considers that:

El flechazo bernaldino no puede ser más certero para la caracterización de este personaje. . . . Dotándola de un pasado como éste y brindándole un alma cristiana, Bernal construye al personaje que será el brazo derecho e inseparable del protagonista principal, . . . Bernal remata este *cuento* . . . , explicando: "y esto me parece que quiere remedar lo que le acaeció con sus hermanos en Egipto a Josef, que vinieron a su poder con lo del trigo." (96, my emphasis)

This pardon of biblical proportions also functions as an act of *anagnorisis* recognizing her forgotten family, a classic strategy commonly used in folktales.

In Esquivel's novel, the constant mention of Malintzin's original name, Malinalli, instead of the more connotative ones, such as Malinche or doña Marina, locates the narration in a nonhistorical past. *Malinche*'s chapter 1 begins:

Primero fue el viento. Más tarde, como un relámpago, como una lengua de plata en el cielo, fue anunciada en el Valle del Anáhuac la tormenta que lavaría la sangre de la piedra. Fue después del sacrificio que la ciudad se oscureció y se escucharon atronadoras descargas, luego apareció en el cielo una serpiente plateada que se vio con la misma fuerza en muy distintos lugares. Enseguida comenzó a llover de una manera pocas veces vista. Llovió toda la tarde y toda la noche y al día siguiente también. Durante tres días no cesó de llover. (1)

This staging locates the character in a mythological beginning that Mircea Eliade calls the *illud tempus*, or sacred time of origin. A technique commonly used in folktales, the formula "once upon a time" used in fairy tales often indicates this tempus. Taking into account the shared structural foundation of folktale and fairy tale, the commonalities between the genres are numerous and frequently repeated: "In every country people began to make a basic collection of national fairy tales. At once the enormous number of recurrent themes struck everybody. The same theme, in thousands of variations, came up again and again" (Von Franz 5).

Examining the underlying structure and themes from *Malinche* reveals a similar pattern of the following sequence: (1) Malinche is born into a privileged family, and her father is a powerful man, a *tlatoani*; (2) at the death of her father, she loses her position in the family and her mother sells her as a slave; (3) thanks to Cortés—cast as a Prince Charming figure—and due to her gifted "tongue," she is elevated from slavery to the best position for a woman of her time: a mediator between the Conqueror (Cortés) and the Emperor (Moctezuma); (4) at the end of the Conquest, when her skills are no longer urgently needed, she marries Juan Jaramillo, a captain in Cortés's army; and finally, (5) she belongs again to a privileged family. Considering its many parallels to the various versions of the fairy tale *Cinderella*, the two stories' similarity is unmistakable. Certain scenes from the novel even reproduce those from *Cinderella*; for example, when her first Spaniard master Portocarrero asks Malinztin to prepare a fire pit, she faces her task as a ceremonial endeavor, and suddenly her deceased grandmother appears like the fairy godmother interrupting Cinderella's castle chores:

> Para avivarlo aún más tomó el soplador. Encender el fuego era una ceremonia importante. Mallinali recordó con una claridad sorprendente la última vez que había encendido el fuego en compañía de su abuela. . . . Sin previo aviso, una lluvia repentina comenzó a caer. La abuela comenzó a reír y con su risa llenó de música la habitación . . . la abuela le habló a su nieta:—La vida siempre nos ofrece dos posibilidades: el día y la noche, el águila o la serpiente, la construcción o la destrucción, el castigo o el perdón, pero siempre hay una tercera oculta que unifica las dos: descúbrela. (53–54)

Since the late nineteenth century, comparative folk studies have identified similar structures among folktales from different cultures. The recurrent topics they share play well into the agendas of global literary markets because they evoke already accepted patterns of female social conduct into a society that might resemble the one readers inhabit through the novel. This friction reveals one of the common dilemmas of our times: "Today women are caught in a dialectic between the cultural *status quo* and the evolving feminist movement, between a need to preserve values and yet accommodate changing mores, between romantic fantasies and contemporary realities" (Rowe qtd. in Hasse 5a). In the case of *Malinche*, the scale tips to the side of romantic fantasies despite certain attitudes of female empowerment. In historical reality, Malinche's uniqueness comes from knowledge and talent, as pointed out by Estrada:

> Cuando unos recaudadores de impuestos de Moctezuma llegan a Cempoala, esta vez para regañar a los caciques de la región por haber hospedado a los extranjeros sin permiso alguno. Al ver que todos los indios se ponen nerviosos y no saben qué hacer, Cortés "preguntó a doña Marina y a Jerónimo de Aguilar, nuestras lenguas" dice el cronista, "que de qué estaban alborotados los caciques desde que vinieron aquellos indios, y quienes eran" (XLVII, 79). . . . Bernal deja ver que su heroína es quien lleva la batuta como intérprete. La pregunta, aunque dirigida a

ambos, solo recibe una respuesta dentro del texto. De repente, Aguilar queda sin habla, "y la doña Marina, que muy bien lo entendió, le contó [a Cortés] lo que pasaba" (XLVII 79). El entendimiento de Marina es superior al de Aguilar, sugiere Bernal. Ella, como nativa de aquella tierra, no sólo entiende la lengua: conoce, además, al revés y al derecho, cómo funcionan las acciones tributarias, los sacrificios humanos, la sumisión absoluta que deben éste y otros pueblos a Moctezuma. (97)

In Esquivel's novel, Malinche's uniqueness also comes from her devoted love for Cortés, whom she confuses with Quetzalcóatl, later confusing Quetzalcóatl with Jesus Christ. In this sense, her love is not an act of affection, but a gesture of loyalty to the god of her childhood: "A su Quetzalcóatl querido, siempre presente. Su gran protector. Desde la primera vez que la regalaron siendo muy niña, Malinalli aprendió a superar su miedo a lo desconocido apoyándose en lo familiar" (15). Her love for Cortés was at once predestined, original, and familiar. Later on the same page divulging her love for him, we read "que era posible su regreso. Como lo era el del señor Quetzalcóatl. Con la diferencia que el regreso de su padre y su abuela sólo la beneficiarían a ella y el regreso de Quetzalcóatl, por el contrario, modificaría por completo el rumbo de todos los pueblos que los mexicas tenían sojuzgados" (15). According to the novel, Malinche's collaboration with Cortés will contribute to a process of political emancipation of the oppressed. Strangely, she does not perceive herself as part of the oppressed because she is predestined to a glorious future. This is another way in which the novel evades any sort of feminist or protofeminist message.

In fact, when Malinalli suffers in the novel, it is not due to her oppressed condition as a slave, because Esquivel constructs her character such that Malinche's life as a slave is later completely erased—including the moment at which she was given to Cortés as war booty. Her sadness at being treated like chattel is expressed in a just few paragraphs that transition into an introduction to memories of her previous life with her beloved grandmother. For example, when being sold by her mother, Malinche's pain lasts only a day, literally: "La tristeza de ese aciago día se aminoró grandemente cuando en la madrugada, cansada de llorar, al observar las estrellas descubrió entre ellas a la Estrella de la Mañana [Quetzalcóatl]" (23). At that time, another male deity came to Malinche's rescue. Despite Malinche's grandmother's significant role in her childhood, Malinche does not hearken to female Aztec deities such as Coatlicue, only to male ones.

In order to replicate the fairy-tale structure, it is necessary that the novel delete or at least cast a shadow over certain historical passages in favor of romantic scenes and exotic scenarios of the Conquest. Again, Malinche's role as a slave is barely mentioned, though during the time in which the novel takes place, slavery included sexual services as well as household chores and hard labor. According to Bernal Díaz's *Historia verdadera*, Malinche was first given to Indians from Xicalango, then to *tabasqueños*; with the Spaniards, she started serving Alonso Hernández de Puertocarrero, then Cortés, and then she was finally awarded to Cortés's soldier Juan Jaramillo. In *Malinche*, Cortés first notices her in her baptism as Marina before he immediately assigns her to Portocarrero: "Al conocer la decisión de Cortés, el corazón de Malinalli dio un vuelco. . . . Si Cortés . . . le ordenaba servir a ese señor que parecía un respetable tlatoani, era porque había visto en ella algo bueno. Claro que a Malinalli le hubiera encantado quedar bajo el servicio directo de Cortés, el señor principal" (49). Erasing her condition as slave serves a hegemonic agenda, as Jean Franco notes:

> En el siglo XVI, la participación en el centro se sellaba por varios "contratos" que daban a la Malinche carta de inclusión—o sea el bautismo que marca su inclusión en la Iglesia universal, la maternidad que la hace un sujeto legal, madre de Martín que es legitimado por el papa, y el contrato de matrimonio con Jaramillo . . . De allí la Malinche-doña Marina marca la hegemonía que reemplaza a la fuerza, una hegemonía basada en un contrato que funciona a raíz de una violencia previa. La hegemonía tiene que operar *como si* los sujetos aceptaran libremente su posición subalterna. (206)

This erasure operation also applies to sexual services performed by Malinche, which are framed in Esquivel's novel as if they were romantic encounters—in some cases, as if they might not have happened at all. For example, the only service Malinche is written to have performed while owned by Puertocarrero regards her setting a fire, the aforementioned chore she treats as a ceremonial rite. After a certain amount of effort, which she reads as a bad sign, she is able to make the fire. This action immediately transports her mentally to the last moment when she shares a fire ceremony with her grandmother. The presence of her grandmother opens a digression of sacred practices and enigmatic predictions till the end of the chapter: "En ese momento la atmósfera se volvió naranja y un estallido de luz envolvió la mente de esas dos mujeres que parecían encantadas, transformadas y levantadas de la gravedad de la vida para flotar en la ligereza de los sueños" (54). No mention of a sexual interaction with Puertocarrero appears.

In the next chapter, Malinche is suddenly under the direct orders of Cortés, but as readers, we are again not exposed to sexual exploitation. In both cases in which Malinche was pushed into sexual service—with Puertocarrero and with Cortés—purifying acts made by wise ancient Indians take the place of concubinage in the text. Violence, in particular sexual violence, has thus been erased. A feminist reading would see in the series of hand-offs from several Indian *patrones* to one conqueror after another a reaffirmation of the "official" history of Malinche as a barragana, contradicting Esquivel's intention to rewrite the manipulative mythical "Chingada Madre." Instead, Esquivel avoids the topic and strictly complies with the rules of the fairy tale: Malinche, like Cinderella—and her modern-day Mexican soap opera counterparts—waits in a pure and ashen intermezzo until the arrival of Prince Charming. Despite scholarly critique arguing that, "as a parable of rape . . . fairy tales—particularly classic tales like *Cinderella, Sleeping Beauty* and *Snow White*—train women to be rape victims" (Brownmiller 309), the novel makes no attempt to elide or to rewrite this tendency in its treatment of Malinche's sexual enslavement.

Nowadays, the idea of fairy tales as a means to "train women to be rape victims" might sound like radical intellectual posturing, but it was not considered so in 1975, when Brownmiller's *Against Our Will: Men, Women and Rape* was published. In *Malinche*, the relationship between fairy tales and social conditioning for female violation is evident, as Esquivel deals with this topic in a problematic fashion. After the massacre of Cholula, in which Cortés extensively abused his power over the entire Mexican population, Malinche starts feeling uneasy about her relationship with the leader, but being pregnant with his child assuages her guilty thoughts. Later, with little Martín in her arms, her doubts return, and one day she confronts and questions Cortés about his abuses of power. He then belittles her and clearly articulates her subjugated role: "acepta que tu misión es simplemente ser mi lengua" (153). Considering Malinche's views on her two contrasting worlds—"el mundo de Cronos" versus "el mundo de Cortés"—having her "put in her place" like this represents a rejection of all indigenous knowledge and its universal order, and the triumph of the imperialistic European vision whose power over us, according to Esquivel, we are all still enduring. The fairy tale's "happily ever after" ending is not possible because Cortés's European vision cannot accept Malinche's

premonitions about herself and Cortés sharing the predestined mission of becoming the foundational couple of the New World:

> Lo que quiero es que despiertes y que aceptes la oportunidad que te ofrezco de ser una familia, de ser un sólo ser. Te ofrezco el beso de los astros, el abrazo del sol y de la luna. Olvídate de esta idea absurda de ir a conquistar las Hibueras, por favor, Hernán, destierra de tu mente esa locura. . . . Cortés la miró y la vio extraña, estaba conmovido. . . . Esa noche, Cortés bebió hasta embriagarse. Había bebido para huir de sí mismo. . . . Para huir de la verdad. (152–53)

Malinche's feminine ways of voicing her opinions lead Cortés to a night of alcohol. In a fit of rage, he offers her to Juan Jaramillo to be his wife. Jaramillo has been in love with Malinche since the voyeuristic moment he saw her being savagely penetrated by Cortés (77). Out of loyalty to his *capitán*, he has abstained from demonstrating his interest in her, but later, "todos fueron testigos de la boda de Jaramillo y Malinalli. . . . Esa misma improvisada noche de bodas, Jaramillo—para entonces ya embriagado y lleno de deseos—la penetró una y otra vez. Bebió sus pechos, besó su piel, se sumergió en su persona, vació en Malinalli todo su ser y se quedó dormido" (156). Graphic sexual encounters such as this one are episodes intended to spice up the story while letting it maintain its fairy-tale frame; they make the novel more appealing to audiences already familiarized with the telenovela, a very popular genre that, as we have suggested, also employs this fairy-tale structure.

Three pages following Malinche's wedding, after giving birth to María, her daughter with Jaramillo, Malinche remembers "el momento en que Cortés la había casado con él y ya no le parecía un recuerdo amargo. . . . En el fondo de su ser le agradecía enormemente que la hubiera casado con Jaramillo. Era un buen hombre. Respetuoso, amable, valiente, leal" (159). Consistent with *machista* standards and the conventions of the fairy-tale genre, it is not considered possible here for a husband to rape his own wife, in spite of spousal rape and domestic abuse today being widely recognized as crimes in contemporary legal systems in the United States and in Mexico. And even if now a woman enduring these actions might still be interpreted by machistas as a type of mandatory spousal duty, presenting a romanticized version of them and then calling the rapist a respectful, good man does not advance any reasonable feminist agenda. In fact, it confirms Brownmiller's proposal that fairy tales prepare women to be rape victims. Malinche was considered a living goddess by the majority of Indians of her

lifetime: "Doña Marina fue una leyenda viva durante los primeros tiempos, fue una figura inmensamente apreciada por los españoles y los criollos, y desde luego fue adorada como una diosa por los indígenas. Se solía destacar su nobleza, su inteligencia y su belleza" (Bartra 198). However, Esquivel's representation of Malinche does not take into account this Indian vision, nor does it carefully contemplate her repeated sexual violation.

On the contrary, Malinche waits for Cortés to seduce her, and her indigenous vision and knowledge are subsumed by their semiconsensual (at best) sexual encounter. In their first sexual meeting, Malinche explains to Cortés the nature of Quetzalcóatl when he starts softly caressing her and ends up possessing her "salvajemente"—"de la manera en que su miembro empujaba y abría la apretada vagina de la niña. No le importaba que su pasión y fuerza lastimaran a Malinalli. . . . En cada arremetida, Malinalli sentía cómo el torso desnudo y velludo de Cortés rozaba sus pechos y le producía placer" (76). Here, Malinche is not a goddess-like figure, but an innocent child seduced and violated by a kind of sadistic Big Bad Wolf. Malinche is also portrayed as enjoying being raped, which is obviously also very problematic. The sentence "abría la apretada vagina de la niña" evokes a scene of a girl being deflowered. It reinforces conservative values of virginity and perpetuates the valuation of women mainly according to the relative purity of their bodies.

At the end of the "erotic" scene of Cortés's rape of Malinche, the narrator explains her following transformation:

> Malinalli, quien por un momento había dejado de ser "La Lengua" para convertirse en una simple mujer, callada, sin voz, una simple mujer que no cargaba sobre sus hombros la enorme responsabilidad de construir con su saliva la conquista. Una mujer que lejos de lo que podía esperarse, sintió alivio de recuperar su condición de sometimiento, pues le resultaba mucho más familiar la sensación de ser un objeto al servicio de los hombres que ser la creadora de su destino. (76)

In this description, Malinche wants to be an objectified woman, to be used rather than to claim any agency. Her two sexual encounters given in detail in this work—that with Jaramillo and that with Cortés—are described as sexual molestation and rape, respectively. In both cases, Malinche—as a simple woman (read as "any woman")—is victimized, but she is also rewarded in both occurrences: from Jaramillo, she obtains honor; from Cortés, pleasure. In *Malinche*, women are not portrayed as possible holders of responsibility and independence. But it is precisely this brave

woman who constructed the Conquest with her tongue who would stress knowledge and talent as relevant values for women heading to positions of power. It was the real-life Malinche's voice, not her silence, that made her an essential and valuable asset to conquerors.

Curiously, some modern women are still, like the heroin of *Malinche*, unable to achieve independence and self-sufficiency, relying completely on men for subsistence and validation. This phenomenon is actually known in popular psychology as "the Cinderella syndrome," a notion popularized in 1981 by Colette Dawling. Says this critic:

> Women's leanings toward dependence are, for the most part, deeply buried. Dependency is frightening. It makes us anxious because it has its roots in infancy, when we were indeed helpless. We do what we can to hide these needs from ourselves—especially now, with the new, socially encouraged thrust toward independence. But that part, buried and denied, is the troublemaker. It affects the way women think and act and speak—and not just some women, but, to varying degrees, *virtually all women.* (Online source, my emphasis)

By exploiting the anxiety shared by many women regarding their self-definition and self-worth in the absence of a male companion, Esquivel reveals more about struggles of contemporary womanhood than it does about a historical Malinche, whose lover Cortés saw his name changed to Capitán Malinche (a fact expressed in the *Historia verdadera*, but barely mentioned in the novel). Esquivel's main character is an ordinary woman, seemingly unruffled by surrendering all agency, rather than the immense historical figure she represents to many.

To be sure, she is portrayed as everywoman, but also as exotic and even eco-oriented—perhaps to appeal to hip, contemporary readers. Unfortunately, most contemporary authors have not considered an appropriation of Malinche from the indigenous perspective:

> Las fuentes de procedencia indígena son efectivamente las que más atestiguan la importancia de Malintzin: nos presentan escenas dramáticas en la que es Malintzin la que convoca, manda, interroga, reclama, negocia, la que fija medidas y condiciones, la que está en el centro de los discursos dotada de insignias y atributos importantes. Aparentemente, esta pre-potencia contribuye a merecerle estatus divino entre los "naturales" de la tierra: Marina fue "tenida por diosa en grado superlativo," comenta el cronista mestizo Muñoz Camargo. (Leitner 234)

Recognizing the views of these sources would actually advance indigenous and female agendas using historical materials that are available but ignored. Indigenous sources would provide historical muscle to a viable narrative that would strongly resist the imposition of a master narrative.

In Esquivel's *Malinche*, the causes of the author's failure to create a new society out of the encounters of two cultures results from the failure to integrate both culture's visions: that of the indigenous and that of the Spaniard. Unfortunately, the indigenous perspective presented in this novel seems based on capriciously selected, nonhistorical sources: "Ahí hallé una viculación del tema con lo que hago . . . con mi interés por las tradiciones sagradas que busco más allá de los libros y de la información usual" (qtd. in Mateos-Vega). Esquivel derives her information more from contemporary Western spiritual movements, like New Age beliefs, than from actual indigenous historical accounts written by Indians or mestizos. In Esquivel's novel, Malinche tries hard to understand and integrate Cortés as her counterpart in an effort to unify the two cultures in her world: she has been Christianized and speaks the language of the Other. But Cortés is just interested in *encomiendas*, political control, and economic success—and not at all in the indigenous cosmovision and beliefs to which Malinche presents him. After Malinche's submission to all "contratos" (to borrow from Franco's citation earlier in this chapter), she still expects Cortés to emulate her, to execute his portion of their allegedly mutual goal of assimilating each other's cultures. As a result, she is portrayed as an extremely naïve *muchachita* for even thinking such a *mestizaje* could occur.

When Cortés fails to honor Malinche's innocent demands to become a legitimate family, the fairy tale becomes a Mexican soap opera:

> Detén el delirio interminable de tu corazón y bebe de la paz para que cese tu ambición y tu delirio. Eso es lo que quiero y está en tus manos entregármelo.
>
> . . .
> —Vuelve a la razón, Marina. No permitas que tus sentimientos envenenen el sentido de nuestras vidas y acepta que tu misión es simplemente ser mi lengua. (152–53)

At her first baptism, Malinche begins with a predestined mission, but after her second one, her aim ends up intertwined with her emotional needs. Malinalli becomes Marina just so she can be an instrument of a man's greed. Her naïveté leads her to fall in love with the wrong man:

Cortés is not in fact Prince Charming, and he in no way represents or embodies a willingness to participate in a mutual goal of mestizaje. At the end of the novel, a disappointed Malinche realizes that Prince Charming does not exist, a truth that would be readily confirmed by all female readers of this novel. But the fantasy of fairy tales and their princesses expands beyond the novel itself; on the book's flap the author is described thusly in capital letters: "LAURA ESQUIVEL, LA PRINCESA DE LA LITERATURA LATINOAMERICANA, ESTÁ DE REGRESO." Suddenly, the figure of Malinche, woman readers of the novel, and even the author herself form a community of princesses in distress.

Malinche: Globalizing a Literary Product

On February 15, 2006, two months prior to *Malinche*'s arrival in Mexican bookstores, the author gave an interview to Mario Alegre Barrios of the Puerto Rican newspaper *El Nuevo Día* titled "Esquivel redime a la Malinche." In this interview,

> la autora de *Como agua para chocolate*, confiesa que no fue a ella a quien se le ocurrió la idea de escribir una novela sobre quien es conocida popularmente como Malinche. . . . "No se me ocurrió a mí, fue a la editorial," señala la escritora. . . . "Me propusieron escribir la biografía de esta mujer tan singular y me sedujo la oferta" (qtd. in Alegre Barrios)

According to the press, *Malinche* was a novel that was commissioned to be written by the popular author of *Como agua para chocolate*, in part at the urging of her press, as Esquivel was already well aware of her commercial success. Later, Esquivel expressed her intention with Malinche as to build a counter-story[1] to repair the identity fractures in Mexico caused by the Conquest.

> "Si el padre se ha perpetuado como ladrón y asesino, y la madre como una traidora, ¿qué somos entonces los mexicanos? Eso ha perpetuado la visión que todavía cargamos en nuestras espaldas y contra la que tenemos que luchar," explica Laura. . . . "Por eso para mí ha sido tan importante revisar y descubrir a una mujer tan apasionante y maravillosa que no fue lo que la historia oficial le atribuye." (qtd. in Alegre Barrios)

Esquivel apparently aspired to question the official "master narrative"[2] by assigning Malinche a destiny based on indigenous interpretations—the

world of Cronos—and far from the official histories that have categorized her. To accomplish this, Esquivel lays down a mythical beginning for Malinche: from the time of her birth, a suite of cosmic forces mainly convened by her paternal grandmother and by her father during her first baptism provides a point of departure for the novel:

> En ese momento, el padre de Malinalli sintió en su mente una inspiración que no le pertenecía y en lugar de continuar con las tradicionales palabras de bienvenida, su lengua habló con otro canto:
> —Hija mía, vienes del agua, y el agua habla. Vienes del tiempo y estarás en el tiempo y tu palabra estará en el viento y será sembrada en la tierra (6).

If Mexican history has unjustly placed Malinche as a treacherous *vende-patrias*, the premonitions in the novel miraculously erase this official version of her historical role.

Malinche erases Cortés's performance as a conqueror, at least at the beginning. He arrives at La Española in 1504, before departing to Tenochtitlán, and while planning his future (he lacks those indigenous powers of fortune telling), he decides to take a walk barefoot on the beach and a scorpion bites him. For three days, he enters a delirium that includes religious visions of a great serpent (possibly Quetzalcóatl, the mythological serpent of Tenochtitlán's founding) and the Virgin of Guadalupe. Rain pours down as he suffers, and we later read, "Algunos lo dieron por muerto . . . pero cuando llegaron al lugar para darle un santo entierro descubrieron que Cortés había abierto los ojos y se recuperaba milagrosamente. Observaron en él una transformación y se dieron cuenta de que su semblante proyectaba una nueva fuerza, un nuevo poder. Todos lo felicitaron y le dijeron que había nacido de nuevo" (10). Again, in a watery atmosphere—water as a symbolic force of new creation—in 1504 the foundational couple has been born/reborn guilt-free to become the emblematic parents of Mexicans and to honor their historical roles in a cosmic order.

Later in the novel, Malinche and Cortés meet in a church while Malinche is receiving baptism, and their first encounter is described in the following terms:

> Y precisamente en el momento en que con más fervor pedía ayuda [while praying], sus ojos se cruzaron con los de Malinalli y una chispa materna los conectó con un mismo deseo. Malinalli sintió que ese hombre la podía proteger [like a father]; Cortés, que esa mujer podía ayudarlo como sólo una madre puede hacerlo: incondicionalmente. (48)

According to Esquivel's interpretation, it seems that our problem as Mexicans has been that our interpretation of history has been based only on political struggles and nationalistic exigencies (understood as a male Eurocentric knowledge), while ignoring the wisdom of Mother Earth—or indigenous knowledge, as Esquivel presents it. Apparently, Malinche's fractures, read broadly as the fractures within Mexican identity, remain open because official history has obliterated pre-Columbian culture. For that reason, all Mexicans are urged to reconcile Eurocentric knowledge and pre-Columbian knowledge and incorporate them in one single vision. As framed by Cortés's rebirthing experience in La Española, the reader is to understand that restoring cosmic order and venerating mestizo deities that look just like Guadalupe-Tonantzin is the solution to historical wounds caused by imperialist forces.

At the end of the novel, Malinche—lacking her counterpart incarnated in Cortés and unable to achieve her goal of establishing an integrated new world—dies and becomes a holistic, energetic body-spirit-mind-god-living creature:

> Ese día Malinalli, sentada en el cerro del Tepeyac, después de enterrar su pasado, se encontró a sí misma, supo que era dios, supo que era eterna y que iba a morir. . . . Ahí en el centro de la Cruz de Quetzalcóatl, en el centro de la encrucijada de caminos, donde se aparecían las Cihuateteo, las mujeres muertas en el parto que formaban la comitiva que acompañaba a Tlazolteotl, a Coatlicue, a Tonantzin— manifestaciones de una misma deidad femenina—ahí en el centro del universo se volvió líquida. . . . Malinalli, al igual que Quetzalcóatl, al confrontar su lado oscuro, fue conciente de su luz. Su voluntad de ser una con el cosmos, provocó que los límites de su cuerpo desaparecieran. (181–82)

Death is not perceived as a finale, but as a transition: the word "transformación," as well as Malinche's various names, are often used to mark the different passages, or rebirths, in the novel: "Fue un trece, el día que Malinalli nació a la eternidad" (183). Throughout the text, nature, deities, the magic of numbers, and the wisdom of the invisible are presented as signs to be interpreted alongside history—and sometimes despite history.

These quasi-mystic, syncretic allusions are not limited to the microcosmos of the novel; they also appear in the marketing and reception of it. Several times during Esquivel's interview with the newspaper *La Jornada,*

these ideas emerge in the discussion of the book itself, its writing and reception:

> *Malinche*, va en camino de repetir y quizá superar el éxito de *Como agua para chocolate* (1989), *opera prima* de esta autora en el mundo de la narrativa. *"Veo los signos,"* señala [la autora] entusiasmada.
>
> . . .
>
> El deseo de escribir sobre la Malinche, reconoce Esquivel, no surgió de ella: "me hablaron de la editorial y me preguntaron si quería escribir sobre el tema, pues deseaban que una escritora lo abordara. Cuando acepté, *pensé que yo misma la atraje."*
>
> . . .
>
> Ha sido una afortunada coincidencia que se haya publicado en Estados Unidos al mismo tiempo que se están dando las movilizaciones de los migrantes. *Nadie lo planeó.* (Mateos-Vega, my emphasis)

Marketing a fiction book apparently enters into the same sphere as that of ancient, sacred premonitions, a world in which chosen people (writers) are called to perform actions (editorial projects) as a result of attracting positive energies.

According to Esquivel, the *Malinche* project materialized on her desk through forces of nature: "lo atraje." However, the assertion "Nadie lo planeó" is hard to believe, particularly if Esquivel's publishing house, Suma de Letras, belongs to Grupo Santillana, with well-known publishing brands such as Alfaguara, Taurus, and Punto de Lectura, which commercialize their books and distribute them globally. The orientations of Grupo Santillana's various subsidiary presses reveal its well-studied analysis of its markets: Alfaguara specializes in publications by Nobel Prize–winning authors and targets an audience interested in highbrow literature. Suma de Letras is the branch in charge of broadening cultural perspectives while providing entertainment to a less informed reader, with historical fictions such as *Conquistadora* by Esmeralda Santiago and *Me llaman la Tequilera* by Alma Velasco, among many others.

On Suma de Letras's website, under the section "Quiénes somos," the publishing house describes itself thusly: "Suma es una editorial que entiende la lectura como el placer del entretenimiento. En nuestras publicaciones encontrará temas fascinantes, países, épocas y situaciones para ampliar su visión del mundo. . . . En Suma queremos que usted quede atrapado desde las primeras páginas, que una trama apasionante le impida cerrar el libro." Editorial intentions are well established: the press publishes

page-turners that include characters who share certain views and concerns with the audience—New Age approaches, long-lost eco-environments, alternative medicine, cures for the soul, passion and love—exotic scenarios that take place during major historical moments. History provides a frame for cultural awareness—"para ampliar su visión del mundo"—but not necessarily for cultural change.

According to Gabriel Zaid's 2006 article, "La lectura como fracaso del sistema educativo," Mexicans on average read 2.9 books per year. His research, based mainly on the analysis of two national surveys on Mexican readership, suggests that Mexicans read books primarily from their childhood to their young adulthood (six to twenty-two years old), essentially during their school years. Therefore, book reading is not seen by adults as a pleasurable experience, but rather as a sort of assigned homework. They spend 2 percent of their income on cultural products as a whole, but not necessarily on books. Gabriel Zaid and Guillermo Sheridan concluded that Mexicans lied to the pollsters: "Al mexicano (el 99.99 por ciento) no le gusta leer. Es más . . . no le gustan los libros ni siquiera en calidad de cosa, ni para no leerlos ni para nada, vamos, ni para prótesis de la cama que se rompió una pata" (Sheridan). With these devastating data regarding Mexico's low percentages of adult readers, how many recent emigrant Mexicans could be considered the book's potential consumers? The anticipated audience must lie beyond Mexico, in the Mexican diaspora.

As Esquivel was already a best-selling author when she published *Malinche*, she did not need to wait long for her work to appear abroad. Actually, the book's publishing house has two slightly different Spanish editions of the book; one titled *Malinche: Novela* entered the U.S. market one month earlier than it did Mexico's, where it was published as simply *Malinche* in March 2006. *Malinche: A Novel*, translated to English, was also released in the United States in March 2006. Actually, Esquivel's "afortunada coincidencia" applies both to the Spanish *Malinche* and to the English *Malinche: A Novel*, but not to *Malinche: Novela*, the Spanish version for the U.S. market.[3] Considering certain recorded comments by Esquivel on Mexican immigrants and the date of the Spanish book's launch in the United States, one can assume that immigrants would consume the Spanish-language cultural product first. As the Spanish edition entered the U.S. market earlier than it did Mexico's, it seems that the primary intended readership was not one focused on Mexicans living in Mexico. Since the novel is directed at the Spanish-speakers of the United States, many of whom are emigrated Mexican nationals, Mexican Americans are precisely the people who have abandoned Mexico and have been assimilated to the United States—to the northern empire. Is *Malinche*'s author a *malinchista*, seeking to please *agringado* audiences (that is, Mexican American émigrés)?

Within the novel, Esquivel's way to counterattack the imperialistic trend toward gearing one's book toward such audiences is through the inclusion of indigenous beliefs and their cosmic vision. Yet she has had in mind participation in globalized capitalistic book production, following closely its marketing patterns; thus, combining her writing with extraliterary artifacts, she has apparently taken a position well summarized in the following argument:

> Las publicaciones de Esquivel muestran además de *su atracción por la mercadotecnia* y el fetiche literario, experimentando más allá del texto. Sus libros incluyen recetas en *Como agua para chocolate* (1989), o el regalo de un CD en *La ley del amor* (1995). En este sentido, *Malinche* ofrece una posibilidad de continuar con ese interés. . . . En esta línea, Esquivel encarga a su sobrino Jordi Castell la elaboración de un códice que siga la historia de la narración de la novela." (Vivancos 114, my emphasis)

As Vivancos points out, "La novela no defrauda a los que esperan leer más de lo mismo" (114).

And as Esquivel herself notes at the end of her interview with *La Jornada*, *Malinche* was also positioned for ease of translation to a mass-media market:

> Mi agente ha empezado a recibir propuestas [cinematográficas]. . . . Claro, vamos a ver, pues para mí sí es muy importante que [la película] se haga en español y aquí en México, punto. Mi ideal sería que fuera en náhuatl y que la producción viniera de España, para que sea un mestizaje cinematográfico" (qtd. in Mateos-Vega).

Esquivel's ideal project would serve two purposes: to resuscitate an ancient language (Náhuatl), a praiseworthy effort, and to utilize the cinematographic infrastructure and distribution platform of Spain. The result would be a self-consciously conceived mestizo project with dialogues in Náhuatl as markers of cultural authenticity (like the Aramaic used in Mel Gibson's *The Passion of the Christ*) that would please the majority of consumers in the international market. The mere mention of a hypothetical film shows the author advancing an outwardly indigenous agenda, but with close management of its marketing. The same applies regarding the novel's ostensible feminist approaches. Literary critic Ryan Long considers Esquivel's construction of female characters to be problematic: "Certainly Esquivel's feminism balances precariously between embracing patriarchy and resisting it" (203). For Esquivel, it is convenient to include certain feminist practices, but not too feminist and not too indigenous.

This precariousness comes from the necessity for the book to satisfy a global market. When Malinche is about to die in the novel, she walks to the Cerro del Tepeyac in search of the Aztec goddess Tonantzin (years later, El Tepeyac will be the site for the apparition of the Virgin of Guadalupe) and prays:

> A ti, madrecita, te pido que seas su reflejo, para que al verte, se sientan orgullosos [the sons of Malinche]. Ellos, que no pertenecen a mi mundo ni al de los españoles. Ellos, que son la mezcla de todas las sangres—la ibérica, la africana, la romana, la goda, la sangre indígena y la sangre del medio oriente—ellos, que junto con todos los que están naciendo, son el verdadero recipiente de Cristo-Quetzalcóatl. (179)

This inclusive idea of Tonantzin/Guadalupe alludes to a contemporary public already familiarized with the Virgin of Guadalupe either as a Catholic figure or as a national emblem, and it also sanctions the idea of the mestizo as the essential Mexican identity. A more committed agenda—be it indigenous or feminist—might discourage potential readers that belong to the Mexican book-buying elite or to the Mexican American middle class. Both groups would prefer a more gradual historical change of vision that does not compromise the status quo. And Esquivel takes into account the need to neither change nor upset these groups by writing a thoroughly unchallenging book.

When Suma de Letras refers to "temas fascinantes, países, épocas," it is alluding to faraway lands and times, and capitalizing on a certain nostalgia for modern readers in search of an authenticity that is located in the recognizable past. Tzevan Todorov, in his chapter "The Journey and Its Narratives," affirms that "the narrator must be different from us, but not *too* different, not, in any case, as different as the people who are the subject of his narrative" (*Morals* 69, my emphasis). While Todorov here refers to travel-writing narrators, a similar notion of the "not *too* different" is present in the globally marketed *Malinche*; Mexico is not a foreign land for its intended readers, but its colonial epoch *is*. The U.S.-printed *Malinche: Novela* opens with a note from the author to clarify the inclusion of a codex: "Es la forma en que intento conciliar dos visiones, dos formas de narrar—la escrita y la simbólica—dos respiraciones, dos anhelos, dos tiempos, dos corazones en uno" (viii). And Vivancos adds: "Está claro que Esquivel aquí está en su papel de traductora del códice a la tradición literaria y la cultura popular de nuestro mundo contemporáneo de telenovela y entretenimiento" (123). Esquivel's aim is to bring this historical period closer to the reader, but not so close that it would lose its exoticism, because production of difference provides comfort to the reader uninformed about Mexico's colonial past.

Moreover, in the Mexican edition of the book, the "note from the author" does not appear; it would seem that reconciling Mexicans with Malinche is somehow not necessary or convenient. In 2009, the newspaper *Reforma* made a survey about reading habits in Mexico, and books whose topics related to history were the number-one preference. It seems obvious that in 2006, Esquivel's editors knew this information: by omitting the word "novel" from the book's Mexican title, leaving out the "author's notes," and including a bibliography with historical titles at the end of the book, the press made the novel appear more national and historical, and less a work of fiction—likely to appeal to an audience seeking a "historical" reading experience.

Nowadays, historical fiction is one of the most popular literary genres because it has the potential to combine page-turners with serious topics associated with important political figures. At the same time, it provides a sense of authenticity that appeals to a reader unaware of the crisis of the archives or the difficulties of historiography in academic circles. Unfortunately, *Malinche's* readers will prolong the mythologization of Malinche— and as a result, the misunderstanding of "who we are" as Mexicans. Clearly, Mexican identity repair requires a titanic cultural effort, and it is naïve to expect a change from a single book, but Esquivel's *Malinche* does not join forces with the Mexican female intellectuals who are producing texts in this vein. Until now, this effort has remained almost completely in the academic world, untranslated into any form of literary representation in Mexican literature, whether popular or not.

Notes

1. From Hilde Lindemann Nelson's *Damaged Identities, Narrative Repair*, I am including the definitions of certain terms, such as *counter-story*, "a story that resists an oppressive identity and attempts to replace it with one that commands respect" (6). "Narrative repair" involves a collection of counter-stories that reclaims moral agency.

2. I also borrowed the term "master narrative" from Hilde Lindemann Nelson, who defines master narratives as "the stories found lying about in our culture that serve as summaries of socially shared understandings. Master narratives are often archetypical, consisting of stock plots and readily recognizable character types, and we use them not only to make sense of our experience but also to justify what we do" (6).

3. Vivancos Pérez's article provides a remarkable mapping of the different editions of Laura Esquivel's *Malinche*.

Works Cited

Alegre Barrios, Mario. "Esquivel redime a la Malinche." *El Nuevo Día*, February 15, 2006. http://www.ciudadseva.com/obra/2006/02/15feb06/15feb06.htm. Accessed March 31, 2013.

Bartra, Roger. "Los hijos de la Malinche." *La Malinche, sus padres y sus hijos*. Ed. Margo Glantz. México, D.F.: Taurus, 2001. 195–99.

Brownmiller, Susan. *Against Our Will: Men, Women and Rape*. New York: Simon & Schuster, 1975.

Díaz del Castillo, Bernal. *Historia verdadera de la conquista de la Nueva España*. 1632. Ed. Joaquín Ramírez Cabañas. México, D.F.: Porrúa, 2007.

Dowling, Colette. "The Cinderella Syndrome." *The New York Times*, March 22, 1981. http://www.nytimes.com/1981/03/22/magazine/the-cinderella-syndrome.html. Accessed March 31, 2013.

Eliade, Mircea. *The Sacred and the Profane: The Nature of Religion*. 1957. Trans. Willard Trask. Orlando: Harcourt Brace Jovanovich, 1987.

Esquivel, Laura. *Malinche*. New York: Atria Books, 2006.

Estrada, Oswaldo. *La imaginación novelesca: Bernal Díaz entre géneros y épocas*. Madrid: Iberoamericana/Vervuert, 2009.

Franco, Jean. "La Malinche y el Primer Mundo." *La Malinche, sus padres y sus hijos*. Ed. Margo Glantz. México, D.F.: Taurus, 2001. 219–46.

Glantz, Margo, ed. *La Malinche, sus padres y sus hijos*. México, D.F.: Taurus, 2001.

Hasse, Donald. "Feminist Fairy-Tale Scholarship." *Fairy Tales and Feminism: New Approaches*. Ed. Donald Hasse. Detroit: Wayne State University Press, 2004. 4–37.

Leitner, Claudia. "El complejo de la Malinche." *La Malinche, sus padres y sus hijos*. Ed. Margo Glantz. México, D.F.: Taurus, 2001. 219–46.

Lindemann Nelson, Hilde. *Damaged Identities, Narrative Repair*. Ithaca, NY: Cornell University Press, 2001.

Long, Ryan F. "Esquivel's Malinalli: Refusing the Last Word on La Malinche." *Laura Esquivel's Mexican Fictions*. Ed. Elizabeth Moore Willingham. Brighton: Sussex, 2010. 197–207.

Mateos-Vega, Mónica. "*Malinche*, de Laura Esquivel se perfila para ser un éxito editorial." *La Jornada*, April 6, 2006. http://www.jornada.unam.mx/2006/04/06/index.php?section=cultura&article=a04n1cul. Accessed March 31, 2013.

Monsiváis, Carlos. "La Malinche y el malinchismo." *La Malinche, sus padres y sus hijos*. Ed. Margo Glantz. México, D.F.: Taurus, 2001. 183–93.

Pratt, Mary Louise. "'Yo Soy La Malinche': Chicana Writers and the Poetics of Ethnonationalism." *Callaloo* 16.4 (1993): 859–73.

"Quiénes somos." Sumadeletras.com. http://www.sumadeletras.com/mx/quienes-somos/. Accessed February 18, 2013.

Rose de Fuggle, Sonia. "Bernal Díaz del Castillo cuentista: La historia de doña Marina." *Actas del X Congreso de la Asociación Internacional de Hispanistas.* Ed. Antonio Vilanova. Barcelona: Promociones y Publicaciones Universitarias, 1992. 939–46.

Sheridan, Guillermo. "La lectura en México 1." *Letras libres* 100 (2007): n. pag. http://letraslibres.com/revista/columnas/la-lectura-en-mexico1. Accessed February 20, 2013.

Todorov, Tzvetan. *The Morals of History.* Trans. Alyson Waters. Minneapolis: University of Minnesota Press, 1995.

Vidal, Mirta. *Women, New Voice of La Raza: Chicanas Speak Out.* New York: Pathfinder, 1971.

Vivancos Pérez, Ricardo F. "Feminismo, traducción y traición en *Malinche* de Laura Esquivel." *Mexican Studies/Estudios Mexicanos* 26.1 (2010): 111–27.

Von Franz, Marie-Louise. *The Interpretation of Fairy Tales.* Boston: Shambhala, 1996.

Zaid, Gabriel. "La lectura como fracaso educativo." *Letras libres* 95 (2006): n. pag. http://www.letraslibres.com/revista/convivio/la-lectura-como-fracaso-del-sistema-educativo. Accessed February 24, 2013.

CHAPTER EIGHT

Transatlantic Revisions of the Conquest in Inma Chacón's La princesa india

Cristina Carrasco

Estas brujas no deberían haber subido al barco.
Después de lo que nos costó librarnos de los moros
y expulsar a los judíos, ahora nosotros llevamos
a estas malditas indias con sus mestizos a cuestas.
Si estuviera en mis manos, ni uno solo entraría en Sevilla.
—LA PRINCESA INDIA (122)

Among the many recent fictionalizations of Mexico's conquest, little has been presented from the point of view of the colonized subject. Although a few notable exceptions to this tendency stand out—such as Carlos Fuentes's *El naranjo* (1993), Ignacio Solares's *Nen, la inútil* (1995), and Carmen Boullosa's *Duerme* (1994)—as literary critic Kimberle López observes, the majority of novels by Latin American authors treating the Conquest produced around the 1992 quincentenary of the Americas portray the conquistadors' point of view, even those that attempt to demystify or distort the conquistadors' original imperialist perspective (4). In Spain, by comparison, very few contemporary novels about the colonization of Mexico (whether from the point of view of the conquered or the conquering) have been published at all, though these few included Arturo Pérez Reverte's *Ojos azules* (2009), José María Merino's *Las crónicas mestizas* (1992), and Matilde Asensi's bestseller *La conjura de Cortés* (2012).[1]

Within this somewhat limited oeuvre one finds Spanish author Inma Chacón's first novel, *La princesa india* (2006),[2] which narrates the journey of an Aztec princess, Ehecatl, who, by traveling to Spain from Mexico, real-

izes that the oppression of the Aztecs in Tenochtitlán mirrors the marginalization of the Jews and Muslims in the Iberian Peninsula. As is well known,
the Catholic monarchs, Fernando and Isabel, used Christianization as an
imperialist tool to conclude the Reconquista of the Iberian Peninsula,
which ended with the expulsion of the Jews in 1492 and was followed by
the colonization of the Americas (Rings 43).[3] The Spanish soldiers and religious who participated in the Reconquista arrived to the Americas with the
idea of conquest culturally present, originating, as Jean Franco points out,
from a society "preoccupied with purity of blood. Having 'cleansed' itself
by expelling the Jews as it would later expel the Moors, Spain found itself
faced with the vast problem of the subjection and conversion of the racially
heterogeneous New World" (xiii). In her novel, Chacón breaks with both
other Spanish novels on Mexico's Conquest as well as with Latin American
fictions, exploring more fully the colonial-era transatlantic obsession with
purity of blood from the Spanish perspective. The novel illustrates how this
Iberian desire was transplanted onto new groups in the Mexican colonial
context, and considers how the indigenous Other could have perceived
of the parallel repression of marginal groups in Spain.

In this chapter, I analyze how *La princesa india* portrays a type of reverse
discovery of the Americas, modeling this fictional inversion through the
geographical and cultural displacement of the protagonist. In *La princesa
india*, it is not the Spanish conquistador who experiences a New World,[4] but
rather the Mexican indigenous woman, a figure who has more often than
not been relegated to a marginal, and silenced, historical space. In the
course of this reversal, the land that Ehecatl discovers is not Tenochtitlán,
but rather a narrow-minded and domineering Extremadura where Jews and
Muslims are treated like the indigenous people in the colonies. The novel
delves into and changes perspective on the obsession with blood purity, and
accompanying demand for Christian expansion, that extended from the
Old World to the New, as seen from the eyes of a conquered native Mexican
inhabitant. In sum, Chacón's novel presents us with what Fernando Aínsa
terms a "revisión crítica de los mitos constitutivos de la nacionalidad" (28),
particularly as the idea of blood purity continues to be problematized in
contemporary Spanish and Mexican national-identity discourses.[5]

Reading the character of Ehecatl in the context of other female archetypes present in Mexican literature, it seems that although the indigenous
protagonist was constructed to demonstrate female agency, her portrayal
unintentionally perpetuates a colonized female archetype. Renowned critics such as the late Luis Leal have confirmed that women in Mexican literature tend to be portrayed either as virgins or as the violated Malinche

(227), whether through myths or as literary icons. Emily Hind agrees with this idea, arguing that the Mexican archetypes of Malinche, the Virgin of Guadalupe, and Sor Juana have continued to flourish in the last decades of the twentieth century (27). Certainly, through their fictions, some female authors—such as Elena Garro and Carmen Boullosa—have rescued relatively more authentic voices of indigenous women that were excluded from official histories (Seydel 22), but their writings are more the exceptions that prove the general rule. In Ehecatl, Chacón rearticulates the Malinche archetype studied by numerous Mexican and Chicana critics, but she does so from a detached, almost voyeuristic angle, consistent with past Spanish fictional reimaginings of figures and events of the Conquest. This author, as we will see, portrays an indigenous Mexican woman who vaguely reminds us of Cortés's lover, the mother of the first mestizo, but Chacón's character is unfortunately a romanticized and exoticized model similar to the protagonist of Laura Esquivel's best seller *Malinche* (2006).

Inma Chacón wrote *La princesa india* in order to fulfill the wishes of her late twin sister Dulce Chacón. Dulce, a popular contemporary Spanish fiction author, wrote many other works—*La voz dormida* (2002) and *Cielos de barro* (2000), among others—that frequently centered on marginalized groups whose voices were not part of Spanish history under Franco. Before Dulce's sudden death in 2003, she had been researching information for more than ten years in order to write a novel about an Aztec princess.

When her sister passed away, Inma Chacón undertook both the project and her sister's narrative thrust, writing a novel that tells the story of a subjugated group from the other side of the Atlantic. In an interview with the Spanish newspaper *El País*, Inma Chacón said of the novel:

> He pretendido contar la conquista de los conquistados. La novela arranca antes de que los españoles arrasaran con la cultura y los credos de aquel pueblo libre. He querido hablar también de los contrastes; de lo que ella se encuentra en España. La princesa llega, con su cultura indígena, a un mundo en el que se le imponía cómo debía vestir o en qué debía creer. Era el mundo de las imposiciones donde la Inquisición mandaba y el miedo marcaba el orden. (Aguilar)

I am particularly interested in how Chacón privileges the Aztec woman's gaze in an attempt to empower a liminal discourse, to voice a peripheral perspective that continues to be neglected in Spanish literature (as well as in Mexican fiction). In the majority of historical accounts of the Conquest, or even in the more recent historical novels that recreate this particular period, we do not usually hear the indigenous woman as we do in Chacón's novel. Although in *The Broken Spears* (1959), Miguel León-Portilla brilliantly writes one of the few historical accounts of the Conquest from the perspective of the indigenous peoples of Mexico, the Aztec woman's point of view continues to be absent. Chacón's novel, then, is an attempt to fill that gap, even if—as I have stated before—the end product is problematic.

La princesa india is divided into two parts. In the first, the author takes us back and forth in time and space, introducing us to its characters and historical context. It starts with the boat trip that Ehecatl (whose name means "wind" in Nahuatl) takes with her husband don Lorenzo—one of Cortés's soldiers—on her way to Spain, after the Conquest. Through various temporal jumps interspersed with the main narrative, an omniscient narrator informs us about the arrival of Spanish colonizers to Mexico in the sixteenth century, providing a historical background for Ehecatl's present situation. This seemingly disorganized—or even unstructured—narrative timeline in the first part of the novel symbolizes the holes that need to be filled when rethinking coloniality in the Americas. Not for nothing does the novel start with Ehecatl's travel to Spain: the Atlantic Ocean is projected as a liminal space that belongs neither to Spain nor to Mexico, and it is as such the most satisfactory environment in which to recreate the history of the Conquest and Spanish colonization of Mexico. Starting out in this neutral zone of the ocean, the Indian princess begins a discovery of her own.

In this first part of the novel, we also learn essential characteristics about the main characters' past and roots: for example, Ehecatl has magical powers, and don Lorenzo's mother, Arabella, was a Moor. We learn that Arabella suffered all her life the rejection from a society that treated her like dirt even after she died: "Se trata de una mora. . . . No puede enterrarse como una cristiana"(36), argues Arabella's stepson don Manuel before her burial; a priori, then, don Lorenzo shares a marginal positionality with his Aztec wife, a facet further developed later in the novel.

In contrast, the second part of the novel is organized linearly and takes place in Zafra, Extremadura, don Lorenzo's native land. Upon her arrival to the Iberian Peninsula, doña Aurora, as Ehecatl is called by the Spaniards, is chased by a merchant who wants to accuse her of witchcraft before the Inquisition because "no sería la primera vez que fijara sus garras en los que vuelven casados con indias" (138). This second part of the novel becomes a diversity of voices, a true heteroglossia, a multiplicity of marginal discourses and points of view that revisit the parallelism between the Spanish Inquisition and the colonization of the Americas. The constant shift from Spain to Mexico through the stories of Muslims, Jews, and various indigenous women mark out similarities in the oppression suffered by these communities over centuries of oppression.

In the first part of the novel, the above-mentioned constant spatial and time inversions immediately grab our attention, as the omniscient narrator travels back and forth from the Aztec empire to Inquisitorial Spain. Both the geographical and temporal destabilizations are characteristic of the new historical novel, of which Ignacio Corona observes that "el manejo mucho menos restringido del tiempo (en un sentido cronológico o histórico) o de los tiempos (históricos y narrativos), en un cuadro maestro de discontinuidades y simultaneismos, convierte a la novela histórica en un discurso con un mayor grado de flexibilidad narrativa" (Corona 93). These inversions rewrite history in alternative ways so as to fill obvious gaps in various historiographical discourses (Barrientos 14). In *La princesa india*, such movements are the textual mechanisms that allow the reader to see the origins of the conquering mentalities experienced firsthand by Ehecatl and to understand the linkages between Spain and the Mexican *colonia*. In Chacón's novel, this chronotropic/chronological play causes the site of oppression to unfold in reverse chronological order: that is, the reader is first exposed to the oppression suffered by the Indians, and is later introduced to that experienced by the Jewish and Moorish women, all of the oppression stemming from the same source.

In the first part of *La princesa india*, the religious discrimination toward the indigenous people of Technotitlán becomes evident when "los nuevos dioses destruyeron el adoratorio. En el mismo lugar, comenzaron a construir uno más pequeño, donde obligaron a todo el pueblo a participar en sus ceremonias sagradas" (57). Later, upon her arrival to Zafra, Ehecatl/doña Aurora is forced to experience an oppressive environment in which blood purity defines one's right to live. As Walter Mignolo points out, the racial formation of the modern and/or colonial world is caused, in part, by shifting various markers of oppression, and even though blood purity is defined "as the absence of Jewish and heretical antecedents" (Martínez 8), this novel shows that this concept is not used exclusively against converted Jews and Muslims, but also against indigenous peoples of the Americas. If, during the Reconquista, the marker of religious belief (whether one was a Jew, a Moor, a *converso*, or a Morisco) was the justification for oppression, then during colonial times, blood purity became the biological and "natural" marker (whether one was an Indian, a black, a mestizo, or a mulatto) (Mignolo 86). Although in most Mexican new historical novels, the referential space is Mexico, Chacón works back from that space and takes us instead to the Iberian Peninsula to show the rigid society in which the Spanish fomented their colonization agenda.[6] In moving from Mexico to Spain, and from the periphery to the center, the evolving question of who, precisely, the Other is, in the scheme of Mexico's colonization, also begins to emerge.

From the very beginning of the novel, we see the subversion of the Othering gaze, first and foremost through Ehecatl's accounts of the Spanish colonizers and their rituals. By placing the actions of the Spanish under Ehecatl's observation, Chacón creates an alternative historical memory such as that found in Mexican novels like Elena Garro's *Los recuerdos del porvenir*, Rosa Beltrán's *La corte de los ilusos*, and the aforementioned *Duerme* by Carmen Boullosa. Ute Seydel well summarizes the idea of this type of memory:

> Las escritoras construyen personajes femeninos que se solidarizan con los marginados, así como con las minorías étnicas y sociales, reivindican el papel del sujeto femenino en los procesos históricos de México para atenuar la invisibilidad de las mujeres en ellos y rescatan las memorias alternativas, entre ellas, las de mujeres, indígenas y otros grupos que quedaron relegados a los márgenes del espacio de la nación y, salvo algunas excepciones, están ausentes del espacio de la memoria. (22)

As Seymour Menton noted of the new Latin American historical novel, usually the writer demystifies a historical character (Menton 22), an observation reflected in the many canonical representations that choose nonindigenous women to rethink history. Chacón's decision to make indigenous women, rather than Cortés and his men (including Ehecatl's husband don Lorenzo), the main characters of the novel changes the interpretive historical framework, privileging the indigenous female perspective over that of the more typical male gaze.

Different types of Othering are also fictionalized in *La princesa india*. In the second half of the novel, Ehecatl and other Aztec individuals are conflated with a more familiar Other (from a sixteenth-century Spanish perspective: the converted Jews or Moriscos). For example, one of the sailors on the ship Ehecatl sails on to Spain says of her and her companions: "¡Estas indias son unas herejes! ¡Están enseñando sus rezos a los niños! Habría que hacer algo. Si estuviéramos en tierra, las denunciaría. Seguro que no cantaban cuando ardieran en la hoguera" (112). In this case, we see an incidence of how the Other's difference was constructed by the Spanish under a set of predetermined ideas. According to Edward Said (96), the

Other is always a mirror image of what is inferior and/or alien in comparison to one's own culture, and this particular example demonstrates how this was the case with the Spanish colonizing gaze in Mexico.

In the same way that Bernal Díaz del Castillo compared Tenochtitlán to Seville or Venice in his *Historia verdadera*, "[prefiriendo] relatar lo desconocido y lo extremo desde su experiencia diaria de los mismos" (Gilman 111), Cortés's soldiers in Chacón's novel compare the Aztec women they encounter to the Jews or Muslims with whom they are familiar. Juan de los Santos, the soldier who marries Ehecatl's slave Valvanera, contemplates his wife and remarks that "le llamó la atención el color de su piel, apenas parecía una india sino una mora nacida de un cristiano" (143). For the Spanish soldier, the only way to describe the Other is through a comparison that reveals the Spanish invaders' racism and xenophobia, minimizing both the individual and the idea to which she is compared.

Given the Otherizing on the part of the Spanish that characterizes their view of the indigenous peoples in this novel, it is unsurprising (and tragic) that Ehecatl and Valvanera are erased as individuals by the Spanish colonizers as soon as they leave their homeland, and that they face constant racism even from the sailors at the bottom of the social ladder. They are called "¡Indias! Como si las letras ardieran en su boca; como si la rabia le obligara a expulsarlas una a una; como si no fueran letras, sino ácido que escuece en el estómago; como dardos" (53). Ehecatl and Valvanera not only have to face these insults, which categorically refer to them as a collective and marginal Other, they also lose their individual identities through their renaming with "Christian" names.

This homogenization was a common de-Otherizing practice on the part of the Spaniards, as we can see from the first colonial documents. However, Chacón does not take the process of renaming for granted and uses it as a tool to deconstruct the rhetoric of Empire (as portrayed in the works of Hernán Cortés and other *cronistas de Indias*). When reflecting on her new name, Ehecatl does not accept it as a natural imposition:

> Muchas veces quiso gritar que los indios tenían un nombre, un nombre que les dieron al nacer y formaba parte de su destino. Un nombre que les robaron sin saber la razón, arrastrado por el agua que derramaron sobre sus cabezas, inclinados, entregados a los dioses que vinieron del mar para salvarles de un tirano. Su nombre. Cada uno tenía su propio nombre. Como lo tuvo ella. Ehecatl. Como el que intentó conservar cuando se lo arrebataron. (54)

Thanks to the ingenious inversion of a traditional point of view of Spanish colonizing via renaming, a characteristic common to many contemporary rearticulations of history (Aínsa 100), although the indigenous subject is deprived of her identity, we are presented her story through the eyes of the colonized and therefore come to understand it differently. Chacón continues to invert this process in other manners as well, Otherizing the Spaniards using the same process that the Spaniards employed to Otherize indigenous Americans, such as when Ehecatl, in referring to the arriving Spanish conquistadors, alludes to the legend of the Spanish being the sons of the Aztec sun-god: "Vienen del mar. Son tan altos como los techos. Todo su cuerpo está cubierto de hierro, solamente aparecen sus caras con largas barbas. Son blancos como de cal" (41). In this case, in parallel to the Spanish preconceptions of the native tribes, which are applied to the Other regardless of their appropriateness or relevance, Ehecatl and the Aztec people also imagine the Other through predetermined paradigms.

Pressing the Otherizing pattern further, and questioning the validity of the assumptions that lie at the heart of such Otherizing, Chacón shows "civilized" Spanish cultural practices as ridiculous and backward—indeed, more "savage" than those of the archetypal Aztec, their hygiene being a case in point. The Spanish foreigners brought with them plagues and illnesses that resulted in "que los enfermos se multiplicaban cada día, algunos morían entre el picor y las quemaduras con que se les llenaban los cuerpos" (106). In contrast, Ehecatl's description of Moctezuma indicates that "Se bañaba tres veces al día" (103). If some colonial chronicles describe the indigenous peoples as barbarians,[7] *La princesa india* subverts the description by using the indigenous woman's gaze to apply those same ideas of barbarism, illogic, and bizarreness to Spanish practices and behaviors.

From the novel's first page, Ehecatl describes the Spaniards and their world in these very terms, opening the novel with her commentary on the absurdity of Spanish-style clothing: "¡Malditos botones! ¡Con lo fáciles que son nuestros lazos! Si esto es una muestra de lo que vamos a encontrar en el nuevo mundo, nos espera un infierno" (1). Her cultural critique of tedious Spanish sartorial practices is emblematic of a more encompassing shock to come: on arriving in Seville, Ehecatl and Valvanera are patently horrified by the Catholic religion and its symbols. On witnessing the Holy Week processions, Ehecatl/doña Aurora interprets the images of Catholicism presented there as a terrifying spectacle: "Doña Aurora escondió su miedo contra el pecho de su esposo y señaló la ventana sin mirarla. Los hombres encapuchados avanzaban hacia el otro lado del río, golpeándose la espalda con manojos de cuerdas terminados en ruedas pequeñas" (171).

When Ehecatl sees the Virgin Mary, she is reminded of "las madres de todos los que murieron a manos de los que pretendían salvarles de los sacrificios sagrados y del fuego del infierno" (172). The savageness that the Spaniards see in the Aztecs when they arrive to Mexico, as represented in the *crónicas*, is reproduced and inverted in Ehecatl's observations of the Spaniards and their Catholic practices in Spain. *La princesa india* overturns the trope of the indigenous savage by conceiving of the Spanish Other as a savage arising from an underdeveloped society, in keeping with Fernando Aínsa's observation that new historical novels often make a historiographical critique through parody, pastiche and, as in the case of the description of the Semana Santa procession, the development of the grotesque.

Throughout the second part of the novel, we continue to see through the indigenous woman's perspective and discover through it shockingly narrow Spanish social and religious practices. Spain, through Ehecatl's eyes, is an oppressive world where religious blood purity determines who is and who is not part of the status quo, who is and who is not the Other. In Spain, she realizes that those who call themselves "cristianos viejos," and marginalize or critique others also are themselves impure of blood. From the perspective of an indigenous woman, Ehecatl is able to articulate the absurdity of the colonizer inflicting the identity of the Other on anyone. While her husband don Lorenzo intends to "lograr el respeto de los que algún día tendrían que olvidar el color de su piel" (39), the indigenous women (Ehecatl and Valvanera) feel proud of their indigenous roots and reject Otherizing homogenization: "La princesa se tranquilizó y bromeó con Valvanera. Habría que vigilar hasta dónde se aclaraban, podría ser que se volvieran blancos y llegaran a tener el pelo dorado como Diamantina" (185). As the novel advances, Spain's obsession with blood purity is shown to be a fallacious and absurd practice, especially since the merchant who later accuses Ehecatl of witchcraft is himself "impure," guilty of the practice of bigamy. At the end of the novel, don Lorenzo confronts the merchant and threatens to take him to the Inquisition court, showing the accuser papers demonstrating that "os casasteis teniendo mujer viva, fingiendo y probando falsamente que había muerto. Y que la acusasteis ante el Santo Oficio cuando la segunda descubrió el engaño. Y que murió inocente, como habría muerto la segunda si hubiera contado lo que sabía" (287). *La princesa india* thus shows different states of Otherness on both sides of the Atlantic and illustrates clearly the absurdity of an "unpolluted" Christian Spain that would determine the "purity" or "savageness" of others.

Ultimately, while most characters in the novel are Otherized in one way or another, women suffer the most from the consequences of this Othering. In spite of the fact that Chacón gives agency to indigenous women and allows them to perform Othering through Ehecatl, women more generally in the novel continue to suffer marginalization inflicted on them for a variety of reasons, principally simply for being women, as well as for participating in "nonstandard" (i.e., non-Catholic) religions. Although the new historical novel often seeks to assert "las diferencias de la historiografía tradicional dando voz a lo que la historia ha negado, silenciado o perseguido" (Aínsa 26), many times, by allowing marginalized characters to surpass or circumvent particular historical conditions, in *La princesa india*, the female characters are not accorded any true authority or social centrality. While Ehecatl and Valvanera are marginalized for their indigenous roots, for being women, and for their religious practices, the Jewish and Moorish women on the Iberian peninsula are also diminished by virtue of their femaleness and their religion. Throughout the novel, these Otherized women are frequently homogenized. Juan de los Santos, for instance, looking at his native wife, exclaims, "El tono de su piel se parecía cada vez más al de las gitanillas y las moriscas" (280). Throughout the novel, the hegemonic representation of the oppressed subject becomes allegorical, since the subaltern appears as a synecdoche of a supposedly homogeneous community (Ballesteros 9). In *La princesa india*, the most marginalized characters fit within both categories. They are women as well as indigenous, Jewish, or Muslim.

Ehecatl's view of the diverse marginality present in Spain, which was enforced by the Spanish Inquisition (an entity, according to Jean Franco, that was "at first mainly concerned with Jews, Protestants, and the occasional Muslim though it also concerned itself with cases of bigamy, witchcraft, obscene and seditious literature" [58]), has the effect of inverting Ehecatl's coloniality and applying it to Spanish subjects, in particular to Spanish women. Through her eyes we see that don Lorenzo's mother, Arabella, was rejected by Spanish society for not been born a Christian. Don Manuel, don Lorenzo's stepbrother, continues to reject his stepmother even after her death, as he does not want Arabella buried with his biological mother. Other female characters also suffer from this type of discrimination. Olvido, a converted Jewish woman who takes care of don Manuel's wife, Diamantina, is required (along with the rest of the women in her family) to wear a sanbenito, or penitential garment, whenever the Santo Oficio conducted an auto-da-fé.[8] Clearly, the colonized marginality Ehecatl

experiences is mirrored in the treatment of other marginal women in Inquisitorial Spanish society.

Valvanera and Ehecatl are not exempted from this type of rejection and
maltreatment; they are part of the group that Jean Franco described, accused of being witches simply because the Spaniards do not know anything about their Aztec religious rituals and beliefs. Viewed under the
Inquisitorial microscope that dominated sixteenth-century Spanish society, Jewish, Moorish, and Indian women are homogenized, and consequently, are marginalized equally.

Chacón focuses on what is perceived by dominant figures in the novel
to thus be a homogenous group of women, and inverts this space of oppression, transforming it into one of empowerment in which Jewish, Muslim, and Aztec women join in the enterprise of rewriting history. This
makes sense within the new historical genre, as (re)writings of history allow room for fragmented and complementary perspectives that challenge
traditional portrayals of history. Consequently, they shift our attention
toward social groups that have been consistently neglected or simply dismissed in various discourses of power (Corona 100). By virtue of this fictional process, peripheral cultural groups unite as a strong collective and
use their powerlessness as a tool of empowerment for women. This idea is
well illustrated when all of the marginalized women join together to help
Ehecatl to escape from the merchant who threatens to inform Inquisitorial authorities that she is a witch.

Shortly after Ehecatl arrives to Spain, a storm kills the mayor of Zafra,
and everybody in town believes that Ehecatl has caused Zafra's death with
her witchcraft. A few days after the incident, Ehecatl/doña Aurora becomes a suspect mainly because of her indigenous origins, but also because she helped a gypsy woman who had been mistreated by Zafra's
mayor. The accusation against her is another example of Ehecatl's marginalization and Otherization, as "Spanish religious authorities saw the
rituals, offerings and divination associated with midwifery and healing as
forms of sorcery and interpreted them as the work of the devil" (Powers
48). Juan de los Santos tries to defend Ehecatl, but the merchant who accuses her, determined to see Ehecatl condemned, uses the incident in-
volving the mayor, the gypsy woman, and Ehecatl as an excuse to publicly
accuse her of witchcraft: "Pero lo que todo el mundo sabe es que tu señora
[Valvanera] le pagó con reales de plata. ¿Sabes tú qué era lo que le estaba
pagando? No me extrañaría que fuera ella quien le enseñó la maldición"
(210). His reasoning is sufficient to bring Ehecatl before the Santo Oficio,
consistent with the Inquisitorial procedures about which Karen Vieira

Powers observes: "Cases of witchcraft were often brought before the Inquisition or other official Church agencies, presumably because they involved activities that were thought to be supernatural and performed in league with the devil" (185). The Inquisitorial process itself accentuates the exclusion of women on the basis of their religious beliefs, for viewing them as supernatural and irrational are means of categorizing women in a way that does not accurately represent them.

Even as Ehecatl is marginalized and persecuted by the Spanish authorities, placing her on the fringes of Spanish society, Chacón valorizes Ehecatl's mystical abilities, giving her agency and turning her into the spokesperson for a collective of marginalized women. Although her witchcraft is one of the reasons she is marginalized, her healing abilities become a private space of empowerment. Jean Franco argues that mysticism becomes a site of empowerment for women in the colonial era; Ehecatl's "witchcraft" similarly builds upon such possibilities and also reflects the practice common in the colonial era, when entire indigenous communities continued their spiritual rites as a strategy of resistance to Spanish authority (Seydel 298). Through the exercise of her alternate belief system, Ehecatl struggles against and challenges notions of oppression, thereby validating her own practices and beliefs.

In several of the novel's episodes, Ehecatl's healing practices are the only way to save particular characters' lives and well-being when all other possibilities have been exhausted or when the person suffering is marginalized and does not have access to the accepted venues of healing. Diamantina, about to die of a badly performed abortion procedure, is brought back to life by Ehecatl's power to staunch the bleeding that threatens to kill her: "Sacó su cesto y comenzó a preparar un emplasto con piedra de sangre para cortar la hemorragia" (194). In another revealing incident, right after Valvanera's baby is born, she demands that Ehecatl "extendiera el libro de la cuenta de los días en el suelo. Debían averiguar el horóscopo de la pequeña Inés para encontrarle su verdadero nombre" (203). Here, Valvanera places implicit value on Ehecatl's knowledge of native cosmology and the rites of indigenous naming practices. As a result of her healing of Diamantina, Ehecatl becomes a figure of authority among the other marginalized women in the novel. Together, the women create a space of their own that allows them to guard their own beliefs and partially empower themselves through their application.

The female characters' empowerment, of course, has its limitations within the novel's historical context, and it is quickly limited and contained by dominant males who enact the principles of an oppressive Inquisitorial

Spanish society, for, as Ruth Behar notes, "while women's witchcraft powers were thought effective on the local level, especially by men who feared they had lost the upper hand in sexual relationships, it is clear that women exercised these powers within a male-dominated system, and thus their resistance was at best limited and piecemeal, as women's own devaluation of their power showed" (200–201). The female characters do eventually, however, create a more stable horizontal solidarity through the sublimation and relocation of their diverse, stigmatized spiritual beliefs to private spaces. The women keep their beliefs and remain true to themselves in the realm of the private, while they concurrently "perform" orthodox norms in the public space ruled by Christian males. Throughout the novel, we observe this pattern of behavior in different groups of women and at different chronological moments, lending a sense of continuity to their public and private practices. Ehecatl/doña Aurora and the Jewish and Moorish women, for example, learn about and co-opt each others' subversive strategies as they preserve and shield their true beliefs:

> Necesitaban demostrar que cumplían con los ritos cristianos, siempre sería mejor pecar por exceso que por defecto. Doña Aurora lo aprendió de los judíos de la calle del Pozo, que construyeron una capilla diminuta aprovechando un hueco entre dos casas para que todo el pueblo supiera que habían abandonando su credo. (251)

Ehecatl also learns that her deceased mother-in-law, the conversa Moor Arabella, only outwardly abandoned her religious practices for Christian ones: "Abrazó la fe de los cristianos por amor a su esposo, pero conservó sus tradiciones en la sombra, como muchos conversos que escondían sus credos a los ojos de los que nunca entenderían que la ley de Dios se puede escribir de distintas maneras" (36). As the female characters protect each other from the Spanish Inquisition's examinations of their private religious practices throughout the novel, the sense of a strong collective female solidarity grows, and Ehecatl becomes the representative for it. Yet it is in this last role that Chacón's triumphant heroine fails, and, perhaps inadvertently, perpetuates the Malinche archetype, with all of its negative connotations.

Malinche, also called doña Marina or Malinalli, depending on the historical source one consults, was a real Nahua woman central in the conquest of Mexico; as most students of the Mexican *colonia* know, she was the conquistador Hernán Cortés's slave, lover, and translator. Over the centuries, she has become an iconic subject of study for historians, anthropologists, and fiction writers. As Margo Glantz points out in her revealing study of this mythical figure, "ya sea como heroína o como traidora, Malinche es sujeto de la historia y objeto de una mitificación" (16).[9] According to Octavio Paz, for Mexicans, she is "La Chingada," who betrays her own people and becomes the symbolic mother of the first Mexican mestizo. For some contemporary Chicana writers, Malinche has evolved into a true heroine,[10] and recent historians such as Ross Hassig highlight her importance as translator and military strategist (Hind 29).

Chacón crafts a variation on this iconic figure through Ehecatl's characterization. On one hand, Ehecatl is depicted as possessing a positive, powerful bicultural identity, echoing Malinche's feminist, resistive formulation by Chicana critics Cherríe Moraga and Gloria Anzaldúa.[11] Unfortunately, though, Chacón's Aztec princess also shares a great deal with the fictional protagonist of Laura Esquivel's best seller *Malinche*. The limited voice of Esquivel's Malinche, explained in Oswaldo Estrada's critique of that novel as one that "mucho se parece al lenguaje de amor que William Prescott le imagina a la Malinche en su voluminosa *History of the conquest of Mexico*" (180), results in the exotification and romanticization of the Malinche character. Something very similar happens in *La princesa india*, in which Ehecatl's historical discourse is both overwhelmed and undermined by the novel's lyricism and use of romantic conventions.[12] The sentimental discourse that inscribes Chacón's new historical fiction removes from Ehecatl and her actions their authority, leading the reader to take them much less seriously than they merit. When we read on the book's last page, for instance, that Ehecatl "desparramó sus trenzas sobre su cuerpo [de don Lorenzo], él le besó la frente, ella los ojos, él buscó sus labios. Y los dos se sumergieron en las profundidades del otro" (318), Ehecatl is transformed through the literary construction of the encounter into a Malinche-like, passive, objectified subject.

Similarly, even as Ehecatl's indigenous practices and beliefs are, as discussed above, a significant source of her empowerment and that of the other marginalized women in Spanish society, Chacón's portrayal of indigenous people as an Other that is inherently more in tune with nature also echoes their problematic presentation in Esquivel's *Malinche*. Estrada's insight into Esquivel's characterization of the indigenous applies as well to Chacón's novel as it does to *Malinche*: "La mayor falla de Esquivel al poner este discurso en boca del adivino es que caricaturiza al *otro* indígena y su mundo oral, como si de nada hubiera servido la labor neoindigenista de José María Arguedas o Rosario Castellanos" (182). *La princesa india* likewise presents us with paratextual elements that perpetuate simplistic and damaging portrayals of native women. The front cover of the first

Alfaguara edition is plastered with Diego Rivera's painting *The Callas Vendor* (1942), and its back cover sells the book as the adventures of "una joven azteca con misteriosos poderes," a disappointing and stereotypical description of what are actually powerful and active abilities exercised by Ehecatl in the novel. The novel ends with Ehecatl's optimistic hope of closing the gap between the two worlds—her indigenous Mexican world and the Spanish world in which she lives and that dominates her culture of origin. When don Lorenzo asks her if she will always love him, she claims, with breathless, exoticized hyperbole: "Mucho más que siempre, hasta que tu mundo y el mío estén tan cerca como nosotros" (318). This moment, unfortunately, has not yet arrived, and the way in which her idea is expressed in the novel diminishes what the novel accomplishes in terms of its historical rewriting of Aztec women. What began with Dulce Chacón's noble proposition to voice and empower the indigenous Other who has been silenced by history's official discourse is undermined by essentialist feminism along with Eurocentric ways of describing the Other.

Undoubtedly, although writers such as Inma Chacón look to Spain's colonial past with the hope of denouncing the marginalization of native women (evidently with uneven success), more needs to be done. In Spain's current literary market, there are hardly any novels that reflect on colonial Mexico, with the exception of those mentioned above in this chapter, and a handful of others.[13] This lack of interest in truly useful reflection makes us rethink the relationship between Spain and its colonial past as it is beginning to be reconceived today. The year 1992, the so-called five-hundred-year anniversary of the discovery of the Americas, was celebrated in Spain at the same time that Barcelona hosted the Olympic Games, and the coincidence of these events with the end of Francoism was seen by many as a starting point for rethinking Spain as a European nation. Part of this Europeanization of Spain involved a symbolic detachment from the country's image as an imperialistic power that had colonized the Americas and beyond. As the Franco regime proudly cultivated a public paean to the Catholic monarchs and their expansionist agenda as an integral part of Spanish identity, the same Europeanizing strategy that sought to remove its fascist image tried to divorce Spain from its colonizing past. Even though Spain has changed a great deal since 1992 (and of course much more so since 1492), the relationship between Mexico and the Iberian Peninsula is still difficult to discuss—even more difficult when dominant discourses seek to "categorizar el colonialismo europeo como cosa del pasado" (Rings 13), and when, as is the generally the case with Latin American culture in Spain, "the other is what eludes our consciousness and knowing, and [remains] outside the sphere of 'our' culture and community" (Chengzhou 13).

For these reasons, my reading of *La princesa india* is ambivalent. The novel is a valid cultural artifact that connects the precolonization oppression of Jews and Muslims in the Iberian Peninsula with the repression of the indigenous people of the Americas, principally through the portrayal of women in each of these contexts. In this sense, Chacón's novel is a unique literary and social contribution to Spanish letters. Seen positively, Ehecatl's romanticized optimism at the end of the novel, "cuando tu mundo y el mío se encuentren" (318), reopens complicated postcolonial negotiations. In practice, however, Chacón's text creates new paradigms of colonialism, homogenizes marginal groups, and creates ambivalent characterizations of the indigenous Other that reflect the nonexistent understanding between Spain and its colonial past. This, unfortunately, clearly illustrates the detachment between the Spanish peninsula and Mexico. If, along with Mexican writer Luis Villoro, we agree that "remitirnos al pasado, dota al presente de una razón de existir" (qt. in Aínsa 69), we need more texts that reflect deeply on the encounter between the Iberian Peninsula and the Americas. Perhaps what is called for are new ways in which to rewrite Spanish and Latin American history in order to establish a deeper and more honest literary dialogue between the two regions. In any case, Inma Chacón's *La princesa india* does offer us a tentative glimpse into an inversion of colonial otherness, showing us a different rewriting of Spanish colonization in Mexico and allowing us to look at the past across an ocean and through the present.

Notes

1. Her "Golden Age saga" includes *Tierra firme* (2007) and *Venganza en Sevilla* (2010).

2. Chacón has also published *Las filipinianas* (2007) and *Tiempo de arena* (2011).

3. For an excellent comparativist study on contemporary cinematic and literary representations of the conquest of the Americas, see Guido Rings's *La conquista desbaratada* (2010).

4. Ute Seydel, Elisabeth Guerrero, and Kimberle López have written excellent books on this topic.

5. Ironically, this Spanish obsession with a unified racial, cultural and religious identity was also prevalent throughout Franco's dictatorship.

6. Ignacio Solares also shows us the Spanish side of colonization in *Nen, la inútil* (1994), and Carmen Boullosa's *Duerme* (1994) allows readers to discover an imperialist Spain in her reconstruction of colonial Mexico.

7. An obvious exception would certainly be Fernández de Oviedo, a *cronista* who calls the Spaniards, as Seydel reminds us, "demonios por su falta de escrúpulos en lo que ellos consideraban función evangelizadora" (391).

8. The sanbenito was either yellow with red St. Andrew's crosses for penitent heretics, or black and decorated with friars, dragons, and devils for impenitent heretics.

9. Glantz's *La Malinche, sus padres y sus hijos* (2001) is one of the most complete works on controversial reinterpretations of Malinche. For further reading, see also Sandra Messinger Cypess's *La Malinche in Mexican Literature: From History to Myth* (1991).

10. For more information about rewritings of Malinche by Chicana writers, read Mary Louise Pratt's "Yo soy la Malinche."

11. For a deeper analysis on the Malinche archetype, see Hind's description of the "Malinche queer" (30) in her book *Femmenism and the Mexican Woman Intellectual* (2010).

12. We see similar portrayals in many of Isabel Allende's novels, and also in Fanny del Río's *La verdadera historia de Malinche* (2010).

13. For a more detailed analysis of these novels in relation to the Spanish colonization of Mexico, see Antonio Gómez-Lopez Quiñones's "La conquista y el problema de la modernidad hispánica."

Works Cited

Aguilar, Andrea. "Inma Chacón rinde homenaje a su hermana Dulce con *La princesa india*." *El País*, May 20, 2005. http://elpais.com/diario/2005/05/20/cultura/1116540005_850215.html. Accessed February 17, 2013.

Aínsa, Fernando. *Reescribir el pasado: Historia y ficción en América Latina*. Mérida: Fundación Centro de Estudios Latinoamericanos Rómulo Gallegos (CELARG)/ El otro, el mismo, 2003.

Ballesteros, Isolina. "Embracing the Other: The Feminization of Spanish 'Immigration Cinema.'" *Studies in Hispanic Cinemas* 2.1 (2005): 3–14.

Barrientos, Juan José. *La nueva novela histórica hispanoamericana*. México, D.F: Universidad Nacional Autónoma de México (UNAM), 2001.

Behar, Ruth. "Sexual Witchcraft, Colonialism, and Women's Powers: Views from the Mexican Inquisition." *Sexuality and Marriage in Colonial Latin America*. Ed. Asunción Lavrin. Lincoln: University of Nebraska Press, 1989. 178–206.

Boullosa, Carmen. *Duerme*. México, D.F.: Alfaguara, 1994.

Chacón, Inma. *La princesa india: Cuando el viento azul*. Madrid: Alfaguara, 2006.

Chengzhou, He, ed. *Representations of the Other: Theory and Practice*. Göttinguen, Germany: Universitätsverlang Göttinguen, 2009.

Corona, Ignacio. "El festín de la historia: Abordajes críticos recientes a la novela histórica." *Literatura Mexicana* 12 (2001): 87–113.

Cypess, Sandra Messinger. *La Malinche in Mexican Literature from History to Myth*. Austin: University of Texas Press, 1991.

Estrada, Oswaldo. *La imaginación novelesca: Bernal Díaz entre géneros y épocas*. Madrid: Iberoamericana/Vervuert, 2009.

Franco, Jean. *Plotting Women: Gender and Representation in Mexico.* New York: Columbia University Press, 1989.

Fuentes, Carlos. *El naranjo.* México, D.F.: Alfaguara, 1993.

Gilman, Stephen. "Bernal Díaz del Castillo y el *Amadís de Gaula.*" *Del Arcipreste de Hita a Pedro Salinas.* Salamanca, Spain: Ediciones Universidad, 2002. 111–13.

Glantz, Margo. *La Malinche, sus padres y sus hijos.* México, D.F.: Taurus, 2001.

Gómez-López Quiñones, Antonio. "La conquista y el problema de la modernidad hispánica. Dos discursos sobre el pasado (post)colonial español." *Anales de Literatura Española Contemporánea* 36.1 (2011): 101–32.

Hind, Emily. *Femmenism and the Mexican Woman Intellectual from Sor Juana to Poniatowska: Boob Lit.* New York: Palgrave Macmillan, 2010.

Leal, Luis. "Female Archetypes in Mexican Literature." *Women in Hispanic Literature: Icons and Fallen Idols.* Ed. Beth Miller. Berkeley: University of California Press, 1983. 227–43.

León-Portilla, Miguel. *Visión de los vencidos: Relaciones indígenas de la conquista.* México, D.F.: UNAM, 1959.

López, Kimberle S. *Latin American Novels of the Conquest: Reinventing the New World.* Columbia: University of Missouri Press, 2002.

Martínez, María Elena. *Genealogical Fictions: Limpieza de Sangre, Religion, and Gender in Colonial Mexico.* Stanford, CA: Stanford University Press, 2008.

Menton, Seymour. *Latin America's New Historical Novel.* Austin: University of Texas Press, 1993.

Merino, José María. *Las crónicas mestizas.* Madrid: Alfaguara, 1992.

Mignolo, Walter. "Dispensable and Bare Lives: Coloniality and the Hidden Political/Economic Agenda of Modernity." *Human Architecture Journal of the Sociology of Self-Knowledge* 7.2 (2009): 69–88.

Pérez Reverte, Arturo. *Ojos azules.* Barcelona: Seix-Barral, 2009.

Powers, Karen Vieira. *Women in the Crucible of Conquest: The Gendered Genesis of Spanish American Society, 1500–1600.* Albuquerque: University of New Mexico Press, 2005.

Pratt, Mary Louise. "'Yo Soy La Malinche': Chicana Writers and the Poetics of Ethnonationalism." *Callaloo* 16 (1993): 859–73.

Rings, Guido. *La Conquista desbaratada: Identidad y alteridad en la novela, el cine y el teatro hispánicos contemporáneos.* Madrid: Iberoamericana/Vervuert, 2010.

Said, Edward. *Orientalism: Western Concepts of the East.* New York: Routledge, 1979.

Seydel, Ute. *Narrar historia(s): La ficcionalización de temas históricos por las escritoras mexicanas Elena Garro, Rosa Beltrán y Carmen Boullosa.* Madrid: Iberoamericana/Vervuert, 2007.

Solares, Ignacio. *Nen, la inútil.* México, D.F.: Alfaguara, 1995.

CHAPTER NINE

También la lluvia

Of Coproductions and Re-Encounters, a Re-Vision of the Colonial

Ilana Dann Luna

The explosions coming out of theoretical,
political, and ethical awareness of the colonial wound
make possible the imagination and construction
of an-other world, a world in which many worlds are possible.
—WALTER MIGNOLO, *THE IDEA OF LATIN AMERICA* (156)

In 1992, at the quincentennial of contact between Europe and the Americas, many artists, critics, and activists questioned the meaning of "discovery" and conquest, interrogating, too, notions of history and the subaltern experiences of these first encounters. Almost twenty years later, following the bicentennial of several Latin American independences, and the centennial of Mexico's revolution, many of the same questions are still pertinent, but critical approaches seem to be shifting. Whose stories are told? How are these stories told? What do Latin American countries have in common beyond a history of shared oppression? A language? A culture? Neoliberal economic policy? While sixteenth-century Spain and its apparatuses of social control (primarily, the Catholic Church) were certainly cast as villainous vis-à-vis Latin America at the quincentennial, more recently there have been shifts that point to a possible rapprochement between Spain and its former colonies, both economically and ideologically.

In this chapter I examine the critically acclaimed Spanish-Mexican-French coproduced film *También la lluvia* (Icíar Bollaín, 2010) as it offers a series of complexities with regard to the question of a "national" product and problematic.[1] Set in Bolivia, starring Mexican superstar Gael García Bernal, directed by well-known Spanish actress and director Icíar Bollaín and written by her partner—Calcutta-born Scotch-Irishman Paul Laverty—the film repositions Spain vis-à-vis its former colonies in a global market and questions the borders and boundaries of national cinemas, while publicizing and fomenting the unity of indigenous struggles of the region through new media circuits. It is a film within a film, in which several international filmmakers (Mexican and Spanish) arrive in Bolivia in the year 2000 with the intent of producing a colonial-period film. The film's story of indigenous resistance by Taíno cacique Hatuey, set in the colony, and the story of the contemporary actor who is playing him, called Daniel, a local agitator in the fight for water autonomy, are intertwined to make explicit the link between colonial oppression and its legacy in neoliberal economic policy in Latin America.

The relationship between the anticolonial Mexican movements and the Bolivian one are quite clear. In fact, David Slater notes the major social shifts that occurred in the 1990s, stating, "It can be argued that Latin America and specifically the Zapatista rebellion had a creative influence on the overall global movement against neoliberalism" (215). He specifically cites the April 2000 Cochabamba "war over water" to demonstrate the violence that is institutionalized in government and private-sector responses to resistance in the global south (218).

The present-day connection between countries and indigenous struggles is mirrored in the film's represented colonial moment as well, utilizing the figure of Hatuey (in the film) to evoke other figures of resistance whose actions echo his defiance of sixteenth-century Spanish invaders in Hispaniola and Cuba; quite explicitly, Cuauhtémoc, who resisted the Spanish in Tenochtitlán. Seymour Menton, in his foundational study of the new historical novel of Latin America notes the specific importance of the "encounter" for authors writing at the close of the century, observing that the approach of the quincentennial propitiated a new consciousness that did not limit itself to Columbus, but also included those who resisted the Conquest, including Hatuey, Cuauhtémoc, and Lautaro (49). It is clear that Bollaín's fictitious filmmaker (García Bernal) reads his imagined Hatuey through the lens of Cuauhtémoc, and Mexico's resistance to colonial rule, thereby uniting the indigenous struggles in the past and present, and creating a genealogy of resistance across Latin America.

Colonial Returns

Returning to the colonial or the historic roots of national trauma is not a new occurrence in contemporary Mexico. Ute Seydel notes that the colonial era—the "discovery" and Conquest—became very important for contemporary Mexican narrative as the quincentennial approached (21). In addition to the proliferation of historical novels, there was a return to the colonial era in filmic narrative as well, producing features that addressed the Conquest, and the years of subsequent Spanish occupation of Mexican territory, culminating in the War of Independence. Many of those films endeavored to vindicate certain subaltern groups within Mexico through their roles as protagonists of a historical "national" drama. The colonial site of trauma, the clashing of cultures, and then, the emergence of a criollo class have offered a rich backdrop onto which filmmakers have projected an alternate history, one that is more inclusive, in which women and vanquished indigenous groups were not relegated, at least momentarily, to the margins of History.

Carrie Chorba notes that the quincentennial prompted a "decolonizing reading of the conquest" (33) among many Mexican intellectuals, one that drew in particular on the legacies of inequity structured from the moment of contact with Spain. Along these lines, Richard Gordon cites several films focusing on colonial themes, the majority of which were produced in the 1990s, including *Retorno a Aztlán* (Juan Mora Catlett, 1990), *Cabeza de Vaca* (Nicolás Echevarría, 1991), *La otra conquista* (Salvador Carrasco, 1998), and *Ave María* (Eduardo Rousoff, 1999). Miriam Haddu cites also *Bartolomé de las Casas* (Sergio Olhovich, 1992) and *Kino* (Felipe Cazals, 1993) (156).[2] I would expand the list to include *Gertrudis* (Ernesto Medina, 1992), one of the only films in Mexican history to portray a female *independentista* as its protagonist (Bloch 30).

If these earlier evocations of the *colonia* select a historically meaningful moment in order to intervene in the collective memory project, creating images where previously there had been lacunae in the historical consciousness of the nation—including points of view and characters that had not entered the popular imaginary as active agents—then this latest "return" to the colonial in *También la lluvia* posits an entirely new set of circumstances. Where the above-mentioned films were revisionist in nature, acting to reinscribe marginalized people into the historical record of popular culture, *También la lluvia* is no less politically motivated. But rather than simply revising history, it breaks history open at the seams in true postmodern form, examining the apparatuses through which film itself is complicit in the construction of "false truths," or (national) myths. Bollaín's film draws explicit (rather than implicit) parallels between colonial practices of enslavement of the indigenous peoples and present-day, neocolonial economic policies that foreground the needs of large, capital-amassing global corporations and relegate the indigenous once more to the margins of economic subsistence.

Simultaneously, the recent trend toward creating economic ties through Spanish–Latin American coproductions is mirrored in *También la lluvia*'s return to the colonial. Its metareferential use of a film within a film, a double "rereading" of the colonial from a place of both personal and political engagement, allows for a complex understanding of the relationship between the conquistadors and the conquered. At the same time that the film reenacts the traumas of colonial history, it acts as a commentary on the very films that were created in the 1990s as a response to the quincentennial of the Conquest. *También la lluvia* grafts the tumultuous present social and political unrest in countries facing extreme poverty, still-marginalized indigenous populations, and evaporating middle classes onto a shared history of colonialism. I argue that while the film critiques the Conquest by Spain of the Americas, it simultaneously proposes possible new alliances between Spain and its former colonies, suggesting that together, there can be a more ethical response to globalization—that a shared linguistic heritage can allow for real understanding. To borrow from José Martí, "Our America" may no longer be confined to the Americas, but it has become a restructuring of alliances between the global south and the north. Spain is no longer being cast as a monolithic enemy, but as a potential ally in an America that represents social movements from below, like those of the Zapatistas in Mexico and the water-rioters in Cochabamba.

Coproduction and Coloniality

I suggest that *También la lluvia*, specifically because of its metafilmic construction, its use of recognizable international film stars—which represent a transatlantic connection between Mexico and Spain—and the specific return to the colonial wound or point of contact all endeavor to question our very understanding of both film and other transnational industries, and the way in which the "national" and "regional" interests of Mexico are implicated in the fate of other Spanish-speaking countries today. While the film unfolds simultaneously in Bolivia and Santo Domingo, colonial

Mexico is also highlighted because of the interventions and questioning of Bartolomé de las Casas's role in the Conquest. Here the "defender of the Indians"—creator of the "black legend," bishop of Chiapas, and contested cultural figure—is put into dialogue with others of his time,[3] connecting Latin American intellectual pursuits in such a way so as to double those occurring in the "outer" film and to call attention to the Zapatista uprisings that took place in city that is his namesake: San Cristóbal de las Casas.

In this vein, Néstor García Canclini argues that in "its colonial period, Mexico City was traversed by economic and cultural movements that stretched well beyond what we today call the country of Mexico. . . . It functioned as a regional capital and as an articulator of links with Spain" (207). He argues that while the globalization of the late 1990s in some respects delocalized capital—thereby stripping film and other cultural industries of their local character and subjecting them to the fancies of commercial criteria of international coproductions—new regional alliances and market adaptations proved to mitigate the denationalizing effects of this new mode (210–13). Thus, the invocation of the colonial in Bollaín's film highlights the larger geographic regional ties, allowing for a critique of the ongoing colonial legacy present in Mexico, Bolivia, and many other parts of Latin America.[4] One of the ways in which national communities are being "imagined" outside the bounds of a circumscribed geographic location is precisely through the identification with nationally marked transnational stars, like Gael García Bernal.[5]

Libia Villazana warns of the danger of viewing coproduction simply as a symmetrical relationship between autonomous nations and industries. In discussing the Spanish–Latin American coproductions of the 1990s she notes the "colonial legacies" still present in the relationship between Ibermedia (Spain's major coproducer) and its Latin American counterparts in their discrete national film industries. She suggests that there is an uneasy interdependence between Spain and its former colonies in the effort to combat the hegemony of Hollywood and the Motion Picture Association of America in international distribution markets and screen time, but that Latin American countries need to be wary of accepting unfavorable coproduction relationships with Spain (81–82). This asymmetrical relationship is questioned and critiqued in Bollaín's *También la lluvia* as it uses the microcosm of the film production to frame larger questions of dependence, exploitation, and the inherent inequality in attempting to speak for the Other.

Because, as Luisela Alvaray has suggested, García Bernal is tied to the "diaspora that has now become a trans-Atlantic star system" (55), because

the "proliferation of films through coproduction potentially multiplies cinematic ways of articulating Latin America in a globalized context" (62),
and because Mexico's film industry has acted as a motor for the production of quality films in other Latin American countries (such as Bolivia)
whose industries are much smaller, Bollaín's metareferential use of García Bernal opens up major potential for a critical view of the nature of
such production relationships with less-established film industries and
economies.[6] His immediate iconicity *as a Mexican superstar*, as well as his
keen understanding of global markets and his relationship with what I will
call commercial activism, make him an ideal character within a character
to engage at once the national (Mexican), the regional (Latin American),
and the global implications of colonialism's most recent offspring: neoliberal economic policies that result in the privatization of public lands and
resources, once again disenfranchising the permanently disenfranchised
of the Americas, its native peoples.

Thus, we can begin to read Icíar Bollaín's film, *También la lluvia*—set
in Cochabamba, Bolivia, which re-creates the Spanish Conquest of Santo
Domingo—as a new spin on returning to the colonial as a critique of contemporary Mexican cultural and economic policy, as much as of Bolivian
and Spanish ones. And the colonial legacy being critiqued is not limited to
the Conquest of Santo Domingo, but also includes that of Tenochtitlán, as
seen in the conflation of Hatuey and Cuauhtémoc in terms of their roles
as tortured resistors.

The Implicit Politics of the Postmodern

The postmodern mode of storytelling that Bollaín's film utilizes can be
read as an overtly political choice. The film takes place in Cochabamba,
Bolivia, in the year 2000. It is an intimate journey, a personal quest of two
friends and collaborators, Sebastián, a Mexican filmmaker (Gael García
Bernal) and Costa (Luis Tosar), his Spanish producer, to create a film that
represents the oppression typical of the early moments of colonial history
in the Americas, as well as the intercessions made by Spaniards for the indigenous cause. Their film is going to provide an epic vision of colonial
times, one that aims to vindicate not only the value of indigenous peoples
and their cultures, but also offers a re-vision of official history in which Columbus was responsible for great cruelty and injustice. At the same time,
because of the favorable laws for film production and the low cost of labor,
their film, eight years in the making (which sets its inception in the year

1992, not accidentally the quincentennial of the Conquest of America, and drawing distinct parallels with films such as Carrasco's *La otra conquista*[7]), is being filmed, not on the island of Santo Domingo, but rather in the Bolivian highlands. The metafilm's setting foregrounds the dire economic straits of the Bolivian government (and the majority of its citizens), reenacting the mass social upheaval that occurred, in reality, in April 2000. The so-called water wars erupted over the privatization of the area's water supply by a transnational company whose usurious charges increased costs by 300 percent for water users. Simultaneously, the government passed laws that denied its citizens the right to collect even the rain. Such a contemporary stranglehold on the native population through controlling its resources recalls Bernal Díaz del Castillo's account in which Cortés cut off the freshwater supply to ultimately conquer Cuauhtémoc and Tenochtitlán.

In the figure of Daniel/Hatuey (played by Carlos Aduviri), two different historical moments are conflated. Daniel is both a leader in the present-day indigenous struggle for social justice, and the inner film's key figure of indigenous resistance in the colonial era, a fierce chief who spit in the face of the Spaniards who tried to make an example of him. This reminds us of Linda Hutcheon's theorizations on historiographic metafiction, as the film within the film represents "not just a world of fiction, however self-consciously presented as a constructed one, but also a world of public experience" (34). Hutcheon describes what she calls "postmodern historiographic metafiction" suggesting that the overt, conscious use of reflexivity, and the mixing of genres and temporalities within a text can force "us to question how we represent—how we construct—our view of reality" (40).

We see this questioning of the constructed nature of history, and its political implications, as Bollaín's filmic text consciously intercalates four discrete narrative levels. The film juxtaposes the historical moment being represented as Columbus's contact with the natives of what are now the Caribbean islands; the filmic moment, or the explicit construction of that historical narrative in which the modern-day characters insist upon the "authority" and textual fidelity to colonial texts (the letters of Columbus, sermons of Montesinos, and writings of Bartolomé de las Casas, to name a few) in their representation of the past; and finally the historical moment in which the film within a film is supposedly being shot: in April 2000 in Cochabamba, Bolivia. And there is a fourth plane as well: by examining the making of a revisionist film, while utilizing García Bernal to enact the role of Sebastián—a Mexican filmmaker—there is a clear harkening back to the proliferation of colonial rereadings that came out of Mexico in the

1990s, ones that attempted to reconcile and revindicate the present with the colonial era, but at the same time elevated certain historical figures to iconic status while, perhaps, erasing contemporary differences among subaltern groups.

This fragmentation of what would normally be the teleological structure of historical fiction films, and the reflection on the constructed nature of whose narrative is told, is perhaps epitomized in the supporting female character, María (Cassandra Ciangherotti)—Mexican, like Sebastián, as evidenced by her accent in the film. She is simultaneously supporting the production of the main film while taking on the responsiblity for obtaining footage for the corollary "Making of . . ." film (a requisite for any international blockbuster, to which Sebastián and Costa's film aspires). María films scenes that the male filmmakers would rather she not show, which highlight their egotism, economic greed, and lack of coherency; but she is also shown to be naïve when it comes to her understanding of Daniel's economic, rather than epistemic, motivation for participation in the film. María, in her own way, attempts to document the "visión de los vencidos" or the vision of the vanquished, but she is sorely underprepared for this task. She is the first to see the potential in filming a "real" documentary on the indigenous resistance when she begins to see the brutality and injustice suffered by Daniel and his community, but she is denied time and funding to pursue this project because Costa refuses to be an "NGO." It is, however, telling that María (as a woman, one whose voice is too often ignored in film industries) attempts to speak for the silenced Bolivian indigenous workers, despite her misreading of their struggle, while Costa (the white, Spanish producer) not only refuses to listen to her, but he refuses to "share" his resources, because his ultimate motivation is profit, not social praxis through art.

Such polyvalency, complexity, and conflicting narratives represent a distinct strategy to destabilize the notions of "truth" that the verisimilitude of film generally offers. As Hutcheon points out, "In a very real sense, postmodernism reveals a desire to understand present culture as the product of previous representations. The representation of history becomes the history of representation" (55). Or, as Walter Mignolo suggests, "You cannot envision alternatives to *modernity* if the principles of knowledge you hold, and the structure of reasoning you follow, are molded by the hegemonic rhetoric of modernity and the hidden logic of coloniality working through it" (114).

También la lluvia's use of metareferentiality compels us to ask whose stories are being told, and how. The scaffolding that is generally hidden from filmgoers is laid bare for the audience to see, and the multiple points of view and levels of filmic narrative uncover the hidden logic of coloniality.[8] The film makes manifest that while historical truth once resided with the Church and the conquering actors, history can be fractured, and new narratives can arise, from below. In this sense, postmodern representations can promote a decolonizing reading of historical events.

Bollaín's film peels back layer after layer, exposing the machinations behind even the most seemingly innocent representations. Her 2010 production telescopes backward, breaking with linear temporal narrative structure to examine not only the nature of physical violence present since colonial times, but that of the continued epistemic violence of the neocoloniality present in neoliberal economic policy in Latin America and in its corollaries, including national and international nongovernmental organizations, that speak for certain groups, instead of making space for them to speak for themselves.

While *También la lluvia* offers some hope of resolution, mutual growth, and understanding, it does so with a very real sense of the difficulty of such a struggle. Couched in an international film language readable for an educated audience, the film highlights one of the too-few positive outcomes achieved by a social movement from below—rather than from top-down economic policies imposed on historically marginalized people—in order to build alliances and garner support for such efforts.

Colonial Complexities: Intercessions and Irruptions

The film opens with dramatic extra-diegetic string music, and scenes of Cochabamba, from inside a van, pass quickly by. The setting is established textually with the words "Cochabamba, Bolivia. Año 2000" in white letters at the bottom of the colorful screen, with squatting street vendors in the background by the side of the road. The camera rests on Sebastián (García Bernal), and then pans back to a long line of people waiting for their chance to be cast in his new film. Outside the van, Sebastián and Costa (Tosar) walk ahead, and María (Cingherotti) trails behind them with her portable camera in hand and begins to film the long line of tired people in their colorful polleras and bowler hats and dusty work clothing. The scene's economic disparity and the sense of desperation are reinforced as Sebastián scrutinizes each person, his white face only inches from their brown ones, while Costa simply attempts to send the majority home because there are too many to deal with.

When Costa's inconsideration meets with resistance, Daniel (Aduviri), whose penetrating gaze and intensity will land him the lead in the film, calls him out, telling him that he must make good on his word of an open casting, and spitting the insult "cara blanquita" at him. Both class and ethnic tensions are established here, as is the central conflict of the film—Costa's (and Sebastián's) inability to really see the people who are pawns in their film. The presence of a low-flying helicopter, trailing a huge, floating wooden cross behind it, breaks the tension of the altercation, and the camera pans up to track its movement across the empty sky. The title flashes across the screen: *También la lluvia*, and the camera cuts to a high angle of a single car speeding along a lonely highway.

In this scene, María shouts for Costa to slow down, and the camera registers a close-up from inside the intimate space of the car as he laughs. The camera turns to Sebastián, but it is suddenly rolling in black and white, suggesting the subjective lens of María's documentary footage. The scene cuts back to María, camera in hand, in color, setting the stage, and Sebastián's reactions to her cynical but accurate assessment of their project. She says, "Estamos en Bolivia, así como que mucho, mucho sentido, pues, no tiene, ¿verdad? Porque, pues, digo, estamos a unos 2,500 metros sobre el nivel del mar, rodeados de montañas, y a miles de kilómetros del caribe." This reflection by María demonstrates the fluidity of Bollaín's film's discourse—its ability to speak of and critique not only one place and time—but many—tying Mexico, Bolivia, the Caribbean, and all of Latin America together in a shared history of colonialism with Spain.

The camera then cuts back to black and white, and Sebastián jokingly responds that Costa (the Spaniard) thinks Columbus landed in the New World by parachute, saying "No, pues, es que acá Costa cree que Colón llegó en paracaídas." Costa intervenes, still in documentary mode, defending himself, "No, perdona, Costa sabe que esto está lleno de indígenas hambrientos y eso significa extras, miles de extras."

Sebastián's displeasure at this gross exploitation is registered in color, and he shakes his head. María is shown playfully wielding her camera, and the shot cuts back to black and white. Costa and Sebastián begin to argue, and Sebastián is worried that the film will fail because the actors' physical features are Quechua, and Columbus has no business talking to indigenous people from the Andes. Costa replies, in essence, that they are all the same—indigenous.

This initial attitude of ignorance—not knowing or caring about the difference between one indigenous group and another—represents what Walter Mignolo claims is the "global idea of 'Latin' America being deployed by imperial states today (the U.S. and the imperial countries of the European Union)" (96). Costa, as European producer, is eager to exploit the cheap labor, exotic scenery, and Otherness that Bolivia has to offer, even if it sacrifices historical accuracy.

María's disbelief mirrors Sebastián's, and she films him signaling for her to cut the filming, but she continues rolling, and the color cam focuses on her asking, "Entonces, ¿la razón es el dinero?" They continue fighting, and debating what can be seen as Costa's insincerity of investment in the "truth" of the project, and his vile capitalism. He claims, "Si hubiéramos rodado en inglés, tendríamos el doble de dinero, tendríamos el doble de público . . ." and Sebastián replies, "No, porque los españoles hablaban español, cabrón." María then interjects with humor, but signaling the discrepancy in Sebastián's argument: "Entonces los españoles hablan español y los taínos que encontró Colón, ¿hablan quechua?" María's questions destabilize both Costa's posture of economic exploitation and Sebastián's pseudo-truths that still favor a colonial view of the Conquest in which Spanish language is the homogenizing factor. In fact, Federico Navarrete Linares notes in his discussion of Mexican historical fiction nearing the quincentennial that there is a real danger in assigning a sole "voice" to the indigenous, because the experiences of the Conquest and the resistance to it were a direct result of the relationship each *pueblo* had to the power structures in place prior to the arrival of the Spaniards; for example, the Tlaxcaltecas and the Aztecs each lived the Conquest in very different manners. This unreflexive conflation of diverse indigenous groups, the erasing of difference, he argues, allows for the celebration of a "common past" that erases the miserable situation that many indigenous peoples suffer in the present (13–14).

María's character here and throughout represents the thrust toward alternate versions of history, ones that were not remembered or recorded in the great books of colonial history. Nevertheless, Bollaín never allows the audience to forget María's relative position of privilege. Later, in a casual off-set filming session, María tapes Daniel in his neighborhood environment. She zooms in on him, while he sits with his friends digging a ditch by the side of the road, with a grainy grayscale Cochabamba in the background, and asks Daniel, "¿Me puedes decir qué fue lo que te motivó para hacer esta película? . . . ¿Como qué fue lo que más te gustó de tu personaje? Tal vez lo que representa como figura de resistencia indígena o plantear la colonización desde un punto de vista diferente." Daniel refuses to allow his version of history to be written by someone foreign to his own cause.

He looks at her, now in color, still digging his ditch, passively resisting her epistemic violence, refusing to capitulate to her version of *his* story. The camera lingers on his not-traditionally film-star face past the point of visual discomfort, and an off-camera voice interjects, with a very particular Bolivian indigenous accent in Spanish, "A él sólo le interesa la plata." And suddenly there is cacophony as his friends start to ask him questions about what it is like to be in the film, if he has to kiss lots of women, or get naked. María gets frustrated and turns off her camera; nonetheless, it will be she that documents Daniel's political activism, and she who attempts to reconcile Sebastián's egocentric goal of making a grandiose (yet ultimately empty) discourse of historical redress, with a coherent condemnation of neocolonialism via neoliberal economics.

The instability of historical truth, and the slippage between colonial abuses, and the continued privilege of the white intellectual in Spain and Mexico (and Bolivia) is also questioned in the conflicts between the present-day actors and their historical characters: Columbus, Montesinos, and Las Casas. In a scene in which the actors are doing a read-through of the script, the lines of temporality are blurred between the represented past and the "real" present. Antón (Karra Elejalde) who is playing Christopher Columbus, begins by reading his script but quickly becomes his character, and the entire cast follows him through their hotel garden. He treats the indigenous woman who is serving as wait staff for their luncheon as if she were a Taína, physically removing her gold earring and demanding to know where there is more gold. There is an intense close-up that registers her uneasiness and Antón's total abandon as he has transformed himself into the greedy, unrelenting conqueror. He breaks the intensity of the moment, laughing and apologizing for his bizarre behavior saying, "Disculpe señorita, los actores somos así, unos puros egoístas." The language used in this scene claims textual fidelity to Columbus's first letter back to Spain, and it comments on the docility and "innocence" of the natives and their supposed lack of the notion of private property, which could be exploited to the benefit of the Crown. There is a decided parallel between his behaviors, for which he apologizes, and those of Columbus.

In the subsequent scene, presumably on set, there is much tension in María's black-and-white documentary between the actors who play Alberto/Bartolomé de las Casas (Carlos Santos) and Juan/Alberto Montesinos (Raúl Arevalo). Alberto argues that his character, Bartolomé de las Casas, is the first to exhort the Crown on behalf of the natives, but Juan, who claims to have done much less research than his fellow actor, insists that his character, Padre Montesinos, lived and died for the indigenous cause, and was a precursor to Las Casas. Juan recites for María—and the audience viewing her putative documentary—a discourse from a sermon that is textually exact and that he repeats several more times throughout the film: "Yo soy la voz de Cristo en el desierto de esta isla y estáis en pecado mortal."[9] A subsequent iteration of this sermon takes place in a replica of a small outdoor chapel, when he is made up and dressed for the actual "filming." The multiple levels of discourse at play utterly destabilize the notion of fidelity to a text and truth. Although textual authority is vehemently cited, the movable nature of the discourse and its multiplicity of deployment suggest that history is a question of interpretation: it can be twisted and positioned where and when it suits the speaker, and it literally represents he who can talk the loudest.

The most significant—and playful—iteration of Juan's/Montesinos's speech is used to break the tension when Antón (Columbus) and Alberto (Bartolomé de las Casas) get into a fight over dinner with the lead cast and crew members. Antón tells Alberto that Las Casas was not as saintly as Alberto would like to believe, and that the priest was directly responsible for African slavery in the Americas. Alberto protests that Las Casas should not be "punished" for one "little" mistake he made in his youth, as if a youthful indiscretion that lead to the murder, torture, and enslavement of a people could be waved away as inconsequential. In fact, Antón criticizes the film and history's demonization of Columbus and quasi-sanctification of Las Casas as the first "humanitarian" in the Americas.[10] This seemingly petty argument underscores real tensions in the ways in which history is recorded and immortalized, thereby undermining the "truth" of history.

Thus, Antón's contradictory character—as a savage and cruel Columbus in the film, and as a drunk teller of uncomfortable truths off screen—serves as a reminder that everything everyone in the film is doing is, in essence, an act of revisionist history; that no one is entirely innocent; and that no single history is the definitive one. No one, especially not the present-day actors, are clean of blood on their hands. This is made evident as the actors interrogate the wait staff about words in Quechua, learning the word "yaku," or water, among others. Antón points out that instead of showing a nominal (and clearly passing) interest in their linguistic heritage, the actors should give the waiters the leftovers from their overindulgent dinner, which is more than their families likely see in a month.

In fact, at the close of the film, when everything has crumbled because of the riots, and the majority of the actors abandon Sebastián at a government checkpoint, Antón (Columbus) acts as the voice of dissent regarding their privileged position as elite, foreign-born actors. He risks real physical violence to offer his drink to a man brutalized by the armed forces, and stays in Bolivia to accompany the bereft Sebastián because the life of acting has left him nothing but spiritual emptiness. Finally, the fragmentation of the once cohesive "master narrative" is demonstrated in the splintering of Sebastián and Costa's friendship and work-team. Sebastián's obsession and egocentrism develop over the course of the film. He reads at first as a leftist intellectual, one whose interest in the indigenous cause coincides with the quincentennial. As previously noted, Sebastián cannot be separated from his alter ego, Gael García Bernal.

Thus, Sebastián acts as representative of Mexico's intellectual or cultural elite. He gives lip service to being "on the side" of indigenous peoples, but in the wash, it is the movie, his *individual* project, that always comes first. He is the character most "connected" to the indigenous cause at first glance, but he is in fact the least able to see their present-day humanity, their *collective* need, as a more important goal than his own personal narrative. His well-meaning public initiatives—as well as the usurpation of the indigenous "image" for his greater artistic vision and leftist political statement—fail because he does not understand the people with whom he is engaging. This appears to be a case of history repeating itself, as we have seen similar usurpation in the 1920s in the government-sponsored discourse of José Vasconcelos's *La raza cósmica*, and in the art of the big three muralists—Diego Rivera, David Alfaro Siqueiros, and José Clemente Orozco—through which a Mexican identity is forged from a mythic indigenous, pre-Columbian past, but is done in a way that, in teleological terms, effectively erases the indigenous people from the present. Mexico "progresses" away from the lived reality of its indigenous people while reifying their origins. Thus, by synecdoche, critiquing García Bernal's character is a critique of Mexico's intellectual class for its lack of concrete solidarity with indigenous rights, at the same time as it more broadly critiques this lack of connection in other parts of Latin America where indigenous populations make up vast underrepresented majorities.

Costa, the Spanish producer, experiences the most transformation throughout the film. The first major step toward an understanding of the indigenous Other in Costa's character comes when he meets with Daniel and his daughter Belén in the warehouse in which they are storing the caravel used in the filming. Belén is acting as Panuca in the film, and is excited to explore the fascinating historical replicas of vast wealth. The inherent inequality of the relationship between Costa and Daniel is made evident as Costa patronizingly tells Daniel in Spanish that he is doing "cojonudo" (Iberian Spanish for "great!"), but he is simultaneously maintaining a conversation in English with a financial backer, saying that Daniel was a problem, but that at least he and the rest of the actors were cheap labor. Costa brags into the phone as Daniel's face registers disbelief, and then quiet rage, that Costa only has to pay the extras two dollars a day, and that Costa finds this fact "fucking great." When Costa returns to Daniel, Daniel responds in English, shaming the producer, and forcing him to address, on a personal level, his imperialist attitude. Daniel tells him that he once worked as a bricklayer in the United Stated for two years and shows that he understands the language of economic domination just as well as Costa—but from below. What Sebastián and María could not achieve, Costa's own shame and guilt could—though not without first selling Daniel out.

Daniel's activism becomes a thorn in Costa's side, and though Costa apologizes to him for his arrogance, their uneasy, economically motivated codependence is exacerbated by Costa's failure to understand the gravity of the local water situation, casting the film as a more urgent priority. Sebastián, although he was nominally Daniel's champion at the beginning of their relationship, is shown as relatively indifferent to the actor's actual lived experience. And when Daniel's social activism gets him captured by the police, Costa and Sebastián's primary concern is for the health of their investment, not for Daniel or his community's well-being.

With dingy yellow lighting to reinforce the sordidness of their behavior, the two wealthy white men are seen in the cramped quarters of a police barracks, greasing the palms of crooked officials who will allow for the release of a bruised and beaten Daniel—only for as long as they need him to finish the filming. In what is to be the culmination of Sebastián's film, the epic scene of indigenous resistance in which Daniel, playing Hatuey, is naked on a cross, spitting in the face of his oppressors, there is a conflation of past and present. Daniel/Hatuey's resistance can be read much as can the noble resistance of Cuauhtémoc in Cortés's *Tercera carta de relación*, in which the fierce Guatimucin (Cuauhtémoc) defends his kingdom and asks to be killed by his captors.[11]

Sebastián and Costa's guilty secrets—their betrayal and abuse of Daniel's trust to further their own interest, as well as their allegiance first to the intellectual pursuit of "social justice" through retelling history, rather than a tangible commitment to the people who suffered the consequences of the perpetual Conquest—are most visibly revealed when the police arrive on set before the filmmakers can finish, or before anyone can warn Daniel that Sebastián and Costa hadn't really paid for his liberation, only for his temporary release—they'd paid for an indentured servitude of sorts.

The blocking and the ethnic marking of these actors echoes a past of crio-llos using natives as cannon fodder in order to maintain their own power, as was the case regarding the independence movements in Mexico and elsewhere in Latin America.

The camera then pans across a field full of crosses, bound and crucified natives, smoke rolling across a misty, lush backdrop, and Daniel/Hatuey having his feet burned as he refuses to submit to the Spanish conquista-dors. The close-ups of his pained but fiercely unwavering gaze elevate him to nobility. Again, Hatuey is read through the lens of Cuauhtémoc's tor-ments; his feet are burned but he will not submit. He will not sell out his people despite the personal sacrifice exacted by the Spaniards.

Costa and Sebastián are confronted with their choice to value the film over the well-being of another human as they nervously watch the police approach, with the roar of "Hatuey, Hatuey" being chanted by the hun-dreds of poorly paid extras. While the police attempt to cuff and remove Daniel, there is a spontaneous rebellion on the very set that reenacts an indigenous resistance ending in death. In real time, however, Daniel escapes with his life. This is another case in which colonial history is pa-limpsestuously "overwritten": by allowing for an escape, by rescuing the water supply, the indigenous resistance is not quashed as in the case of the total decimation of the Mexicas and defeat of Cuauhtémoc and destruc-tion of Tenochtitlán. Daniel/Hatuey is neither killed nor captured by the occupying forces, offering an equally brutal but ultimately more hopeful reading of white/indigenous relations moving into the future.

The crux of the film lies in the way that the characters' choices, their initial failures to take ethical stands, affect each one differently. As the water riots escalate in the city, so too does the urgency to complete the film. Sebastián tries to rally the dubious actors, fearful for their lives, be-hind his last-ditch effort to film his epic. In a final moment of desperation, as they attempt to flee the city and the site of actual indigenous resistance, Sebastián ultimately decides that making the film is more important than anything else, but Costa cannot ignore the pleas of Belén's mother when she begs for his help to save the injured girl.

Meanwhile, after the riots and the heroic sacrifice that Costa makes of the film in order to save Belén's life, the camera pans slowly down over a razed and empty Cochabamba street. There are bricks strewn everywhere, and Costa's jeep approaches. This scene is undoubtedly reminiscent of the devastation of Tenochtitlán, and these colonial echoes are, as I have ar-gued, no accident. Costa descends, and the camera takes a 360-degree pan of him and his surroundings, registering both high-rises and refuse, trees and buildings, as well as a telephone pole that mimics the cross that Costa helped the underpaid crew lift early in the film. As he looks up at the occupied "Agua de Bolivia"[12] building, which is covered in graffiti with slogans like "El agua es vida, carajo" and "Cabrones" covering the transnational company's sign, he asks of an indigenous occupier, "¿Dónde está el ejército?"—to which he receives no reply. There is a close-up of his pained and puzzled face as he hears a bell ringing and a cry: "Detengan la lucha, el agua es de ustedes." The camera cuts to a mid-range backlit shot of a priest, dressed in his habit—an outfit that differs very little from those of the sixteenth-century friars—swinging his bell in the vast emptiness. Smoke swirls up around him, and he is silhouetted as he laments the world's tragic nature in an unoccupied street. The symbolism is clear: the role of the Church, like the role of the conquistadors, has changed with the popular uprisings, and any attempts to mediate between the powerful elite and the oppressed masses are, if anything, an ineffectual afterthought. There is nobody listening, and any attempts at "intercession" are destined to fail, ultimately echoing those attempts made by the likes of Montesinos and Fray Bartolomé de las Casas, but with a revised outcome.

Instead of a move to seamlessly rewrite history, Bollaín's film highlights the collaborative nature of both film and history. The work underscores an urgent connection between the past of Spanish colonial rule and the present and continued subjugation of indigenous people, and the most vulnerable members of disparate societies—such as the indigent in Bolivia and Mexico—in which wealth is polarized and transnational corporations rule. Simultaneously, it attempts to reconcile Spain's role in both the past and present situation in Latin America. Through metonymic relation with Costa and his personal growth, the film allows Spain (and an international audience that has bought into the myths of "discovery") to take responsibility: exposing the legacy of its own role in both the institutionalization of slavery[13] and—in the contemporary predatory corporate practices of the privatization of natural resources—in water, food distribution, and the film industry, to name only a few.

In its own small way, *También la lluvia* not only highlights a realized victory of "social movements from below"; it embodies, precisely through coproduction, a postcolonial or "de-colonial" perspective. While the Ejército Zapatista de Liberación Nacional is not directly named in the film, the demands for basic human rights outlined by the Zapatistas of that group were, only a few years before, present in the enactment of the water riots on screen. Subcomandante Marcos considered it an urgent imperative in the struggle to control ideas to "disseminate alternative visions of indigenous struggles" (Slater 206), and Bollaín's film strives to do just that.

Carlos Aduviri, the Bolivian would-be filmmaker and first-time actor who leads as both Daniel, the political agitator, and Hatuey, the indigenous leader, speaks to the importance of the film for telling "their story."[14] He sees the film as a way to spread the message of resistance to a wider audience, citing the international reach of Bollaín, Laverty, Tosar, and García Bernal as the key to guaranteeing the film's wide distribution and potential penetration.

In the closing sequence of the film, Costa, the once-ignorant, exploitative Spanish producer, has been changed to a degree. In the same warehouse in which Costa first embarrassed himself by making assumptions about Daniel's education and his willingness to work for a pittance, the two men say an emotional goodbye. After having saved Daniel's daughter Belén through an explicit intervention of money and power, there is yet a true sense of caring between the two men, despite their disparate fates. Costa states that it is not likely that he will ever return, and Daniel laments that despite their "victory," the highest price is always paid by his own community, the indigenous majority that still, after five hundred years, are the most vulnerable. Daniel gives Costa a gift in a small wooden box. And Costa walks away while we watch Daniel watch him grow smaller, crossing a backlit threshold and disappearing. This highlights that the Spaniard can still return to his homeland, free from the "dangers" of the underdeveloped nation, reaping all the benefits of his privilege, while the indigenous character is left to muddle through the remnants of his shattered life, to care for his crippled daughter the best he can with what little resources he has been able to defend.

In a technical nod to the cyclical nature of the film's narrative, there is a cut to Costa from inside a taxi cab, returning to his previous life, with colorful markets whizzing by in the background, much like the opening scene that focalized on Sebastián. The camera cuts to Costa's hands, working out knots, revealing what is inside the carefully tied-up, coffin-like box Daniel gave him. There he holds the enormity of Daniel's gift in his hand: a tiny perfume bottle filled with the most precious resource for life—water. He lifts it up and utters the Quechua word he learned, "yaku," and the tired, indigenous eyes of the cab driver are seen registering surprise, or perhaps a wary uncertainty, in the rearview mirror. The gaze lingers, much like Daniel's first penetrating gaze on the screen tests. While Daniel's action of giving a gift to Costa feels somewhat forced and complacent, what saves this film from entirely collapsing into a self-satisfying narrative of the white-savior complex is that the gift is a symbolic reminder to the producer—as well as the international audience, likely to identify with him—of their extreme privilege. The transformation in Costa and all he represents, *También la lluvia* suggests, is truly the gift of being able to see one's own privilege, be it the privilege of being European in Latin America, or being among the social and cultural elite in Mexico. It says to its international audience: the choice is yours; another world *is* possible.

Notes

1. This film was on the Oscar short list. It won a Silver Ariel in Mexico for Best Latin American Film, Best Fiction Film at the Berlin International Film Festival, Best Cinematography, Best Director, Best Film, Best Score, and Best Screenplay at the Cinema Writers Circle Awards in Spain, and many, many other honors (Internet Movie Data Base).

2. Precursors to these films were *El Santo Oficio* (Arturo Ripstein, 1974) and *Nuevo Mundo* (Gabriel Retes, 1976).

3. On the quincentennial of Bartolomé de las Casas's birth, José María Muría wrote a volume, *Bartolomé de las Casas ante la historiografía mexicana*, that outlines the wildly disparate views of Las Casas between historians from colonial times to the time the book was produced (1974), considering Las Casas one of the most controversial figures in the history of Mexico (10).

4. García Canclini suggests, drawing the idea of a colonial-era Mexico City into dialogue with contemporary media production, that "media circuits support the bulk of weight once shouldered in Mexico City by traditional central spaces of congregation, and these circuits convey information and imaginaries of urban life no longer [responsive] solely to national projects" (212).

5. García Bernal, along with Diego Luna and the filmmaking trio—Alfonso Cuarón, González Iñárritu, and Guillermo del Toro (with screenwriter Guillermo Arriaga)—are perhaps the driving force behind the explosion of international screen time that Mexican film has won during the last decade.

6. Gael García Bernal as an actor is an indisputable international superstar. Interestingly, however, he has not limited himself to just acting. For example, his production company Canana Films acted as executive producers of the award-winning film, *Cochochi* (Israel Cárdenas, Laura Amelia Guzmán, 2007), which was filmed in the Tarahumara highlands of Chihuahua. As a producer, García Bernal acts as a public intellectual/activist in support of social equity through his sponsorship of quality film projects. In fact, Canana has been exploring many new media tactics, including "view-on-demand" media, to promote and distribute their films and others from Latin America on a Pan-Latin platform, to connect across previously discrete and disconnected national markets (Hopewell).

7. Haddu notes that Carrasco's film, started in 1992, took six years to complete "because of the financial burdens of seeing through an ambitious project with limited funding" (156).

8. In fact, in the "The Making of *También la lluvia*," Paul Laverty notes his personal fascination with the question, "¿Quiénes son los dueños de la gran narrativa de la Historia?"

9. This sermon, attributed to Dominican Fray Antón de Montesinos on December 21, 1511, was recorded by Fray Bartolomé de las Casas and appears in volume 2 of his *Historia de las Indias* (441–44).

10. Lewis Hanke, in his introduction to Bartolomé de las Casas's writing, notes both the contradictory nature of his place in history and his truly pan-Latin Americanness: "Se convirtió en célebre campeón de los indios y durante medio siglo fué una de las relevantes figuras de la época que España ha conocido nunca. Desde su gran despertar en Cuba en 1514 hasta su muerte en Madrid en 1566, a la edad de 92 años, fué sucesivamente reformador en la corte española, fracasado colonizador en Venezuela, fraile en La Española, obstructor en Nicaragua de guerras que él consideraba injustas, combatiente en pro de la justicia para los indios en acerbos debates con los eclesiásticos en México, promotor del plan para conquistar y cristianizar a los indios de Chiapas en Guatemala por medios pacíficos solamente, afortunado agitador en la corte del emperador Carlos V a favor de las Nuevas Leyes, y obispo de Chiapas" (XI).

11. Lira González writes an exhaustive study on the different ways in which Cuauhtémoc's capture was reported in the historiographic chronicles of the colonial era.

12. In the real protests of April 2000, the transnational company that privatized the water was called "Aguas del Tunari."

13. Bollaín explains in "The Making of *También la lluvia*" that she wished to highlight not Columbus's mythical status as a visionary and an explorer, but rather the often ignored historical fact that he was not only a "discoverer" but also among the first to govern in the Spanish colonies, and he was directly responsible for the systems of subhuman treatment of indigenous slaves and the imposed tribute extracted from their natural resources.

14. In "The Making of *También la lluvia*," Aduviri discusses the fact that he *has* made some short films, but because of economic factors, he had not (yet) been able to make his own feature-length film. Bollaín discusses, in a dialogue that parallels one in the script, that Aduviri was chosen for her film precisely because of his "unconventional" looks, small stature, and "untrained/unspoiled" quality. He was chosen over transnational stars from Peru, just as in Sebastián's film within a film.

Works Cited

Alvaray, Luisela. "National, Regional, and Global: New Waves of Latin American Cinema." *Cinema Journal* 47.3 (2008): 48–65.

Bloch, Catherine. "La güera Rodríguez y Gertrudis Bocanegra." *La ficción de la historia: El siglo XIX en el cine mexicano.* Ed. Ángel Miquel. México, D.F.: Cineteca Nacional, 2010. 30–35.

Chorba, Carrie C. *Mexico, From Mestizo to Multicultural: National Identity and Recent Representations of the Conquest.* Nashville: Vanderbilt University Press, 2007.

Cortés, Hernán. *Cartas de relación.* 1522. Ed. Ángel Delgado Gómez. Madrid: Castalia. 1993.

D'Arcy, David. "Director Icíar Bollaín on Her New Film *También la lluvia.*" *San Francisco Chronicle.* http://www.sfgate.com/entertainment/article/Director-Iciar-Bollain-on-her-new-film-Even-the-2476349.php. Accessed February 13, 2011.

García Canclini, Néstor. "From National Capital to Global Capital: Urban Change in Mexico City." Trans. Paul Liffman. *Public Culture* 12.1 (2000): 207–13.

Gordon, Richard A. *Cannibalizing the Colony: Cinematic Adaptations of Colonial Literature in Mexico and Brazil.* West Lafayette: Purdue University Press, 2009.

Haddu, Miriam. "The Power of Looking: Politics and the Gaze in Salvador Carrasco's *La otra conquista.*" *Contemporary Latin American Cinema: Breaking into the Global Market.* Ed. Deborah Shaw. Lanham, MD: Rowman and Littlefield Publishers, 2007. 153–72.

Hanke, Lewis. "Bartolomé de las Casas, Historiador." Introduction, *Historia de las Indias.* Bartolomé de las Casas. Ed. Agustín Millares Carlo. México, D.F.: Fondo de Cultura Económica (FCE), 1950. ix–lxxxvi.

Hopewell, John, and Emilio Mayorga. "Canana Looks to Manana." *Variety*, February 15, 2010. http://variety.com/2010/biz/news/canana-looks-to-manana-1118015254. Accessed October 18, 2012.

Hutcheon, Linda. *The Politics of Postmodernism.* New York: Routledge, 2003.

Internet Movie Database. http://www.imdb.com/?ref_=nv_home. Accessed November 19, 2012.

Las Casas, Bartolomé de. *Historia de las Indias.* Vol. 2. 1875. Ed. Lewis Hanke. México, D.F.: FCE, 1965.

Lira González, Andrés. "Las palabras de Cuauhtémoc en la historiografía de los siglos XVI a XIX." *Relaciones* 47 (1991): 61–84.

"The Making of *También la lluvia.*" *También la lluvia.* A. V. H. San Luis S. R. L., 2010. DVD.

Menton, Seymour. *La nueva novela histórica de la América Latina, 1979–1992.* Trans. Seymour Menton. México, D.F.: FCE, 1993.

Mignolo, Walter. *The Idea of Latin America.* Malden, MA: Blackwell, 2005.

Muriá, José María. *Bartolomé de las Casas ante la historiografía mexicana.* México, D.F.: SEP, 1974.

Navarrete Linares, Federico. "Historia y ficción: Las dos caras de Jano." *El historiador frente a la historia: Historia y literatura.* México, D.F.: UNAM, 2000. 7–39.

Seydel, Ute. *Narrar historia(s): La ficcionalización de temas históricos por las escritoras mexicanas Elena Garro, Rosa Beltrán y Carmen Boullosa.* Madrid: Iberoamericana/ Vervuert, 2007.

Slater, David. "'Another World is Possible': On Social Movements, the Zapatistas and the Dynamics of 'Globalization from Below.'" *Geopolitics and the Post-Colonial: Rethinking the North-South Relations.* Malden, MA: Blackwell, 2004. 197–222.

También la lluvia. Dir. Icíar Bollaín. Dir. A. V. H. San Luis S. R. L., 2010. DVD.

Villazana, Libia. "Hegemony Conditions in the Coproduction Cinema of Latin America: The Role of Spain." *Framework: The Journal of Cinema and Media* 49.2 (2008): 65–85.

CHAPTER TEN

Children's Literature on the Colonia

La Nao de China, the Inquisition, Sor Juana

Emily Hind

Mexican colonial histories for children published after the year 2000 concern this volume in terms of three themes: first, the maritime trade route between Acapulco and the Philippines; second, the Tribunal of the Holy Inquisition; and finally, the biography of Sor Juana Inés de la Cruz. The present analysis pays attention to both the use and suppression of a gothic mood as it affects the three thematic groupings. On an international level, gothic styling has become so familiar that the aesthetic "is probably more popular now than it has ever been" (Heiland 156). This global popularity reflects the power of the gothic to contradict the rational impulse of the Enlightenment, since the shadows, mysteries, and unknowable yet enclosed spaces of the gothic mode provide relief from the demands of a contrasting, rational progress narrative (Anolik 2). In terms of Mexican literary tradition, that eerie tone characterizes Heriberto Frías's turn-of-the-previous-century chapbooks on Mexican history, available in the eighty-five installments of the Biblioteca del Niño Mexicano (1899–1901) and illustrated by José Guadalupe Posada (Alcubierre Moya 121).[1] Frías finds the colonia memorable largely for its horrors. About a century later, the post-2000 histories for children show that gothic narrative tactics can be used, on the one hand, in texts that represent the colonia as a period of appalling cruelties that must never be repeated, and, on the other hand, in texts that warn that contemporary realities engage the colonia and thus enclose the past within the present. These two approaches call upon familiar gothic moods by emphasizing themes of transgression and monstrosity, as well as enclosure and persecution. These topics create fear in the reader, and as Frías knew, suspense keeps an audience engaged with a story.[2] Despite what could be termed a "gothic creep," suggesting that the eerie is continually edging into many colonial histories, the three topics in the more recent histories sometimes attempt to sidestep the spooky with troublingly dry results. For example, work on La Nao de China that would avoid the gothic mode largely eliminates human figures. The Inquisition lessons that would evade the gothic tactic look to numbers to quantify events, and when it comes to Sor Juana, biographies that would refuse the gothic tend to insist on the wholly admirable, and consequently inaccessible, nature of the poet-nun's timeless, undead model. The contradiction that wavers between treating children as "special" readers who would require character-infused, gripping, gothic-tinged narratives, or addressing children as mature readers who can handle a stricter, more factual approach, hints at a larger debate in our time regarding the disputed divisions between childhood and adulthood. It is not clear which group ultimately proves the more "innocent" when it comes to the difficult legacy of Mexican colonial history.

Manila Galleons in Mexican Children's Literature

Recent Mexican narratives for children on the subject of the colonial trade route tend to emphasize maps and objects, rather than characters and adventure; thus, their young readers are imagined to possess a high tolerance for factual information.[3] Even the summaries of these texts can bore, and thus before reviewing the titles, it makes sense to acquaint the reader with a radically different approach to similar topics. The lively British series of history books for children whose titles begin with some variation of the phrase "you wouldn't want to" show that accurate history of maritime activities, to name only one topic covered, can be enthralling. In these English-language books, humorous cartoon figures in the midst of a busy layout convey excitement and humor and create a sense of progressive sequence. The books always begin by giving the reader instructions on taking on a starring role. For example, in *You Wouldn't Want to Sail with Christopher Columbus! Uncharted Waters You'd Rather Not Cross* (2004), the first lines directly address the reader: "The year is A.D. 1492. The place is Palos, a harbor town in southwestern Spain. . . . You're ten years old and it's time for you to find a job to help support your family" (Macdonald 5). The reader's explicit engagement finds further incentive in a fun, cartoonish aesthetic that can be described as "only flirting" with the gothic. Despite endless grotesque details drawn from eras that predate modern medicine and human-rights law, the histories never tip into the fully creepy, because their details amuse more than they horrify. That is, the British series does not participate in the same gothic tone found in some Mexican texts, mostly thanks to the giggling foreign books' upbeat illustrations. Furthermore, the humorous British books never suggest that beyond the parameters of each book, young readers should want to go back to the past and reside in its setting, or that the present operates as a faithful reflection of this past. In the European histories, the past seems delightfully and thankfully *past*. Not so in the Mexican books.

In contrast to the sequential delivery of disturbing details that make for a rip-roaring good time *and* a history lesson in the British series, *El galeón de Manila: Los objetos que llegaron de Oriente* (2005), by Rosa Dopazo Durán, features statically serene and collage-like drawings of ships, maps, and vague people, along with some final images from the collection in the Franz Mayer museum, where the author works. Two more contemporary-styled illustrations in the text mercifully present a brief appeal to more playful sensibilities. One picture shows human legs sticking out of the ocean surface near a shark fin, and another portrays Posada-like skeletons strewn about on a galleon deck. However, most of the text seems only loosely aimed at a young audience, if younger audiences can be assumed to prefer stories with engaging plots and specific characters. For example, consider the unexciting conclusion that means to relate the trade route to the present time:

> Y más allá de intercambios comerciales y artísticos, esa línea que se tendió de Acapulco a Manila, influyó de manera determinante en nuestra cultura, pues además de los objetos, llegaron también chinos y filipinos que trajeron consigo tradiciones y costumbres, formas de vestir, de hablar y de comer, y que formaron familias que probablemente todavía encuentren en sus recuerdos el eco del mar que atravesó el Galeón de Manila. (47)

The fact that no image of the aforementioned families appears suggests the abstract nature of the human relations portrayed. A stronger sense of humor—but the same generally dry approach—characterizes Claudia Burr and Rebeca Orozco's *Lo que va y lo que viene: La Nao de China* (2006). This book takes inspiration from the writings of Gerónimo Monteiro, an admiral from the mid-eighteenth century. Unfortunately for children in

search of a heroic protagonist, Monteiro does not appear in the text until the notes at the end, which seem focused on informing teachers instead of entertaining youngsters. In a second, perhaps more regrettable move for younger readers, the authors use images taken from the colonial period, and the visuals concentrate not on humans but ships, without developing a sequential sense of action from page to page. Still, an occasional touch of humor manages to interrupt the rather inert transmission of data, as a "you wouldn't want to" moment occurs with the mention of scurvy. The authors confide that dozens of people onboard died after losing their teeth to the disease, since the stricken travelers could not swallow or chew (Burr and Orozco n.p.). Unfortunately for child readers inclined to gaze upon historical horror, the above lines accompany a placid drawing of a ship.

Interest in the trade route between Acapulco and the Philippines is not new, and in a history text for young readers published in 1900, Heriberto Frías takes a different tack when he enthuses, "¡Se llamaba la *nao de China*! ¡Con qué delicia era esperada en México aquella maravillosa *nao*!" (*Los crímenes* 10). In contrast to Frías's merry enthusiasm when it comes to telling children about the trade ship, the title of the relevant chapbook, *Los crímenes y las epopeyas de México colonial*, emphasizes law-breaking and strikes a chord closer to the delicious frisson of the "you wouldn't want to" British series. A gothic aesthetic more plainly characterizes another of Frías's history titles, *El fantasma carnicero* (1900). The promise of a scary tale seems likely to hook readers, and Frías doubtless believed that the dreadful tone would convince an otherwise reluctant audience to read about the colonia. The contradictions of this approach bear emphasizing: somehow, a portrayal of the colonia as a disagreeably violent period of history was intended to cast that time as a more attractive subject. The fact that Frías felt he had to overcome audience disinterest in the colonia appears in his lamentation from *Los crímenes y las epopeyas de México colonial*, in which he exclaims that grown men had elected to protect their ignorance of the period: "Fueron pasando los años, los años unos tras otros, sin que ninguno de los hombres . . . quisieran [*sic*] saber los estupendos hechos de la vida de México durante la dominación de los virreyes! [*sic*]" (5–6). Frías implies that his young audience exercises greater intellectual bravery, in a tactic reminiscent of the British books that grant young readers trusted maturity to learn "what you wouldn't want to." In Frías's texts, the dynamic pits children's willing loss of innocence against adults' refusal to read about colonial history. Still, a framework of historic optimism applies, because Frías contends that the past matters because it is *not* the present. His turn-of-the-century Manichaeism simplistically

splits the colonia from Mexican Independence by calling one unhappy and the other righteous. For example, in *El fantasma carnicero*, Frías writes,

> ¡Ay amiguitos mexicanos que leéis estas líneas en que se os traza por mano amiga, algo como el cuadro de aquellas tristezas de nuestros antepasados pobres, sabed que en México durante la época que se ha llamado *Colonial* y es aquella en la que gobernaron los *virreyes*, época que duró muy cerca de trescientos años . . . durante esos tres siglos, siempre la vanidad, el orgullo y la crueldad de los ricos españoles, privaron sobre los dolores y trabajos del indio . . . (5)

This hypnotic prose, with long sentences and many ellipses, manages to create tension for the young reader by giving a "friendly" hand to a creepy presentation of Spanish cruelty. The touted optimistic vision of Mexican Independence as a cheery solution to the colonia aligns Frías with the official nationalist efforts that celebrated a progress narrative for Mexican history.

Today, Mexican authors who write for a young audience continue to fight the perception that knowledge of the colonia is unnecessary or unpleasant, and that to know a little about the period is already to know too much. In his history book for young people published in 2004, Alfonso Miranda Márquez explains that readers avoid the subject of the colonia because they associate it with the Conquest: "Frecuentemente, sólo nos quedamos con una terrible imagen violenta, aunque hay mucho más. Cuando analicemos correctamente este periodo, podremos conciliarnos con nuestra propia historia y liberarnos del pesado lastre de la incomprensión" (7). Miranda Márquez seems to blame writers like Frías for perpetuating the negative reputation of the colonia. The point on which Miranda Márquez and Frías coincide relates to the idea that knowledge of the colonia results in freedom. In an approach also critical of the Manichaeism wielded by writers like Frías, Estela Rosselló writes her children's history book, published in 2007, to express misgivings regarding the portrayal of the colonia as three centuries of immobility and obscurantism, succeeded by the heroic years of the Mexican Independence (44). Rosselló champions the renewed study of the colonia that would link the present with that foundational time: "Por más lejana y diferente que nos parezca la sociedad virreinal, lo cierto es que muchas de nuestras costumbres, ideas, creencias, formas de relacionarnos, instituciones, expresiones al hablar o manifestaciones artísticas datan, precisamente, de la época colonial" (44). Rosselló follows a trend supported, to varying degrees, by fellow children's history writers when she hints that the colonia relates to the future as a reflection of the past. The gothic potential in the suggestion that the present is enclosed in the past, and is thus gloomily foretold, may catch the interest of a younger public eager for a ghost story, and thus Roselló's narrative, perhaps somewhat unintentionally, ends up echoing Frías's technique.

Another relatively recent text that repeats Frías's gothic lure is *El Tombuctú* (2000) by Edna María Orozco. This illustrated story tells of two Spanish boys in the capital of New Spain who imagine their canoe, *El Tombuctú*, to be a vessel worthy of the adventures had by La Nao de China.[4] The eeriness arrives with Melchora, the black slave who can conjure the "soul" that all things have (24). During perilous floods in the capital, the slave magically calls El Tombuctú to her so that she, her "amitos," and her *amitos*' family can escape the rising waters. The slave does not attempt to achieve an overarching solution to stop the bad weather; instead, she seems satisfied with the small group's escape (31). It remains unclear whether Melchora cannot speak to the soul of the rain, or whether she simply refuses to, and here arises the ambiguity of depicting a slave who rescues her "little owners" with comfortingly "white" magic. In spooky conflict that underscores the racism of "white" and "black" magic, Melchora's powers always retain a suspicious connotation of "black" enchantment for the privileged Spanish family, whose members help to perpetuate the "black" legend of New Spain. By no means does Melchora reassure the reader conscious of the horror of slavery when she says "softly" to the boy who asks about the canoe as a means of rescue, "Todo puede pasar, mi querido pichoncito" (11). The possible threat contained in that line probably occurs to at least some young Mexican readers. In harmony with the enigmatic persecutions that underpin the gothic tradition, *El Tombuctú* never deciphers Melchora's underlying intentions and thereby allows the reader to determine the possible level of aggression contained in the slave's actions.

The gothic potential inherent in the idea that the past continues to "live," spectrally, in the present, by way of a ghost story or some other uncanny transgression, works to combat the daunting distance of the colonial topic. The alien nature of the colonia surfaced in emails by the aforementioned child-history authors Claudia Burr and Rosa Dopazo Durán, who generously responded to my query about whether the topic of the commercial trade route between Acapulco and Manila in their works was meant to acknowledge implicitly the recent wave of Asian immigration to Mexico. Dopazo Durán gave a blunt answer, to the effect that the two time periods

have nothing to do with one another: "No tiene nada que ver con la po-
blación creciente de orientales [*sic*], sólo que hay fenómenos sociales que
se repiten en la historia." For her part, Burr did not answer the specific
question, but she did spell out the difficulty of writing about that era: "La
Colonia para los niños de hoy tiene poco o nada que ver con su cotidiani-
dad." Nonetheless, Burr and Dopazo Durán showed they believe that
knowledge of the colonia matters when it comes to an adequate compre-
hension of Mexican history. Even though the prospect of learning about
La Nao de China might at first seem irrelevant to young, technologically
savvy cybernauts, these authors believe in the importance of supplying the
information.

Aside from the gothic possibility, a second possible point of interest for
children who would study the colonial trade route has to do with a central
contradiction in children's literature, as pointed out by Perry Nodelman,
who notes that in order to learn about the securities of home, a child must
leave. This movement provokes a kind of contamination that spoils adult
ideas about children's obedience, immobility, and innocence (81). Thus,
one way to interest young readers in the topic of the high-seas trade would
be to play up the aspect of human adventure. Because contemporary
youths spend increasing amounts of time indoors, they might especially
enjoy the possibility of reading about the shipping routes. While it may be
understandable that Mexican history writers today do not readily use the
gothic aesthetic when talking about the cultural significance of La Nao
de China, it does perhaps seem surprising that writers similarly avoid the
gothic, even when exploring the matter of the Inquisition for young
readers.

Inquisition by the Numbers

Rather than using the gothic aesthetic, children's texts on the Inquisition
usually approach the subject through facts, such as the start and end dates
of the event. Even in the midst of the fictionalized narrative in Agustín
Ramos's *El preso número cuatro* (2000), the page layout includes inserted
boxes of factual text. The fates of the four prisoners, perhaps due to dis-
couraging wordiness, turn out to be less interesting than the inserted selections of precise historical data. One of the text boxes explains that the
Tribunal of the Holy Inquisition was formed in 1571, and that between
1522 and 1820, the Inquisition executed 296 prisoners (12). The numbers
also clarify that "El Tribunal de la Acordada llegó a tener dos mil quinientos

tenientes o comisarios al mando de un capitán, que ejercían el terror, principalmente sobre los pobres. En menos de un siglo, entre 1719 y 1813, la Acordada ejecutó a ochocientos ochenta y ocho prisioneros" (23). The historic sources on the Inquisition may promote this reliance on numbers, although the urge to avoid turning history into a gothic horror show may also influence the paint-by-numbers technique. A second example of the number-intensive data appears in Carmen Saucedo Zarco's history, which includes a news item from the *Gazeta de México* from 1730, which informs readers of the date on which an "auto de fe" was carried out with four prisoners (*La Nueva España* 36). Of course, this parade of dates and sums can support distinct interpretations. In Roselló's history, the numbers seek to minimize the horrors of the Inquisition:

A diferencia de lo que ocurría en Europa en los siglos XVI y XVII, en la Nueva España, la Inquisición no quemó ni ejecutó a un gran número de personas. Se dice que durante los trescientos años de su existencia, el Santo Oficio no condenó a muerte a más de cincuenta personas; sin embargo, el miedo, la amenaza y la tortura sí fueron mecanismos muy utilizados por el tribunal para lograr que las personas se delataran entre sí o se autoacusaran. (19)

Roselló also uses a comparative perspective to diminish the gruesomeness of the numbers, and she mentions the witches of Salem, New England—where, in four months, more than 150 people accused of witchcraft were tried, and ultimately nineteen of them were hung (18). This mathematical approach to history risks leaving the young reader with the interpretive burden, which hints that if the adult historian does not seem to know what the numbers mean, less expert youngsters might not know what to do with the information, either.

In another example of the numerical approach, Alejandro Rosas uses the children's history *De Tenochtitlán a la Nueva España* (2007) to explain that the first "auto de fe" occurred in 1574, with punishment imposed on eighty-nine people accused of crimes against the faith, of whom five were burned (77). The narrative surrounding the numbers means to compensate for the weak interpretive content of the hard data—and Rosas specifies, for example, that the Monte de Piedad building is the present-day site of some Inquisitorial events; he also notes that the colonial convictions were carried out in today's Alameda (77). This spatial reference brings the past into the present with the effect of issuing a gothic invitation to view the historic center of Mexico City through the gloomy filter of the Inquisition. Thus, in between the almost unspoken meanings of the numbers and the apparently unspeakable details of the tortures, there remains a more accessible interpretive option of enclosing the present in the past. This example of the "gothic creep" shows that even in the midst of a would-be factual presentation, the effort to bring the colonia into young readers' daily lives does not shy away from harnessing the sensationalism of the gothic mood.

A review of the legal changes that occurred between the times of the early practices of the Inquisition and the later habit of duels concerns Elisa Speckman Guerra's unlikely, yet entertaining illustrated book on the history of Mexican law for young readers, *¿Quién es criminal? Un recorrido por el delito, la ley, la justicia y el castigo en México (desde el virreinato hasta el siglo XX)* (2006). That text concludes by recognizing the ongoing evolution of the law: "Este libro—al igual que todos los que describen las ideas y las instituciones de nuestra sociedad—todavía no se ha acabado de escribir" (70). Since this legal evolution has no ending or stable interpretation, it appears to insist on a tradition of error that characterizes the past, and at the same time, through linking the present to the past, the text implies the inevitability of further error. Significantly for this odd journey "back to the future" for young readers, the recent children's histories of the colonia are populated almost entirely by adults. At first glance, this emphasis seems like a fortunate tendency, given that one way to cordon off the colonial past and thus "liberate" the future for young readers might be to focus on adult historical characters. Ultimately, however, it seems that the division between past and present, or adult historic protagonists and present-time child readers, can set up a gothic trap. In the recent colonial histories, the national Mexican project does not seem to create the country in a foundational way, but instead merely recreates it, and this recreation tends to hint that young readers' futures are trapped in history. That is, if the endeavor of founding the nation originally inspired the saying, "Gobernar es poblar," now it would seem that to govern is to resettle. For children, this means that the prospect of growing "up" into Mexican citizens might also connote the notion of growing "down" by extending roots into tradition and historical folly.

To illustrate the potential trap of growing "backward" into the celebrated and yet notoriously imperfect adult figures of the past, I turn to the free national textbook *Formación cívica y ética* for the second grade, (2010).[5] In this text, required for *all* second-graders in Mexico, an activity titled "Me esfuerzo por ser mejor persona" asks readers to work in groups and research one of four historical personalities: Cuauhtémoc, Sor Juana

Inés de la Cruz, Benito Juárez, or Carmen Serdán (47). The impression of a gothic return grows stronger on the next page, on which the reader finds the second-person instruction to ponder the qualities appreciated in these "héroes y las heroínas de tu país" (48). These exercises do not automatically presume the value of innocence in readers because they require children to locate themselves among the adult heroes of the past, who saw particularly difficult, even bloody, events. The self-improvement exercises that propose a future in history ask second-grade readers to meditate on their personal flaws that do not match up with those of the historic characters, with the aim of having children assimilate their behavior into that of the named national heroes.[6] This task suggests a certain defiance of the notion of freely willed personal improvement, given that under the gothic schematic, the effort to know oneself can lead to self-identification as a reincarnated Other, as in the sometimes school-assigned novella *Aura* (1962) by Carlos Fuentes, to name an example drawn from Mexican fiction.

The degree to which Mexican history authors admit that their texts ask children to imagine themselves as part of the community of adults that resides in the historic past understandably presents a tricky operation. It bears emphasizing that under this aesthetic, to aspire to grow "up" into a person like Cuauhtémoc or Sor Juana is really to imagine evolving back through time. The ambivalence that young readers might feel in response to this injunction to seek self-betterment among deceased and evidently imperfect national heroes, perhaps unexpectedly, actually contradicts Heriberto Frías's reassurance that young readers need not return to the horrors of the colonia in life, but only in narrative. In contrast to Frías's optimism, the post-2000 tendency in Mexican histories for children is to recognize with ambivalence that the colonia persists. As an additional contemporary snare, Mexican history, as presented by Mexican writers, is full of mistakes and injustices committed by adults. Thus, the future that returns to the past hints at an odd bargain that would have children build a future in the past—and on a foundation of known mistakes. The loosening of authority in the history books for children accompanies the admission of historical error evident in practices such as slavery and all those related to the Inquisition. This new interpretive flexibility leads to another reason why the histories of the new millennium do not promise an authentic liberation from the past for children: historians can no longer easily affirm the motto of the Iberoamericana University, with its ominous future tense, "La verdad os hará libres." That is, the recent histories of the colonia cannot support the foregone freedoms of univocal truth ("la verdad") or its implied progressive plot. What historians now tend to promote for young

Mexicans involves multiple versions of truth that generally engage one another in unresolved contradictions and nevertheless continue to structure the future.

Another Inquisition history for children appears with Santiago Cortés Hernández's *El hombre que se convirtió en toro y otras historias de la Inquisición* (2006). This sophisticated book makes use of many colorful illustrations to explain itself—mercifully, in light of the density of the texts taken from the Archive of the Inquisition in Mexico City (57). The drawings help the reader visualize a pact with the devil that turns out to be illusory, since the Inquisition determines that the story in question is groundless rumor (39). The story's lack of a univocal truth—or any truth at all—emerges when the character Cortés Hernández casts suspicion on the veracity of the protagonist, that is, the man turned into a bull by diabolic influence: "Muy probablemente era un acusado imaginario que tal vez ni siquiera existió" (39). Instead of dismissing or making fun of colonial history-cum-folktales, Cortés Hernández counsels that narrative is valuable in itself and was useful to the illiterate people who related to these archival stories differently than did the literate Inquisitorial researchers. This literary value connects to the contemporary reader's present: "Tal vez nos sorprenda encontrar que todas las historias, las nuestras y las suyas, las de entonces y las de cualquier época, tienen una misma lógica, unos temas parecidos y una manera semejante de encerrar enseñanzas y entretenimiento" (55). In tune with our media-saturated times that thwart children's innocence, contemporary children's books on the Mexican colonia do not debate the principle of young readers' innocence per se, but rather the degree of influence that the past works on the present.

The matter of children's innocence is worth reviewing, since it underpins one current of thinking regarding the reasons for writing books for children, rather than simply asking children to read books also written for adults. In *The Disappearance of Childhood*, Neil Postman argues that the "Western" concept of childhood developed as a consequence of the spread of the printing press and the subsequent division between those who could read and those who could not; this new rift between children and adults based on literacy skills created the notion of childhood, which in Postman's analysis peaked in the century lasting from 1850 to 1950 (18, 67). With the arrival of television in the mid-twentieth century, the adult secrets kept in books were no longer so removed from children's reach, and the nonliterate group became less "childish" as a result (80). The difference that Mexico presents with this version of "Western" history turns on an alternate reading scene. At the very time that Frías was optimistically writing for children, literacy rates rose slowly in Mexico: between 1895 and 1910, they grew from 14.4 percent to 19.7 percent (Gonzales, citing Vaughan 526). Thomas Greer clarifies that not until 1960 did the Mexican national literacy rate hit 62.2 percent; working backward, one may see that in 1950, the percentage stood at 55.9 percent, in 1940 at 44.8 percent, and in 1930 at 33.4 percent (467). This different pattern of literacy rates may explain why relatively little research on children in general has been carried out in Mexico. Barbara Potthast and Sandra Carreras's edited volume on children in Latin America recognizes this lacuna. Potthast and Carreras regret that despite academic interest in topics related to homeless children, delinquents, and child labor, broad studies of infancy and youth in Latin America remain in short supply (7). The lack of generalized interest in children suggests that perhaps Mexican literature for young readers never widely imagined the audience as innocent, or especially distinct from adult audiences, and therefore Frías's delighted exploration of the ghastly side of colonial history may have postulated itself as an appeal to young, but not necessarily immature, readers. Now, more than a century later, the "innocence divide" might even be understood to favor adults over children. While historians still wrestle with ways in which to present unpleasant facts to young readers, some adults in the media, both foreign and Mexican, appear to conform to the "see-no-colonia adults" of Frías's above-mentioned complaint when the grown-ups argue that "today" is the least moral time of all, and that a vaguely defined "yesterday" used to safeguard proper morality, a notion that no child reader of colonial history could support.

Given the factual forthrightness evident in Mexican colonial histories for young audiences, Nodelman's observations on double meanings or shadow narratives in English-language children's literature require retooling for the Mexican context (77). While it would not be accurate to claim that no shadow narrative exists in books for young students of Mexican history, it does seem that few double histories on the colonia (that is, texts with denser information available to those able to catch the implications available "between the lines") have been published, even for young readers. Perhaps because the twentieth-century Mexican government never saw fit to glorify the colonia, the period does not inspire the multiple versions of history that narrate periods such as that of Mexican Independence and the Mexican Revolution, which consequently might better lend themselves to shadow narratives. Not only, then, do children know as much as adults when it comes to the colonial topic, it seems possible that the children may know even more than adults will admit to understanding about that time.

Ghostly Sor Juana: Transcending Linear Time

In one exception to the rule of imagining the past as a place of error, the image of Sor Juana in recent children's literature conjures a more positive figure. However, because the poet-nun appears as utterly nonnormative, her imagined model quashes any realistic hope of children becoming (like) her. Oddly, since Sor Juana never dies in a definitive way in the recent histories of the colonia for children, she belongs to a strange temporality of inimitable, transcendent exception. Therefore, her image promises one way out of the gothic trap (the problem of living in the past by virtue of existing in a doomed present), but this solution, due to Sor Juana's peerless nature, does not apply to the young reader in a shared escape. As Blanca Martínez-Fernández writes in spectral terms for her biography of the nun for children, supposedly narrated by Sor Juana herself: "Mi vida fue muy interesante y bonita" (41). Of course, the statement, "My life *was* . . ." denies the normative finality of death. The same strange, but nice, time appears in the surprisingly lengthy text by Irene Livas, awkwardly illustrated by amateur painters ages nine through fourteen. To begin at the ending, the biography placed at the conclusion of the fictional plot reads, "Érase una vez una niña muy inteligente y con mucha voluntad . . . ," and the same page gives the year 1651 as that of Sor Juana's birth (Livas). The "Once upon a time" that begins precisely in 1651 captures this aspect of strangely suspended time that facilitates Livas's fictional text, which consists of letters that a young narrator writes to Sor Juana. The letters always begin in intimate style, "Querida Juana Inés," and the reader never sees Sor Juana's reply. Given Sor Juana's fantastic achievements as a woman, intellectual, and artist in the colonia, her biography for children might be expected to engage one of two traditional genres: the fairy tale or the fable. In fact, neither genre completely informs the biographies. Due to the suspended time that denies Sor Juana a mortal end, her biography does not participate fully in the tradition of a fairy tale, since that genre concludes with the famous "happy ending." On the contrary, the Sor Juana of contemporary children's literature "lives on" without ever really dying.

The approach in children's literature to Sor Juana's undead life does not represent a fable, either, since the moral lesson that would need to emerge is not clear. The new biographies for children suggest that one would have to *be* Sor Juana in order to match her accomplishments, and that goal is impossible given that learning to read at age three, absorbing Latin and mathematics almost by osmosis, and performing both as a beautiful social star at court and a brilliant intellectual dedicated to the convent, are events that simply happen to someone as much as someone can make them happen. Although a child might strive to imitate Sor Juana by becoming a writer, that possibility is not emphasized because the children's histories do not tend to classify Sor Juana primarily as a poet. In an attempt to straddle the line between the roles, Roselló includes Sor Juana in the category of "Religion in New Spain" and imagines the "poetisa" leading a tranquil life in the convent, surrounded by silence and the company of her books (15). Other biographies conceive of Sor Juana's life as more sociable. In the chapter on education in *La Nueva España: Siglos XVII y XVIII* (2009), Carmen Saucedo Zarco presents the poet's life as more agitated, and in a second text, *Sor Juana y don Carlos: Una amistad entre genios* (2007), indicated as meant for lower reading levels, the historian offers noninnocent details. In the latter illustrated text, Saucedo Zarco reveals that upon entering the convent Sor Juana received a slave as a dowry from her mother (23). Saucedo Zarco also explains that Sor Juana's father never recognized her, and thus she did not use the paternal last name until joining the convent (14). This contemporary effort to demystify the poet for children, however, does not quite achieve its goal because there is no way to combat positively the transcendence of Sor Juana's image in Mexico. That is probably why she figures in so many history books for children not so much as a writer, but mostly as an unrivaled celebrity.

In sum, recent biographies of Sor Juana for young readers defy the genre of fables because the texts do not hint that the future can be improved by behaving like a nun, nor that the young Juana learned a moral lesson. The presentation also avoids the fairy-tale model, which insists that wishes can come true, because obviously they did not for the nun. In point of fact regarding the unpleasantness, Livas's book has an imaginary pen pal grasp the threat of Inquisitorial violence:

Querida Sor Juana:
　Se me hace tarde para la escuela. Te escribo a toda prisa, aunque sea un recadito, porque es urgente que sepas algo: tu confesor es de la Inquisición.
　Ay, Juana Inés, me apena decírtelo, pero el padre Antonio, tu consejero querido es tu enemigo. Sí, ese hombre que hace tantos años te dijo que entraras al convento para que tuvieras tiempo de escribir a gusto, ahora anda diciendo que hacer obras de teatro es pecado. (approx. 103)

This missive is the third letter of the book that treats the Inquisition. Although the narrative voice first learns of the institution through the invisible letters from Sor Juana, by this third letter the young student is competent enough to warn the nun about her confessor's political loyalties. However, no lesson can come of these warnings, since Sor Juana's story is already determined. The lack of a moral point to the biography indicates the difficulty of deciding which "facts" in the poet's life matter. One seeming point of agreement is the importance of Sor Juana's birth year, and the date appears in a startling number of texts. Cortés Hernández ends his book about the Inquisition with a colonial chronology that announces 1651 as Sor Juana's birth date (59). A chronology in the fourth-grade free textbook *Historia* (2010) places the iconic black-and-white Sor Juana in a nun's habit next to the year 1651. Despite the nearly universal emphasis on the date, not all scholars agree on exactly which year is correct. The book from the same governmental series for sixth-grade students of *Español* (2010) gives the poet's birth year as 1648.

Martínez-Fernández's lively biography anchors the events of Sor Juana's life at every turn in specific, although perhaps incorrect, dates, continuing with this historical tic until the end of the book, listing "important facts for school" that span a period from 1890 to 1980, or from the passageway of the train through Sor Juana's family property in Nepantla and the destruction of part of the house where Sor Juana lived, to the institution of the Mexican National Day of the Book (43). None of these bookish events may strike some readers as worthy of memorization, or even mention, and thus the chronology may seem to aid mainly the school that would ignore the more fundamental, though perhaps more abstract, information that would connect the poet's political time with that of the children. This disengagement with the heart or "artery" of the history by way of distracting the reader with "capillary" details, which by their very nature lead to nowhere especially central, allows studious children a release from the potential of the gothic trap, because young readers are not likely to understand why the rambling story matters to their futures. In the unlikely case that the nun's long-ago birth year does mean something to young readers in the twenty-first century, it might make sense to include the poet-nun's year of death as well. That date does not appear as often, likely due to the fact that a death date would threaten Sor Juana's magically continued life in suspended time. Interestingly, although Sor Juana never really seems to die, her image seems self-contained, outside the consumer culture that the children readers inhabit. The poet's exceptionality when it comes to now-strange practices, such as always wearing the same outfit in canonical images, leads me to the contentious dividing line between adult and young readers as regards the select population in Mexico today that can afford to buy history books. Specifically, this line of separation has to do with consumption power.

Children, Colonial History, and the New Consumers

Children's books published in Mexico after the year 2000 give surprisingly candid coverage of many colonial topics. Even so, the texts tend to omit reference to some historic phenomena, such as abandoned children and drug use. These omissions probably fail to signal a principal intention of protecting young readers' innocence, given the visibility of these themes in Mexico today. From the street level, children in Mexico can easily observe homeless peers and the use of drugs. Thus, Mexican literature for children may operate not so much according to a dynamic of knowing and not knowing, but as a principle of obstructed participation. The saying "El que calla otorga" suggests that by avoiding meaningful explorations of certain topics in histories of the colonia, such as drugs and sex, the historians end up giving tacit approbation for these phenomena. A cynical view could conclude that children must engage with the censored material, if Mexican society is to continue functioning as it has been. The most gothic aspect of the past enclosed in the present, then, may have to do with the material excised from the histories. The explicit lessons for children in the negative thematic of the colonia deal with forms of violence such as racism, slavery, corruption, and torture, while the topic of Sor Juana allows the additional admission of colonial sexism. These themes recognize the continued relevance of violence and discrimination, and they deliver an implicit reproach to children who would become involved in these practices, since the activities are not viewed positively in the texts. But sex, drugs, and to some extent poverty go untreated in the histories and thus could be erroneously imagined by young readers to represent temptingly new forms of rebellion.

Nevertheless, for the most part, rather than segregation according to literacy levels, or levels of knowing and not-knowing, the dividing line today between children and adults may be centered on the economic. Young people with access to television and Internet today may not so much lack information as they do a means of supporting themselves. Thus, even as childhood disappears, the notion of dependence remains. Mexicans call the young people who today neither study nor work the "ni-ni" generation. Scholars of comparable youthful experience in the United States write about "Guyland" (Kimmel) and "men turning into boys" (Cross) and find the perceived modern (male) immaturity disturbing. Today, across the globe, kids—perhaps especially boys—cannot win, because they are neither innocent children nor satisfactory adults, but something hybrid. Given the probably unprecedented sophistication of contemporary youth when it comes to accessing information, perhaps the disappointment that these still unfamiliar generations present to older adults today has less to do with what kids do or do not know and more to do with what they can or cannot consume, a reality that in one way or another affects how many and what kinds of history books they can read. In a last example of these texts for children, I want to mention the project financed by the General Consulate of the United States, written by Arturo Curiel Ballestero, *Del cacao al dólar* (2007). The book begins with an image by illustrator Felipe Dávalos of a cacao plant with its roots in a credit card. Regardless of the agenda that the book's U.S. backers may have had for the image, it speaks to me of hopeful environmental possibilities. The inability of young people today to consume at the level that adults might wish suggests a path toward sustainability, from a valuable, living plant to an even more purely abstract, "electronic" form of currency. In this image the gothic threat of reliving the past seems, at least potentially, to find a solution. If young readers today cannot buy or travel (e.g., colonize) their way out of their predicaments, they will need to try to think their way out and avoid mistakes already delineated in the history books. Good luck to them!

Notes

1. In spite of Frías's early example, as recently as the 1980s, relatively few Mexican books for children existed. One article reports that from 2000 to 2007, an employee at the Guadalajara bookstore Gandhi saw the children's area expand, as well as noticing that the demand for Mexican children's books rose by some 50 percent (Félix 12). By 2007, according to the same article, the children's area of the Fondo de Cultura Económica bookstore in Guadalajara had expanded from 9 to 200 meters.

2. Heiland observes that the gothic "at its core" is about transgression, of all sorts, and that gothic novels aim "above all" to create fear (3, 5).

3. Histories of the colonia for young people that mention the trade route include those by Rosas (69), Roselló (24–25), and Saucedo Zarco (*La Nueva España* 52, 70, 71).

4. The volumes in the series by Fondo de Cultura Económica are two books in one, with the second book printed upside-down from the first. For example, on the other side of *El Tombuctú* one finds *El preso número cuatro*.

5. *Formación cívica y ética*, for the fourth grade, also reviews Sor Juana's biography and mentions her literary contribution (60).

6. The cues that propose change for second-graders are: "Decido en qué quiero mejorar," "Reflexiono sobre qué quiero lograr," "Para lograr mi propósito voy a realizar las siguientes acciones," and "El tiempo en que voy a alcanzar las metas mencionadas es . . ." (48).

Works Cited

Alcubierre Moya, Beatriz. *Ciudadanos del futuro: Una historia de las publicaciones para niños en el siglo XIX mexicano.* Mexico, D.F.: El Colegio de México; Universidad Autónoma del Estado de Morelos, 2010.

Anolik, Ruth Bienstock. "Introduction: Diagnosing Demons; Creating and Disabling the Discourse of Difference in the Gothic Text." *The Gothic Other: Racial and Social Constructions in the Literary Imagination.* Ed. Anolik and Douglas L. Howard. Jefferson: McFarland, 2004. 1–20.

Burr, Claudia. Message to the author. November 13, 2011. E-mail.

——, and Rebeca Orozco. *Lo que va y lo que viene: La Nao de China.* México, D.F.: Ediciones Tecolote, 2006.

Cortés Hernández, Santiago. *El hombre que se convirtió en toro y otras historias de la Inquisición.* Illustrations by Edgar Clement. México, D.F.: Ediciones Castillo, 2006.

Cross, Gary. *Men to Boys: The Making of Modern Immaturity.* New York: Columbia University Press, 2008.

Curiel Ballesteros, Arturo. *Del cacao al dólar.* Illustrations by Felipe Dávalos. Guadalajara: Consulado General de los Estados Unidos y Petra Ediciones, 2007.

Dopazo Durán, Rosa. Message to the author. November 25, 2011. E-mail.

——. *El galeón de Manila: Los objetos que llegaron de Oriente.* Illustrations by Diego Álvarez. México, D.F.: Ediciones Castillo, 2005.

Español: Sexto grado. 2010. México, D.F.: Secretaria de Educación Pública (SEP), 2011.

Félix, Marcela. "Crece literatura infantil." *Mural,* December 26, 2007: 12.

Formación cívica y ética: Cuarto Grado. 2008. México, D.F.: SEP, 2010.

Formación cívica y ética: Segundo Grado. 2008. México, D.F.: SEP, 2010.

Frías, Heriberto. *Los crímenes y las epopeyas de México colonial.* Biblioteca del niño mexicano. 3rd series: Después de la Conquista. México, D.F.: Maucci Hermanos, 1900.

——. *El fantasma carnicero o el pavor de los verdugos.* Biblioteca del niño mexicano. 3rd series: Después de la Conquista—Virreinato. México, D.F.: Maucci Hermanos, 1900.

Gonzales, Michael J. "Imagining Mexico in 1910: Visions of the Patria in the Centennial Celebration in Mexico City." *Journal of Latin American Studies* 39.3 (2007): 495–533.

Greer, Thomas V. "An Analysis of Mexican Literacy." *Journal of Inter-American Studies* 11.3 (1969): 466–76.

Heiland, Donna. *Gothic and Gender: An Introduction.* Malden, MA: Blackwell, 2004.

Historia: Cuarto Grado. Libro de texto gratuito. 2010. Mexico, D.F.: SEP, 2011.

Kimmel, Michael. *Guyland: The Perilous World Where Boys Become Men.* New York: HarperCollins Publishers, 2008.

Livas, Irene. *Los niños de Nuevo León conocen a Sor Juana.* México, D.F.: Consejo para la Cultura y las Artes de Nuevo León, Consejo Nacional para la Cultura y las Artes (Conaculta), 2002.

Macdonald, Fiona. *You Wouldn't Want To Sail with Christopher Columbus! Uncharted Waters You'd Rather Not Cross.* Illustrations by David Antram. Series creator and designer David Salariya. New York: Franklin Watts, 2004.

Martínez-Fernández, Blanca. *Sor Juana Inés de la Cruz.* Mexico, D.F.: Selector, 2004.

Miranda Márquez, Alfonso. *Historia de México: Conquista, virreinato, independencia.* México, D.F.: Panorama, 2004.

Nodelman, Perry. *The Hidden Adult: Defining Children's Literature.* Baltimore, MD: Johns Hopkins University Press, 2008.

Orozco, Edna María. *El Tombuctú.* Illustrations by Fabricio Vanden Broeck. Introduction by Rodrigo Martínez. Historias de México, Vol. 6.1. Mexico, D.F.: Fondo de Cultura Económica (FCE), 2000.

Postman, Neil. *The Disappearance of Childhood.* New York: Delacorte, 1982.

Potthast, Barbara y Sandra Carreras. "Introducción: Niños y jóvenes entre la familia, la sociedad y el Estado." *Entre la familia, la sociedad y el Estado: Niños y jóvenes en América Latina (siglos XIX–XX).* Ed. Barbara Potthast and Sandra Carreras. Frankfurt: Vervuert, 2005. 7–24.

Ramos, Agustín. *El preso número cuatro.* Illustrations by Fabricio Vanden Broeck. Introduction by Rodrigo Martínez. Historias de México, Vol. 6.2. México, D.F.: FCE, 2000.

Rosas, Alejandro. *De Tenochtitlán a la Nueva España.* Illustrations by Erika Martínez. México, D.F.: Nostra Ediciones, 2007.

Roselló, Estela. *La sociedad novohispana: Vivir y compartir.* México, D.F.: Random House Mondadori/Conaculta/Instituto Nacional de Antropología e Historia, 2007.

Saucedo Zarco, Carmen. *La Nueva España siglos XVII y XVIII.* Illustrations by Alejandro Magallanes. México, D.F.: Nostra Ediciones, 2009.

———. *Sor Juana y don Carlos: Una amistad entre genios.* México, D.F.: Random House Mondadori, 2007.

Speckman Guerra, Elisa. *¿Quién es criminal? Un recorrido por el delito, la ley, la justicia y el castigo en México (desde el virreinato hasta el siglo XX).* Illustrations by Alejandro Magallanes. Coord. La otra escalera. México, D.F.: Ediciones Castillo, 2006.

PART FOUR

Into the Nineteenth-Century Colonia

CHAPTER ELEVEN

Rethinking the Nascent Nation

Historical Fiction and Metanarrative in Pablo Soler Frost's 1767

Anna M. Nogar

Esto es una novela. Es una novela sobre un hecho real, la tristísima expulsión de los jesuitas de la Nueva España, dictada por un déspota ilustrado. Escribir una novela es como enfrentarse a un enemigo que esgrime un hacha a nuestra izquierda y viene armado hasta los dientes; hay que fintar y esquivar y mantener siempre la vista fija en sus movimientos, no sea que erremos y seamos derribados.

—PABLO SOLER FROST, 1767

The straight lines of "historical" novels can fairly be reconstructed from the efforts to bend them.

—DORIS SOMMER, *FOUNDATIONAL FICTIONS*

In a 2008 piece in *Letras libres,* Mexican author Pablo Soler Frost speculated in reference to his novel *1767* that "para poder formular siquiera la pregunta '¿y si no hubiera sido expulsada la Compañía de Jesús del orbe indiano, que habría pasado?' es preciso hacer un ejercicio de imaginación histórica demasiado complejo, casi monstruoso. . . . Es una tarea, me repito, imposible e inútil." Instead of a conjectural past "imposible e inútil" in which the Jesuit order remained in the Spanish colonies in the eighteenth century, Soler Frost's curious 2004 novel recounts a fictionalized history of the Jesuits in Mexico before, during, and after their 1767 exile on the orders of the Spanish Crown. And in this aim, it is successful, and even emblematic of the historical novel. But what lends the novel its engaging and disquieting tenor is its variation from the norms of the genre, its subtle deviation from the very construct it so carefully establishes for the reader. If he or she has the strange sensation while reading the novel that it is somehow more than it portends on its surface to be, that feeling is with good reason, since a parallel metatext within enriches and complicates the reading of *1767* as a purely historical novel.

Needless to say, this has not been the predominant critical reading of the novel to date. Christopher Domínguez Michael's 2004 analysis of the novel centered on *1767*'s apparent narrow focus on the events of the Jesuit expulsion, and on its "transparent" political and religious sympathies. He critiqued the book for its artless reiteration of "la versión jesuítica de la expulsión," which he suggested was limited, "absteniéndose de someterla a examen." In Domínguez Michael's estimation, *1767* was a conservative generic turn from Soler Frost's previous work, shifting "del exotismo al tradicionalismo" from the literary experimentation of the author's preceding works to the staid (but bestselling) genre of the historical novel. The reader unfamiliar with Soler Frost and his work is further cautioned not to imagine that the book is "una broma postmoderna," twisting the historical novel into making fun of itself or of the reader for believing it to be such a text. Domínguez Michael asserts unequivocally that "no lo es"; *1767* is, in his reading, a historical novel played straight, its implicit allegiances and motives consistent with that genre.

While I agree that *1767* is no postmodern tease, neither is it solely the conventional historical novel it portrays itself to be. Rather, the novel functions as two complete literary entities: an actual historical novel, and also a metatext that shares several characteristics of the new historical novel as defined by Seymour Menton and whose purpose is to antagonize the popular historical novel genre. The two entities depend on one another to successfully perform their independent agendas, and in accomplishing this, the novel belies its own stated premise. The interplay of these two elements creates a destabilizing tension for the reader: the focused perspective of the historical novel presents a positive view of the Jesuits and their influence over colonial Mexican society, reproaching the enlightened Spanish Crown's preening and imperious mandate of exile for the order. Meanwhile, the floor shifts under the feet of the historical novel, as the second text, a narrative about the motives for Mexico's independence from Spain, emerges from beneath. The technical means by which Soler Frost accomplishes this feat is the focus of this chapter—that is, how he constructs an authentic historical novel while at the same time subverting it through its own metatext. It is with good reason that Domínguez Michael follows Soler Frost's writing career "con mayor devoción," for the author accomplishes the subtle effect of making the reader question how the genre is constructed, even as he or she reads the text itself.

The success of Soler Frost's project lies in the early and consistent assertion of *1767* as a historical novel. To understand how he accomplishes this, an idea of what that genre comprises is helpful. Elisabeth Guerrero finds the nineteenth-century historical novel (to which Domínguez Michael likens *1767*) "stylistically straightforward, generally including a linear chronology" (4). I take this second point to mean additionally that the novel hitches its plot advancement to the chronology of the historical events narrated. In contrast with contemporary historically based fictions that "invite the reader to reflect upon the creation of the text itself" (Guerrero 4), traditional historical fictions ask the reader to enter the fictional world presented without questioning its production. Ute Seydel, in summarizing Brian McHale's analysis of classic or traditional historical novels in his *Postmodernist Fiction* (1987), finds that historical fictions conform to three general tenets: "la restricción de no desmentir la historiografía oficial, la de no producir anacronismos y, por último, la de no contradecir la lógica y las leyes naturales" (146–47). In clarifying McHale's first point, Seydel notes that "al reconstruir los repertorios del mundo real correspondientes a una época pasada éstos solamente podían insertarse en la ficción histórica cuando no contradecían a la historia oficial" (146–47); that is, the historical fiction must be consistent in its refabrication of the past with an "official" history of some sort. Regarding the last of the three qualities of the historical novel, "era indispensable que las ficciones históricas tradicionales respetaran las convenciones escriturarias del modelo realista-mimético" (Seydel 147–48); the inventive "ficción histórica fantástica" (Seydel 147–48) that inverts chronologies or imagines pasts or futures that did not or could not exist are not part of a traditional historical fiction's repertoire. As explained below, *1767* builds upon these characteristics and others in marking itself out as a historical fiction.

As this chapter's epigraph by Doris Sommer suggests, determining the parameters of a historical novel can also be accomplished by establishing what it is not, or how other, similar genres relate to it. Unlike historically based metafictions and new historical fictions, which use particular literary qualities to engage the reader in disquieting traditional historical readings, historical fictions are characterized by the absence of such tropes. As noted in *Colonial Itineraries of Contemporary Mexico's* introduction, the new historical novel outlined by Menton sets itself apart from a traditional historical novel based on six fundamental parameters: the premising of the novel on the unknowability and circularity of history; the deliberate alteration and manipulation of known historical narrative; the protagonization of prominent historical actors; the implementation of metafictive techniques to underscore the self-aware process of creating fiction; the incorporation of other literary works structurally or as cited sources (intertextuality); and, finally, the deployment of particular Bahktinian characteristics (the dialogic, carnivalesque, parody, and heteroglossia) throughout the text (23–25). While *1767* does implement some of these elements, the sense the novel initially and pervasively impresses upon the reader is that the text will not be participating in the new historical fiction's literary gamesmanship in the same manner that, for example, Enrique Serna's *Ángeles del abismo* (2004) does. Instead, in *1767* the reader is led to understand that he or she will be reading a historical novel, and that, in contrast to the reading experience involved in a new historical novel, his/her role is not to question the events and histories portrayed, but rather to buy into them as they unfold. To this effect, the novel deploys the conceits of historical fiction throughout, but never more convincingly than through the framing of its title and paratexual materials.

1767, as the book's title, anchors the novel temporally in the year the Jesuit order was expelled from Spain's colonies, including Mexico. But beyond that fact, while a book more in keeping with Domínguez Michael's "broma postmodernista" would have manipulated or reread the date, or assigned it a different meaning altogether, *1767*'s subtitle leads unequivocally down the path of the historical novel, stating that the book is "Una novela sobre el destierro de los jesuitas mexicanos." This frank positioning of the novel assures that it is not be read with irony; the title is a directive that informs and models the historical fiction to come.

This declaration of the book's genre is reinforced on its back cover, which reads in part: "Los jesuitas llegaron a México de noche, para pasar desapercibidos y que no se interrumpiera su misión con encargos y festejos. Doscientos años después los desterraron, también de noche, esta vez para evitar que los mexicanos se pusieran de su lado . . . terminaron alucinando al despótico gobierno español, quien, para asombro del universo, decide expulsar a la Compañía de Jesús de todo su imperio en 1767. Esta novela trata de esos meses de 1767." This cover material expresses not only the novel's historical fiction approach, but also the particular sympathies the narrative will assume and which, in keeping with readings of historical fiction, the reader likewise takes on or reacts to upon reading. In this second sense, the book's allegiances are aligned with those of the Mexican Jesuits, who "se granjearon el afecto de las generaciones" and whose "paciencia frente a las adversidades se hizo ciencia, y en el exilio compusieron algunos de los mejores libros mexicanos." Although the back cover concludes discussing the protagonist Pablo Rayón's experience with the Jesuits' exile, which leaves him "completamente transformado"—an allusion to the book's metanarrative—it is just as explicit in its specification that the book is about the events immediately leading to, shaping, and following the Jesuits' expulsion from Mexico. In keeping with Guerrero's definition of the historical novel, the title and back cover propose a straightforward style, recounting a past that is, as Seydel proposes, consistent with a particular historical perspective of those events.

The novel's "Nota" at the end of the book further elaborates this premise by thoroughly documenting the historical sources incorporated throughout the book. The "Nota" explains (with a bit of downplayed cheek, in light of the book's self-deconstructing metanarrative) that the reasons for the meticulous attention to the citation of these materials is to avoid the appearance of plagiarism: "Sabiendo que en estos tiempos es fácil perecer víctima de la acusación del plagio . . . he querido exponer en este aparte los textos que, entrados en mi novela, pudieran tener un poco demasiado que ver con textos de otras personas, y citar, uno por uno, al pie, los que van entrecomillados, de modo que cualquiera pueda consultar dichos textos" (197). The "Nota" continues in this vein, naming the authors whose historical texts are used in the book chapter by chapter. Most were written by exiled Mexican Jesuit friars—including well-known works by Francisco Javier Alegre, Rafael de Zelis, and Mariano Cuevas—and others are secondary sources on the Jesuits, written by contemporary historians. Although many other recent, historically based novels such as *Yo, la peor* by Mónica Lavín, *Malinche* by Laura Esquivel, and *Nen, la inútil* by Ignacio Solares, also include citations or bibliographies of historical sources, *1767*'s "Nota" takes this tendency toward scholarly-style documentation several steps beyond simple citation. It rushes to assure the accuracy of the historical portions of the novel, and elucidates to an almost unnecessary degree that the historical sources used are authentic (they are actual historical writings), that they are cited in the book as they appear in the original texts (they are not distorted), and that their incorporation into the text is consistent with their original gist or message. Through these techniques, the "Nota" differentiates the novel as a whole from postmodern historically based fictions, its proposition adhering to the historical novel's restriction to "no desmentir la historiografía oficial." This distancing from the tendencies of postmodern historically based fictions in terms of how they use historical sources in the text stresses *1767*'s assertion that it is to be read as a historical novel.

Furthering this same tendency to hyperidentify the novel as a work of historical fiction, the "Nota" specifies precisely which historically plausible plot points were imagined by the author, to set them apart from actual historical episodes. The inclusion of these invented elements is explained and justified as a plot device that the reader could have feasibly distinguished as fiction if only because they were not causally possible: "Los dos primeros [episodios ficticios] son imposibles históricos, e improbablemente pudiera haber sucedido el tercero, pero creo que muy difícilmente podría uno haber prescindido de estos episodios en la consecución del relato" (199). This marking out is unusual not so much for what it actually describes—the insertion of fictional characters into two historically real episodes, and the invention of a meeting between the Jesuits and the English—but rather for the fact that the "Nota" discusses them at all. In doing so, it enacts a radical conformity to the historical-fiction genre, explicitly explaining to the reader that there are moments in the text that are completely fictional, and, further, how to distinguish them from fact. Differentiating between the two as the "Nota" does would be irrelevant or even slightly bizarre in a work of new historical fiction, given its characteristic altering of historical events, but 1767's careful division of fact from fiction hearkens back to a nineteenth-century notion of the historical novel as genre distinct from history itself. The insistence of the "Nota" on scrupulously minding the borders of historical fiction underscores McHale's definition of the genre: that in the course of the text, fictional elements may not contradict official histories. As Seydel explains, "La libertad del escritor se limitaba en el siglo XIX a improvisar acciones y propiedades de los personajes históricos, así como de imaginar todos los demás aspectos relacionados con una determinada coyuntura pretérita en torno a los que el recuento oficial no tenía nada que reportar, ya que eran desconocidos o secretos" (147). Ultimately, the parsing of historical elements from fictional ones in the "Nota" not only dramatically frames 1767 as historical fiction, it also compels the reader to explicitly imagine him/herself as a reader of that type of narrative.

1767's stylization of its table of contents and chapter headings further cultivates the sense of the novel as a nineteenth-century vintage historical fiction. Menton contrasts many nineteenth-century titles with new historical fictions in his book, and Domínguez Michael specifies 1767's resemblance to works by nineteenth-century Mexican authors Manuel Payno and Vicente Rivas Palacio. Like Payno's *El Hombre de la situación* (1861), 1767's Índice and chapter headings feature brief, suggestive plot summaries narrating the action of the chapter, many of which are posed from a highly subjective viewpoint and all of which leave the reader with the feeling that his or her interpretation of the contents of the chapter are secondary to those laid out by the table of contents. Worked in among the more pedestrian outlines that include character names ("La descripción del padre Lazcano," "El padre Alegre"); places ("Tepozotlán," "El rancho de don Martín Sánchez Vinuesa"); or general plot movements ("Camino a Veracruz," "Una visita familiar"), one finds more evocative synopses: "¿De dónde procede la autoridad?" "La compañía, ¿sediciosa?" "Nadie los quiere," and "José de Gálvez, hombre de tripas de verdugo." These short summaries, as well as remaining consistent with nineteenth-century stylization, also suggest the omniscient (and biased) third-person narrator that, for Guerrero, defines the traditional historical novel, although the actual narrator(s) of the novel interrupt that sense. Most suggestive of the synopses is chapter 8's "La flor del maguey," which—while on its surface is not of particular interest—gains meaning when elaborated by the chapter's narrative voice: "Imagino a la Compañía como si fuera la flor del maguey, alta, fuerte, hermosa, que preludia la muerte de la radiante planta. Se iban [los jesuitas], y nosotros nos quedábamos sin ellos" (115). Speaking in metaphor, the narrator invokes the symbolic maguey plant to manifest the connection between the Jesuit order's departure and its impact on Mexican citizens, emphasizing the relationship between the two that is laid out more generally in the brief plot summary. For a contemporary reader, the chapter summaries make the book feel like a nineteenth-century historical fiction, and they invoke the type of reading demanded by such texts: straightforward and through the lens of a subjective narrator.

These structural and paratextual elements undeniably frame *1767* as a historical fiction; moreover, the text itself also behaves as such, as it both cleaves close to a particular historical record and presents a distinct bias in how the historical events are portrayed. *1767* as a whole therefore conforms with this major conceit of the historical novel, for, as Menton notes, citing Léon-Francoise Hoffmann, the historical novel may be defined as "a novel in which the precise events taken from history determine or influence the development of the plot and provide it to a great extent with the referential background" (15). The historical record, the sources for which are specified in the "Nota," draws the plot forward, and delivers on *1767*'s stated subject matter. The novel leads the reader through a great deal of explanation about the series of events leading to the Jesuit order's exodus from various sites in New Spain, and to its eventual expulsion from the colony; the political machinations in Mexico, Spain, and Rome that led to and accompanied the expulsion; the resigned response of the order to the edict to leave; the personalities and characteristics of some of the historical and fictional Jesuits; and the eventual fate of the friars once abroad, and, of course, the documents they produced that provided the raw historical material for the novel itself.

These novelistic events recall the Jesuits' abrupt removal from New Spain, where they arrived in 1572 as a result of the lobbying efforts of the bishop of Michoacán, Vasco de Quiroga (Santos Hernández 20). As Jesuit historian Ángel Santos Hernández points out, the relatively new order (officially founded in 1540 by Spaniard St. Ignatius Loyola) was oriented toward the mission field, Ignatius himself urging his representatives in Spain to send friars to New Spain: "Al México envíen [los padres jesuitas], si les parece, haciendo que sean pedidos, o sin serlo" (20). After establishing the Colegio Máximo de San Pedro y San Pablo in 1573 in Mexico City, the main Jesuit seminary in Mexico, the order continued to expand, founding other colleges, establishing missions and schools among native groups in central Mexico, and creating fourteen other missions in Mexico's far northwest regions (Durango, Sinaloa, Nayarit, and Baja California), since missionization and conversion was a priority for the order in the New Spanish theater. By the time the edict of expulsion was issued by the Spanish Bourbon Crown, the Mexican Jesuits numbered almost seven hundred (Santos Hernández 61), and had entered into many facets of New Spanish public life. The result of anti-Jesuit sentiment in Europe (arising mainly in Portugal, France, and Italy), accusations against the order in New Spain centered on allegations of wealth in their remote missions, "sobre todo a la adquisición de perlas en las misiones de California y en las minas ocultas que se decía explotaban en las de Sonora" (Santos Hernández 62). The consequences not only of the expulsion of the Jesuits, but also of the Bourbon Reforms more generally were a series of eight rebellions in 1767 and a resulting harsh imposition of monarchical authority at those sites (Castro Gutiérrez 115–74). The unrest resulting from these events nonetheless set the stage for imminent changes to New Spanish governance and Mexican identity.

In the course of the novel's linear plot progression, there is no misquoting of original historical documents; neither are imagined, ersatz-historical texts (testimonies or accounts represented as historical documents but written by fictional characters), or fictional historical texts (invented documents presented as though written by real historical actors) included alongside the real historical sources. These mock-historical techniques, common in new historical novels, cast doubt on or question the validity of original historical works, create metahistorical discourses about the nature and construction of historical narrative, or invent alternate histories altogether. In contrast, the earnest implementation of a verifiable historical record in 1767 distinguishes the novel as one that views history as fixed and nonnegotiable.

The events relating to the expulsion of the Jesuits are evoked in 1767 in the chronological order in which they occurred, mapping out the movement of the Jesuits from distant reaches of Mexico as they moved southward toward the port of Veracruz, their point of departure from New Spain. In cases in which historical sources are not cited directly, historical materials and historical frameworks provide the stabilizing structures for the inner musings of the fictional characters. For example, that the transmission of the expulsion order from Spain was supposed to remain confidential (the main preoccupation of the sailor Maturino Cuévano in chapter 5, who inadvertently breaks the royal seal on the expulsion order and reads the document while en route to Mexico) is consistent with Santos Hernández's assertion that, historically, "no se le quería dar publicidad, por temor a reacciones contrarias, pretendiéndose proceder con el mayor sigilo" (62). Another case in point is the fictional first-person musing of Pope Clement XIII, the pontiff at the time of the Spanish Crown's decree, in chapter 13. While his reflections do not include direct citations of historical sources, they are deeply interlaced with historical references to the historical events in Europe that led to the expulsion order, most prominently the Spanish War of Succession (1701–1714), which ultimately ended Hapsburg rule and ushered in Bourbon reign in Spain. Clement XIII also ruminates on expanding Bourbon and British interests in Europe, his thoughts about which are substantiated by a footnote quoting the 1625 writing of Englishman John Chamberlain. The historical record provides shape and gives weight to Clement XIII's reflections on the reasons for the Spanish Crown's attack on the Jesuits, which he was unable (as the text presents him) or unwilling to prevent:

> ¿Quién en su sano juicio hubiera pensado que el Rey de España despediría de sus dominios a una orden religiosa que el resto del mundo, tengo al obispo de York como testigo, piensa que es demasiado española, piensa que actúa por España. El mismo lord Chesterfield escribió a su hijo Stanhope: "¿habrías imaginádote que esos godos ignorantes se hubiesen atrevido a desterrar a los jesuitas?" (150)

The balance of the chapter explains the chain of historical events, narrated from Clement XIII's perspective, which precipitated the pontiff's decision not to intervene in the Jesuits' expulsion from Spanish territories with the hope of retaining English Catholics, justifying his actions: "La Sagrada Escritura dice claramente que es mejor ser un perro vivo que un león muerto, [Clement XIII], que no se sentía ni perro ni león . . . hubiera preferido dejar de ver todo como velado" (153). As chapter 13 demonstrates, even inaction in the plot derives from historical sources, which consistently inform the progression of the novel.

As Guerrero specifies for the historical novel, *1767* clings fast to the historical record and does not create a counter-narrative about it. The historical documents cited in the text are actual historical sources, as in the official declaration by the Marquis de Croix regarding the expulsion of the Jesuits from Mexico (87–88), and the veracity of their contents are presented so as to be read without any doubt. Similarly, chapter 5's excerpts from the writings of Antonio López de Priego and Francisco Javier Alegre, both themselves exiled Jesuit priests, frame the chapter's narration of the residence of the protagonist (the Mexican Jesuit novice Pablo Rayón) in Puerto Santa María, Spain, with the rest of the exiled Jesuits:

> un espectáculo que sacaba lágrimas, aun a los más indiferentes, ver . . .
> formadas divisiones donde recogerse los hermanos coadjutores, los estu-
> diantes y aun algunos de los sacerdotes. En el puerto se notificó otro
> real decreto, con pena de la vida a los no sacerdotes y a los sacerdotes,
> de reclusión perpetua, si de cualquier modo volvían a los dominios de
> España. (citing Alegre 125)

Neither the framing by the narrative voices, nor the placement of citations such as the above within the novel lead readers to wonder about whether such historical sources are to be read precisely as they are presented. This selective citation reinforces a particular historical narrative about the expulsion of the Jesuits from New Spain. In doing so, *1767* behaves in the most absolute sense as a historical novel, creating a reading that deeply conforms to the historical source material. The expected result of this, therefore, is that *1767*'s narrative is guided by a single historical perspective, in this case, one that is as well-disposed toward the Jesuits' history in Mexico as it is critical of Enlightenment and/or Bourbon views and politics.

Throughout *1767*, the narrative's allegiances openly unfold, exhibiting a distinct sympathy for the Jesuits and their plight and a valorization of the Jesuits' social role in the Mexican *colonia*. In most instances in the text, the Jesuit order is depicted as above reproach or critique and beloved by most New Spanish citizens, particularly indigenous and criollo groups, whose affection for the order the novel extensively details, as it does in describing the Jesuits' departure from Pátzcuaro (98–100). In addition to the consistent depiction of the Jesuits' positive presence in Mexico, such as in the description of the tranquil and idealized Jesuit hacienda in Xal-molonga—"alrededor de la hermosa iglesia levantados los arcos que sostenían los claustros interiores. . . . Había casas para los indios que allí laboraban, bien medidas y limpias" (38), the New Spanish citizens' response to the edict of expulsion is intended to illustrate the close relationship between the Mexicans and the Jesuits, and the tragedy of their uprooting:

> Podían prohibirlo todo, con el despótico lenguaje que acostumbraban los que se creen asistidos de absoluta razón; no podían prohibir que la gente llorase. Y en la capital del imperio mexicano se lloró, amargamente. Y de repente un indio se echaba a llorar de pronto en medio de la calle, o a una señora se le anegaban los ojos de lágrimas mientras hacía cualquier cosa, o a un canónigo lo acogotaban unos sollozos capaces de partirle el corazón a cualquiera con tal que no fuera ilustrado, que a esos señores nada parecía poder quebrarles. (94)

The friars' dealings among themselves and with Spanish authorities are likewise discreet, humble, and in conformation with the vows of obedience to their order and to the Spanish Crown, and promotion of the well-being of the Mexican citizens who would defend them. When the community of Páztcuaro planned to resist the Jesuits' removal, Padre Rector José Meléndez negotiated with them to prevent a fight against the soldiers sent to remove the friars from the college; when unsuccessful in negotiation, Meléndez "se arrodilló . . . y con lágrimas en los ojos, le pidió [al cacique de la comunidad] como última muestra del afecto que siempre había mostrado a la Compañía, no como sumisión a una orden de afuera . . . permitiera al comisionado cumplir con su cometido" (99). The machinations originating in Spain and throughout Europe that precipitated the Jesuit expulsion are presented as beyond the order's sphere of influence, as emphasized in chapter 9's description of an edict circulated in Portugal in 1759 declaring that "desde aquella fecha quedaban *exterminados, desnaturalizados, proscritos y expelidos* los padres de la Compañía" (69, original emphasis). The Jesuits in New Spain, aware that their expulsion represents a major diminishment of their order, are portrayed as the victims of forces largely out of their control, but they do not resist, out of obedience to the Crown and to protect their faithful. Although as Domínguez Michael notes, this does produce the sense that 1767 is "un libro devoto dedicado a vindicar los sufrimientos de los padres de la Compañía de Jesús," its opinionated take on the events of the expulsion is yet another characteristic consistent with the historical novel genre.

Based on the characteristics described above, we must conclude that 1767 is a historical novel that radically cleaves to the characteristics of that genre, and that makes this conformity patent to its readers, demanding that they understand it on those literary terms. The book's unusual subject matter no doubt provides a small thrill for students of the Mexican colonia, who recognize that many important episodes of the period, like the expulsion of the Jesuits, are passed over in contemporary fiction in favor of more iconic figures (Malinche, Cortés, Sor Juana) or events (La Noche Triste, El Grito de Dolores, etc.). As a historical novel, 1767 is an affecting, personalized fictionalization of the Jesuits and their plight, one that "acaba por ganarse al lector, a ese lector escéptico, o indiferente en material de religión" (Domínguez Michael, online source).

But even as 1767's historical fiction trappings are fully developed, the undertow begins to shift beneath that traditional (and commercially viable) surface with the introduction of subtle and significant narrative interventions. This intentional subversion creates a sense of instability from within the historical novel, a sort of pebble in the reader's shoe that acutely distracts from that genre and leads the reader to focus sharply on the interruption. It persistently proposes a different story altogether that proceeds in parallel to, and intersects, the narration of the Jesuit's exile from New Spain. In doing so, this second novel implements several, but not all, of the characteristics of Menton's new historical novel, including the use of metafiction (through direct references to the creation and nature of the novel) and heteroglossia (via the insertion of several different narrative voices). These two elements, along with the characterization of Pablo Rayón as the prototypical eighteenth-century Mexican criollo, as well as the staging of certain paratexts aside from those already discussed, define and characterize this metatext. Some other tropes of the new historical novel are notably absent in the metatext, namely those that run explicitly contrary to the aims and construct of the historical novel (such as the manipulation of the historical record and the Borgesian ruminations on the circularity or inevitability of history). 1767's metatext complicates the novel's identity as a historical fiction, and—more significantly—the way(s) in which the reader finally grasps the work.

When juxtaposed against the historical novel, the new historical elements that 1767 presents produce a reading experience that destabilizes the historical novel genre, while at the same time engaging with the historical novel as a means of hypothesizing about historical events and conditions. In this book's case, the metafictive narrative concerns the formation of a Mexican national consciousness that emerges in reaction to the impositions of the Spanish Crown on its New Spanish citizens. The nature of that domination is articulated through the order of expulsion of the Jesuits from the Spanish kingdoms. In turn, the Jesuits' obedience to that order, and their resignation in the face of the Crown's coercive power, stand for the New Spanish citizens' submission to Spanish authority, an acquiescence that becomes increasingly unacceptable and is eventually defied. Pablo Rayón's changing allegiances, represented in his changing roles from conformist Jesuit novice to uneasy secular criollo, lie outside the paradigms of the historical novel. No longer a Jesuit at the novel's end, Pablo Rayón's brooding unease with "algo" (290) is the key representation of a growing Mexican self-awareness and dissatisfaction with Spanish rule that marked the end of the Mexican colonia, a moment presaged by Pablo Rayón's realization in earlier chapters that, in spite of his own expectations to the contrary, "era capaz de pensar" (102). This narrative undertow, every bit as compelling as the historical novel 1767 explicitly shows itself to be, is artfully deployed, leaving the historical novel largely intact, but deeply disturbed.

The destabilizing metanovel consistently emerges in the text through the manipulations of the narrative voice. First, the novel makes use of polyvocality as it switches among several different voices in the text. In addition to a dominant narrator, which appears to be that of a highly educated Mexican criollo familiar with secular and religious texts, other narrators intervene. In chapters 5 and 9, the first-person narration of Maturino Cuévano, a Spanish marine lieutenant raised by his Jesuit uncle who delivers the order of expulsion to the Mexican viceroy, voices a Spanish perspective supportive of the Jesuits, but which also fears the Spanish Crown. When, in chapter 13, the primary narrative voice gives way to the interior thought processes of Pope Clement XIII, another internal perspective is expressed. This movement among different narrative voices (there could be more than those identified above, as Maturino Cuévano's is the only voice that identifies itself), whose relationship to one another is not articulated, ruffles the historical novel's smooth waters by decentralizing its message and presenting the multiple perspectives that the straightforward historical novel normally eschews. However, far more subversive than the several interwoven narrative voices are the first-person incursions of the predominant narrator, whose self-reflexivity and ongoing conversation with the reader provide the important first entry into the narrative beyond the historical novel.

This voice, which is referred to here in the singular because its tone, language usage, and political perspectives are more or less consistent across the novel, inserts itself fleetingly but regularly into the text as a meta-authorial figure. It comments explicitly on the construction and composition of the novel, implying that it is aware of and, to a degree, controls the text produced. The voice is complicit with the reader and demonstrates narrative selectivity in deciding which scenes, sites, or elements to include or exclude in the metatext: "Don Luis y Daniel iban hablando en voz muy baja. Oigámosles, ya que ése es el privilegio de la novela" (34). In a footnote regarding the citation of Marcelino Menéndez Pelayo in chapter 9, the voice assumes a more traditional tone, one almost more consistent with the nineteenth-century historical novel: "el mismo . . . a quien, con la venia del lector, se citará largamente en este capítulo" (69). The voice discusses how to pace a novel; that is, to what extent the narrative voice should comment upon the novel's action as it unfolds. "Pero basta de teorizar y de moralizar. La novela exige otro ritmo" (76). It also refers explicitly to the role of the author in creating the narrative and in the decisions he or she makes in doing so, in a self-referential manner: "Es justo que luego de hablar del carácter de Pablo Rayón, y sus primeros años en el primer patio y del carácter de los criollos en general como lo trae un muy prudente autor, describamos el famoso Colegio" (44). Finally, and most subversively in relationship to the historical novel's earnest invocation of the historical record, the narrative voice emphasizes that even the selection of such texts is a metanarrative choice, alluding to the process by which such determinations shape and advance the text: "Y aquí, para dar idea mejor de la partida, y como no tiene caso que uno escriba mal lo que ya bien escribió otro hombre, citaré [a Fray] Antonio López de Priego" (113). These insertions imply that the narrative voice has already molded the historical novel that the reader is currently reading, revealing the hands that are operating the strings controlling this carefully staged historical novel.

These various invocations of the metanarrative voice worry the historical novel genre by drawing attention to the novel as a literary construct. The very nature of the historical novel depends upon the lack of a self-aware narrative voice that participates in the creation of the text, as Guerrero suggests. The primary narrator in 1767 is anything but detached from the novel, constantly referring to a collective "nosotros" or a "yo"— "Retrotraigamos ahora nuestra narración al año de 1765" (47)—and inserting subjective opinions reflective of his personal perspective into the narration: "[El señor se llamaba] don Segismundo Güolde, o Gúlde o un nombre así de raro" (22); "ocurre muchas veces cuando uno se despide que los demás se aprovechan la ocasión para hacer lo mismo" (33). The tension between the historical novel and metanarrative voice induces an awareness on the part of the reader of an additional layer of textual complexity, which in turn translates into a questioning of the reading of the novel itself as a purely historical novel. As the novel progresses, the increasingly unsettling cohabitation between the historical novel and a narrator whose assertive existence subverts that particular genre of writing provides the strange sensation of reading a historical novel while being made completely aware of how it was put together.

This major structural element creates porosity within the historical novel, and allows for the metanovel, a commentary on Mexican independence from Spain, to edge out from behind it. These reflections are set out in the book's paratextual materials. Immediately following the novel's close, and before the "Nota," is the first chapter of what is presented as the next book in a series, *Libro segundo*, a progression in which the reader was not previously aware he or she was participating. Its "capítulo I," sampled as a conclusion to the novel, is subtitled "Un padre llamado Hidalgo." Fray Miguel Hidalgo's reflections, which open the mini-chapter, point to the expulsion of the Jesuits from Mexico as the precipitating event that galvanized Mexican political will to seek independence from Spain:

El cura de Dolores [se acordó] de la rabia que había sentido al verse impotente ante el infame decreto . . . aún hoy, año de la Redención del Mundo de 1820, le hervía la sangre. Aquélla había sido la primera vez que había comprendido que estábamos sujetos a la Corona, y que las órdenes dadas allá se aplicaban aquí . . . y recordaba esto cuando un septiembre salió a la noche y al tumulto, y a lo que vendría después, enarbolando el estandarte de la Virgen de Guadalupe, dispuesto a morir por ver a su nación independiente. (195–96)

More of a coda to *1767* than an entry to a new work, the para-chapter's dovetailing of the preceding novel with the Independence movement in the projected *Libro segundo* is the essential clue needed for reading between the lines of the historical novel. The scant two paragraphs of the forthcoming text also cite Melchor de Talamantes, a Mercederian friar involved in the Mexican Independence movement, and eventually imprisoned for his participation in it. Though Soler Frost's choice of another religious historical source in proposing this next novel is the subject for ongoing analysis of the author's oeuvre, the important detail to observe here is that the footnote crediting the source is numbered continuously with those of the rest of the book. This (along with the fact that no *Libro segundo* following up *1767* has yet been published) suggests that the supposed leading of *1767* into a follow-up novel about Mexican Independence is likely an intentional move designed to shape the "preceding" text. The decisiveness of this addition in the context of the other suggestive narrative and structural elements modifies the reading of the historical novel from primary text to framing device.

When seen in this way, the meta-incursions into the preceding novel serve another purpose: to ensure that the reader is aware that he or she is being drawn toward a discussion of nascent Mexican identity and independence in the midst of the historical novel's exposition of the Jesuits' expulsion. The historical novel thus creates anticipation, establishing motive for what will become a resistance to and overthrowing of colonial authority. In other words, it is not the Jesuit's expulsion—the ostensible subject of *1767*—that is the impetus for Mexican Independence; rather, it is the forced capitulation by New Spanish citizens to harsh and unwelcome Spanish orders (in the form of the expulsion) that catalyze the formation of a Mexican national consciousness and the refusal of colonial authority. A look backward into the novel in light of this articulation illustrates how its two internal texts—historical fiction and metatext—fit together.

The Mexican Independence theme is presaged in *1767*'s conclusion, which takes place at the end of the eighteenth century. While in seminary as a novice, Pablo Rayón becomes aware of the expanse of knowledge available to him, and "por primera vez [comprendió] que México era un gran reino y nación" (57). Later, shortly before leaving the community of exiled Jesuits living in Italy, at the end of the novel, Pablo Rayón and his co-novice Jerónimo de Celaya engage in a conversation that demonstrates the type of questioning about Spanish rule over New Spanish citizens toward which the metanovel builds. Pablo Rayón wonders to Jerónimo, "Pero si la autoridad no viene a los reyes de Dios, no deviene entonces en la pura 'fuerza, la astucia, la tiranía, nada de razón, nada de justicia; necesidad quizá de someterse, obligación ninguna'" (157). Jerónimo replies to Pablo Rayón's reflections, citing St. Thomas Aquinas, "No reina sobre los hombres la voluntad de otro hombre, no reina su simple razón . . . cuando las leyes son injustas no obligan en el fuero de la consciencia . . . que las leyes son injustas cuando son contrarias al bien común" (157–58). Later, as Pablo Rayón stands on the precipice of leaving the Jesuit order, he is reassured by his friend and co-novice José María de Castañiza, ordained to the priesthood in exile, that outside of the religious life, there are ways to make one's life a worthwhile endeavor, for "hay otras formas de santificarse y una de ellas es en medio del mundo" (173). Through conversations between these men, the stirrings within the metatext cohere, though they are purposefully left incompletely expressed, anticipatory, until we are closer to the novel's conclusion.

After departing the order and returning to Mexico as a married landowner, a fundamental paradigm shift occurs for Pablo Rayón: "Algo (llamémoslo fidelidad al trono) se había quebrado en él: algo le molestaba, algo que había en el aire de Europa y que veía reflejado en los insufribles fastos y en la despótica autoridad de los funcionarios y de los eclesiásticos españoles" (190). Eventually, Pablo Rayón and his pregnant Irish wife Catalina leave their first home in Mexico City, as "algo los desasosegó . . . algo extraño" (191), to return to their family holdings and to Pablo Rayón's mother doña Serafina in San Ambrosio Chalmita, the bindings tying Pablo Rayón to his previous "fidelidad al trono" permanently loosened and replaced with undefined and inchoate sensibilities. The narrator avows that, in the midst of growing turmoil in Mexico, the former exiled Jesuit and his family "se estuvieron, rutinaria, felizmente" (191), yet he also brings Pablo Rayón and his stirrings of inquietude to bear in the "next" book. As the novel ends, in the shadow of Mexican Independence, the narrative voice seems to lead the protagonist directly into the succeeding *Libro segundo*— "dejando para mejor ocasión el resto de la historia, abandono la pluma, prometiendo continuar la vida de Pablo Rayón en otro volumen, si Dios me presta vida" (191). That the historical novel's narration of the Jesuit expulsion was perhaps as metaphorical as it was literal here materializes, and with it, so does the representative figure of Pablo Rayón, a proxy for Mexican political will for independence. A closer examination of the protagonist further elucidates the metanovel's meaning.

Pablo Rayón is an ordinary man, not a famous historical character, the typical protagonist of most new historical novels. He comes from a wealthy family, dominated by a strong mother, and the family as whole is dyed-in-the-wool criollo. This very ordinariness makes interpreting him as a metonym for Mexican citizens (or at least for New Spanish criollos) feasible, the better to understand him in a metatextual context. Looking more closely at his character, we see that Pablo Rayón's unusual name is suggestive of a breaking with the past, or with changes on the brink of manifesting themselves. His second name, Rayón (for he is always referred to as "Pablo Rayón") seemingly derives from the verb "rayar," meaning variously to cross out ("tachar"), to mark out the limits between two entities (perhaps Mexico's colonial past and its impending independence), and to dawn ("rayar el día/alba") or to light up ("rayar la luz"). Any possible reading into "Rayón" via "rayar" alludes to change and/or the demarcation of a different state of affairs. The augmentative suffix "-ón" added to "rayar" not only creates an impression of emphasis or urgency, but, more importantly, a sense of agency for Pablo in engaging in or embodying the verb's paradigm-shifting action; in other words, Pablo Rayón is he who breaks through, marks out, or causes to emerge. Looking back over the text, then, Pablo Rayón himself has been the covert messenger of the book's metanarrative, the impetus for the shifting movements underpinning the historical novel.

In the case of *1767*, the novel's most intriguing characteristic is not so much that it manipulates the historical novel's "straight lines," as suggested by Sommer—indeed, its stated purpose is to be a model historical novel—but rather that it simultaneously balances a completely different metanarrative against the model historical novel's restrictive boundaries. The net effect of the relationship between the two pieces is that the historical novel itself is in some sense undermined; it is less a bending of the genre and more a low-level, ongoing, and earthquake-like rattling of its foundations. The book's trick lies in convincing the reader to buy into the conceits of the historical novel, and then actually leading him or her through just such a text, only to deliver a message that deeply troubles the genre itself, as the events of the historical novel become the means and justification for the motives of the metatext. If the Jesuits are the long-suffering heroes of the historical novel, this does not hold for the metatext, in which their exploits are symbolically important, but in which the emblematic figure is actually Pablo Rayón.

Though it is tempting to categorize the interplay between the two genres as itself a parodic metaliterary game, a lampooning of the historical novel genre via a more subtle and complex metanarrative, this interpretation does not quite hold in the face of *1767*'s execution of the historical novel. There is a little too much of that straight-laced genre in comparison to the metaliterary interludes to read the whole book as a satire. Instead, the overall effect of *1767* is to present two intermeshed texts at once, the more subversive and technically involved story about Mexico's growing desire for liberation from Spain edging through the holes created in the traditional historical novel's conservative conventions by the first-person narrative voice.

As Soler Frost states in the "Nota," anticipating the movements of *1776* involves guessing at its tricky narrative gestures: "Hay que fintar y esquivar y mantener siempre la vista fija en sus movimientos, no sea que erremos y seamos derribados" (199). In using his or her interpretive ability to dance with, dodge, and duck the novel's movements, the reader may conclude, with Bolívar Echeverría, that "hay, podría decirse, una relación de interioridad entre esas dos historias, una gravitación recíproca entre lo que hace la Compañía de Jesús y lo que es la historia del mundo latinoamericano durante todo este tiempo [the seventeenth and eighteenth centuries]" (50). The intermingling of the two narratives does expose the reader to that singular notion, and, in so doing, maps out an intriguingly innovative discourse on the ending of the Mexican colonia and the impetus for Mexican Independence.

Works Cited

Castro Gutiérrez, Felipe. *Nueva ley y Nuevo rey: Reformas borbónicas y rebelión popular en Nueva España*. México, D.F.: Universidad Nacional Autónoma de México (UNAM), 1996.

Domínguez Michael, Christopher. "Retrato de un moderno." *Letras Libres*, October 31, 2004. http://www.letraslibres.com/revista/letrillas/retrato-de-un-moderno. Accessed October 10, 2012.

Echeverría, Bolívar. "La Compañía de Jesús y la primera modernidad de América Latina." *Barrocos y modernos: Nuevos caminos en la investigación del Barroco iberoamericano*. Ed. Petra Schumm. Madrid: Iberoamericana/Vervuert, 1998. 49–65.

Guerrero, Elisabeth. *Confronting History and Modernity in Mexican Narrative*. New York: Palgrave, 2008.

Menton, Seymour. *Latin America's New Historical Novel*. Austin: University of Texas Press, 1993.

Santos Hernández, Ángel. *Los jesuitas en América*. Madrid: Editorial Mapfre, 1992.

Soler Frost, Pablo. *1767: Una novela sobre el destierro de los jesuitas mexicanos*. México, D.F.: Joaquín Mortiz, 2004.

———. "Los jesuitas no son expulsados: La república del espíritu." *Letras Libres*, October 31, 2008. http://www.letraslibres.com/revista/convivio/los-jesuitas-no-son-ex pulsados-la-republica-del-espiritu. Accessed October 10, 2012.

Seydel, Ute. *Narrar historia(s): La ficcionalización de temas históricos por las escritoras mexicanas Elena Garro, Rosa Beltraán y Carmen Bullosa*. Madrid: Iberoamericana/Vervuert, 2007.

Sommer, Doris. *Foundational Fictions: The National Romances of Latin America*. Berkeley: University of California Press, 1991.

CHAPTER TWELVE

Out of Bounds in 1822

Humoring the Limits of Colonial Mexico

Stuart A. Day

By act and word he strives to do it;
with sincerity, if possible;
failing that, with theatricality.
— *OXFORD ENGLISH DICTIONARY*

The beginnings of Mexican Independence were marked by the presence of Spanish forces in Veracruz, a Mexican emperor (Agustín de Iturbide) who had in fact battled brutally on the side of Spain for most of his military career, and the unpleasant sensation among many that the more things change, the more they stay the same. Flavio González Mello's play *1822: El año que fuimos imperio*, the smash hit first staged in 2002 and the focus of this chapter, interrogates the space between colony and coloniality—the powerful vestiges of colonialism after ties with Spain were officially but incompletely severed—by bringing to life a host of characters, including Iturbide and Fray Servando Teresa de Mier, a priest who questioned an event (or image or miracle or machination) that justified conquest: the timing and circumstances (if not the veracity) of the apparition of the Virgin of Guadalupe, who is sometimes referred to in political terms as the Queen of Mexico and Empress of the Americas. The apparition both promoted and hindered Independence and would continue to validate political theatrics through Vicente Fox's 2000 presidential campaign and beyond.

In the nineteenth century, as Spain became more liberal under the Spanish Constitution of 1812, Mexican elites rallied under the banner of the Virgin of Guadalupe in order to unite conservative forces and to form the first Mexican empire. In the second half of the twentieth century, as the Partido Revolucionario Institucional (PRI) haltingly succumbed to the fault lines created in large part by the 1968 massacre of students, the political right once again used explicit religious imagery, especially that of the Virgin of Guadalupe, to unite Mexico under the flag of religion. In both cases the *guadalupana* image, which had originally justified the conquest of Mexico, set it on a course that promoted the extension of colonial structures, including the role of the Catholic Church in the political arena, and avoided a seemingly more achievable, progressive path for the nation. *1822: El año que fuimos imperio*, without explicit reference to the present—though the link to present-day politics was seemingly impossible for the audience to ignore in the four hundred-plus representations of the play, and in the film version of the play produced by the National Autonomous University of Mexico—parodies the use of farcical theatrics and religious imagery in politics. Perhaps more importantly, the play underscores the residual effects of colonial Mexico in the two hundred years since the famous Grito de Dolores, the cry for independence uttered in the town of Dolores by a parish priest. One version of the words Miguel Hidalgo used to inspire his followers has continued to prove germane beyond (but inclusive of) its important religious manifestations: "¡Viva la Virgen de Guadalupe!"

Playwright González Mello had been mulling over a piece on the first Mexican empire—the year and a half (1821–1823) during which the arrogant Iturbide had European tailors designing his regal clothes, and when newly imported etiquette required that his hand be kissed—since before the election of Vicente Fox in July 2000: "En realidad es un proyecto que había empezado a escribir varios años atrás, a principios de los noventa y que luego fui retomando a lo largo de esa década. El elemento que le faltaba me lo dio el año 2000 cuando vino el momento del cambio político en el país, la salida del PRI y las elecciones donde finalmente ganó Vicente Fox" (76–77). In particular, González Mello refers to the "twin" historical processes that led to the governments of Iturbide and Fox, noting that his play is about "la 'cruda' después de la consumación de la Independencia. . . . Los tres años que lleva en cartelera la obra han coincidido, hasta cierto punto, con lo que ocurrió en ese otro proceso de transición; las cosas no cambian tan espectacularmente como uno esperaría en el momento del clímax" (77).

As he penned the play in the 1990s, González Mello surely took note that members of the Partido Acción Nacional (PAN) used a key symbol of Mexican unity, the Virgin of Guadalupe, as a driving force to promote a business-oriented, conservative Catholic government. Though not new to Mexicans (or Chicanos, for that matter, since the farmworker movement, led by César Chávez and supported by Luis Valdez and the Teatro Campesino, used the Virgin of Guadalupe strategically to attract people to the movement and to harness the public-relations power of religion) the use of *guadalupana* imagery was divisive. During the 1999 presidential campaign, Mexican journalist Sergio Sarmiento portrayed the opinion of Mexicans from a spectrum of political viewpoints on the deployment of Mexico's Virgin:

> El panista Vicente Fox se las arregló para irritar tanto a católicos como a no católicos, a religiosos y a laicos, a conservadores y a liberales, con su decisión de ondear un estandarte de la Virgen de Guadalupe en el acto de campaña que llevó a cabo el 10 de septiembre en la ciudad de León, Guanajuato. En México existe, por supuesto, una larga tradición de uso político de la imagen de la Virgen de Guadalupe. A falta de otros símbolos nacionales, el cura Miguel Hidalgo utilizó una imagen de la Virgen de Guadalupe para atraer el apoyo de indios y mestizos al comenzar su levantamiento en contra de las autoridades virreinales en 1810. El propio Francisco I. Madero también emplea a la Virgen como símbolo de unidad en su cruzada democrática en contra de Porfirio Díaz. La gran pregunta es si hoy la sociedad mexicana puede aceptar esta imagen sacra como bandera de un movimiento político. (*Siempre!*)

When González Mello conjures the image of the Virgin of Guadalupe on the theatrical stage, in this case specifically as an oversized image behind the congressional podium and through the words of Teresa de Mier (who sought a more egalitarian, pre-Columbian origin for the apparition of the Virgin), *1822: El año que fuimos imperio* enters full force into a complex historical debate. In doing so, González Mello also follows in a long line of Mexican playwrights and performance artists who take as their trope the history of Mexico—including many re-interpretations of the Virgin of Guadalupe and other historical figures—and tinge their creations with subtle or not-so-subtle references to the present, a modus operandi that has resonated with Mexican audiences for decades. The representation/negotiation/critique of key historical watersheds and icons, coupled with powerful theatrical iterations located well beyond the walls of the theater, is one of the defining characteristics of Mexico's most compelling plays and performance pieces of the twentieth and twenty-first centuries, brief examples of which I will consider as I analyze González Mello's play and the way the author uses humor and theatrical devices to interrogate the boundaries—and the seemingly boundless power—of (colonial) history.[1]

It may seem odd to hint at the influence of theater in contemporary Mexico, especially in a high-tech, cable-TV, social-media, information-overload era in which art in its traditional formats can seem ancillary at best. How can the present-day status of the stage compare, for instance, to the crucial role of theater, broadly defined, before the Conquest or in early colonial times? Take, for example, the sociopolitical significance, the centrality, of the festival of Quetzalcóatl that Adam Versényi describes: "This being a ritual performance, its ultimate end was transformational, the convergence of the community in worshipping the god. The theatre's division between spectator and actor was nonexistent in pre-Columbian indigenous display. What the subsequent evangelical theatre retained and developed were the spectacular and transformational aspects of ritual performance, wedding them to Christian theological and political concerns" (11). This transformational theatre (and politics) was carried out sans irony, as one might guess, or at least without the intention of a double-voiced discourse that would undermine the status quo. And it was far from tangential in its importance as a tool to impose, and perhaps at times to negotiate, colonial hegemony. Joseph Roach (also via Versényi) underscores the importance of theatricality to the Conquest: "The communication between Spanish conquistadors and the Mesoamericans *relied on* reciprocal stagings and theatrical devices" (146, my emphasis). Yet despite the apparent diminishing effectiveness of theatre in contemporary Mexico, many would argue that it is anything but *transformational* or *relied on* by society; one can find abundant examples of artists in the theater and beyond who use performance to communicate their ideas in much wider arenas than one might expect.

It is clear, for example, that the federal government, which subsidizes some theater in Mexico and has over the years officially or semi-officially censored plays, entered the entertainment industry to paint Mexico's war on drugs in a positive, if unbelievable, light through the TV show *El equipo* precisely because officials saw the power of acting and fiction to mold opinion—even if the show couldn't attract nearly as many viewers as a soap opera.[2] Television is removed from theater, no doubt, but as my analysis of *1822: El año que fuimos imperio* and other examples along the way will make clear, creative boundaries, like the temporal boundaries of history mentioned above, are often obscured much earlier than our academic categories are. The same people who work on the Mexican stage often earn their living on or behind the small and large screens, and the lifespan of a play is no longer and by no means limited to the staging it-self, and to the few-and-far-between performance reviews. Indeed, one could argue that the intellectual "crime" regarding a play is not missing its live performance—though there is still nothing quite like its elegant ephemerality—but ignoring the extended, complementary life that plays often have through YouTube, Facebook, public television, DVDs, and other digital media. It may be that these iterations will always play the role of a surrogate, to use Roach's term, for the real experience of watching a play—albeit with a slight twist. They are stand-ins that are—and are not—"authentic," in some ways parallel to the actors in Nahuatl sacrifice under-stood by Roach: "Like the Iroquois, the Aztecs addressed their doomed victims 'with kinship terms' and even mourned their deaths. In *The Conquest of America*, Todorov draws attention to the duality of the victim: taken from among outsiders but assimilated by the period of preparation, the surrogate becomes familiar enough to stand in for his hosts but at the same time remains sufficiently strange to stand apart from them" (148).[3]

Sarah Bay-Cheng, in "Theatre History and Digital Historiography," makes a case for an open view of digital technology, observing that "if we look closely at either Joseph Roach's surrogation of performance or Tay-lor's repertoire, we find resonances of the moving image and, more signifi-cantly for historiography, the echoes of the digital as it becomes assumed into daily life" (128). Bay-Cheng does not see digital media itself as a sur-rogate for live performance, per se, yet her ideas are crucial for under-standing the ways in which Mexican theater lives on—but also beyond—the formal stage and retains an important place in Mexican society, often in digital form and playing the part of court jester, provocateur, watchdog. These are the exact roles that the character Padre Mier represents (jester, provocateur, watchdog) in *1822: El año que fuimos imperio*, enacting a microcosm of the most iconoclastic aspects of Mexican theater. Unlike some members of regal courts, however, he has adopted a status as a pesky, irreverent "court jester" who is by all counts unsanctioned and generally unwelcome, which offers him less protection for speaking his mind than, say, an authorized jester specifically chosen by a king or emperor. It is through his cunning, humor, a few of his allies, and his position in the Church (though admittedly precarious) that he keeps the "off-with-your-head" commands—the supposed fates of many a jester—at bay. Who else, one wonders, would have the gall to supply an "incorrect" response to Iturbide's affirmation, "Yo, como Jorge Washington, sólo aspiro a darle la libertad a mi país, y retirarme a la vida privada"? But of course Padre Mier does, with a deadpan delivery that communicates a truth Iturbide prefers not to hear and that creates humorous complicity with the audience: "Bueno, pues la libertad ya se la dió. ¿Qué lo detiene?" (13). Padre Mier is indeed quick to call Iturbide's bluff, to question the depth of his political briefing and the depth of his knowledge:

ITURBIDE. ¡Hasta que se me hace conocerlo, Fray Servando!
MIER. "Padre Mier," por favor. Me secularicé hace veinte años.
ITURBIDE. Déjeme decirle que desde que leí sus escritos lo admiré profundamente.
MIER. ¿Usted ha leído mis libros?
ITURBIDE. Por supuesto. Cualquiera que se precie de estar interesado en su Patria tiene que haberlo hecho.
MIER. ¡Vaya! ¿Y cuáles leyó, General?
ITURBIDE. ¿Eh? Pues . . . ése, donde habla de . . . la libertad, y . . . y ése otro, de la independencia, ¿no? (12)

In *Fools are Everywhere*, Beatrice K. Otto explains that "the court jester is not as universal a figure on stage as he is in court life but his presence is widespread, and where he does feature as a clearly recognizable character in a play, many of his functions are taken over by others" (187). González Mello very well may not have conceived of his character as a jester figure, though his version of Teresa de Mier clearly shares affinities with other fictional and real court jesters—whether or not their motley attire is of the acting profession (distinctive clothes, distinctive headwear) or the clergy (distinctive clothes, distinctive headwear). As Otto notes, and as the character Padre Mier exemplifies, "the theatrical court jester and his impersonators generally serve the same purpose as the court jester in real life. They amuse and entertain, stand on the sidelines and observe, and act as a control against which to measure the folly of others" (187).

To the historical Teresa de Mier, of course, the foolishness of early nineteenth-century Creoles was to allow Spain to retain political control of the Virgin of Guadalupe. He made this clear on December 12, 1794, when he argued a different lineage for Mexico's Virgin of Guadalupe. The soon-to-be exiled doctor of theology affirmed—in a sermon on the very day Guadalupe is honored each year, and only two years after he, as a Dominican, had received a permit to preach—that Guadalupe's image appeared not on the cloak of the mestizo Juan Diego, but on that of Saint Thomas the Apostle.[4] He was put on trial with the utmost expediency by the New Spanish Inquisition for following in the theological and political footsteps of earlier theologians, with a few twists of his own, and promptly exiled to a *patria* he never knew: Spain.[5] To situate the audience, and to hint at the puppet Congress that Iturbide set up in order to legitimize his opportunities, the play offers an early intersection of history, wit (seen more clearly in the performance, but present in the text), and Padre Mier's intractable charm:

> RAMOS ARIZPE. Es una pequeña formalidad. Sólo tienes que decir que te arrepientes de haber negado la existencia de la Virgen de Guadalupe.
> MIER. ¡Yo nunca negué su existencia! Lo que negué fue la leyenda de las apariciones a Juan Diego, nada más.
> GÓMEZ FARÍAS. ¡Nada más!
> MIER. En mi sermón demostré que mucho antes de la Conquista, la Virgen ya era venerada por los antiguos mexicanos, y que la imagen no está impresa en el ayate de Juan Diego, sino en la capa de Santo Tomás Apóstol, que vino a predicar en estas tierras en el primer siglo de nuestra era y fue conocido con el nombre de Quetzalcóatl.
> GÓMEZ FARÍAS. ¡Qué disparate!
> MIER. ¡Al contrario! Disparate hubiera sido defender esa fábula de las apariciones, tan inverosímil y llena de incongruencias, que de ella se agarraban los españoles para poner en duda continuamente la existencia de la Guadalupana. Yo, en cambio, quise brindar al milagro guadalupano un fundamento histórico que callara para siempre a los que pretenden escatimarnos la gloria de haber sido señalados por la madre de Dios como sus especiales protegidos. ¿Eso es negar su existencia? . . .
> RAMOS ARIZPE. Es un asunto delicado, Servando. El Congreso acaba de nombrar a la Virgen de Guadalupe Patrona y Protectora del Imperio. ¿Qué pierdes reconociéndola tú también? Acuérdate que uno de los dos verbos de la política es ceder . . .
> MIER. ¿Y el otro?
> RAMOS ARIZPE. Esperar.
> MIER. Pues ya llevamos tres horas haciendo política aquí. ¿Por qué no nos vamos? (10–11)

The historical José Miguel Ramos Arizpe knew what it meant to wait (he, like Mier, had spent time jailed in Spain), as well as to cede politically—Ramos Arizpe would, based in part on his participation in Spain's political future, be willing to yield just enough power to the states to become known as Mexico's Father of Federalism.[6] Padre Mier's other question ("¿Eso es negar su existencia?") is, in historical terms, spot on, and for some taking a stand against the interests of Spain was equivalent to—or made to look equivalent to—negating the existence of the Virgin of Guadalupe. The seriousness of Padre Mier's words, when considered along with more humorous sections of the piece, provide a picture of the historical Mier, one of whose letters related to the debate about the apparition, as described by Santa Arias, can serve to describe his life: "La seriedad del asunto está aliviada por el típico humor servandino" (6).

Before Mier takes the stage to defend and ostensibly clarify his position, the audience witnesses a scene that (like others in the play) would no doubt lead to a comparison with today's Congress, in which insults are common and fistfights can be viewed on video. Hinting at the Mexican tradition of the *albur* seen in other parts of the play, González Mello's congressional characters demonstrate their "verbal acumen" and the fact that the state of the nation is not always on the top of the priority list. Diputado Torrejas questions Diputado Calvillo's excuse for absence: "El recado del diputado Calvillo es una mentira infame y vil, pues esta mañana al pasar por la calle del Apartado yo mismo pude constatar que no estaba enfermo, sino borracho, armando escándalo y acompañado por tres señoras que no merecen ese nombre. En virtud de lo cual, propongo que se desafore al diputado Calvillo por haber dado muestras contundentes de su disipación y poco recato, y por haber intentado engañar a este Soberano Congreso" (16). To this, Diputado de la Lagaña replies, "¡Conciudadanos! Protesto enérgicamente por las calumnias del diputado Torrejas, y solicito de la manera más enérgica que no sea puesta a votación su insidiosa propuesta, pues sentaría el pésimo precedente de hacer que prevalezcan sobre el fuero de un representante de la Nación los chismes inventados por cualquier hijo de vecino; y más aun: por cualquier hijo *ilegítimo* de vecino, pues todos estamos al tanto del bastardo origen de su apellido, diputado Torrejas" (16, emphasis in original). When order is finally restored ("Se somete a votación la propuesta de no someter a votación la propuesta de desaforar al diputado Calvillo," 16), Mier explains himself in front of an increasingly incredulous group of politicians: "Se ha difundido una versión en el sentido de que esa vez yo habría negado la existencia de la Virgen de Guadalupe. Pues bien . . . he de decirles que . . . *(Carraspea. Mira con incomodidad la enorme imagen a sus espaldas)* . . . que niego haber afirmado dicha negación, y en este acto afirmo mi negativa rotunda a afirmar nada de lo que hubiera negado. Es todo" (20). It seems that Padre Mier is the consummate politician, adept at preserving—somehow and despite the odds—his complex intellectual honor, a process best honed when words are censored or censured in debates, in writing, in the theatre of politics.

In her article "De Fray Servando Teresa de Mier a Juan Bautista Muñoz: La disputa guadalupana en vísperas de la independencia," Santa Arias explains that the guadalupana debate occupied much of the oral and written communication of Mexican and Spanish intellectuals who saw, as Mexican Independence came closer and closer to a political reality, the critical importance of defending their positions. Arias also reminds the reader of the recent, official outcome of the centuries-long debate and the myriad offshoots of guadalupana imagery: "Con la canonización de Juan Diego y las publicaciones recientes sobre el fenómeno guadalupano (como fenómeno que ha cruzado fronteras físicas, lingüísticas y culturales), vemos cómo los elementos del debate original continúan siendo los mismos" (13). It follows that part of the reason colonial figures loom large in the present is because so much of Mexico's cultural present is so deeply haunted, for better and for worse, by the past; and addressing the colonial-era topic of the Virgin of Guadalupe, as González Mello does in his play, guarantees that a work of art will get some attention. Laura G. Gutiérrez writes that "there is no icon that has achieved greater importance in the realm of *mexicanidad* than that of the Virgin of Guadalupe, who, in fact, may very well be the stick by which Mexicanness is measured" (21).

The (attempted) control of the powerful image of the Virgin of Guadalupe, perhaps the most common artistic colonial touchstone after Sor Juana, is, as one can imagine, of concern to many. Gutiérrez exemplifies the efforts to censor guadalupana imagery in *Performing Mexicanidad* by noting, for example, that

> the director of the Museo de El Carmen, Alfredo Martín Gutiérrez, told the artist of the piece *La comandante Lupita* (*Lupita, the Commander*), Polo Castellanos, member of the Tepito Arte Acá collective, that his piece could not be exhibited in the show *Promesas guadalupanas* (*Guadalupana Promises*) because it contained "political overtones." Simultaneous with the Mexican act of censorship, across the border, the Centro Cultural Aztlán's Cultural Arts Gallery in San Antonio, Texas, decided to not exhibit Anna-Marie López's *Virgin* during its annual *Celebración a la Virgen de Guadalupe* (*Celebration of the Virgin of Guadalupe*) apparently because it featured a naked (and pregnant) Virgen de Guadalupe with her blue mantle and a snake wrapped around her body. (62–63)

The potency of historical/mythical figures is crucial to forming a basis on which to project social changes either to promote new directions or to solidify the status quo. Diana Taylor reminds us that "several of the of the best performance artists in Latin America—Jesusa Rodríguez and Astrid Hadad, to name two Mexican performers—have chosen to play with and reexamine some of the most 'Latin American' of icons. Their work to subvert the stereotypical images that have regulated the formulation of gender identity for Mexican women, from the sainted mother (the Virgin of Guadalupe or Coatlicue, the Mexica 'mother' of all Mexicans) to the macho woman with high heels and spurs" (220).

The unrelenting returns of icons like Sor Juana and Guadalupe are rivaled perhaps only by political leaders in their appearance in Mexican performances: in Mexico City there is always a present or former leader—or a thinly veiled version of one—on stage, as well as one of the founding women—for example, Coatlicue, Sor Juana, Frida Kahlo, or the Virgin of Guadalupe. These (feminist) touchstones seem well worn to some, yet they signal the residual colonialism that underpins the present. Taylor, writing about comments she elicited after a New York performance by Brazilian performance artist Denise Stoklos, explains the result of a tendency to find performances too European, as if "Latin Americans do not belong to the West," or, alternatively, "too Latin American" (221). To revisit colonialism—to recognize coloniality—for these and many other artists (including González Mello) is to take the most staged icons and to address the overlay of the twentieth- and twenty-first centuries and colonial Mexico as they challenge stereotypes and expose political appropriations, laying bare the mythical power of the past. One important distinction separates the work of artists like Rodríguez and Hadad from González Mello: the latter follows a long tradition (with innumerable exceptions from both female and male artists) of male authors who stage Mexican men in power, showing their fatal flaws and/or repeating (either for the sake of historical accuracy or as a representation of their present-day sentiments) social patterns that date to colonial times and before. In real life, from the *colonia* to today, as in González Mello's play, the Virgin of Guadalupe has been *debated* mostly by men and *reinterpreted* mostly by women.

As in the case of other well-known figures who appear on stage, many reimaginings of Guadalupe share two traits: the accessibility to audiences (on the stage and well beyond) that familiar figures allow, and the sense that there is unfinished business in present-day Mexico. These colonial remains speak to the promises of post-Independence and post-Revolution society, a theme seen in canonical Mexican plays of the twentieth and twenty-first centuries that offer dozens of historical characters who in one way or another speak to unrequited (political) passion. A very few examples include *La venganza de la gleba* (1905), by Federico Gamboa, which presents the plight of the dark-skinned campesino; Rodolfo Usigli's *El gesticulador* (1938), a play that underscores postrevolutionary duplicity and corruption, but could also—easily—apply to post-Independence; *El eterno femenino* (1975) by Rosario Castellanos, a farce that questions the confines of society for women centuries after Sor Juana retired to her cell and gave up her library; Sabina Berman's *Entre Villa y una mujer desnuda* (1993), which includes a Villa who, along with his contemporary sidekick Adrián, is rendered socially impotent by his machismo; or the many Sor Juana performances on stage and beyond that point out the dealings of "hombres necios" in a variety of present-day contexts that at times are indistinguishable from colonial Mexico.

Thus it is no surprise that the perennial, political use of Guadalupe, combined with the propensity of Mexican playwrights to take the most recognizable figures from history to the stage, makes pertinent an alternative version of the Guadalupe legend. The real life Padre Mier's colonial-era repositioning of *Guadalupe* continues to be politically salient, though while there is little doubt that his bold revisions of the past served Mexico during the quest for independence, post-Independence Mexico paid little heed to its indigenous past. This theme is subtly foreshadowed in *1822: El año que fuimos imperio* as characters routinely reinforce economic and ethnic categories that point to anything but equality—some of the unfinished business that underpins coloniality. As Enrique Krauze puts it, "Needless to say, when independence became fact in 1821, the new nation did not reinstate the Mexican empire. But the country took its name from the original tribal name of the Aztecs, and for the emblem on its flag it used the mythical symbol of the foundation of the city of Mexico-Tenochtitlán: an eagle perched on a nopal cactus holding a writhing serpent in its beak" (28–29). In name (and image) only is indeed one way the "fact" of Mexican Independence was seen by many Mexicans. The above-cited symbols adorned Mexico but did not change the country's colonial power structure, as Aníbal Quijano argues: "The national homogenization of the population could only have been achieved through a radical and global process of the democratization of society and the state. That democratization would have implied, and should imply before anything else, the process of decolonizing social, political, and cultural relations that maintain and reproduce racial social classification. The structure of power was and even continues to be organized on and around the colonial axis" (568). In *1822: El año que fuimos imperio* we see both the rupture and continuity of post-Independence Mexico, which is aided (and abetted) by the historically (in)appropriate humor of the secularized priest Mier. González Mello's rendition of Mier and other historical characters, which is enhanced by tremendous acting and by multiple references to theatricality (*sainetes*, comedias, etc.) that underscore the efficacy of humor and underpins the playful tone, provides a metatheatrical thread that unites the play and serves to highlight key instances of coloniality.[7]

One of the many successes of *1822* is the dramatic duplication of the complex Mier character—he is humorous without being a caricature. It is a respectful parody that still provides for a critique of the historical Mier, a possibility Linda Hutcheon clarifies, noting that "parodic art comes in a wide variety of tones and moods—from the respectful to playful to scathingly critical—and because its ironies can so obviously cut both ways [it is] a form of repetition with ironic critical distance, marking difference rather than similarity" (xii). Hutcheon also underscores the "tension between the potentially conservative effect of repetition and the potentially revolutionary impact of difference" (xii), an apt description of the forces at play in *1822*. In conjuring up a parody of Mier, the double-edged voice of irony referred to by Hutcheon catches the famous historical persona in his history, and what is essentially an *elogio* has its negative side: coloniality by definition is made up of the same players, the same social components, and in this case not even the names (e.g., Iturbide, Santa Anna, Guadalupe Victoria) have changed. And Mier is implicated (as we will soon see), yet the audience is likely to let him off the hook; the jester plays the same role with the audience that he does with Iturbide (and other characters) so that neither will skewer him.

The quick, biting wit necessary for survival is present from the very beginning of the play, when Padre Mier covers up his attempted escape from the infamous prison/castle in the Mexican city of Veracruz, San Juan de Ulúa, one of the places the real-life Mier spent time in prison. After explaining to the character Dávila, governor of the Spanish Crown's holdout in Veracruz, that he was simply trying to "repair" the bars of his cell (with a nail) because the cell is crumbling, a not-so-subtle reference to the sole remaining bastion of Spanish power in Mexico, he offers an oral curriculum vitae, presented with the verbal acumen seen previously, as a defense:

MIER. Señor Gobernador, no le otorgará más crédito a los chismes de este limpiarretretes que a la palabra de don Servando Teresa de Mier, Noriega, Guerra y Fernán-González, doctor en sagrada teología por la

Real y Pontificia Universidad de México; protonotario apostólico y pre-
lado doméstico del Sumo Pontífice; caballero hijodalgo de casa y solar
conocido descendiente de los primeros conquistadores e hijo de quien
fuera Gobernador del Nuevo Reino de León.

DÁVILA. A ver los títulos.

MIER. Se los entregué a mis jueces, junto con mis escritos y el resto de
mis pertenencias. Todo debe constar en autos.

DÁVILA. *(Revuelve los papeles de su escritorio y extrae un pliego, que re-
visa)* Aquí lo único que dice es que con usted hay que andarse con
mucho cuidado, porque al menor descuido está intrigando . . . *(Lee
por encima)* "Crimen de lesa majestad . . . apostasía . . . escritos
invitando a la sedición . . . prácticas masónicas . . . concesión no
autorizada de indulgencias . . . piratería . . ." ¡Ah, aquí está! "Fuga
e intento de fuga de diferentes prisiones civiles y eclesiásticas, con un
total de catorce reincidencias . . ." *(Moja su pluma en el tintero y en-
mienda el documento)* Y con ésta, ya son quince . . . (2–3)

The list of offenses Dávila reads is long, though surprisingly it omits
many of the accusations leveled against the historical Mier over the years,
not to mention the bulk of his myriad adventures. Still, one could argue
that he ended up on the right side of Mexican history. Héctor Ortega, the
actor who played Mier, winning a best actor award for the role, refers to
the historical Mier and to his own role in the production:

Yo creo que todavía no hemos rescatado lo suficiente a Fray Servando;
nada más hay por ahí una calle con su nombre. . . . Es un apasionado
por la libertad; éste es un personaje que quise representar y me encon-
tré con una maravilla de obra, escrita por Flavio González Mello. . . .
Estuvimos tres años y me entusiasmó el personaje porque es el
nacimiento de la República en una oposición total al imperio de Iturbide, para construir una patria que no tuviera como principio el colonialismo y menos el autoritarismo. (Cano)

Seeing the play in the 2000s, of course, audiences might view Ortega's
idea of the birth of the Republic through a different lens: on the one hand,
Mexico shook off the visible chains of the Spanish Crown in 1821; on the
other, the idea that Mexico will escape/has escaped colonialism and au-
thoritarianism is undermined at every turn in the play, as Padre Mier
corrects Iturbide, who has just tried to make it clear that he, Iturbide, is
Mexico's only hope by referring to an erroneous Aztec past: "¿Quién,

quién tendría los méritos suficientes para heredar el solio de Moctezuma, el último emperador azteca?" (13). In sharp lines that show González Mello's parodic prowess, Mier supplies, as the jester, true but unwanted answers:

> MIER. Querrá decir Cuauhtémoc . . .
>
> ITURBIDE. ¿Eh? . . . Sí, perdón: Cuauhtémoc . . . ¿Quién podría ocupar tan grave sitio? . . . Guerrero, a pesar de su nula educación, estoy seguro que sería un espléndido gobernante; pero creo que ninguno de nosotros ve a un mulato sentado en el trono de México, ¿o sí? . . . Bravo es un patriota intachable, pero sabemos que la corona le quedaría grande; y además, con sus múltiples enfermedades no creo que nos dure mucho . . . ¿Quién, entonces? Si el Rey de España nos desaira, el Congreso tiene una tarea harto difícil que resolver. Pero aun así, don Valentín, don Miguel, padre Mier, convendría que ya no postergaran más la discusión del asunto, porque se rumora que en este mismo momento, aquéllos a quienes ofrecimos el cetro fraguan con la Santa Alianza una expedición para reconquistarnos. Y nada ayudaría más a sus planes que encontrar al Imperio sin cabeza coronada. Es necesario que la nave mexicana tenga quién la conduzca en las tormentas que se avecinan.
>
> MIER. Le faltó mencionar al candidato más importante de todos, General.
>
> ITURBIDE. *(Con falsa modestia)* ¿Quién, padre?
>
> MIER. Don Guadalupe Victoria. (13)

Padre Mier is right in the first instance (Cuauhtémoc, not Montezuma was the last Aztec emperor), as well as in the second, though there would be some delay in Mexico before Guadalupe Victoria, who escaped to the jungle after being imprisoned by Iturbide, and whose pseudonym proclaimed his goal and his allegiance to—and desire to achieve victory in the name of—Mexico's Virgin of Guadalupe, would become Mexico's first president. To the royal ready to hear only the words he desires, none but the jester can question authority (this in contrast to Iturbide's comedic but cowardly entourage, which includes Colonel Pío Marcha, Goyo, the court painter, and a French tailor). Inserted into the above-cited dialogue is also race, an intended "entre nous" on the part of Iturbide that, despite their differences, Padre Mier does not refute. Indeed, Padre Mier's own references to the Mexican people leave little room for new social structures. In "protecting" the *léperos*, the uneducated masses, from the manipulative machinations of Iturbide and his supporters, Mier shows both his despair at witnessing the farcical "representation" of the masses and the fact that he cannot envision a political structure much beyond that offered by colonial Mexico. That is, the fierce proponent of Independence who sees hope in Mexico's indigenous history is forced to propose that the decision on Mexico's next "ruler" be made by state leaders and in secret:

> MIER. Lo que procede es turnar la propuesta a las legislaturas de los estados, para que cada uno se pronuncie y de este modo la decisión final exprese realmente el sentir de toda la Nación, y no la de un puñado de comparsas a los que difícilmente podemos llamar "el pueblo."
> *(Por el ingreso de público entran varios LÉPEROS, atropellando al UJIER que intentaba contenerlos, y ocupan la gradería superior del teatro lanzando vivas a Agustín Primero. Los DIPUTADOS se ponen de pie para ver mejor el espectáculo. Durante un momento todo es confusión)*
> MIER. ¡Señor Presidente! Solicito que haga desalojar las graderías.
> *(Los LÉPEROS le responden con una rechifla)*
> UJIER. ¡Sin más hombres que los que tengo no puedo hacer nada, Su Señoría!
> MIER. Entonces exijo que la sesión se suspenda hasta que el Congreso se haya mudado a un recinto donde pueda sesionar en secreto.
> GÓMEZ FARÍAS. No veo por qué tendríamos que andar escondiéndonos. Yo, al menos, no tengo nada que ocultarle a la Nación. ¿Usted sí, padre?
> MIER. Insisto en que no ventilemos la discusión frente al leperaje, que es tan fácilmente manipulable.
> *(Los LÉPEROS le vuelven a responder con una rechifla)*
> GÓMEZ FARÍAS. ¡Señor presidente! Ya fue mucho para moción, ¿no? Éste quiere hacer discurso.
> MIER. Le recuerdo que yo estaba en uso de la palabra cuando todo este sainete empezó.
> GÓMEZ FARÍAS. ¡El asunto ya está suficientemente discutido! ¡Que se vote!
> SECRETARIO. *(desesperado)* ¡Se suplica a los señores diputados que tengan la bondad de hablar un poco más despacio, que no me da tiempo de escribir todo lo que dicen!
> *(Un murmullo se apodera de la sala: por el ingreso de público acaba de entrar ITURBIDE, acompañado por MARCHA y un piquete de SOLDADOS. Los LÉPEROS vuelven a corear vivas a Agustín Primero. ITURBIDE sube a la tribuna).* (19–20)

The words "comparsas," "espectáculo," and "sainete" follow other instances in which Padre Mier signals the farcical nature of politics, in a scene that could perhaps remind Mexicans of some of the more colorful stagings in Mexico's present-day congress (e.g., several famous fistfights). While the play itself has some farcical elements (for example, the arrival of Iturbide to the port of Veracruz dressed as a woman, or Mier's ability to trick a soldier by pointing at the soldier's foot and then escaping), it is Mier's affirmation that a farce is being played out in Mexican politics that hits home with readers or spectators. At one point, Mier refuses to attend Iturbide's coronation, indicating that "La Iglesia me prohíbe asistir a las comedias" (27). And in a conversation with Guadalupe Victoria, the character Padre Mier quotes the real-life Mier: "Entre los hombres no se necesitan sino farsas porque todo es una comedia. Seamos realistas, General . . ." (39). This conversation is telling not only as an example of histrionic politicians, but also in that Padre Mier is willing to use his own theatrics to his gain, as he did in real life.

In her study on farce in Latin American theater, Priscilla Meléndez walks a fine line when she asserts that "one of Spanish American farce's most complex aspects and its central force lies in its attempt to transgress the traditional perception that it is an anti-aesthetic, anti-intellectual, anti-critical, unrealistic, unpretentious, solely humorous and playful genre, stripped of political agendas, while simultaneously questioning the attempt to stress farce's more serious and 'meaningful' purposes" (28). As mentioned above, 1822 is historical theatre and farce—but it is not solely either. Yet the metafarces, like the foolhardy congressional sessions, allow the author to present the best of both worlds: from farce (and from the historical Mier), González Mello borrows playful passion; through historical theatre,[8] he taps into the Mexican tradition of serious, generally straightforward political criticism through the lens of the past. Timothy G. Compton captures this combination (farcical metatheatre, if we consider the present-day Mexican Congress to be a space that brackets off a play within a play, and historical theatre):

Despite the disheartening self-serving politics of almost all of Mexico's early politicians and caciques portrayed in 1822, it also showed the antidote in the person of Fray Servando Teresa de Mier, who spoke bluntly of abuses, punctured balloons of self-adulation, and put love of country and fellow men above love of self. Far from being a history lesson, although the basics of Mexican history were clearly accurate, 1822 had obvious repercussions for modern Mexico which were not lost on audience members sitting near me, as I heard them mutter "Salinas de Gortari" several times. . . . My favorite scenes were the hilarious portrayals of sessions of Congress. Actors took seats in the audience during these scenes so their flamboyant outbursts, their impassioned ironic speeches, their petty and self-serving proposals, and their off-the-record comments erupted like fireworks right next to spectators. (106)

The metatheatrical elements of the play serve to entertain, and it is fun to be in on the joke, pleasing to watch along with the characters in the *palcos* (box seats) as they watch a variety of scenes, to be an audience member who "gets" the play within a play—but these elements also serve to underscore the theatricality (in the devious sense) of Iturbide's intrigues. Compton explains the set design, which allowed for the most obvious example of metatheatre: "Since the play required nine different settings, ranging from interiors of palaces, castles, theatres and houses, to city streets and the deep jungle of Veracruz, most of the set work designed by Mónica Raya consisted of exquisite two-dimensional backdrops which could be raised and lowered instantly. During the second act, politicians watched parts of the historical drama unfold from replicas of box seats from the Teatro Santa Anna from Mexico City's 19th century" (106). The various metatheatrical scenes in Act II, one of which involves a conspiracy to overthrow Iturbide in favor of Santa Anna, provide for the above-mentioned distancing and—as Compton mentions—frame action that takes place elsewhere.

A case in point concerns a scene in which Mier, Ramos Arizpe, and an indigenous guide take to the jungle to search for Guadalupe Victoria, an expedition that also provides insight into colonial structures. The expedition scenes are some of the most comical and troubling; as the search party heads into the jungle they also enter a past that is very much present, a foreign locale that is very much local: "*MIER y RAMOS ARIZPE caminan dificultosamente entre la vegetación; un GUÍA indio les va abriendo paso con su machete; atrás, un par de INDIOS, antorcha en mano, vienen cargando las provisiones. Todos se detienen a descansar, exhaustos. RAMOS ARIZPE se la pasa matando mosquitos y rascándose las ronchas que cubren su cuerpo*" (32).

The potential political savior (and Mexico's real-life first president), whose pseudonym—as mentioned above—was chosen carefully to represent Mexican Independence, is eventually found by Mier and the other members of the search party. While the historical Guadalupe Victoria did indeed spend time hiding in the jungles of Veracruz, and while he indeed suffered from epilepsy, the parodic key in *1822: El año que fuimos imperio* is that Mier and company retrain him to speak Spanish; that is, they attempt to rid him of the tempestuous trapping of years lived with beasts and "indios."

The first clue that the search party is making progress is finding a footprint. To Ramos Arizpe's question, "¿Y cómo sabe que es de español?" the guide responds, "Porque el pie tiene forma de zapato" (33). It turns out that Guadalupe Victoria has not been eaten by "la bestia," as Ramos Arizpe conjectured, yet his grunting (not to mention his words in Nahuatl) are of grave concern. They listen to the beastly Other as his words are translated by guides and as he terrifies his first meta-audience (Mier, Ramos Arizpe), his second meta-audience (Iturbide and others in the palcos of the theater, who clap slowly), and those of us who have purchased a ticket to see the play. Concluding this frenetic scene is an epileptic seizure—duplicating a symptom of the real-life illness of Guadalupe Victoria—of which he does not die, of course, and in fact it takes just about seven theatrical minutes for the character to go from Nahuatl-speaking cave dweller/beast to Spanish-speaking Independence leader of "indios" and "campesinos," separated from them in some cases by language, in some case by lineage (despite his relatively humble origins), and in some cases by both. Mier helps with the transition:

VICTORIA. ¡Ndependeciomuert, ndependenciomuert!
MIER. "Independencia . . ."
VICTORIA. ¡Novoantregar ralistjoeput! ¡Ndependeciomuert!
MIER. ". . . Independencia . . . ¿o muerte?"
VICTORIA. ¡Svaientesnosesinan!
MIER. ". . . Los valientes . . ."
VICTORIA. ¡Svaientesnosesinan!
MIER. ". . . Los valientes no asesinan . . ."
VICTORIA. ¡Lapatresprimer!
MIER. ". . . La patria es primero . . ."
VICTORIA. ¡Iaméxico! ¡Iaméxico! ¡Iaméxico! (36)

In the video version of the play, the Victoria Guadalupe character does not speak the words, "I am Mexico" (Iaméxico), at least not intelligibly, though other references point to a future colonial conundrum, for example Mier's stance against state's rights: "¡Vendan! ¡Vendan Texas, y si pueden, también lo demás! Hay que aprovechar que los estados todavía no se han separado de nosotros. Con ese disparate del federalismo, no nos queda mucho tiempo. ¡A vender! ¡Pronto! ¡Rematen todo!" (49). This is a world far removed from the "los fieros y los monos" of the jungle, far removed from Nahuatl and tinged with English: it is the new modus operandi (similar to the old modus operandi) that Mier encourages Guadalupe Victoria to accept by signing Santa Anna's Plan de Tres Puntos:

VICTORIA. ¿Qué opinan?

RAMOS ARIZPE. Yo creo que es un plan espléndido.

VICTORIA. *(a MIER)* ¿Y usted?

MIER. *(observando el documento)* Sí, bueno . . . convendría darle una buena corregidita . . . "Soberanía" no se escribe con "z," brigadier. Y "América" va sin "h."

SANTA ANNA. ¿De veras?

VICTORIA. ¿Pero . . . piensa que debo firmar?

MIER. . . . Sin duda. Y cuanto antes, mejor.

VICTORIA. *(señala a SANTA ANNA)* Pero él también era realista.

MIER. General . . . creo que el fin superior que perseguimos amerita que olvidemos esas pasadas diferencias.

VICTORIA. Está bien. Todo sea por la . . . la . . . ¿cómo se llama, esto . . . lo que estamos intentando salvar . . . ?

MIER. Pellejo, don Lupe. (42)

As words (and structures) are restored to Victoria Guadalupe's memory, so too are the colonial baggage they carry. *Orden* and *Patria* (not to mention *raza*, a word not spoken in the play) serve to reify the past. For Mier, this represents the lesser of two evils, and in a society on the brink of war, the conservative European male path often wins out. Yet he again plays the jester (briefly) to Guadalupe Victoria, telling him in no uncertain terms, "Pues tu nombre es tan ridículo como tu victoria, y tan falso como las leyendas de tu Guadalupe" (52). As Mier puts it, "Ahora los habitantes de estas tierras se llaman 'ciudadanos,' pero soportan los mismos vicios y la misma opresión que cuando eran súbditos de la corona. . . . La diferencia entre 'México' y 'Nueva España' es la misma que hay entre Guadalupe Victoria y José Miguel Fernández . . ." (51). José Miguel Fernández was Guadalupe Victoria's original name, and through parodic repetition, a nod to Mexican traditions (farce, historical theater), and a metatheatrical staging that reminds the audience of different levels of theatricality, González Mello signals the (almost) inevitable result of political transitions in Mexico and elsewhere (and the only option for those who want to promote change): theatricality.

For colonial structures that remain unchanged, for residual *porfirismo*, for stalled revolutionary changes, and for political transitions, it may be that the only antidote is not the acts of politicians but of artists, the self-conscious theatricality that exposes naturalizing theatrics. And of course a bit of biting drama is always in order, as seen in Mier's self-administered last rites: "A los mexicanos les heredo una patria independiente y republicana, aunque infestada de parásitos y a punto de desmembrarse, para que se arreglen con ella lo mejor que puedan . . . *(Da un brinco y desaparece en la fosa que estuvo cavando. Obscuro lento)* (53–54). By "humoring the limits" of colonial times—and by reviving Teresa de Mier's dark, biting humor, González Mello highlights the colonial structures that endure in Mexico.

Notes

1. Another play written and directed by González Mello, *Lascuráin, o la brevedad del poder*, interrogates temporal boundaries. The satire takes place during the forty-five minutes during which the lead character, based on the Mexican president Pedro Lascuráin, who very briefly held office in 1913, is corrupted by power—at least as González Mello imagines the short reign. The critical portrayal of a presidential placeholder between the betrayed Francisco I. Madero and the soon-to-take-power Victoriano Huerta was staged outside the National Palace in 2005 and again a half-decade later but, similar to *1822: El año que fuimos imperio*, "'mientras actuábamos [en 2005], afuera las cosas estaban candentes, acababan de desaforar a Andrés Manuel López Obrador.' El montaje sigue vigente ya que retrata el presidencialismo mexicano que ha determinado el rumbo de este país política y económicamente en los últimos 150 años, explicó. 'No cambié nada para hablar de lo que pasa actualmente. Hay pasajes que en 2005 le venían muy bien al gobierno de Fox, y en estos momentos la trama también es pertinente, pues demuestra una conducta reiterada en el actuar de los políticos mexicanos'" (Balerini Casal).

2. A *New York Times* article informs readers that the government of Felipe Calderón, as part of the political theatrics employed by all political parties, likely subsidized (and at the very least facilitated, by offering extensive access to high police facilities) the production of a TV show that glamorized a group of antinarcotics agents. Clearly, people view acting—art—as retaining the ability to play a central role in politics. In this case the artistry is not new: "[Secretary of Public Security] Mr. García Luna does enjoy the theatrical side of his job. In one famous case in 2005, when he was the federal police chief, he admitted to staging the arrest of an alleged kidnapping ring so morning news broadcasts could show a 'live' police action. And after the arrest last year of a top cartel operator, Edgar Valdez Villarreal, known as La Barbie, the public security ministry circulated DVDs of the interrogation. It made for riveting television but did nothing to help the legal investigation" (Malkin).

3. Adam Versényi also writes of the double role of the *actor*: "The festival of Quetzalcóatl presents us with a type of experience, the sacred rite, that the modern theatre

has explored from Artaud to Growtoski. It is the seed of, though by no means the same as, one of the recurring fascinations of twentieth-century theatrical technique: the continuing explorations of the duality inherent in acting itself, where the person portraying a role can either ask us to enter into the fiction of the actor's character with him, or can present that character to us as a fabrication, commenting upon it as he or she does so" (10–11).

4. Teresa de Mier was born in Mexico (the city of Monterrey), and in 1763, he entered the Dominican order. While his counter-history about the Virgin of Guadalupe, delivered in front of the clerical crème de la crème of Mexican society, is clearly his most impressive, iconoclastic act, Mier was also a prolific writer and something of an escape artist who spent time in a variety of prisons in France, Spain, and Mexico.

5. Enrique Krauze details Teresa de Mier's assertion: "The seed of nationalism bore its first political fruit toward the end of the eighteenth century, when Fray Servando Teresa de Mier produced his theological conjectures geared toward claiming the creole right—based on their native birth—to the political and economic power then monopolized by fifteen thousand Spaniards in a country of six million. Clavijero had compared the Aztec past with the Greek and Roman world. In his famous sermon delivered at the Colegiata of Guadalupe . . . Fray Servando went even further. Considering himself a direct heir of the mendicant friars and inspired particularly by Fray Bartolomé de las Casas, he built a mythological bridge linking the creoles to the Aztecs and denying the divine rights of the Spanish Crown after the Conquest. Fray Servando asserted that the root of the Náhuatl word *mexi* was the same as the Hebrew word for Messiah. As some sixteenth-century scholars had maintained, the ancient Mexicans might be none other than one of the lost tribes of Israel. And Quetzalcóatl, who had visited and instructed the Indians and then gone away again—Servando asserted—must have been the Apostle Thomas. . . . From claims like this it was only a small political distance to the demand for independence" (81–82).

6. "From its inception, the Second Constituent Congress faced the thorny question of the limitations placed on the delegates by the provinces of Jalisco, Zacatecas, Guanajuato, and Yucatán. . . . Since the provinces, most of which now called themselves states, had determined that Mexico must have a federal republic, debate in the congress focused on the critical issue of who was sovereign: the nation or the states. Extreme defenders of states' rights . . . argued that only the states possessed sovereignty, a portion of which they collectively ceded to the union in order to form a national government. . . . Their opponents, men such as Servando de Mier . . . believed that only the nation was sovereign. . . . Midway between these extremes stood those who, like Ramos Arizpe, believed that the national government and the states must share sovereignty" (Rodríguez O. 77–78).

7. Timothy G. Compton, in his summary of the performance for the *Latin American Theatre Review*, writes: "All of the actors performed marvelously, but special commendations are in order for Mario Iván Martínez for his portrayal of the regally two-faced Iturbide, Hernán del Riego for an unforgettable version of Guadalupe Victoria completely demented after hiding in the jungle, Mario Zaragoza for his wicked embodiment of a contemptible early congressman and his inspired portrayal of a guide in the jungle, and Héctor Ortega for injecting grace and humor into the role of Padre Mier even as he showed his great dignity and integrity. As did *La prisionera, 1822* proved that intelligent, relevant theatre can be artistic, receive

strong reviews, and attract strong audiences (without any nudity, foul language, or cheap humor)" (106).

8. In an interview with Katia de la Rosa, González Mello explains that "el género histórico es uno de los géneros más socorridos del teatro mexicano aunque por momentos se deja un poco de lado. Luego se retoma porque hay una tradición al respecto, desde luego con Usigli, Magaña, Ibargüengoitia—este último le da una perspectiva diferente al teatro histórico en *El atentado, la conspiración vendida*—y también con la que considero mi generación. David Olguín tiene una constante preocupación por los temas históricos. Por supuesto Ignacio Solares, que tiene este tríptico histórico político maravilloso: *El jefe máximo*. Esa tradición nunca ha dejado de ser un tema. Hay gente a la que jamás le entusiasmará y no lo escribirá, pero no ha quedado clausurado. Ha quedado clausurado en el cine, por ejemplo. Ahí sí te puedo decir que por un prejuicio absurdo, en términos de que es muy caro hacer películas históricas, el tema de la Historia quedó prácticamente desterrado del cine nacional y, las pocas veces que se aborda, es desde una perspectiva poco afortunada. En el teatro difícilmente creo que desaparezcan los temas históricos. Shakespeare acudía a ellos porque son un abrevadero de situaciones, de personajes, una fuente natural. *1822 el año que fuimos imperio* es una obra más política que histórica. Por eso se conecta con el público, esa temática une la Historia con la actualidad."

Works Cited

Arias, Santa. "De Fray Servando Teresa de Mier a Juan Bautista Muñoz: La disputa guadalupana en vísperas de la independencia." *Revista Iberoamericana* 222 (2008): 6–13.

Balerini Casal, Emiliano. "Lascuráin o la brevedad del poder, retrato del presidencialismo." *Milenio*, September 24, 2010.

Bay-Cheng, Sarah. "Theatre History and Digital Historiography." *Theater Historiography: Critical Interventions*. Ed. Henry Bial and Scott Magelssen. Ann Arbor: University of Michigan Press, 2010. 128.

Cano, Natalia, and Julio Alejandro Quijano. "Recuerda actor censura en representar héroes históricos." *El Universal*, September 16, 2005. http://www.eluniversal.com .mx/espectaculos/64561.html. Accessed November 8, 2012.

Compton, Timothy G. "Mexico City Theatre: Spring 2002." *Latin American Theatre Review*. 36.2 (2003): 103–16.

González Mello, Flavio. *1822: El año que fuimos imperio*. MS.

Gutiérrez, Laura. *Performing Mexicanidad*. Austin: University of Texas Press, 2010.

Hutcheon, Linda. *A Theory of Parody: The Teachings of Twentieth-Century Art Forms*. Champaign: University of Illinois Press, 1985.

Krauze, Enrique. *Mexico, Biography of Power: A History of Modern Mexico, 1810–1996*. Trans. Hank Heifetz. New York: Harper Collins, 1997.

Malkin, Elizabeth. "Mexican Cops: These Are Their Stories." *New York Times*, June 10, 2011. http://www.nytimes.com/2011/06/12/arts/television/el-equipo-mexi cos-television-police-drama.html?pagewanted=all&_r=0. Accessed November 8, 2012.

Meléndez, Priscilla. *The Politics of Farce in Contemporary Spanish American Theatre.* Chapel Hill: North Carolina Studies in the Romance Languages and Literatures, University of North Carolina–Chapel Hill, 2006.

Otto, Beatrice K. *Fools are Everywhere.* Chicago: University of Chicago Press, 2001.

Quijano, Aníbal. "Coloniality of Power, Eurocentrism, and Latin America." *Nepantla: Views from South* 1.3 (2000): 533–80.

Roach, Joseph. *Cities of the Dead: Circum-Atlantic Performance.* New York: Columbia University Press, 1996.

Rodríguez O., Jaime E. "Constitution of 1824 and the Mexican State." *The Origins of Mexican National Politics: 1808–1847.* Ed. Jaime E. Rodríguez O. New York: Rowman & Littlefield, 1997. 65–84.

Rosa, Katia de la. "1822: El año que fuimos imperio: Entrevista a Flavio González Mello." *Revista de la Universidad de México* 14 (2005): 76–77.

Sarmiento, Sergio. "Fox y la Virgen de Guadalupe: Imagen usada ni Segob la quita." *Siempre!* September 16, 1999. Web. Accessed June 18, 2012.

Taylor, Diana. *The Archive and the Repertoire: Performing Cultural Memory in the Americas.* Durham: Duke University Press, 2003.

Versényi, Adam. *Theatre in Latin America: Religion, Politics and Culture from Cortés to the 1980s.* Cambridge: Cambridge University Press, 1993.

CHAPTER THIRTEEN

A Postcolonial Quartet, 2006–2008

Seymour Menton

In my 1993 book on Latin America's new historical novel, I presented empirical evidence that this subgenre predominated between 1979 and 1992. Although the trend was undoubtedly inspired by the five-hundredth anniversary of what is commonly known as Columbus's discovery of the New World, Latin America's first new historical novel was actually Alejo Carpentier's *El reino de este mundo*, published in 1949. What is even more amazing is that Carpentier's novel was preceded by Virginia Woolf's *Orlando*, published in 1928 and translated into Spanish by Jorge Luis Borges in 1936 and 1937. Although *Orlando* shares with the new historical novel its carnivalesque mood, its intertextuality, and its metafiction, I would not give it credit for the flourishing of Latin America's new historical novel between 1979 and 1992.

Just as the new historical novel predominated with incredible precision between 1979 and 1992, it ended with similarly brusque precision in 1992. Although I have read more than 150 Latin American novels published between 1993 and 2011, I have observed that "the new historical novel" I studied in the early nineties has almost disappeared—the only exceptions, to my knowledge, are *Rasero* (1993) by the Mexican chemist Francisco Rebolledo and *Margarita, está linda la mar* (1998) by the Nicaraguan short-story writer, novelist, and former Sandinista vice-president Sergio Ramírez. However, several varieties of the historical novel continue to enjoy great popularity among writers and readers.

Although I have given many lectures on the historical novel, new and otherwise, in the past eighteen years, I am deeply indebted to my fellow

Mexicanist Oswaldo Estrada for presenting me with a new challenge for this collection. I am eager to comment on four Mexican novels set in the nineteenth century that were published between 2006 and 2008, and that are linked to the Mexican *colonia: Península, península* (2008) by Hernán Lara Zavala; *Juárez, el rostro de piedra* (2008) by Eduardo Antonio Parra; *Expediente del atentado* (2007) by Álvaro Uribe; and *Las grandes lluvias* (2006) and *Tocar el fuego* (2007), the first two volumes of Eraclio Zepeda's tetralogy, a muralistic vision of Chiapas based on the four ancient Greek elements of water, fire, earth, and air. Though these novels all have different degrees of experimentation, none can be classified as *new* historical novels.

The semijustification for including them in a volume devoted to novels with colonial themes is that my colleague Jaime Rodríguez has insisted in many publications that Mexico was better off politically and economically in the pre-Independence period than in the post-Independence period. If so, it might be said that the colonial period extended through the Santa Anna Anarchy, the War of Reform (1857–1860), and the French Invasion of 1862 followed by the establishment of the Maximilian-Carlota Empire. It was not until Porfirio Díaz's dictatorship, with all its faults, that Mexico really embarked on the road to modernization. Furthermore, if I don my theoretical fedora, I could apply the Early Modern (instead of Golden Age) label to the late colonial period (the "enlightened absolutism," for example, of Carlos III, 1759–1788) and the Porfiriato's "orden, paz y progreso" (1876–1911), and reserve the beginning of the modern period for the presidency of Miguel Alemán (1946–1952). Perhaps this chapter could be considered a transition to a second volume devoted to a reconsideration of the Mexican canonical novels of the twentieth century.

Because I am dealing with four novels set in the nineteenth century, I cannot resist the temptation to divide the "operatic" quartet of my title into two duets. Individual differences between the first two novels not withstanding, these novels, *Península, península* and *Las grandes lluvias*, share a panoramic geographical, political, and ethnic base (they take place in Yucatán and Chiapas), while *Juárez, el rostro de piedra* and *Expediente del atentado* are biographically based (the former, obviously, focused on Juárez, the latter on Porfirio Díaz and Federico Gamboa).

Península, península and *Las grandes lluvias*, in addition to their muralistic orientation, project their authors' ideological messages. Although Mexico's Aztec heritage was glorified both by the 1964 opening of the Museo Nacional de Antropología by the Partido Revolucionario Institucional (PRI), and by the highly publicized 1992 pro-Indian march down the Paseo de la Reforma to the chant of "Cristóbal Colón al paredón," Mexico's Hispanic heritage was touted for perhaps the first time in Vicente Leñero's play *La noche de Hernán Cortés*, in Carlos Fuentes's call for an equestrian statue in honor of Cortés, and in Octavio Paz's support for a more balanced view of Cortés, all in the same year of 1992. Mexico's dual ethnic heritage is even more clearly trumpeted in *Península, península*. The title refers to Yucatán and Spain, and the characters are descendants of the Mayans as well as of the Spanish conquistadors intertwined in the Caste War of 1847–1849. Although the Mayan rebels distrust the *hacendados* because they never fulfill their promises, don Quintín, the one individualized hacendado, albeit a relatively minor character, is not portrayed negatively. Even more significantly, the bishop of Yucatán, Campeche, and Cozumel, don Celestino Onésimo, is one of the novel's real heroes, in spite of his name. He judiciously solves a dilemma for Lorenza when her marriage to the novel's "author" José Turrisa is threatened by a letter from her long-believed-dead first husband Genaro, who is obviously planning to blackmail her. In a previous chapter, Bishop Onésimo criticized colonial Bishop Landa for burning the Mayan codices.

On the other hand, in socialist Zepeda's novel, the clearcut villain is the hacendado don Desiderio, and don Lino García, a high official of the Cathedral with a very minor role, is portrayed negatively in contrast to the positive role of the young, recently ordained *presbítero*, who becomes a good friend to—and eventually the lover and husband of—the heroine Juana.

Rather than continue with the parallelisms between the two novels— Plutarch's (Parallel) *Lives* is actually mentioned in *Las grandes lluvias*— it would probably be better at this point to delve more deeply into *Península, península,* the more complex of the two. A very rich muralistic text, Hernán Lara Zavala's novel has a title that heralds its dualistic structure. In keeping with its nineteenth-century setting, detailed descriptions reminiscent of Balzac as well as some sentimental and melodramatic plot elements predominate, which are explicitly justified by the revelation toward the end of the novel that the "author" is José Turrisa, the pseudonym of the Romantic mid-nineteenth-century novelist Justo Sierra O'Reilly. In one of several passages of metafiction, Lara explains his approach: "¿Nos encontramos ante una novela histórica? . . . ¿Cómo escribir una novela basada en hechos reales del siglo XIX sin rendirse a las convenciones de la novela decimonónica?" (79). He also occasionally confides to the reader that he is sitting at his computer in Cambridge or Cuernavaca working on this book.

In addition to the racial conflict between Indians and criollos shown in the novel, the split within each group is actually more important: that between the Mérida centralist followers of Governor Miguel Barbachano and the Campeche federalist followers of Governor Santiago Méndez; Cecilio Chi; and that between leader of the Indians in the eastern area of Valladolid, and Jacinto Pat, leader in southern Yucatán.

Two very different foreigners reinforce the dual structure of the novel. In an example of intertextuality with Carlos Fuentes's *Gringo viejo*, the Englishwoman Miss Bell teaches the children of the wealthy landowner don Quintín. In her diary, she provides Lara with the opportunity to insert into the novel some details of Mayan history and culture, which she is studying, along with two other examples of dualism: the colonial conflicts between Dominicans and Jesuits, and Obispo Landa's burning of the Mayan codices, which previews the burning of José Turrisa's manuscripts by his political enemies, the supporters of Yrigoyen whose rivalry with the supporters of Barrera echoes the rivalry between the previous generation's Méndez and Barbachano. In the novel's epilogue, the reader is told that the contemporary author Lara reconstructed Turrisa's charred manuscript. Miss Bell, in the course of the novel, falls in love with the mestizo José María, and they eventually marry and go to live among the Indians.

The Irish Dr. Fitzpatrick, the other important foreigner in the novel, always followed by his dog Pompeyo, is kidnapped by Mayan leader Jacinto Pat in order to have the doctor tend to the wounded during the uprising. Perhaps in keeping with Lara's questioning Mexico's official Indian ethnic image, he characterizes Dr. Fitzpatrick as being antirevolutionary, both in Ireland and in Yucatán, as well as a nonbeliever, in contrast to the prototype of the revolutionary Irish Catholic. Padre Turrisa, novelist José's brother, helps Dr. Fitzpatrick escape from Valladolid. Father Turrisa later meets up with Jacinto Pat, who helps the doctor escape to Belize, where he boards an English launch on his way to England. However, Dr. Fitzpatrick probably dies, melodramatically, when he dives into the water in order to save his beloved dog from being eaten by a crocodile.

Although the novel's specific setting is Yucatán's Caste War, national and international contexts are also inserted, albeit briefly. Allusions are made to the roles played by Santa Anna and Juárez, the occupation of Mexico City by the United States, the request for American arms by Governor Méndez, and the shipment of arms from the British colony of Belize (British Honduras) to the Indians.

May I divulge any critical comments? During my student days in Mexico in 1948–1949, I once turned in an overly positive analysis of Gregorio López y Fuentes's novel *Entresuelo* to Professor Francisco Monterde. The kind and gentle Monterde praised my paper and then, with a smile, flabbergasted me with a question I have never forgotten: "How could the author have improved the novel?" In the case of *Península, península,* although the historical and fictitious elements are well integrated with a judicious degree of experimentation, the overabundance of characters prevents any of them from standing out as protagonists. In a sense contradicting myself, I would still say that if the story of Gonzalo Guerrero, the shipwrecked sailor who probably fathered Mexico's first mestizo, had been inserted, it would have provided an interesting challenge to Octavio Paz's interpretation of the Mexican psyche based on the story of La Malinche in *El laberinto de la soledad.*

To return to the comparative approach, just as Lara's *Península, península* projects a muralistic view of nineteenth-century Yucatán, Eraclio Zepeda's *Las grandes lluvias* does the same for Chiapas, with an incredible number of similarities between the two novels, a fact that does not discount their very significant differences. Both novels are set in specific historical periods, 1847–1849 and 1837–1839, respectively, with "tentacles" that reach back to the Conquest and colonial periods and forward to the present. In *Las grandes lluvias,* mention is made of a transoceanic canal through Tehuantepec, while in *Península, península,* Dr. Fitzpatrick alludes to a canal through Nicaragua. Likewise, both novels are centered geographically in their respective state capitals of Mérida and San Cristóbal, with the action moving to other cities (Valladolid and Tuxtla Gutiérrez) and to a multitude of towns that are at times gratuitously named. Even Belize plays a minor role in both novels.

The muralistic or panoramic approach is also applied in both novels to social classes and ethnicities. The rivalry between conservative and centralist Governor Barbachano supported by the Meridians, and liberal federalist Governor Méndez supported by the inhabitants of Campeche in *Península,* is mirrored in *Lluvias* by the conflict between Governor Sandoval, the conservative centralist allied with the Scottish Freemasonry Lodge in San Cristóbal, and Joaquín Miguel Gutiérrez, the liberal federalist allied with the York Freemasonry Lodge in Tuxtla (Tuxtla Gutiérrez today). The national political scene in both novels is dominated by Santa Anna: the U.S. Invasion of 1845 in *Península* facilitated the Indian uprising in Yucatán, while the San Cristóbal upper classes in *Lluvias* discuss Santa Anna's role in the 1836 Texas War of Independence and the loss of his leg in the frivolously named Pastry War of 1838.

Both novels begin with the introduction of the principal upper-class characters in large parties: a farewell for Governor Miguel Barbachano, who has resigned in favor of his rival Santiago Méndez in *Península* and in *Lluvias*, and the wake for Governor Mariano Montes de Oca, whose child bride Juana quickly becomes the protagonist of the entire novel. After becoming a widow, she gives early signs of becoming the forerunner of the twentieth-century liberated woman by organizing a weekly *tertulia* in her "Salón de los visibles." There the young scholarly Manuel Larráinzar lends her a copy of Plutarch's *Parallel Lives*, which might well symbolize Juana's three friends, who represent three components of society, and whose first names all begin with the letter M: Manuel the politician, Manuel Galindo the army lieutenant, and Mariano Mejía the young priest.

As Juana rides on horseback through the streets of San Cristóbal, she observes the differences between the neighborhoods of the wealthy, the former mulatto and Negro slaves, and the Indians. Author Zepeda also makes a point of distinguishing between the different Indian groups: the Tzotziles, also called *murciélagos*, the Zinacantecos, the Chamulas, and the Zoques. The Indian Xun is individualized as Juana's accomplice in her trysts with Lieutenant Galindo and later avenges Galindo's assassination, planned by Juana's father don Desiderio. Although blacks and mulattos play a folkloric role in the novel, the two dancers Gog and Magog later help Juana deliver a confidential letter destined for Senator Manuel Larráinzar in Mexico City.

The two foreigners in *Lluvias*, Juana's German friend Mühlenpfordt and the American Dr. McKinney, are not as prominent in the novel as the two in *Península*. In *Lluvias*, Dr. McKinney, called Santiago Maquenes, helped Guatemala cope with a cholera epidemic before curing Juana of her unidentified fever. He also spoke to Juana, somewhat gratuitously, about his famous countrymen, the archaeologist John Lloyd Stephens and the English painter Frederick Catherwood, who were on their way to explore the Mayan ruins of Palenque.

In *Las grandes lluvias*, the protagonist Juana is punished by her hacendado father for becoming pregnant out of wedlock. She is forced to live in a hut with the Indians and to dress and eat like them. However, Zepeda goes further than Lara by actually describing how Juana happily adapts to Indian life and learns their language. In a June 7, 2006, interview published in *El Universal*, Zepeda recognizes the influence of Rosario Castellanos, "quien describe una cultura milenaria sojuzgada y oprimida durante siglos, que un día clamó por su derecho a existir, en un grito que captó la atención del mundo el 1 de enero de 1994 [due to the Zapatista uprising led by Subcomandante Marcos]" (Licona).

In terms of a comparative literary evaluation, both novels succeed in creating a broad view of their respective states, with the occasional fault of inserting too many historical and geographical details. The historical aspect of *Península, península* has greater impact than that of *Las grandes lluvias* because of the importance of the Caste War of 1847–1849. On the other hand, the novelistic aspects of *Lluvias* have greater unity because there is only one protagonist, Juana, who consistently displays her independence and strong character. After meeting and falling in love with Lieutenant Manuel Galindo, she takes the lead in captivating him, and by the seventh chapter, she dances the first *rigodón* in Chiapas with Galindo. During the absence of her father and her brother, she visits Galindo's barracks and takes a special interest in the conditions of the *soldaderas*. The very next day, with Xun's assistance, she sets up a rendezvous with Galindo in a nearby farm cabin, where they have the first of their five sexual encounters during her father's absence. From the seventh chapter on, the novelistic plot gathers speed as, little by little, dialogue becomes more important. In the seventeenth chapter, probably the most dramatic chapter of the entire novel, Juana boldly confronts her father, telling him that Galindo, who by this time has been killed, is the father of her child. When he slaps her in the face, she grabs his arms and overpowers him. He calls her a *puta* and she replies that he tried to make her a puta when he married her to the aged Governor Mariano Montes de Oca. It is at this moment that don Desiderio has the servants drag her off to live with the Indians.

In 1839, eight months after the death of Lieutenant Galindo, and after Juana has given birth to Galindo's son, she begins to fall in love with Mariano Mejía, the *presbítero*. Given her previous behavior, the reader can accept this improbable turn of events. However, what cannot be accepted as realistic are the events resulting in the excessive biblical symbolism in the thirty-third and final chapter of the novel. Juana and Mariano take refuge from the torrential rains in a cave where they are joined by several animals, in an evocation of Noah and the biblical flood. The presence of a snake evokes the beginning of the world, a Paradise in which Juana and Mariano will constitute the figurative first couple. The torrential rains in this chapter reinforce the leitmotif spelled out in the title *Las grandes lluvias*, and excessively repeated in the poetic "weather reports" that initiate the majority of the chapters.

The second volume of Eraclio Zepeda's tetralogy, *Tocar el fuego* (2007) is very disappointing and merits few comments. The title symbolizes the

1862–1867 war against the French troops of Napoleon III, but there is no real novelistic conflict or tension, nor is there sufficient development of the new characters introduced. The protagonist is Ezequiel ("Cheque"), the oldest child of Juana and Mariano Mejía, who rapidly rises up through the ranks of the Mexican army, but the characters from *Las grandes lluvias* are excessively reviewed. Benito Juárez and Porfirio Díaz are mentioned briefly. The third volume, yet to be published, is anticipated with the discovery of gold and petroleum below the surface of Juana's ranch or *land*. The leitmotif of the fourth volume, *air*, will undoubtedly be represented by . . .

In contrast to the similarities between *Península, península* and *Las grandes lluvias*, the differences between Eduardo Antonio Parra's *Juárez, el rostro de piedra* and Álvaro Uribe's *Expediente del atentado* could not be greater. Whereas *Juárez* is a biographical novel with a minimum of fiction, *Expediente del atentado* concentrates on only one historical episode in the life of Porfirio Díaz—the failed attempt to assassinate him in 1897—and fictionalizes it.

How can I possibly add anything to Christopher Domínguez Michael's comments on *Juárez* the novel, Parra the author, Juárez as portrayed by historians and previous novelists, and Juárez as exploited by governments of the Mexican Revolution, published in the April 2009 issue of *Letras Libres*? I agree with the critic's interpretation and evaluation of Parra's work and admire his placing it within its literary and political contexts. *Juárez* continues to be relevant, as well as controversial, in Mexico in the twenty-first century. Domínguez Michael reports that when Vicente Fox, the Partido Acción Nacional presidential candidate, took office in 2000, one of his sons handed him a crucifix, which was met by cries of "Juárez, Juárez!" from a group of *diputados*. Fifty-two years earlier, an American student, who was walking past the Alameda on Avenida Juárez, was shocked to see the Juárez Monument painted black, an annual insult to one of Mexico's most revered heroes, perpetrated by the Fascist *sinarquistas*. As a testimony to this American's fascination with Mexican history, his first book, published in 1955, was *Saga de México*, a textbook anthology of selections from Mexican novels, short stories, plays, and essays, embellished with illustrations. The sixth chapter of that volume, "Juárez y Maximiliano," includes selections from Héctor Pérez Martínez's popular novel *Juárez el impasible* (1934), with an impressive portrait of Juárez by Diego Rivera. The reader of this volume will surely realize that the young author of *Saga de México* is the same individual who penned *Latin America's New Historical Novel*, published in 1993.

Although Domínguez Michael condemns the biographical novel as an "híbrido lamentable," he does praise Parra's "orden narrativo juicioso, sin ser lineal," as well as his thorough research: "Todo lo que tenía que leer Parra lo leyó notoriamente." My only addition to Domínguez Michael's essay, and a minor one at that, is to recognize Parra's probable indebtedness to Carlos Fuentes's *La muerte de Artemio Cruz* for anchoring the novel in the year of Juárez's death, 1871–1872, and complementing that relatively short period with alternating chapters that capture the most dramatic moments in Juárez's political life from 1853 to 1867, but not in chronological order. Parra's challenge in writing a biographical novel about "el mexicano más importante de la historia" (Domínguez Michael) is to humanize the highly revered "Stoneface," while at the same time capturing his interaction with the key historical figures of the Reforma, the invasion by the French Army of Napoleon III, and Maximilian and Carlota's empire. By devoting nine of the nineteen chapters to Juárez's impending death in the years 1871 and 1872 in the Palacio Nacional, Parra goes a long way in achieving this goal. It is also appropriate that Juárez's death in the nineteenth chapter is preceded by Maximilian's execution in the eighteenth chapter. What is probably less apparent is that the only odd-numbered chapter that does not deal with Juárez's impending death is the ninth—almost the novel's exact midpoint, and its most dramatic chapter of all, "Las tinajas de San Juan de Ulúa"—which, according to Domínguez Michael, provides the author with the opportunity to "pintar, con olores y colores revueltianos [à la José Revueltas] un infierno." In this chapter, Juárez is taken prisoner by Santa Anna's bastard son and cast into the damp dungeons of the most infamous of Mexico's prisons.

Although the humanization of Juárez is achieved principally in the nine chapters that take place in 1871–1872 in the Palacio Nacional, it is certainly reinforced throughout the novel. In fact, it is actually suggested in the ironic subtitle *El rostro de piedra*. In Parra's novel, Juárez is a man who is not only capable of feeling, he is also capable of self-doubt. The author's intermittent use of second-person narrative to address Juárez as Pablo—his full name was Benito Pablo Juárez García—draws a distinction between the national hero and the former Zapotec-speaking shepherd boy. Juárez himself never forgets his humble origins. As he crosses the northern desert fleeing from the invading French army in 1865, he contrasts his role as president with his situation at that moment: "De frente al desierto no era sino un pobre indio zapoteco" (331). The use of the name "Pablo" is also linked to the prominent role of Juárez's Zapotec-speaking

Indian servant Camilo, who listens to the president's dying recollections of his childhood in the Oaxacan sierra.

Juárez's wife Margarita Maza, twenty years his junior, is a great source of strength for him, and he is devastated by her death in 1871. Although his marriage was instrumental in his being accepted by Oaxacan and Mexican society, in the final chapter of the book, the reader discovers that, ironically, she was the adopted daughter of the Mazas, a fact known by Juárez but not by her. In today's parlance, Juárez would be called a "workaholic." However, in spite of being driven by his mission to create a better Mexico after the successful revolt against Santa Anna in 1855 until his death in 1872, Juárez is portrayed as a sincere family man who loved his wife and children deeply, with a love that was reciprocated.

What is even more effective in the humanizing process is Juárez's frequent moments of self-doubt. To what extent did he really want to create a democratic Mexico with strict adherence to the Constitution of 1857—or was he obsessed with climbing to the top of the "pirámide del poder"? (428) In the thirteenth chapter, titled "Lo llamaban Huitzilopochtli (Palacio Nacional 1871)," Juárez himself recognizes that "tu crimen es el poder mismo, esa droga a la que eres adicto desde el año 59" (280). Juárez says this to himself because in spite of his ill health, he is running for reelection, even though the supporters of the constantly named "el buen Porfirio," Juárez's fellow Oaxacan and "adopted son," have risen up in arms. When Juárez's Minister of War Ignacio Mejía reports to Juárez with great enthusiasm that he has won the election, Juárez knowingly inquires, "¿Ganamos con limpieza?" (239).

Porfirio Díaz is only one of Juárez's former friends or supporters who have abandoned him or who have become his enemies. Aside from his family and the ever-loyal Camilo, his only stalwart friend was Melchor Ocampo, he of the "eterna sonrisa irónica en los labios" (159). In the delightful eighth chapter titled "Jugadas en el tablero (Veracruz 1860)," Juárez and Ocampo discuss the strategy of the McLane-Ocampo Treaty as they move their pieces on the chessboard. Although Ocampo complains that he was forced to resign as secretary of foreign relations because he was called a "vendepatria," Juárez explains to him that he signed the treaty knowing full well that the U.S. Senate would not ratify it. The treaty would have given the United States the perpetual transit rights to the Isthmus of Tehuantepec and parts of northern Mexico in exchange for four million dollars. Juárez points out that the money and the loan of the U.S. corvette enabled the Mexican liberals to defeat the conservatives in the Guerra de la Reforma. Juárez credits Ocampo with having been his mentor. In 1861, "El año ne-

gro," Juárez becomes distraught upon hearing that Ocampo has been captured and then executed by the conservative "Tigre de Tacubaya,"
Leonardo Márquez. Nonetheless, he resists the temptation to retaliate by
executing the conservative prisoners, which is what Márquez wanted him
to do.

However, what really depresses Juárez is the realization that "en política
no existen lealtades permanentes" (375). Guillermo Prieto, the well-known
poet who saved Juárez's life, is no longer his friend, and the character who
provokes these thoughts more than any other is Jesús González Ortega,
one of the outstanding heroes of the Guerra de la Reforma, who, after becoming vice president, conspires to replace Juárez as president. Although
Juárez outwits him and destroys his reputation, Juárez seems to have
second thoughts. He imagines General Zaragoza's asking him: "Pero el
remate contra don Jesús, ¿no le parece excesivo e innecesario? ¿para qué
declararlo desertor . . . ¿no le parece que es ensañarse demasiado con al-
guien a quien usted y yo tanto admirábamos?" (374). Juárez also resists the
temptation to compare himself to Abraham Lincoln upon hearing the
news of the latter's assassination. He cannot help but make the comparison recalling, after thinking of Plutarch's *Parallel Lives* (363), that he, like
Lincoln, celebrated his victory in a civil war by going to the theater, in
1860, but he decides that the similarities between him and the U.S. president
are insufficient.

To sum up, Parra's biographical novel is an excellent blend of Juárez the
feeling man and Juárez the reputedly stonefaced national hero. One of its
most successful ingredients is the emphasis on Juárez's approaching death
in 1871–1872, which prompts him to review in a nonchronological, somewhat emotional manner the most important events of his life.

Returning to Domínguez Michael's article, the critic does not "damn
[Parra's novel] with faint praise" but perhaps quite the opposite. He alludes
to books on Juárez by Bulnes, Justo Sierra, Roeder, and Pérez Martínez
before surprising the reader with the following words: "Me sorprendí pen-
sando que sería inverosímil escribir una novela sobre Juárez distinta a la
de Parra." However, he then retracts his praise somewhat with a brief comment on Franz Werfel's 1924 "drama magnífico," *Juárez y Maximiliano.* I
recall reading and enjoying Werfel's play, but it was so many years ago that
I hesitate to make a comparative judgment today.

Nonetheless, I am thankful to Domínguez Michael for giving me the
opportunity to promote my interpretation of magic realism. In my book *Historia verdadera del realismo mágico*, I indicate that in Franz Werfel's 1926
short story "Saverio's Secret" (written in German), the narrator observes that

in all the Parisian art galleries on the Rue de la Boétie, the latest style is magic realism, thus confirming my thesis that magic realism was not an exclusively literary movement indigenous to Latin America, but rather one closely linked to European painting, as well as literature (212). Of course, I would be the last one to deny the world's debt to Gabriel García Márquez and other Latin American writers for the movement's huge success.

To close this section of my chapter on Parra's *Juárez* in a lighter vein, when I saw the Juárez Monument painted black in 1948, I was living at Melchor Ocampo 403 in the Colonia Anzures.

Whereas in Parra's biographical novel, Juárez is constantly "on stage," in Álvaro Uribe's complex and ingenious *Expediente del atentado*, Porfirio Díaz for the most part remains a less central character in the narrative. As the work's title indicates, it is essentially a dossier about the assassination attempt. Although the novel initially focuses on the former president's would-be assassin in Englishman Peter Gay's "Bar-room," on the morning of September 16, 1897, it gradually expands to provide a rather accurate picture of the Díaz dictatorship, at least in Mexico City, by using a great variety of literary devices, some of which stem from the detective story. Federico Gamboa, Mexico's most important late nineteenth- and early twentieth-century novelist, actually mentions the failed assassination attempt in the September 16 entry of his *Mi diario*. In the apocryphal entry for the following day, Gamboa secretly confides to the reader that he is opening an extraofficial dossier on the event that he may well convert into a "novela-*reportaje*" (124). In other words, Gamboa's projected novel is effectively declared to have become Álvaro Uribe's novel.

Gamboa's "novela-*reportaje*," which he later calls "mitad novela y mitad pesquisa periodística y aun policial" (251), bears resemblances to a good detective story in which the reader is confronted with some puzzling questions from the very beginning that prevent him or her from laying the book aside, no matter how sleepy the reader may be. For example, why did the alcoholic Arnulfo Arroyo hate Dictator Porfirio Díaz so much that he wanted to kill him? Why did one of Arroyo's drinking companions in the Bar-room plunge the dagger into the table? Why does the first chapter end with that companion looking ferociously at Arroyo after the assassination attempt fails?

In the dossier's second of three "file folders," Arroyo's failed assassination attempt is overshadowed by his "lynching" at the hands of seven masked men, a crime organized by Inspector General Eduardo (Lalo) Velázquez.

Some other puzzling questions for the reader are: Why did Velázquez disobey dictator Díaz's order to keep Arroyo alive? Why did Antonio Villavicencio, the police chief, urge his superior Velázquez to let him kill Arroyo by the rules of "la ley fuga"? Why does Cordelia suspect that her fiancé, the very same Velázquez, may have committed suicide, not so much for having ordered Arroyo's "lynching" as for having discovered her infidelity with his friend Federico Gamboa (or "F. G.," as the novel familiarly refers to him)?

In the dossier's third and final file folder, entitled "Villavicencio y los demás," the pace picks up as the view of the Díaz regime is expanded. Almost all the loose ends are strongly tied together. The leitmotif "por órdenes superiores" points to Ministro de Gobernación González del Río as the true author of the "lynching." Nevertheless, the word "almost" in the next-to-the-last sentence indicates that there is still one question to be answered: Who was the third of the drinking companions in Peter Gay's Bar-room, the most elegantly dressed of the three, and the head of the assassination plot—and what was his motive?

The novel has a plethora of outstanding techniques, not the least of which are its variety of speech patterns, their sources ranging from stuffy official proclamations to romantic love letters to down-to-earth Mexican slang; its "architectural" structure so strong that not even a 7.5 earthquake would make it tremble; and an occasional light touch of humor, like the oxymoronic name of Judge Generoso Guerrero. However, for the sake of brevity, I'll try to concentrate on the characterization of Porfirio Díaz and F. G.

Although Porfirio Díaz the *caudillo* appears rather infrequently, by the end of the novel, the reader is left with strong impressions both of the individual and of his thirty-five-year regime. In the novel's very first chapter, the omniscient narrator portrays him as "majestuoso y erecto a pesar de sus sesenta y siete años cumplidos en la víspera" (17). His notorious self-control is displayed in the superb description of how he regains it after his initial reaction to the chaos caused by Arroyo's assault, which makes him stumble as his plumed bicorne is knocked off his head: "Se había ocupado con parsimonia en recuperar del suelo su bicornio, sacudirle a manotadas el polvo que le mancillaba las plumas y volverlo a acomodar sobre su altiva cabeza" (22). He then surprises the sycophants who surround him with his great magnanimity: "Que no se le haga nada a ese hombre. Cuídenlo. Ya pertenece a la justicia" (25).

In spite of—or perhaps because of—his alcoholism, Arroyo is the only character in the novel who is openly critical of the "viejo taimado" (25) with those "ojos abismales de esfinge" (25), "tirano que disponía de un país entero como si se tratara de su propiedad privada" (25). Since Arroyo's hatred was subjective, "con un odio filial" (24), the reader soon finds out that Arroyo hated both his "fathers." He treated his biological father with contempt because that man was a mediocre tailor, and Arnulfo, particularly after surpassing his wealthy classmates in law school, was ashamed of him: "Había adoptado al héroe victorioso de 1876 como el padre enérgico y sapiente que mi padre verdadero nunca fue" (59). However, once he began to frequent the law courts, he quickly realized that "la única ley válida para los funcionarios porfiristas es la ley del más fuerte" (59). As he became disillusioned with the official slogan of "Order, peace, and progress," he felt "condenado a la orfandad" (60).

The caudillo's relative invisibility in this novel stands out all the more because the visibility of F. G. increases. Out of the novel's thirty-six chapters, F. G. stars in seventeen, including the final one—either as a first-person narrator, as the author of letters sent to his mistress, the promiscuous widow Cordelia, or as the recipient of her sentimental letters, addressed affectionately with the popular vulgar term "Querido Pájaro" or "Pajarito añorado." In addition to praising Porfirio Díaz as the man who put an end to the disastrous decades of military uprisings (150), F. G. reinforces his image as a strong, brave, and upright leader in contrast to his own cowardice. In the novel's second chapter, entitled "Un desafecto," when F. G. finds out that the would-be assassin was his childhood classmate, he fears that someone might have witnessed his unpleasant encounter in the street with the alcoholic aggressor and might report him to the police as being an enemy of the government. F. G.'s fear increases as he finds himself doubly linked to Inspector Velázquez, a former classmate and Cordelia's fiancé. By coincidence, Arroyo had also been one of Cordelia's lovers, and the three classmates were all thirty-three years old, and perhaps therefore, like Jesus, condemned to die—Arroyo by "lynching," Eduardo by suicide, and F. G. by putting an end to his life as a bohemian.

Such coincidences continue at the beginning of the first chapter of the third file folder, entitled appropriately "Pura casualidad," with a snapshot of Arroyo's capture, taken by nobody knows who. This is still another version of the failed assassination attempt, two of which appear in the first file folder: the autobiographical version, titled "Un hombre invisible," in which Arroyo divides his life in two, "sólo puedo decir que no soy sino fui Arnufo Arroyo" (57); and the biographical one, written by his mother in a typically Mexican dialect after the "lynching": "Miren ustedes nomás cómo me lo dejaron" (93).

It is not until the third file folder that the true story of the assassination attempt is almost completely revealed. Of the three drinking companions in Peter Gay's bar, the leader seems to be the most elegantly dressed, and he also seems to be motivated to obtain a position of greater importance in the Federal District government. And why not in the Secretaría de Gobernación? adds Villavicencio (293), insinuating that the elegantly dressed man may be following the orders of the Ministro de Gobernación in doing the crime they plan to commit. In other words, they are planning to "crucify" Arnulfo Arroyo in order to be rewarded by the ministro, and he, perhaps, by the caudillo. As Villavicencio's accomplice Genovevo Uribe (the author chose the family name with a sly wink), explains: "La única falla al cumplir mis instrucciones, una falla garrafal que echó todo a perder, no se debió a un error mío. Se debió, como a lo mejor no podía ser de otra manera, a un acierto del Primer Magistrado de la Nación" (307–8).

In the same autobiographical chapter, Genovevo Uribe gives an eyewitness account of probably the most cruel event in the thirty-five years of Porfirio Díaz's dictatorship: the massacre and deportation of the Yaqui Indians from Sonora to Yucatán. This episode makes a great impact on the reader because it is the only one that occurs outside of the capital and because the narrator is a forced recruit—"Me agarraron de *leva*, como a casi todos" (304)—who tells in his own language how he participated in the execution of the Indians, in hanging them from the tree branches, in riddling their bodies with bullets from his pistol and wounds from his sword . . . without tempering the violence by explaining the historical circumstances, but with a deliberate reinforcement of the leitmotif "por órdenes superiores": "Las mejores y las peores cosas se hacen en el ejército porque las manda hacer un oficial. Y a ese oficial lo manda otro. Y a ése, otro más. Y así hasta mero arriba" (304). Without actually saying so, it seems that the soldier Uribe and the author Uribe are holding Porfirio Díaz personally responsible for the massacre of the Yaquis.

The linking in the same chapter of the soldier Uribe in Sonora with the policeman Uribe, who participated in the "lynching" of Arroyo in Mexico City, anticipates the linking of Porfirio Díaz and F. G. in the later chapter entitled "Las mismas palabras." F. G. says, "Acabo de darme cuenta de que hoy perdí para siempre una entrañable amistad" (314) to his superior Ignacio Mariscal in regard to his breakup with Cordelia. Mariscal then tells F. G. that the same words were pronounced to *him* by General Díaz—but the reader will not discover the identity of don Porfirio's friend until the following chapter, which is titled "Los que saben" (3). In this chapter, Ministro de Gobernación Felipe González del Río realizes that don Porfirio

290 · *Into the Nineteenth-Century* Colonia

suspects that he was responsible not only for Arroyo's attack on him, but also for Arroyo's "lynching" and Inspector Velázquez's suicide. Don Felipe falls ill: his nerves, his liver, and his heart are all failing. Sly don Porfirio terrorizes his friend by visiting him in his home unexpectedly. Nevertheless, with his usual adulation, the Ministro de Gobernación declares himself "algo repuesto por el efecto milagroso de esa inmerecida visita" (320). After don Felipe recovers sufficiently to attend a cabinet meeting, he hears the president announce that the Ministro is going to resign in order to take over a Mexican legation in Europe.

Just as Porfirio Díaz's character is etched in stone by the way he manipulates his friend don Felipe, in the novel's final chapter—titled "Tiro de gracia"—F. G.'s admitted cowardice is twice confirmed. Instead of marrying Clotilde for love, he prefers "un matrimonio decente" and instead of "poner mi pluma al servicio de la verdad; elijo el destino menos azaroso del escritor indecente" (325). How ironic that these words should come from an author who, in a previous chapter, called Zola "mi admirado maestro" and wondered whether he, too, could become "un *acusador*" ("J'accuse") (124).

To put the finishing touches on this chapter I would like to comment briefly on the chapter titled "Órdenes superiores," a one-act theatrical farce in which Arroyo's murderers are tried. The defense lawyer justifies their killing of Arroyo because of the great threat from international anarchists, who are mentioned throughout the novel. The invisible crowd shouts, "¡Mueras!" to Velázquez, to Villavicencio, "*a la policía toda y, acallados en el acto, al mal gobierno*" (282–83). The nine members of the people's jury find most of the accused guilty and sentence them to death by hanging. However, in the novel's colophon, the omniscient narrator reports that in 1903, while Porfirio Díaz was still president, a new trial was held, and all the condemned men were absolved and freed, confirming the farcical nature of Porfirian justice, which was exactly what Arnulfo Arroyo had discovered several years before.

Here is my own colophon to these comments on *Expediente del atentado*: just as F. G. deposited his dossier of the assassination attempt in his trunk and locked it tight, I deposited my New York University doctoral dissertation on Federico Gamboa in my trunk and locked it tight after receiving a letter in 1953 from Antonio Castro Leal, former director of the Instituto Nacional de Bellas Artes, in which he apologized for not being able to fulfill his promise to publish it . . . "por órdenes superiores." Fifty years later, Conaculta published the complete seven volumes of Gamboa's *Mi diario*, edited by . . . Álvaro Uribe.

Works Cited

Domínguez Michael, Christopher. "*Juárez: El rostro de piedra*, de Eduardo Antonio Parra." *Letras Libres* 129 (2009): 80–82. http://www.letraslibres.com/revista/libros /juarez-el-rostro-de-piedra-de-eduardo-antonio-parra. Accessed January 13, 2013.

Lara Zavala, Hernán. *Península, península*. México, D.F.: Alfaguara, 2008.

Licona, Sandra. "Inicia saga literaria sobre San Cristóbal de las Casas." *El Universal*. June 7, 2006. http://www.eluniversal.com.mx/cultura/48993.html. Accessed November 17, 2012.

Menton, Seymour. *Historia verdadera del realismo mágico*. México, D.F.: Fondo de Cultura Económica (FCE), 1999.

———. *Latin American's New Historical Novel*. Austin: University of Texas Press, 1993.

———, ed. *Saga de México*. New York: Appleton-Century-Crofts, 1955.

Parra, Eduardo Antonio. *Juárez, el rostro de piedra*. México, D.F.: Grijalbo, 2008.

Uribe, Álvaro. *Expediente del atentado*. México, D. F.: Tusquets, 2007.

Zepeda, Eraclio. *Las grandes lluvias*. México, D.F.: FCE, 2006.

———. *Tocar el fuego*. México, D.F.: FCE, 2007.

Specifically Mexican, Universally American

Tales of Colonial Mexico and Their Legacies

Rolena Adorno

The vastness of Mexico—its privileged place in the early modern European imagination and its later-modern, Latin American, and also Anglo–North American counterparts—has fomented its status as a site of the unusual, the unexpected, and the ever-unique. Mexico has been the site of the creation of one of the great, all-time pan-American stories, that of "going native." Although the first mestizo communities were created by Spanish expeditionaries who became renegades in the early Hispanic Caribbean well before the Spanish Conquest of mainland Mexico,[1] Mexico has been imagined as the ur-site of Europeans and other Westerners "going native" in the Americas.

Whether originating in actual events or in the whispers of fearful gossip and wild imaginings, accounts of "going native," be they historical, fictional, or mythical, emerged long ago in Mexico and have been ever since a staple of fictional and artistic representation, first in elite, and more recently, in popular and mass culture. I recall here two early sixteenth-century cases—one historical, one not—that have enjoyed long-lived legacies after emerging from the chronicles of the Indies, where the transition from historical to literary narrative took place.

In the spring of 1536, Álvar Núñez Cabeza de Vaca and his three companions, Andrés Dorantes, his North African slave Estevan ("Estevanico"), and Alonso del Castillo Maldonado arrived in Spanish-held territory in northwestern Mexico. They had walked from eastern coastal Texas over the course of the previous ten months, and they had been separated from all their countrymen for the previous eight years.[2] Living with native Amerindian communities, exposed to the elements during all that time and, "like serpents," changing their skins twice a year, as Cabeza de Vaca later reported, they must have been a sight to behold by the startled Spanish slaving party that received them in today's Sinaloa.[3]

The Mexican filmmaker and director Nicolás Echevarría, and his collaborator, the screenwriter Guillermo Sheridan, interpreted that event in the feature-length film *Cabeza de Vaca* (1990).[4] I saw that film when it debuted two decades ago, but it is not the reunion scene that stands out in my memory. It is instead a single, brilliant cinematographic moment when Cabeza de Vaca, who had spent four of those eight years alone with native groups and no one speaking his language, confronts his existential anguish by butting his head against a post in utter despair verging on madness. What always has tantalized me is: What if it all didn't actually happen the way Cabeza de Vaca later reported it to the emperor? But the more pertinent question is: How could Cabeza de Vaca *possibly* have been accurate in his reporting of events that occurred over the span of the previous decade, from the Pánfilo de Narváez expedition's departure from Spain in 1527 to conquer the vast territories rimming the Gulf of Mexico, known by the Spanish as La Florida, through Cabeza de Vaca's return to his homeland in 1537?

From my own investigations, I know that Cabeza de Vaca's solo report, published in 1542 under the title *Relación*, better known since its 1555 edition as *Naufragios*, diverges from the joint report that he and his two Castilian hidalgo companions filed with the Real Audiencia of Santo Domingo, to whose jurisdiction La Florida belonged.[5] At Santo Domingo, the Spanish administrator and historian Gonzalo Fernández de Oviedo relied on the men's joint report to write his own account of the Narváez expedition for his *Historia general y natural de las Indias*.[6] Later, in 1547, Oviedo read Cabeza de Vaca's published *Relación*. He added a chapter to his own account based on Cabeza de Vaca's information, but he remarked that he still preferred the three men's collective report.[7]

It was not that Oviedo was so "objective": If Cabeza de Vaca in his own account made himself the protagonist of many episodes in which he had not been so featured in the joint report, Oviedo greatly embellished as miraculous the events (the curing episodes) about which Cabeza de Vaca had been modest if not circumspect.[8] So there was plenty of room, as Natalie Zemon Davis identified it in other circumstances, for "fiction in the archives," and Cabeza de Vaca's experience has been reinterpreted if not rewritten into forms that include elements that emanate, in Roberto González Echevarría's felicitous phrase, from both "myth and archive."[9] Jorge Luis Borges and Juan José Saer have written fictionally on the topic of the American or the European living separated from Western civilization, voluntarily or as a captive, with native Amerindian groups, and Abel Posse has done so, explicitly re-creating the figure of Cabeza de Vaca.

These twentieth-century fictions are agreeable and seductive—agreeable because their topic, if not a historical one familiar to all readers, is definitely familiar as a theme: the white man lives in the wilderness among aboriginal peoples who make possible his physical survival but who also reinforce the bonds of his captivity, of being separated from all he holds dear. The aborigines' presence underscores the white stranger's deep anguish, which Nicolás Echevarría cinematographically captures in Cabeza de Vaca's moment of self-punishing solitude, all the while living in the company of others unlike himself.

Such narratives are seductive because they inevitably invite the reader to speculate on what he or she would do in similar circumstances. The current rage for reality TV adventure series that focus on physical survival, psychic toughness, and the elimination of rivals (who are not aborigines but rather versions of oneself) also play into these fantasies. All these are New World (now, New Age) versions of ancient Old World trials of mythical heroes that have appeared from Homer's *Odyssey* onward. To wit, Odysseus's multiyear captivity by the nymph Calypso (in post-Homeric ancient versions of his narrative, she bore him children), as well as the assault on his ships and men by the cannibalistic Laestrygonians on his homebound journey after the Trojan War, provide the "bones" of the story.

Still and all, these old stories are ever new and renewable, especially so because of the real-life, fifteenth- and sixteenth-century addition to the world's geography of its theretofore unknown "fourth part": the Americas. Spanish exploration and conquest hold priority of time and place over those of other nations in other languages that followed. In fact, the Spanish-language accounts were quickly translated and published by other European aspirants to transatlantic expansion—in Italian by Gian Battista Ramusio, in English by Richard Hakluyt and Samuel Purchas, to name a few. But these compilers and translators were seeking information about the New World, not offering food for imaginative speculation—except, of course, to enliven the speculating, that is, the economic imaginations of potential investors and adventurers.

The question at this point is: Why have these "ancient" sixteenth- and later-century accounts of the Spanish piqued the interest of Latin American and other writers and readers of our centuries? It is in part because their themes dramatize and put to the test humanity's major impulses: physical survival, personal valor, altruistic do-gooding, entrepreneurial greed, and imperial glory. They satisfy our common human interest in the success of individual survival and its recognition by society. But what has made possible the mythifying and fictionalizing? At the level of language, I argue, it is the figure of grammatical construction known as ellipsis. It is not always the ellipsis of deliberate omission; it is sometimes the ellipsis created by the inexpressibility of the phenomena to be described, or, more mundanely, by the paucity of information available. Gabriel García Márquez once explained that in his novel *El general en su laberinto* (1989) he chose to write about the final weeks of Simón Bolívar's life because they were the least well documented, that is, there were many ellipses. Yet to write convincingly about Bolívar, at least to satisfy his own demanding criteria, García Márquez had to spend two years reading the "torrential documentation" left by the Liberator in the wake of his life.[10] In other words, to be filled in plausibly, ellipses have to be informed by as much knowledge about the literary subject as possible.

But Bolívar was a nineteenth-century phenomenon, and the sixteenth-century figures, with some exceptions, did not leave such long or thick documentary trails. History's secrets are hinted at, but not told, in narrative accounts like Cabeza de Vaca's. As a narrator, the sixteenth-century historical protagonist is not generally a well-rounded figure; he conceals more than he reveals, in part intentionally and in part in spite of himself. The slim notice of the survivor of the Pánfilo de Narváez expedition who was christened Álvar Núñez and took the distinguished maternal surname of Cabeza de Vaca was historical, but he was much less well known in his person than in the deeds he narrated. His historical actions have become stylized and narrowed as those of the Christian caballero lost in the wilderness, then devoting himself to settling and civilizing Indians in North America and later supervising a disastrous governorship in the South American province of Río de la Plata, all the while serving a demanding but grateful monarch.

With respect to Cabeza de Vaca, my co-author Patrick Pautz and I spent years ferreting out the documentary evidence to write a modest monograph that we titled "The Life of Cabeza de Vaca."[11] On the basis of the primary sources at our disposal, we could not presume to claim our work to be a biography. For that reason, Cabeza de Vaca's profile, even his portrait, has been susceptible to reinvention. (Ironically, completely fictional characters, if exquisitely crafted, are harder to reformulate and reinvent;

their contours and outlines are often too well chiseled, too finely detailed, for readers to be convinced by any attempts to simulate them afresh.) Yet the paucity of information about Conquest-era historical figures also serves as the very invitation to fictionalize their imagined lives. Such fictional works comprise essays on the problems of memory and representation as much as they constitute novels or short stories.

As a result, the best meditations on the "gone-native" phenomenon are produced by writers of fiction. If the historian is caught up in the obsessive search for data, the novelist reveals the folly of such a craving. With such sensibilities in mind, the novelists Juan José Saer and Abel Posse, in *El entenado* (1983) and *El largo atardecer del caminante* (1992), respectively, took up the theme of the quintessential experience of the European lost in the wilderness of the Americas and living among its native peoples. Both Saer and Posse wrote their novels from the perspective of the protagonist writing his memoirs decades after his life-altering experience. Saer's inspiration for his protagonist, a former ship's cabin boy (*grumete*), was not Cabeza de Vaca's account, but Posse's protagonist is Cabeza de Vaca himself. Not surprisingly, as we can also see with Nicolás Echevarría's filmic Cabeza de Vaca, the interior, unknown experiences of the protagonists are those that ring truest, that is, that succeed in creating verisimilitude in the eyes of the reader.

By creating an anonymous protagonist, Saer focuses on the challenge that his witness/survivor/narrator faces in attempting to describe the customs and contradictions of the native group with whom he had lived long ago and for whom he felt both compassion and repugnance. Once out of captivity, his inability to recapture their essence, if he ever understood it, was further confounded by the theatrical representation he produced about them. He abandoned the theater company when he could no longer abide the falseness of his creation. At the same time, he recognized that his status as an authentic survivor playing the role of himself added considerable dramatic force to the theatrical spectacle.[12]

In the end, his attempts to write about his former captors and companions revealed only himself, because the dramatic enactments he created relied on an inevitable combination of the "true" and the "false": his historical role as survivor and his fanciful characterization of his subject. Saer's creation of his protagonist's dilemma reveals the hopeless tangle into which both "real" and "fictional" dimensions of remembered (and misremembered) experiences inevitably fall.

In contrast, by giving his novel's protagonist the name and identity of the historical figure Cabeza de Vaca, Posse focuses not on the opaqueness of the native communities the Castilian hidalgo encountered (the synchronic dimension) but, diachronically, on the irretrievability of the events and interactions he experienced. Posse's aging Cabeza de Vaca dispatches the desire of his curious interlocutors for the real "facts" of his captivity, and he highlights as well the impossibility of reproducing them. One of the protagonist's interlocutors challenges him with the taunt, "They say you have a secret version, a third version of your travels or journey" (30). Reflecting on this assertion some time (and pages) later, the old Cabeza de Vaca replies, to himself, "I have no patience for the prestigious lie of exactitude" (35). His reflection conceals the problem not only of what he *did not* or *would not* say, but also of that which he simply *was incapable of* expressing. Posse dramatizes through his protagonist's silent, scoffing dismissal of his questioner the double impossibility of possessing certitude in the knowledge of one's own experience and of being able to communicate it accurately.

With characteristic economy and elegance, Jorge Luis Borges earlier had offered the most convincing dramatization of these matters in his short story, "El etnógrafo" (c. 1969).[13] The leanness of his narrative account and the simplicity of his protagonist's remarks, uttered in direct dialogue, illuminate the significant silences of any retrospective (or prospective) "Cabeza de Vaca." This one is named Fred Murdock. Borges begins, "I was told about the case in Texas, but it had happened in another state" (334). Murdock, a graduate student of aboriginal cultures, followed the recommendation of his professors and devoted himself to the study of Amerindian languages by spending two years on an Indian reservation in some U.S. state in prairie country. Upon returning to his university, he announced to his mentor that he would not be writing his anticipated doctoral dissertation because, he says, "I learned something out there that I can't express"(335).

When asked if perhaps the English language was incapable of communicating what he had learned, Murdock answers, "That's not it, sir. Now that I possess the secret, I could tell it in a hundred different and even contradictory ways. I don't know how to tell you this, but the secret is beautiful, and science, *our* science, seems mere frivolity to me now" (335). After a pause, he adds, "And anyway, the secret is not as important as the paths that led me to it. Each person has to walk those paths himself" (335). When asked somewhat mockingly if he plans to go back and live with the Indians, Murdock replies, again in the negative, "No. I may not even go back to the prairie. What the men of the prairie taught me is good anywhere and for any circumstances" (335).

Borges thus sets forth in a few succinct sentences the conundrum: Murdock's possession of the knowledge has changed him, and he is possessed (or liberated, we ask?) by it. He can communicate the specific knowledge gained in a hundred different ways, and it can be applied universally; still, the result obtained pales in the face of the quest to achieve it. Unlike the aging protagonists created by Saer and Posse, Borges's has been less confounded than enlightened by his experience. The key to keeping the new knowledge, Murdock knows, is not to write about it (neither in dissertation nor in memoirs) but rather to live it, and to live with it. Borges's fictional response via Fred Murdock postulates the timelessness that emanates from experience that can be understood only through its unmediated self, not through any interpretive scheme or utterance.

Murdock keeps his significant silences. After the conversation and cacophony of his now-failed marriage, Murdock opts for divorce and the silence of solitude. Silence, too, characterizes his workaday world: Borges's Fred Murdock "is now one of the librarians at Yale" (335). We imagine Mr. Murdock spending his days and years classifying an endless miscellany of books, all of them marked by imprecision and incertitude, some of them aimed at giving testimony to the types of experience that Saer's anonymous narrator, Posse's Cabeza de Vaca, and Borges's Murdock would not, could not utter. All that remains, Borges makes clear, is the archive and the nameless, timeless myths it contains as imperfect reminders of ineffable experience.

Also in Mexico and in three locations, there is a spectacular sculptural ensemble whose stone figures have stepped straight out of hearsay and myth into history and art.[14] Its central figure is "Gonzalo Guerrero," who inhabits the chronicles of the Spanish Conquest of Mexico and is constituted entirely by the collection of tales told and written about him. Still, like the indisputably historical Christopher Columbus, "Gonzalo" is memorialized in stone. His statue, spear in hand, is accompanied by that of his Maya wife, who, seated at his feet, gazes up at him and nurses an infant, the youngest of their three mestizo children. Their first-born child, a son, clings to his father's side, and a little girl, seated on the ground, is absorbed at play with the Spanish military helmet once used by her father.

The brochure prepared in 1975 for the opening of the Club de Exploraciones y Deportes Acuáticos de México, where the Akumal ensemble stands, interprets the scene as follows [my translation]:

> Gonzalo contemplates the sea; the wind of the Caribbean rustles his
> hair. He is a sailor, and his gaze is a mixture of melancholy and chal-

lenge. . . . He is no longer alone but is bound by amorous ties to the children of the union with the noble Maya woman who calmly and serenely lifts her gaze to him while she nurses the youngest of their children. . . . A small boy embraces his father, and he, too, scrutinizes the distance, innocent of the imminent fall of his people before the foreign faith imposed with his people's blood. . . . Completing the scene is the small girl who, without knowing its origin, plays with the old helmet of her father. . . . She is open to the sun, the air, and the water. She was born free and happy. (Club de Yates Akumal Caribe, *Gonzalo Guerrero* 6–7)

This late-twentieth-century sculpture and its verbal description summarize two principal dimensions of the Gonzalo Guerrero story as realized in its sixteenth-century plenitude: the new domestic configuration of the mestizo family and the warrior Gonzalo's heroic defense of his adopted Maya homeland. Although the alleged Gonzalo's conduct was seen as traitorous and was condemned as heretical in his own day, he becomes here a figure of 1960s-style, counterhegemonic cultural liberation, appearing in this domestic tableau much more like a peace-loving "flower child" than a militant activist advocating violence.

The Gonzalo Guerrero of the chronicles of conquest is a figure, as I have demonstrated, whose existence is owed to a few lines written down some two decades after the fact.[15] In 1534 and 1536, there appeared accounts about a possible shipwreck survivor, marooned in Yucatán since 1511, whose name was never known with certainty and who was never subsequently encountered, much less rescued.[16] "Gonzalo" nevertheless emerged from the pens of the chroniclers in ever more vivid hues as a hero of Maya resistance and the cause of the Spaniards' decades-long failure to conquer Yucatán.

Drafting his account of the Spanish Conquest of Yucatán for his *Historia general y natural de las Indias* in 1542, Oviedo was the first chronicler to give the full outline of the story, naming the shipwreck survivor "one Gonzalo, a mariner," and attributing to him a "conversion to being an Indian and worse than an Indian" (3: 232), being married to a Maya woman, siring her children, and bearing Maya body markings and perforations; Oviedo flatly condemns "Gonzalo" as a traitor and heretical apostate.[17] A decade later, now a full forty years after the newly named sailor allegedly disappeared into the peninsula's dense forests, Francisco López de Gómara, in his *Historia general de las Indias y la conquista de México* (1552), gave "Gonzalo" the surname of "Guerrero" (=warrior). Following Gómara's account and writing in the same decade, Bernal Díaz del Castillo brought

"Gonzalo Guerrero" fully to life in his posthumously published *Historia verdadera de la conquista de la Nueva España* (1632).

Much more widely read today than either Oviedo or Gómara, Bernal Díaz's influential work merely embellished the details of their earlier accounts. His tour de force, nevertheless, was to dramatize as a fully drawn historical figure the shadowy Spanish sailor, endowing him with a vivid domestic life by "putting words into" Gonzalo's mouth and that of his Maya wife: Bernal Díaz invents for them speeches that memorably reject Spanish civilization and reaffirm the sovereign rights and ways of the Yucatec Maya.

More than any other period source, Bernal Díaz's was the voice that made possible the creation of the 1970s sculptural ensemble. Bernal Díaz's Gonzalo declares to his fellow shipwreck victim, the newly rescued Jerónimo de Aguilar, who attempts to persuade Gonzalo to flee with him: "Brother Aguilar, I am married and have three children, and [the Mayas] have me as a lord and captain when there are wars; go yourself with God, for my face is tattooed and my ears are pierced. What will those Spaniards say about me if they see me looking like this!" (98 [ch. 27]). His wife, gleefully incarnated by Bernal Díaz as a shrew-like, haranguing female, puts it more bluntly: "Look at the promises this slave [Aguilar] makes to my husband! Get out of here and don't bother us with more speeches!" (98 [ch 27]).

The old Indies-hand Bernal Díaz furthermore welcomes the mestizo family into the fold of Spanish creole society. Mestizos are fondly portrayed in Bernal Díaz's Gonzalo's tender remarks, again directed to Aguilar: "And you now see these my children, how handsome they are! On your life, man, give me some of those green glass beads for them, and I will say that my brothers send them to me from my homeland" (98 [ch. 27]). The pride that Bernal Díaz expresses on behalf of Gonzalo for his mestizo progeny would have been unthinkable to Oviedo and Gómara; Bernal Díaz here reveals his understanding of creole society "from within," including the likelihood that he himself sired mestizo offspring of whom he was fond. The conversion of the Spaniards' glass trading beads into children's playthings rounds out Bernal Díaz's vivid creation of Gonzalo's rejection of Spain and the grandiosity of its imperial schemes, reduced here to the paltry, useless trinkets that were worthy of serving only as children's toys.

Appearing in chronicles and histories that stretched from the sixteenth through the eighteenth centuries, Gonzalo more recently appeared in Tzvetan Todorov's best-selling *The Conquest of America* (1982), where he is featured as a historical case of crossing over into the land and life of the Other.[18] The Gonzalo story always has been taken as a bona fide historical phenomenon, and it has figured in historical monographs up to the present day. Meanwhile, Gonzalo's imagined life has been the object of at least two mutually contradictory "autobiographies," both proclaiming themselves as true, "discovered" in the last quarter of the twentieth century.[19]

"Gonzalo Guerrero" is presented insistently to this day as a historical figure, despite the fact that there is no basis on which to postulate with certainty even the *name*, much less the actual *survival* of the rumored 1511 shipwreck victim. Created by gossip, speculation, and hearsay, Gonzalo was never actually seen by any of the Spanish reporters who commented on him, starting with the first recorded statement, which had been made by Hernán Cortés, trying to recall what he had heard nearly twenty years earlier. Still, none of these factors has proven to be an obstacle to the vitality and persistence of the Gonzalo story and the scholarly and popular promotion of its mythic qualities.

In sum, the twentieth-century narrative accounts about the historical Cabeza de Vaca and the phantom shipwreck survivor "Gonzalo Guerrero" show how literary authority can overpower and erase, paradoxically, the lack of historical evidence. The figure of Cabeza de Vaca proved irresistible to subsequent explorers, historians, and myth makers.[20] The threat of an alleged renegade rebel belatedly dubbed "Gonzalo Guerrero" reveals how gossip and hearsay reporting about historical events can pass straight into history, then fiction (or fiction-as-history), constituting a skewed segue from an authority assumed to be historical when in fact it was literary and fictional. Bernal Díaz's re-creation and embellishment of the Gonzalo Guerrero figure shows that the literary record can and does trump the historical record, and that in this passage from paper phantom to flesh-and-blood hero, the literary tradition of Latin America was born, nourished by the powers of the narrative imagination.

The tales about the likes of Cabeza de Vaca and Gonzalo Guerrero that continue to be spun today seem to emerge from the historical archive, but their origins lie elsewhere. Their sources are the hopes and aspirations about human experience in its quintessential and yet, somewhat contradictorily, unique manifestations. Their inspiration comes from strands of myth that have survived from the Old World and, brought into the New, have become uniquely American, turning on ideas of captivity and "going native." Cabeza de Vaca goes native briefly but remains entrenched in his Christian, Spanish imperial ideology and identity (a latter-day version of Homer's pagan but faithful Odysseus). "Gonzalo Guerrero" goes native and never comes back. Both are American stories; both are quintessential myths of America.

Postscriptum to the postscriptum: The abundant production of fictional works that re-create and reinvent the Spanish colonial world illuminate theoretical problems of significance for the study of colonial Latin American letters. These new fictions (the texts that present themselves as such, as well as those that insist on their historicity) have a double value for the colonial-studies field. In the first place, they set forth the importance of the ever-present past and, consequently, the pertinence of research and criticism in colonial literary and historical studies. Second, these new writings help us to read the colonial experience in new ways. That is, to the degree that scholarship and interpretation are advanced when new questions are formulated about familiar objects of study, fictional reformulations of the past invite new reflections—and identify new conundrums— regarding "the prestigious lies of exactitude" and the place of the work of literary and historical interpretation generated by narrative itself.

Notes

1. Alejandro Lipschutz, *El problema racial en la conquista de América* (1963); Magnus Mörner, *Race Mixture in the History of Latin America* (1967); and Stuart B. Schwartz, "Spaniards, *Pardos*, and the Missing Mestizos" (1997) document and discuss this phenomenon.

2. Their experiences and the historical and literary traditions informing them are analyzed in Rolena Adorno and Patrick Charles Pautz, *Álvar Núñez Cabeza de Vaca* (1999).

3. Cabeza de Vaca's account is transcribed and translated into English in Adorno and Pautz, *Álvar Núñez Cabeza de Vaca* (1: 14–279). The quoted text is: "a manera de serpientes mudábamos los cueros dos vezes en el año" (1: 170–71).

4. Directed by Echevarría on the basis of Sheridan's screenplay, *Cabeza de Vaca* was co-produced by Producciones Iguana and the Instituto Mexicano de Cinematografía; see Guillermo Sheridan, *Cabeza de Vaca* (1994).

5. As a slave, Estevan ("Estevanico") was not permitted to provide testimony for the joint report. For differences between the joint report and Cabeza de Vaca's *Relación*, see Adorno and Pautz, *Álvar Núñez Cabeza de Vaca* (3: 31–39, 78–81).

6. The joint report and Oviedo's use and interpretation of it are analyzed in Adorno and Pautz, *Álvar Núñez Cabeza de Vaca* (3: 12–13, 31–45).

7. "Pero en alguna manera yo tengo por buena la relación de los tres é por más clara que estotra que el uno solo hace e hizo imprimir" (Oviedo, *Historia general y natural de las Indias* 4: 315 [bk. 35, chap. 7]). Oviedo (*Historia* 4: 287 [proem to bk. 35]) had been the first to use the term "naufragios" in reference to Cabeza de Vaca's experience, metaphorically characterizing the Narváez expedition by its dangers and calamities (not literally shipwrecks).

8. On the respective interpretive "embellishments" made by Oviedo and Cabeza de Vaca, see Adorno and Pautz, *Álvar Núñez Cabeza de Vaca* (3: 43–45, 58–64).

9. I refer to Natalie Zemon Davis's *Fiction in the Archives* (1999), and Roberto González Echevarría's *Myth and Archive* (1998).

10. Gabriel García Márquez, "Gratitudes," *El general en su laberinto* (271–72).

11. In titling our monograph, which appears in Adorno and Pautz, *Álvar Núñez Cabeza de Vaca* (1: 295–413), we followed the sixteenth-century designation of "life," which narrated the public deeds, not the private lives, of their subjects.

12. Juan José Saer, *El entenado* (106–12).

13. "The Ethnographer" was originally published in the collection *Elogio de la sombra* (1969).

14. Created by the sculptor Raúl Ayala Arellano, in Ciudad Juárez, Chihuahua, in 1974, the casting I have seen and studied is located in Akumal in the state of Quintana Roo on the Yucatán Peninsula. Another is erected in a traffic circle (*glorieta*) on the extension of the Paseo Montejo in Mérida, Yucatán, and a third is reported as being located in Mexico City.

15. I have surveyed the appearances of "Gonzalo Guerrero" in "La estatua de Gonzalo Guerrero" (1996); *De Guancane a Macondo* (207–29); and *The Polemics of Possession* (220–45).

16. Hernán Cortés first mentioned such a shipwreck survivor, whom he identified by the name "Morales," in a 1534 account he prepared for the official investigation (*residencia*) of his tenure as governor of New Spain. In 1536, the civil and military governor of Honduras-Higueras, Andrés de Cereceda, reporting on Pedro de Alvarado's failed attempt to conquer Yucatán, mentioned a certain "Aroza" or "Azora," whose military leadership, according to the account, he claimed, of the Maya cacique Cizumba, had been responsible for Francisco de Montejo's earlier failed attempts to conquer Yucatán; see Adorno, *The Polemics of Possession* (226–29).

17. Oviedo, *Historia* (3: 404, 405, 415; 4: 9 [bk. 32, chaps. 3 and 6; bk. 33, chap. 1]).

18. Although attractive to us today, the radical concept of the Other was an impossibility for the Spanish at the time, because of the Orthodox Christian view that all humanity was one and all souls could be saved. That is why Oviedo, according to that world view, dismissed "Gonzalo" as an infidel, an apostate, or heretic, when—if a good Christian—he should have brought his Maya wife and children into the Christian fold.

19. These "memoirs" appear in Mario Aguirre Rosas, *Gonzalo de Guerrero* (1975) and Joseph de San Buenaventura, *Historias de la conquista del Mayab* (1994). I analyze these alleged autobiographical accounts in *The Polemics* (242–45).

20. Eighteenth-century chroniclers, in particular, attributed to Cabeza de Vaca and his companions a nearly mythic status, making them retrospectively the harbingers of later settlement in northern and northwestern Mexico in areas through which the Cabeza de Vaca party probably never passed. See Adorno and Pautz, *Álvar Núñez Cabeza de Vaca* (3: 168–71).

Works Cited

Adorno, Rolena. "La estatua de Gonzalo Guerrero en Akumal: Íconos culturales y la reactualización del pasado colonial." *Revista Iberoamericana* 176–77 (1996): 905–23.

——. *De Guancane a Macondo: Estudios de literatura hispanoamericana.* Sevilla: Renacimiento, 2008.

——. *The Polemics of Possession in Spanish American Narrative.* New Haven, CT: Yale University Press, 2007.

Adorno, Rolena, and Patrick Charles Pautz. *Álvar Núñez Cabeza de Vaca: His Account, His Life, and the Expedition of Pánfilo de Narváez.* 3 vols. Lincoln: University of Nebraska Press, 1999.

Aguirre Rosas, Mario. *Gonzalo de Guerrero, padre del mestizaje iberoamericano.* Introd. Alfonso Taracena. México, D.F.: Jus, 1975.

Borges, Jorge Luis. "The Ethnographer." *Collected Fictions.* Trans. Andrew Hurley. New York: Viking Press, 1998. 334–35.

Club de Yates Akumal Caribe. *Gonzalo Guerrero.* Quintana Roo, México: Bush Juárez, Sociedad Anónima, n.d.

Davis, Natalie Zemon. *Fiction in the Archives: Pardon Tales and their Tellers in Sixteenth-Century France.* 1987. Stanford, CA: Stanford University Press, 1999.

Díaz del Castillo, Bernal. *Historia verdadera de la conquista de la Nueva España.* Ed. Carmelo Sáenz de Santa María. 2 vols. 1632. Madrid: Consejo Superior de Investigaciones Científicas, 1982.

García Márquez, Gabriel. Gratitudes. *El general en su laberinto.* 1989. Buenos Aires: Sudamericana, 1993.

González Echevarría, Roberto. *Myth and Archive: A Theory of Latin American Narrative.* 1990. Cambridge: Cambridge University Press, 1998.

Lipschutz, Alejandro. *El problema racial en la conquista de América.* 1963. México, D.F.: Siglo Veintiuno, 1975.

Mörner, Magnus. *Race Mixture in the History of Latin America.* Boston: Little Brown, 1967.

Oviedo y Valdés, Gonzalo Fernández de. *Historia general y natural de las Indias.* Ed. José Amador de los Ríos. 4 vols. Madrid: Real Academia de la Historia, 1851–1855.

Posse, Abel. *El largo atardecer del caminante.* Buenos Aires: Emecé, 1992.

Saer, Juan José. *El entenado.* México, D.F.: Folios, 1983.

San Buenaventura, Joseph de. *Historias de la conquista del Mayab, 1511–1697.* Ed. Gabriela Solís Robleda and Pedro Bracamonte y Sosa. Mérida: Universidad Autónoma de Yucatán, 1994.

Schwartz, Stuart B. "Spaniards, *Pardos,* and the Missing Mestizos: Identities and Racial Categories in the Early Hispanic Caribbean." *New West Indian Guide* 71.1–2 (1997): 5–19.

Sheridan, Guillermo. *Cabeza de Vaca, inspirada libremente en el libro* Naufragios, *de Álvar Núñez Cabeza de Vaca.* Prologue by Álvaro Mutis. Introduction by Nicolás Echevarría. México, D.F.: El Milagro, 1994.

Contributors

Rolena Adorno earned her PhD from Cornell University and is now Sterling Professor of Spanish and chair of the Department of Spanish and Portuguese at Yale University. She holds the title of honorary professor (*profesora honoraria*) at the Pontificia Universidad Católica del Perú in Lima. Her teaching and research focus on colonial Spanish American literary and cultural history and the nineteenth-century origins of Hispanism in the United States. Her books include *Colonial Latin American Literature: A Very Short Introduction* (Oxford University Press, 2011); *De Guancane a Macondo: Estudios de literatura hispanoamericana* (Renacimiento, 2008); *The Polemics of Possession in Spanish American Narrative* (Yale University Press, 2007), which was awarded the Katherine Singer Kovacs Prize by the Modern Language Association; *Álvar Núñez Cabeza de Vaca: His Account, His Life, and the Expedition of Pánfilo de Narváez* (University of Nebraska Press, 1999), which received prizes from the American Historical Association, the Western Historical Association, and the New England Council of Latin American Studies; and *Guaman Poma: Writing and Resistance in Colonial Peru* (University of Texas Press, 1986, 2000). She is the author of critical editions of the works of Cabeza de Vaca (print) and Guaman Poma (print and digital). In 2009, she was appointed by President Barack Obama to membership on the National Council on the Humanities, the advisory board of the National Endowment for the Humanities. Adorno is a member of the American Academy of Arts and Sciences.

Irma Cantú is an assistant professor at Texas A&M International University. She obtained her PhD in Hispanic literature from The University of Texas at Austin. Her research focuses on in-transit writing, including notions of mobility such as travel, exile, and migration in literature from Spanish colonial narrative to contemporary Mexican literature. She has studied extensively the works of Octavio Paz influenced by his six-year residence in India as Mexican ambassador, and she has recently published articles and book chapters on Juan Villoro and Cristina Rivera Garza.

Cristina Carrasco teaches Spanish language and literature at the University of North Carolina at Chapel Hill. She holds an MA in comparative literature from the University of Iowa and a PhD in Hispanic literature from The University of Texas at Austin. Her research focuses on twentieth- and twenty-first-century Spanish and transatlantic literature, film, and culture. She has published on hybrid genres in contemporary Latin America and Spain and is currently working on recent immigration and redefinitions of national identities on both sides of the Atlantic. She has recently published articles in *Romance Notes, Transitions: Journal of Franco-Iberian Studies, Revista de Humanidades*, and *Cuaderno Internacional de Estudios Humanísticos y Literatura*.

Stuart A. Day, PhD, is an associate professor of Spanish at the University of Kansas and editor of the *Latin American Theatre Review.* He also serves as department chair and managing editor for LATR BOOKS. His book *Staging Politics in Mexico: The Road to Neoliberalism* was published by Bucknell University Press (2005). He has published anthologies of Mexican plays and co-edited, with Jacqueline E. Bixler, the collection *El Teatro de Rascón Banda: Voces en el umbral* (Escenología Ediciones, 2010). Day recently completed an edited volume on Mexican public intellectuals with Debra A. Castillo (Palgrave, 2014) and has published several book chapters on Mexican theater, as well as numerous articles, play introductions, and interviews in a variety of journals.

Guillermo de los Reyes-Heredia is an associate professor of Latin American Literature and cultural studies in the Department of Hispanic Studies at the University of Houston. He is currently the director of undergraduate studies and associate director of the Women's, Gender, and Sexuality Studies Program at the same institution. He holds both a PhD and an MA from the University of Pennsylvania, as well as an MA and a BA from the Universidad de las Américas-Puebla. He is the author of *Herencias secretas: Masonería, política y sociedad en México* (Benemérita Universidad Autónoma de Puebla, 2009) and is working on a second book project, with the working title The Inventions and Transgressions of Sexual and Gendered Discourses in Colonial Mexican Society. His work focuses on gender and sexuality, colonial Mesoamerica, queer theory, Latin American cultural studies, and secret and fraternal societies.

Linda Egan, PhD, is a professor at the University of California, Davis, and specializes in twentieth-century fiction and nonfiction, as well as Mexican poetry and colonial studies, particularly sorjuanine scholarship and the chronicle of the Indies. She has published the book *Diosas, demonios y debate: Las armas metafísicas de Sor Juana* (Biblioteca de Textos Universitarios, 1997) as well as two monographs on the contemporary chronicle: *Carlos Monsiváis: Culture and Chronicle in Contemporary Mexico* (University of Arizona Press, 2001; translation Fondo de Cultura Económica, 2004) and *Monsivaisiana: Aforismos de un pueblo que quiere ser ciudadano* (Martin Meidenbauer of Munich, 2010). She co-edited the critical anthology, *Mexico Reading the United States* (Vanderbilt University Press, 2009). She is the author of numerous articles on Monsiváis, Sor Juana, Carlos Funtes, colonial writers in general, and other Mexican topics. Her most recent book is *Leyendo a Monsiváis* (Universidad Nacional Autónoma de México, 2014).

Oswaldo Estrada, PhD, is an associate professor of Latin American literature at the University of North Carolina at Chapel Hill and the editor of *Romance Notes*. His research focuses on the rewritings of history, historical memory, gender formation and transgression, and the construction of dissident identities in contemporary Mexico and Peru. He has published numerous articles and book chapters in Latin America, Spain, and the United States on colonial and contemporary literature, specifically on subjects from Bernal Díaz del Castillo and Sor Juana Inés de la Cruz to Rosario Castellanos, Carlos Monsiváis, Elena Poniatowska, Manuel Scorza, and Mario Vargas Llosa, among others. He is the author of *La imaginación novelesca: Bernal Díaz entre géneros y épocas* (Iberoamericana/Vervuert, 2009), and the editor and co-author of *Critina Rivera Garza: Ningún crítico cuenta esto . . .* (Eón, University of North Carolina at Chapel Hill, UC-Mexicanistas, 2010).

Josué Gutiérrez-González is a doctoral candidate in the Department of Hispanic Studies at the University of Houston. His research interests include twentieth- and twenty-first-century Mexican narrative and politics, regional disparities, cultural policy in the Americas, and U.S. Latino immigration literature. His dissertation focuses on the representation of enclosure and confinement in recent Mexican novels. He works for the Recovering the U.S. Hispanic Literary Heritage Project at the University of Houston and collaborates with *Literal Magazine*.

Emily Hind, PhD, is an associate professor at the University of Florida. She specializes in Mexican studies and has published *Entrevistas con quince autoras mexicanas* (Iberoamericana/Vervuert, 2003), *Femmenism and the Mexican Woman Intellectual From Sor Juana to Poniatowska: Boob Lit* (Palgrave Macmillan, 2010), and *La generación XXX: Entrevistas con veinte escritores mexicanos nacidos en los 70; De Abenshushan a Xoconostle. Entrevistas* (Eón, 2013). Hind has written numerous articles on Mexican literature and film, with concentrations on topics such as children's literature, pirates, and celebrity culture, and the genre of the essay. She is currently writing on drug trafficking and the theory of drugs, ageism, and specters, as well as the Mexican novel and disability studies. Hind's analysis on lesbianism in the work of Rosario Castellanos won the Feministas Unidas Essay Contest in 2005. She has written on Carlos Fuentes and Guadalupe Amor, Mario Bellatin, Carmen Boullosa, Bernardo Esquinca, and Guadalupe Loaeza, and many other Mexican writers.

Ilana Dann Luna is an assistant professor of Latin American Studies at Arizona State University's School of Humanities, Arts, and Cultural Studies. She holds a doctorate in Hispanic languages and literature with an emphasis on translation studies from the University of California, Santa Barbara. Her work centers on Latin American literature and film, specifically focusing on issues of gender and sexuality, themes of adolescence and national allegory, women filmmakers, and film adaptation in Mexico. Her work has appeared in various collections in the United States and Mexico, as well as publications such as the *Revista de Crítica Literaria Latinoamericana*, *Hispanófila* and *La Gaceta de la Universidad Veracruzana*.

Seymour Menton, PhD, studied and wrote on Spanish American fiction for more than sixty years. His best-known book is *El cuento hispanoamericano*, originally published in 1964 with several updated editions, the latest one in 2009. He also published books on the novel and/or short story of Guatemala (Editorial Universitaria de Guatemala 1960, 1985), Costa Rica (University of Kansas Press, 1964), Cuba (University of Texas Press, 1975), Colombia (Plaza y Janés, 1978, 2007), and Mexico (Universidad Autónoma de Tlaxcala; Universidad Autónoma de Puebla, 1991). His last four books are *Latin America's New Historical Novel* (University of Texas Press, 1993), *Historia verdadera del realismo mágico* (Fondo de Cultura Económica, 1998), *Caminata por la narrativa latinoamericana* (2002), and *Un tercer gringo viejo: Relatos y confesiones* (Universidad Veracruzana and Fondo de Cultura Económica, 2005). In 2011, he published *A Mystical Journey* (Gaon Books), a translation of Angelina Muñiz Huberman's historical novel *Tierra adentro*. Menton taught at Dartmouth College, the University of Kansas, and the University of California, Irvine, where he was the founding chair of the Department of Foreign Languages and Literatures in 1965. He also taught at the Universidad de San Carlos in Guatemala, the Universidad de Costa Rica, and the Instituto Caro y Cuervo in Bogotá.

Anna M. Nogar earned her PhD at The University of Texas at Austin and is now an assistant professor at the University of New Mexico specializing in colonial Mexican and Mexican American literature and culture. She has published in *Confluencia*, *Trans-*, *Renaissance Quarterly*, and *Revista de Estudios Hispánicos*, among other periodicals. She is the author of a monograph on seventeenth-century nun and author Sor María de Jesús de Ágreda, which is forthcoming with the University of Notre Dame Press, as is a bilingual children's book on the nun's mystical travels to New Mexico, forthcoming with the University of New Mexico Press.

Jeremy Paden, PhD, is an associate professor of Latin American literature at Transylvania University. He has published on Gonzalo Fernández de Oviedo, Sor Juana (including contemporary treatments), and Sigüenza y Góngora. His articles have appeared in the *Colonial Latin American Review, Calíope: Journal of the Society for Renaissance and Baroque Hispanic Poetry*, and other journals. He was a guest editor for a volume of the *South Atlantic Review* titled *Reflections on Empire: Latin American Depictions of Colonization in Literature, Film, and Art*. He is also a poet. His poems have appeared in *Beloit Poetry Review, Rattle*, and *Atlanta Review*, among other journals, and in such anthologies as *Abuelas hispanas desde la memoria* and *So Spoke the Earth: The Haiti I Knew, the Haiti I Know, the Haiti I Want to Know*. His chapbook *Broken Tulips* was published by Accents Publishing in 2013.

Vinodh Venkatesh, PhD, is an assistant professor of Latin American literature and culture at Virginia Tech. His research is primarily centered on issues of gender, subjectivity, and the urban space in contemporary Latin American narrative and cinema. He has published articles in such journals as *Chasqui, Hispanic Review, Revista de Estudios Hispánicos*, and *Latin American Literary Review*, in addition to several chapters in critical editions. His current research focuses on expressions of masculinity in a neoliberal climate.

Tamara R. Williams earned her PhD from the University of Michigan and is professor of Hispanic studies at Pacific Lutheran University in Tacoma, Washington. She is the coordinator of the bilingual edition of Ernesto Cardenal's *The Doubtful Straight/ El estrecho dudoso* (Iowa University Press, 1995), co-editor of *Literatura a ciencia cierta: Homenaje a Cedomil Goic* (Juan de la Cuesta Hispanic Monographs, 2011), as well as author of numerous articles focused on the new Latin American epic and on poetic rereadings of Latin America's colonial past. These include articles on Cardenal, Antonio

Cisneros, Nicolás Guillén, and Pablo Neruda. She is co-editing with Sarah Pollack (the City University of New York) an anthology of critical essays on the works of Fabio Morábito. More recent publications and current research entail an emphasis on the construction of masculinities in contemporary Mexican poetry and fiction, generally, and on the work of Luis Felipe Fabre and Juan Villoro, in particular.

Index